Individualized
Instruction and Learning

Individualized Instruction

compiled and edited by

Madan Mohan and
Ronald E. Hull

and Learning

Professional/Technical Series

nh Nelson-Hall Co.
Chicago

ISBN: 0-88229-113-0

Library of Congress Catalog Card Number:
73-89605

Contents

Section V: Evaluating Cognitive and Affective Outcomes of Individualization

Foreword

Pleasure and a sense of accomplishment accompany me as I write the foreword to this book. I am flattered in having been asked by the editors and contributors, Madan Mohan and Ronald Hull. Also, I derive much professional satisfaction from adding in this small way to the publishing endeavor of so many educators and colleagues whom I count as close friends.

For over one hundred years American public education depended largely upon single-purpose institutions, called teachers colleges, for their yearly outpouring of two-, three-, four-, and five-year graduates. The lack of status of these institutions among the ranks of other and usually larger multipurpose colleges and universities was their distinctive characteristic. Directly under state education department authority, their mediocrity seemed precisely the role that state power structures desired. They were cheap and usually readily accessible places of educational opportunity for the nonelitist high school graduates whose aspirations were to stand timidly on the fringe of the white-collar carpet.

The fact of this book and other distinguished publications authored by outstanding faculty members from former teachers colleges is but one indication of the rise in excellence in these colleges of an earlier era. Indeed, within less than twenty years, many of the former teachers colleges now rank high by comparison with public and private colleges and universities long known for their excellence.

This book well symbolizes the expanding mission of the Fredonia State College. Its subject, *Individualization*, focuses directly on the teaching-learning process and examines a problem rooted deeply in an institution with a past history of single purposefulness—the preparation of teachers. At the same time, the book also illustrates the dynamic change that has taken place in this institution which now has come fully into the academic arena.

Beyond the expansion of institutional mission at Fredonia has been the evolutionary movement of teacher education. This movement is mentioned here because the authors hold rank in what has emerged as a consequence of teacher education keeping pace with the rapid expansion and increasing quality of the newer college programs. The Teacher Education Research Center is the only one of its kind in the State University of New York. It was formed in 1967 as a consequence of closing the ninety-nine-year-old campus school, and it serves as the research and development arm of an expanded teacher education program.

The subject of this publication is, indeed, indicative of our continuing desire that through the combined efforts of the Education Department, the Teacher Education Research Center, and cooperating public schools, teachers will be taught in a manner that will enable them to apply understanding and skill in such a way that the motto of the State University of New York may rightly be placed before the entrance of each public elementary and secondary school as well: "Let each become all he is capable of being."

I believe an appropriate introduction to the subject of this book is the quite poignantly expressed sentiment from *Letters to My Teacher* by Dagobert Runes:

> No teacher has the right to stigmatize a child as being inferior because its memory is less formidable than that of others. No teacher has the right to mark a child

low or lower because its apparatus of comprehension works in a slower manner than that of others. No teacher has the right to point out the child or mark it publicly because its strength of concentration or span of attention operates on a different depth or length.

If anyone objects to my using the term "publicly," may I explain that to the pupil his colleagues and friends in the classroom are his peers, that is, his public, as your colleagues and friends are your public. He has to spend ten or twenty years of his life in the classroom, labeled by *public* tests and *public* evaluations as an inferior individual.

Dallas K. Beal
President
State University College
Fredonia, New York

Develop teacher talent, not grade it
Don Davies

Preface

Our purpose in editing and compiling this book is to provide useful guides and suggestions for those concerned with individualized instruction and individualized learning. The book consists of a collection of thirty-one articles and addresses, as well as appendices which guide the reader to pertinent references, materials, and programs of individualized instruction.

The criteria used in choosing articles were: (1) relevancy, (2) recency, and (3) identification of techniques, skills, and programs which have facilitated the individualized treatment of students and staff. There are bound to be repetitions of concepts in a volume of this kind, especially as no editorial changes were made in the articles published previously. However, by selecting and arranging the best thinking on individualized instruction, we hope to increase interest among school personnel in this area. Our book is also intended as a reference work for any student interested in formal educational programs. The book will be a useful supplementary textbook and an impetus for further reading and research.

The book is organized in five sections. Each section consists of several articles with a preface by the editors.

Only those materials were included which received a positive reaction from consultants and teachers who are now in the processes of individualizing their own instructional programs.

We do not emphasize any one technique over others; nor do we recognize any one writer as having a monopoly on ways to individualize instruction. The emphasis has been on the process of individualized instruction, the conditions under which it occurs, and ways it may be facilitated.

Many friends generously helped, advised, and encouraged us. It is not possible to list all of them. However, we are greatly indebted to two men, John B. Bouchard and Kenneth G. Nelson, who have been most supportive of our efforts at State University College, Fredonia, New York. They first focused our attention on the exciting concept of individualized instruction and constantly encouraged us in our efforts to learn more. Special thanks are due Chris Halas and Marian Anderson for their assistance in the preparation of the manuscript.

We will feel rewarded if this book helps the reader toward the goals so precisely expressed by Don Davies of the United States Office of Education, who has stated that educators must "develop teacher talent, not grade it."

SECTION **I**

Philosophy and Rationale for Individualization

In this section we have attempted to compile original source materials on the philosophy and rationale for individualized instruction. The five articles included communicate most effectively the personality of each author and his thinking on the need for matching learning environments to the unique requirements of each child. We believe that the reader will get the "feel" of the need for individualized instruction by reading these essays.

Benjamin Bloom in his article, "Learning for Mastery," contends that our present school system presumes many students will fail, when 90 percent could master subject material if not compelled to work at a certain rate and in a certain way. He develops ideas related to five variables that may be adjusted to permit mastery of learning for each child. These variables are: (1) aptitude for particular kinds of learning, (2) quality of instruction, (3) ability to understand instruction, (4) perseverance, and (5) time allowed for learning. Each of these factors has been explained in easy-to-understand language. A strategy for mastery learning and its cognitive and affective consequences are pointed out.

John Carroll's article, "A Model of School Learning," places time at the center of learning experience. Carroll maintains that, given enough time, all students can attain mastery of a learning task. Such a formulation has the most fundamental implication for individualized instruction. The model involves five elements. Three of these elements —aptitude, ability to understand instruction, and perseverance—reside in the individual. The remaining two elements—time allowed for learning and the quality of instruction—stem from external conditions. The model has generated research. This is nowhere more evident than in the first article, in which Bloom has tried to explicate the various elements in the model and supports the model on the basis of his research. The article, at times, may make for difficult reading because of mathematical terms. However, the material presented is highly relevant to individualized instruction and the reader should persevere to grasp the meaning.

In his article, "The Science of Learning and the Art of Teaching," B. F. Skinner discusses some recent advances in the control of learning processes. These advances are in the area of reinforcement in learning. According to the author, the designing of techniques by which reinforcement can be manipulated has implications for individualized instruction. He points out that perhaps the most serious criticism of the current classroom is the relative infrequency of reinforcement, and he suggests that the results of his experimental work in the field of learning can be applied to help children achieve mastery learning. He recommends the use of mechanical devices to solve learning problems and deals with the advantages of and objections to their use.

The reader will note that Professor Skinner has added another variable, reinforcement, not mentioned explicitly in the first two articles.

Harold E. Mitzel, in "The Impending Instruction Revolution," briefly reviews the history of individualized instruction and five different concepts of individualization. He points out that these concepts of individualized instruction have been fairly well arrested at the level of encouraging the learner to vary and control his task completion time. The use of computer-assisted instruction (CAI) as an individualizing technique is discussed, and individual difference variables which are considered to be more promising for CAI are discussed.

The reader will find the article addressed to problems at the college/university level. However, what the author says about the use of CAI and his identification of psychological variables more amenable to individualizing instruction can be applied profitably to the elementary and secondary levels.

In "Individuals and Learning: The New Aptitudes," Robert Glaser discusses developments in psychology which promise new directions in the individualization of instruction in the preschool and elementary school years, although the developments have applications to all levels of our educational system. Some exemplary studies in which cognitive process variables are highly related to performance of various tasks are mentioned. Glaser supports the importance of cognitive and noncognitive process variables for individualization of instruction with evidence from other studies.

1

Learning for Mastery

Benjamin S. Bloom

Each teacher begins a new term (or course) with the expectation that about a third of his students will adequately learn what he has to teach. He expects about a third of his students to fail or to just "get by." Finally, he expects another third to learn a good deal of what he has to teach, but not enough to be regarded as "good students." This set of expectations, supported by school policies and practices in grading, becomes transmitted to the students through the grading procedures and through the methods and materials of instruction. The system creates a self-fulfilling prophecy such that the final sorting of students through the grading process becomes approximately equivalent to the original expectations.

This set of expectations, which fixes the academic goals of teachers and students, is the most wasteful and destructive aspect of the present educational system. It reduces the aspirations of both teachers and students; it reduces motivation for learning in students; and it systematically destroys the ego and self-concept of a sizable group of students who are legally required to attend school for 10 to 12 years under conditions which are frustrating and humiliating year after year. The cost of this system in reducing opportunities for further learning and in alienating youth from both school and society is so great that no society can tolerate it for long.

Most students (perhaps over 90 percent) can master what we have to teach them, and it is the task of instruction to find the means which will enable our students to master the subject under consideration. Our basic task is to determine what we mean by mastery of the subject and to search for the methods and materials which will enable the largest proportion of our students to attain such mastery.

In this paper we will consider one approach to learning for mastery and the underlying theoretical concepts, research findings, and techniques required. Basically, the problem of developing a strategy for mastery learning is one of determining how individual differences in learners can be related to the learning and teaching process.

Background

Some societies can utilize only a small number of highly educated persons in the economy and can provide the economic support for only a small proportion of the students to complete secondary or higher education. Under such conditions much of the effort of the schools and the external examining system is to find ways of rejecting the majority of students at various points in the educational system and to discover the talented few who are to be given advanced educational opportunities. Such societies invest a great deal more in the prediction and selection of talent than in the development of such talent.

The complexities of the skills required by the work force in the United States and in other highly developed nations means that we can no longer operate on the assumption that completion of secondary and advanced education is for the few. The increasing evidence, Schultz (1963) and Bowman (1966), that investment in the education of humans pays off at a greater rate than does capital investment suggests that we cannot return to an economy of scarcity of educational opportunity.

Whatever might have been the case previously, highly developed nations must seek to find ways to increase the proportion of the age group that can successfully complete both secondary and higher education. The problem is no longer one of finding the few who can succeed. The basic problem is to determine how the largest proportion of the age group can learn effectively those skills and subject matter regarded as essential for their own development in a complex society.

However, given another set of philosophic and psychological presuppositions, we may express our concern for the intellectual and personality consequences of lack of clear success in the learning tasks of the school. Increasingly, learning throughout life (continuing learning) will be necessary for the largest proportion of the work force. If school learning is regarded as frustrating and even impossible by a sizable proportion of students, then little can be done at later levels to kindle a genuine interest in further learning. School learning must be successful and rewarding as one basis for insuring that learning can continue throughout one's life as needed.

Even more important in modern society is the malaise about values. As the secular society becomes more and more central, the values remaining for the individual have to do with hedonism, interpersonal relations, self-development, and ideas. If the schools frustrate the students in the latter two areas, only the first two are available to the individual. Whatever the case may be for each of these values, the schools must strive to assure all students of successful learning experiences in the realm of ideas and self-development.

There is little question that the schools now do provide successful learning experiences for some students—perhaps as high as one third of the students. If the schools are to provide successful and satisfying learning experiences for at least 90 percent of the students, major changes must take place in the attitudes of students, teachers, and administrators; changes must also take place in teaching strategies and in the role of evaluation.

The Normal Curve

We have for so long used the normal curve in grading students that we have come to believe in it. Our achievement measures are designed to detect differences among our learners, even if the differences are trivial in terms of the subject matter. We then distribute our grades in a normal fashion. In any group of students we expect to have some small percent receive A grades. We are surprised when the percentage differs greatly from about 10 percent. We are also prepared to fail an equal proportion of students. Quite frequently this failure is determined by the rank order of the students in the group rather than by their failure to grasp the essential ideas of the course. Thus, we have become accustomed to classify students into about five categories of level of performance and to assign grades in some relative fashion. It matters not that the failures of one year performed at about the same level as the C students of another year. Nor does it matter that the A students of one school do about as well as the F students of another school.

Having become "conditioned" to the normal distribution, we set grade policies in these terms and are horrified when some teacher attempts to recommend a very different distribution of grades. Administrators are constantly on the alert to control teachers who are "too easy" or "too hard" in their grading. A teacher whose grade distribution is normal will avoid difficulties with administrators. But even more important, we find ways of convincing students that they can only do C work or D work by our grading system and even by our system of quiz and progress testing. Finally, we proceed in our teaching as though only the minority of our students should be able to learn what we have to teach.

There is nothing sacred about the normal curve. It is the distribution most appropriate to chance and random activity. Education is a purposeful activity and we seek to have the students learn what we have to teach. If we are effective in our instruction, the distribution of achievement should be very different from the normal curve. In fact, we may even insist that our educational efforts have been unsuccessful to the extent to which our distribution of achievement approximates the normal distribution.

"Individual differences" in learners is a fact that can be demonstrated in many ways. That our students vary in many ways can never be forgotten. That these variations must be reflected in learning standards and achievement criteria is more a reflection of our policies and our practices

rather than the necessities of the case. Our basic task in
education is to find strategies which will take individual
differences into consideration but which will do so in such
a way as to promote the fullest development of the individual.

The Variables for Mastery Learning Strategies

A learning strategy for mastery may be derived from the
work of Carroll (1963), supported by the ideas of Morrison
(1926), Bruner (1966), Skinner (1954), Suppes (1966),
Goodlad and Anderson (1959), and Glaser (1968). In presenting these ideas we will refer to some of the research
findings which bear on them. However, our main concern
here is with the major variables in a model of school
learning and the ways in which these variables may be
utilized in a strategy for mastery learning.

Put in its most brief form the model proposed by
Carroll (1963) makes it clear that if the students are normally distributed with respect to aptitude for some subject
(mathematics, science, literature, history, etc.) and all the
students are provided with exactly the same instruction
(same in terms of amount of instruction, quality of instruction, and time available for learning), the end result will be
a normal distribution on an appropriate measure of achievement. Furthermore, the relationship between aptitude and
achievement will be relatively high (correlations of +.70 or
higher are to be expected if the aptitude and achievement
measures are valid and reliable). Conversely, if the students are normally distributed with respect to aptitude, but
the kind and quality of instruction and the amount of time
available for learning are made appropriate to the characteristics and needs of each student, the majority of students
may be expected to achieve mastery of the subject. And, the
relationship between aptitude and achievement should
approach zero. It is this basic set of ideas we wish to
develop in the following.

Aptitude for Particular Kinds of Learning

We have come to recognize that individuals do differ in
their aptitudes for particular kinds of learning and over the

years we have developed a large number of aptitude tests to measure these differences. In study after study we have found that aptitude tests are relatively good predictors of achievement criteria (achievement tests or teacher judgments). Thus, a good set of mathematic aptitude tests given at the beginning of the year will correlate as high as +.70 with the mathematics achievement tests given at the end of the course in algebra, or some other mathematics subject.

The use of aptitude tests for predictive purposes and the high correlations between such tests and achievement criteria have led many of us to the view that high levels of achievement are possible only for the most able students. From this, it is an easy step to some notion of causal connection between aptitude and achievement. The simplest notion of causality is that the students with high levels of aptitude can learn the complex ideas of the subject while the students with low levels of aptitude can learn only the simplest ideas of the subject.

Quite in contrast to this is Carroll's (1963) view that aptitude is the amount of time required by the learner to attain mastery of a learning task. Implicit in this formulation is the assumption that, given enough time, all students can conceivably attain mastery of a learning task. If Carroll is right, then learning mastery is theoretically available to all, if we can find the means for helping each student. It is this writer's belief that this formulation of Carroll's has the most fundamental implications for education.

One type of support for this view is to be found in the grade norms for many standardized achievement tests. These norms demonstrate that selected criterion scores achieved by the top students at one grade level are achieved by the majority of students at a later grade level. Further support is available in studies where students can learn at their own rate. These studies show that although most students eventually reach mastery on each learning task, some students achieve mastery much sooner than do other students (Glaser, 1968; Atkinson, 1967).

Can all students learn a subject equally well? That is, can all students master a learning task at a high level of complexity? As we study aptitude distributions in relation to student performance we have become convinced that there are differences between the extreme students and the remainder of the population. At the top of the aptitude distribution (1 percent to 5 percent) there are likely to be some students who have a special talent for the subject. Such students are able to learn and to use the subject with greater fluency than other students. The student with special aptitudes for music or foreign languages can learn these subjects in ways not available to most other students. Whether this is a matter of native endowment or the effect of previous training is not clear, although this must vary from subject to subject. It is likely that some individuals are born with sensory organs better attuned to sounds (music, language, etc.) than are others and that these constitutional characteristics give them special advantages in learning such subjects over others. For other subjects, special training, particular interests, etc. may develop these high level aptitudes.

At the other extreme of the aptitude distribution, we believe there are individuals with special disabilities for particular learning. The tone deaf individual will have great difficulty in learning music; the color blind individual will have problems in learning art; the individual who thinks in concrete forms will have special problems in learning highly abstract conceptual systems such as philosophy. Again, we believe these may constitute less than 5 percent of the distribution, but this will vary with the subject and the aptitudes.

In between are approximately 90 percent of the individuals where we believe (as does Carroll) that aptitudes are predictive of rate of learning rather than the level (or complexity) of learning that is possible. Thus, we are expressing the view that, given sufficient time and appropriate types of help, 95 percent of students (the top 5 percent + the next 90 percent) can learn a subject up to a high level of mastery. We are convinced that the grade of A as an index of mastery of a subject can, under appropriate conditions, be achieved by up to 95 percent of the students in a class.

It is assumed that it will take some students more effort, time, and help to achieve this level than it will other students. For some students the effort and help required may make it prohibitive. Thus, to learn high school algebra to a point of mastery may require several years for some students but only a fraction of a year for other students. Whether mastery learning is worth this great effort for the students who may take several years is highly questionable. One basic problem for a mastery learning strategy is to find ways of reducing the amount of time required for the slower students to a point where it is no longer a prohibitively long and difficult task for these less able students.

We do not believe that aptitude for particular learning tasks is completely stable. There is evidence (Bloom, 1964; Hunt, 1961) that the aptitude for particular learning tasks may be modified by appropriate environmental conditions or learning experiences in the school and the home. The major task of educational programs concerned with learning to learn and general education should be to produce positive changes in the students' basic aptitudes. It is likely that these aptitudes can be most markedly affected during the early years in the home and during the elementary years of school. Undoubtedly, however, some changes can take place at later points in the individual's career.

However, even if marked changes are not made in the individual's aptitudes, it is highly probable that more effective learning conditions can reduce the amount of time required to learn a subject to mastery for all students and especially for the students with lower aptitudes. It is this problem which must be directly attacked by strategies for mastery learning.

Quality of Instruction

Our schools have usually proceeded on the assumption that there is a standard classroom situation for all students. Typically, this has been expressed in the teacher-student ratio of 1-30 with group instruction as the central means of teaching. There is the expectation that each teacher will teach the subject in much the same way as other teachers. This standardization is further emphasized by textbook adoption which specifies the instructional material to be provided each class. Closely related to this is the extensive research over the past 50 years which seeks to find the one instructional method, material, or curriculum program that is best for all students.

Thus, over the years, we have fallen into the "educational trap" of specifying quality of instruction in terms of good and poor teachers, teaching, instructional materials, curriculum—all in terms of group results. We persist in asking such questions as: What is the best teacher for the group? What is the best method of instruction for the group? What is the best instructional material for the group?

One may start with the very different assumption that individual students may need very different types and qualities of instruction to achieve mastery. That is, the same content and objectives of instruction may be learned by different students as the result of very different types of instruction. Carroll (1963) defines the quality of instruction in terms of the degree to which the presentation, explanation, and ordering of elements of the task to be learned approach the optimum for a given learner.

Much research is needed to determine how individual differences in learners can be related to variations in the quality of instruction. There is evidence that some students can learn quite well through independent learning efforts while others need highly structured teaching-learning situations (Congreve, 1965). It seems reasonable to expect that some students will need more concrete illustrations and explanations than will others; some students may need more examples to get an idea than do others; some students may need more approval and reinforcement than others; and some students may even need to have several repetitions of the explanation while others may be able to get it the first time.

We believe that if every student had a very good tutor, most of them would be able to learn a particular subject to a higher degree. A good tutor attempts to find the qualities of instruction (and motivation) best suited to a given learner. And, there is some evidence (Dave, 1963) that middle-class parents do attempt to tutor their children when they believe that the quality of instruction in school does not enable their children to learn a particular subject. In an unpublished study, the writer found that one-third of the students in an algebra course in a middle-class school were receiving as much tutorial instruction in the home in algebra as they were receiving group instruction in the school. These students received relatively high grades for the algebra course. For these students, the relationship between their mathematics aptitude scores (at the beginning of the year) and their achievement in algebra at the end of the year was almost zero. In contrast, for the students who received no additional instruction other than the regular classroom instruction, the relationship between their mathematics aptitude scores and their algebra achievement scores was very high (+.90). While this type of research needs to be replicated, it is evident in this small study that the home tutoring help was providing the quality of instruction needed by these students to learn the algebra —that is, the instruction was adapted to the needs of the individual learners.

The main point to be stressed is that the quality of instruction is to be considered in terms of its effects on individual learners rather than on random groups of learners. Hopefully, the research of the future may lead to the definition of the qualities and kinds of instruction needed by various types of learners. Such research may suggest more effective group instruction since it is unlikely that the schools will be able to provide instruction for each learner separately.

Ability to Understand Instruction

In most courses at the high school and college level there is a single teacher and a single set of instructional materials. If the student has facility in understanding the teacher's communications about the learning and the instructional material (usually a textbook), he has little difficulty in learning the subject. If he has difficulty in understanding the teacher's instruction and/or the instructional material, he is likely to have greater difficulty in learning the subject. The ability to understand instruction may be defined as the ability of the learner to understand the nature of the task he is to learn and the procedures he is to follow in the learning of the task.

Here is a point at which the student's abilities interact with the instructional materials and the instructor's abilities in teaching. For the student in our highly verbal schools it is likely that this ability to understand instruction is primarily determined by verbal ability and reading comprehension. These two measures of language ability are significantly related to achievement in the majority of subjects and they are highly related (+.50 to +.60) to grade point averages at the high school or college level. What this suggests is that verbal ability (independent of specific aptitudes for each subject) determines some general ability to learn from teachers and instructional materials.

While it is possible to alter an individual's verbal ability by appropriate training, there are limits to the amount of change that can be produced. Most change in verbal ability can be produced at the pre-school and elementary school levels with less and less change being likely as the student gets older (Bloom, 1964). Vocabulary and reading ability, however, may be improved to some extent at all age levels, even though there is a diminishing utility of this approach with increasing age. Improvements in verbal abilities should result in improvements in the individual's ability to understand instruction.

The greatest immediate payoff in dealing with the ability to understand instruction is likely to come from modifications in instruction in order to meet the needs of individual students. There is no doubt that some teachers do attempt to modify their instruction to fit a given group of students. Many teachers center their instruction at the middle group of their students, others at the top or bottom group—these are, however, reflections of the teacher's habits and attitudes. They are, by no means, determinants of what it is possible for a teacher to do. Given help and various types of aids, individual teachers can find ways of modifying their instruction to fit the differing needs of their students.

Group study procedures should be available to students as they need it. In our own experience we have found that small groups of students (two or three students) meeting regularly to go over points of difficulty in the learning process were most effective, especially when the students could cooperate and help each other without any danger of giving each other special advantages in a competitive situation. Where learning can be turned into a cooperative process with everyone likely to gain from the process, small group learning procedures can be very effective. Much depends on the composition of the group and the opportunities it gives each person to expose his difficulties and have them corrected without demeaning one person and elevating another. In the group process, the more able students have opportunities to strengthen their own learning in the process of helping another person grasp the idea through alternative ways of explaining and using the idea.

Tutorial help (one to one relations between teacher and learner) represents the most costly type of help and should be used only where alternative procedures are not effective. However, this type of help should be available to students as they need it, especially where individuals have particular difficulties that can't be corrected in other ways. The tutor, ideally, should be someone other than the teacher, since he should bring a fresh way of viewing the idea or the process. The tutor must be skillful in detecting the points of difficulty in the student's learning and should help him in such a way as to free the student from continued dependence on him.

Another approach to variations in the students' ability to understand instruction is to vary the instructional material.

Textbooks may vary in the clarity with which they explain a particular idea or process. The fact that one textbook has been adopted by the school or by the teacher does not necessarily mean that other textbooks cannot be used at particular points in the instruction when they would be helpful to a student who can't grasp the idea from the adopted textbook. The task here is to be able to determine where the individual student has difficulty in understanding the instructions and then provide alternative textbook explanations if they are more effective at that point.

Workbooks and programmed instruction units may be especially helpful for some students who cannot grasp the ideas or procedures in the textbook form. Some students need the drill and the specific tasks which workbooks can provide. Other students need the small steps and frequent reinforcement which programmed units can provide. Such materials may be used in the initial instruction or as devote the amount of time he needs to the learning task but also that he be allowed enough time for the learning to take place.

There seems to be little doubt that students with high levels of aptitude are likely to be more efficient in their learning and to require less time for learning than students with lower levels of aptitude. Whether most students can be helped to become highly efficient learners in general is a problem for future research.

The amount of time students need for a particular kind of learning has not been studied directly. One indication of the time needed comes from studies of the amount of time students spend on homework. In our review of the amount of time spent by 13-year-old students on mathematics homework in the International Study of Educational Achievement (Husen, 1967), we find that if we omit the extreme 5 percent of the subjects, the ratio is roughly 6 to 1. That is, some students spend 6 times as much time on mathematics homework as do others. Other studies of use of time suggest that this is roughly the order of magnitude to be expected.

If instruction and student use of time become more effective, we believe that most students will need less time to learn the subject to mastery and that the ratio of time required for the slower and the faster learners may be reduced from 6 to 1 to perhaps 3 to 1.

In general, we find a zero or a slightly negative relationship between final grades and amount of time spent on homework. In the International Study (Husen, 1967) the average correlation for twelve countries at the 13-year-old level is approximately $-.05$ between achievement test scores in mathematics and number of hours per week of homework in mathematics as reported by students. Thus, the amount of time spent on homework does not seem to be a very good predictor of achievement in the subject.

We are convinced that it is not the sheer amount of time spent in learning (either in school or out of school) that accounts for the level of learning. We believe that each student should be allowed the time he needs to learn a subject. And, the time he needs to learn the subject is likely

students encounter specific difficulties in learning a particular unit or section of the course.

■ *Audiovisual Methods and Academic Games*—Some students may learn a particular idea best through concrete illustrations and vivid and clear explanations. It is likely that film strips and short motion pictures which can be used by individual students as needed may be very effective. Other students may need concrete material such as laboratory experiences, simple demonstrations, blocks, and other relevant apparatus in order to comprehend an idea or task. Academic games, puzzles, and other interesting but not threatening devices may be useful. Here again, the point is that some ways of communicating and comprehending an idea, problem, or task may be especially effective for some students although others may not use or need such materials and methods. We need not place the highest priority for all on abstract and verbal ways of instruction.

With regard to instructional materials, the suggestion is not that particular materials be used by particular students throughout the course. It is that each type of material may serve as a means of helping individual students at selected points in the learning process—and that a particular student may use whatever variety of materials are found to be useful as he encounters difficulties in the learning.

Throughout the use of alternative methods of instruction and instructional material, the essential point to be borne in mind is that these are attempts to improve the quality of instruction in relation to the ability of each student to understand the instruction. As feedback methods inform the teachers of particular errors and difficulties the majority of students are having, it is to be expected that the regular group instruction could be modified so as to correct these difficulties. As particular students are helped individually, the goal should be not only to help the student over particular learning difficulties but also to enable him to become more independent in his learning and to help him identify the alternative ways by which he can comprehend new ideas. But, most important, the presence of a great variety of instructional materials and procedures should help both teachers and students to overcome feelings of defeatism and passivity about learning. If the student can't learn in one way, he should be reassured that alternatives are available to him. The teacher should come to recognize that it is the learning which is important and that instructional alternatives exist to enable all (or almost all) of the students to learn the subject to a high level.

Perseverance

Carroll defines perseverance as the time the learner is willing to spend in learning. If a student needs to spend a certain amount of time to master a particular task, and he spends less than his amount in active learning, he is not likely to learn the task to the level of mastery. Carroll attempts to differentiate between spending time on learning and the amount of time the student is actively engaged in learning.

Perseverance does appear to be related to attitudes toward and interest in learning. In the International Study of Educational Achievement (Husen, 1967), the relationship between the number of hours of homework per week reported by the student (a crude index of perseverance) and the number of years of further education desired by the student is +.25.

We do believe that students vary in the amount of perseverance they bring to a specific learning task. However, students appear to approach different learning tasks with different amounts of perseverance. The student who gives up quickly in his efforts to learn an academic subject may persevere an unusually long time in learning how to repair an automobile or in learning to play a musical instrument. It would appear to us that as a student finds the effort rewarding, he is likely to spend more time on a particular learning task. If, on the other hand, the student is frustrated in his learning, he must (in self-defense) reduce the amount of time he devotes to learning. While the frustration level of students may vary, we believe that all students must sooner or later give up a task if it is too painful for them.

While efforts may be made to increase the amount of perseverance in students, it is likely that manipulation of the instruction and learning materials may be more effec-

tive in helping students master a given learning t spite of their present level of perseverance. Freque reward and evidence of success in learning can increa student's perseverance in a learning situation. As stu attain mastery of a given task, they are likely to inc their perseverance for a related learning task.

In our own research we are finding that the dem for perseverance may be sharply reduced if student provided with instructional resources most appropriat them. Frequent feedback accompanied by specific hel instruction and material as needed can reduce the time (perseverance) required. Improvement in the quality instruction (or explanations and illustrations) may red the amount of perseverance necessary for a given learn task.

There seems to be little reason to make learning difficult that only a small proportion of the students c persevere to mastery. Endurance and unusual perseve ance may be appropriate for long-distance running—the are not great virtues in their own right. The emphas should be on learning, not on vague ideas of discipline an endurance.

Time Allowed for Learning

Throughout the world schools are organized to give group instruction with definite periods of time allocated for particular learning tasks. A course in history at the secondary level may be planned for an academic year of instruction, another course may be planned for a semester, while the amount of instructional time allocated for a subject like arithmetic at the 5th-grade level may be fixed. Whatever the amount of time allowed by the school and the curriculum for particular subjects or learning tasks, it is likely to be too much for some students and not enough for other students.

For Carroll, the time spent on learning is the key to mastery. His basic assumption is that aptitude determines the rate of learning and that most, if not all, students can achieve mastery if they devote the amount of time needed to the learning. This implies that the student must not only

to be affected by the student's aptitudes, his verbal ability, the quality of instruction he receives in class, and the quality of the help he receives outside of class. The task of a strategy for mastery learning is to find ways of altering the time individual students need for learning as well as to find ways of providing whatever time is needed by each student. Thus, a strategy for mastery learning must find some way of solving the instructional problems as well as the school organizational (including time) problems.

One Strategy for Mastery Learning

There are many alternative strategies for mastery learning. Each strategy must find some way of dealing with individual differences in learners through some means of relating the instruction to the needs and characteristics of the learners. We believe that each strategy must include some way of dealing with the five variables discussed in the foregoing.

Were it not so costly in human resources, we believe that the provision of a good tutor for each student might be one ideal strategy. In any case, the tutor-student relationship is a useful model to consider when one attempts to work out the details of a less costly strategy. Also, the tutor strategy is not as farfetched as it may seem at first glance. In the pre-school period most of the child's instruction is tutorial—usually provided by the mother. In many middle-class homes the parents continue to provide tutorial help as needed by the child during much of his school career.

Other strategies include permitting students to go at their own pace, guiding students with respect to courses they should or should not take, and providing different tracks or streams for different groups of learners. The nongraded school (Goodlad and Anderson, 1959) is one attempt to provide an organizational structure that permits and encourages mastery learning.

A group of us at the University of Chicago have been doing research on the variables discussed in the previous pages. In addition, some of us have been attempting to develop a strategy of teaching and learning which will bring all (or almost all) students to a level of mastery in the learning of any subject. Our approach has been to supplement regular group instruction by using diagnostic procedures and alternative instructional methods and materials in such a way as to bring a large proportion of the students to a predetermined standard of achievement. In this approach, we have tried to bring most of the students to mastery levels of achievement within the regular term, semester, or period of calendar time in which the course is usually taught. Undoubtedly, some students will spend more time than others in learning the subject, but if the majority of students reach mastery levels at the end of the time allocated for the subject, mastery will have affective as well as cognitive consequences.

We have had some successes and some dismal failures with this approach. We have been trying to learn from both the successes and the failures. In the near future we hope to have some of these ideas applied to a large number of classrooms in selected school systems. Initially, we have chosen to work with subjects which have few prerequisites (algebra, science, etc.) because we believe it is easier to secure mastery learning in a given time period in such courses. In contrast are subjects which are late in a long sequence of learning (6th grade reading, 8th grade arithmetic, advanced mathematics, etc.). For such subjects, it is unlikely that mastery learning can be attained within a term for a group of students who have had a long history of cumulative learning difficulties in the specific subject field.

In working on this strategy we have attempted to spell out some of the preconditions necessary, develop the operating procedures required, and evaluate some of the outcomes of the strategy.

Preconditions

If we are able to develop mastery learning in students, we must be able to recognize when students have achieved it. We must be able to define what we mean by mastery and we must be able to collect the necessary evidence to establish whether or not a student has achieved it.

The specification of the objectives and content of

instruction is one necessary precondition for informing both teachers and students about the expectations. The translation of the specifications into evaluation procedures helps to further define what it is that the student should be able to do when he has completed the course. The evaluation procedures used to appraise the outcomes of instruction (summative evaluation) help the teacher and student know when the instruction has been effective.

Implicit in this way of defining the outcomes and preparing evaluation instruments is a distinction between the teaching-learning process and the evaluation process. At some point in time, the results of teaching and learning can be reflected in the evaluation of the students. But, these are separate processes. That is, teaching and learning are intended to prepare the student in an area of learning, while evaluation (summative) is intended to appraise the extent to which the student has developed in the desired ways. Both the teacher and the learner must have some understanding of what the achievement criteria are and both must be able to secure evidence of progress toward these criteria.

If the achievement criteria are primarily competitive, i.e., the student is to be judged in terms of his relative position in the group, then the student is likely to seek evidence on his standing in the group as he progresses through the learning tasks. We recognize that competition may be a spur to those students who view others in competitive terms, but we believe that much of learning and development may be destroyed by primary emphasis on competition.

Much more preferable in terms of intrinsic motivation for learning is the setting of standards of mastery and excellence apart from interstudent competition, followed by appropriate efforts to bring as many students up to this standard as possible. This suggests some notion of absolute standards and the use of grades or marks which will reflect these standards. Thus, it is conceivable that all students may achieve mastery and the grade of A. It is also possible in a particular year in a specific course for a few or none of the students to attain mastery or a grade of A.

While we would recommend the use of absolute standards carefully worked out for a subject, we recognize the difficulty of arriving at such standards. In some of our own work, we have made use of standards derived from previous experience with students in a particular course. In one course, students in 1966 were informed that the grades for 1966 would be based on standards arrived at in 1965. The grades of A, B, C, D, and F would be based on an examination which was parallel to that used in 1965 and the grades would be set at the same performance levels as those used in 1965. The students were informed that the proportion of students receiving each grade was to be determined by their performance levels rather than by their rank order in the group. Thus, the students were not competing with each other for grades; they were to be judged on the basis of levels of mastery used in 1965.

We do not believe this is the only way of arriving at achievement standards, but the point is that students must feel they are being judged in terms of level of performance rather than a normal curve or some other arbitrary and relative set of standards. We are not recommending national achievement standards. What is being recommended are realistic performance standards developed for each school or group, followed by instructional procedures which will enable the majority of students to attain these standards.

One result of this way of setting achievement standards was to enable the students to work with each other and to help each other without being concerned about giving special advantages (or disadvantages) to other students. Cooperation in learning rather than competition was a clear result from this method of setting achievement criteria.

In the work we have done, we attempted to have the teacher teach the course in much the same way as previously. That is, the particular materials and methods of instruction in the current year should be about the same as in previous years. Also, the time schedule during the course was about the same. The operating procedures discussed in the next section supplemented the regular instruction of the teacher. We have proceeded in this way because we believe a useful strategy for mastery learning should be widely applicable. If extensive training of teachers is necessary for a particular strategy, it is less likely that it will receive widespread use.

Operating Procedures

The operating procedures we have used are intended to provide detailed feedback to teachers and students and to provide specific supplementary instructional resources as needed. These procedures are devised to insure mastery of each learning unit in such a way as to reduce the time required while directly affecting both quality of instruction and the ability of the student to understand the instruction.

■ *Formative Evaluation*—One useful operating procedure is to break a course or subject into smaller units of learning. Such a learning unit may correspond to a chapter in a textbook, a well-defined content portion of a course, or a particular time unit of the course. We have tended to think of units as involving a week or two of learning activity.

Using some of the ideas of Gagné (1965) and Bloom (1956) we have attempted to analyze each unit into a number of elements ranging from specific terms or facts, more complex and abstract ideas such as concepts and principles, and relatively complex processes such as application of principles and analysis of complex theoretical statements. We believe, as does Gagné (1965) that these elements form a hierarchy of learning tasks.

We have then attempted to construct brief diagnostic-progress tests which can be used to determine whether or not the student has mastered the unit and what, if anything, the student must still do to master it. We have borrowed the term Formative Evaluation from Scriven (1967) to refer to these diagnostic-progress tests.

Frequent formative evaluation tests pace the learning of students and help motivate them to put forth the necessary effort at the appropriate time. The appropriate use of these tests helps to insure that each set of learning tasks is thoroughly mastered before subsequent learning tasks are started.

Each formative test is administered after the completion of the appropriate learning unit. While the frequency of these progress tests may vary throughout the course, it is likely that some portions of the course—especially the early sections of the course—may need more frequent formative tests than later portions. Where some of the learning units are basic and prerequisite for other units of the course, the tests should be frequent enough to insure thorough mastery of such learning material.

For those students who have thoroughly mastered the unit, the formative tests should reinforce the learning and assure the student that his present mode of learning and approach to study is adequate. Since he will have a number of such tests, the student who consistently demonstrates mastery should be able to reduce his anxiety about his course achievement.

For students who lack mastery of a particular unit, the formative tests should reveal the particular points of difficulty—the specific questions they answer incorrectly and the particular ideas, skills, and processes they still need to work on. It is most helpful when the diagnosis shows the elements in a learning hierarchy that the student still needs to learn. We have found that students respond best to the diagnostic results when they are referred to particular instructional materials or processes intended to help them correct their difficulties. The diagnosis should be accompanied by a very specific prescription if the students are to do anything about it.

Although we have limited evidence on this point, we believe that the formative tests should not be assigned grades or quality points. We have marked the tests to show mastery and nonmastery. The nonmastery is accompanied by detailed diagnosis and prescription of what is yet to be done before mastery is complete. We believe that the use of grades on repeated progress tests prepares students for the acceptance of less than mastery. To be graded C repeatedly prepares the student to accept a C as his "fate" for the particular course, especially when the grades on progress tests are averaged in as part of the final grade. Under such conditions there must come a point when it is impossible to do better than a particular grade in the course—and there is little value in striving to improve. Formative evaluation tests should be regarded as part of the learning process and should in no way be confused with the judgment of the capabilities of the student or used as a part of the grading process.

These formative tests may also provide feedback for the teacher since they can be used to identify particular points in the instruction that are in need of modification. The formative evaluation tests can also serve as a means of quality control in future cycles of the course. The performance of the students on each test may be compared with the norms for previous years to insure that students are doing as well or better. Such comparisons can also be used to insure that changes in instruction or materials are not producing more error and difficulty than was true in a previous cycle of the course.

■ *Alternative Learning Resources*—It is one thing to diagnose the specific learning difficulties the student has and to suggest the specific steps he should take to overcome these difficulties. It is quite another thing to get him to do anything about it. By itself, the frequent use of progress tests can improve the achievement of students to a small degree. If, in addition, the student can be motivated to expend further effort on correcting his errors on the progress tests, the gains in achievement can be very great.

We have found that students do attempt to work on their difficulties when they are given specific suggestions (usually on the formative evaluation results) as to what they need to do.

The best procedure we have found thus far is to have small groups of students (two or three) meet regularly for as much as an hour per week to review the results of their formative evaluation tests and to help each other overcome the difficulties identified on these tests.

We have offered tutorial help as students desired it, but so far students at the secondary or higher education level do not seek this type of help frequently.

Other types of learning resources we have prescribed for students include: a. reread particular pages of the original instructional materials; b. read or study specific pages in alternative textbooks or other instructional materials; c. use specific pages of workbooks or programmed texts; and d. use selected audiovisual materials.

We suspect that no specific learning material or process is indispensable. The presence of a great variety of instructional materials and procedures and specific suggestions as to which ones the student might use help the student recognize that if he cannot learn in one way, alternatives are available to him. Perhaps further research will reveal the best match between individuals and alternative learning resources. At present, we do not have firm evidence on the relations between student characteristics and instructional materials and procedures.

Outcomes

What are the results of a strategy for mastery learning? So far we have limited evidence. The results to date, however, are very encouraging. We are in the process of securing more evidence on a variety of situations at the elementary, secondary, and higher education levels.

■ *Cognitive Outcomes of a Mastery Strategy*—In our work to date we have found some evidence of the effectiveness of a strategy for mastery learning. Our best results have been found in a course on test theory where we have been able to use parallel achievement tests for the course in 1965, 1966, and 1967. In 1965, before the strategy was used, approximately 20 percent of the students received the grade of A on the final examination. In 1966, after the strategy was employed, 80 percent of the students reached this same level of mastery on the parallel examination and were given the grade of A. The difference in the mean performance of the two groups represents about two standard deviations on the 1965 achievement test and is highly significant.

In 1967, using the same formative evaluation tests as used in 1966, it was possible to compare the 1966 and the 1967 results after each unit of learning. Thus, the formative evaluation tests become quality control measures. Where there were significant negative differences between the results on a particular test from 1966 to 1967, the instructor reviewed the specific learning difficulties and attempted to explain the ideas in a different way. The final results on the 1967 summative evaluation instrument, which was parallel to the final achievement tests in 1965 and 1966, were that 90 percent of the students achieved mastery and were given grades of A.

Similar studies are underway at different levels of education. We expect to have many failures and a few successes. But, the point to be made is not that a single strategy of mastery learning can be used mechanically to achieve a particular set of results. Rather, the problem is one of determining what procedures will prove effective in helping particular students learn the subject under consideration. It is hoped that each time a strategy is used, it will be studied to find where it is succeeding and where it is not. For which students is it effective and for which students is it not effective? Hopefully, the results in a particular year can take advantage of the experience accumulated over the previous years.

■ *Affective Consequences of Mastery*—We have for the past century conceived of mastery of a subject as being possible for only a minority of students. With this assumption we have adjusted our grading system so as to certify that only a small percent of students (no matter how carefully selected) are awarded a grade of A. If a group of students learns a subject in a superior way (as contrasted with a previous group of students) we still persist in awarding the A (or mastery) to only the top 10 or 15 percent of the students. We grudgingly recognize that the majority of students have "gotten by" by awarding them grades of D or C. Mastery and recognition of mastery under the present relative grading system is unattainable for the majority of students—but this is the result of the way in which we have "rigged" the educational system.

Mastery must be both a subjective recognition by the student of his competence and a public recognition by the school or society. The public recognition must be in the form of appropriate certification by the teacher or by the school. No matter how much the student has learned, if public recognition is denied him, he must come to believe that he is inadequate, rather than the system of grading or instruction. Subjectively, the student must gain feelings of control over ideas and skills. He must come to recognize that he "knows" and can do what the subject requires.

If the system of formative evaluation (diagnostic-progress tests) and the summative evaluation (achievement examinations) informs the student of his mastery of the subject, he will come to believe in his own mastery and competence. He may be informed by the grading system as well as by the discovery that he can adequately cope with the variety of tasks and problems in the evaluation instruments.

When the student has mastered a subject and when he receives both objective and subjective evidence of the mastery, there are profound changes in his view of himself and of the outer world.

Perhaps the clearest evidence of affective change is the interest the student develops for the subject he has mastered. He begins to "like" the subject and to desire more of it. To do well in a subject opens up further avenues for exploration of the subject. Conversely, to do poorly in a subject closes an area for further study. The student desires some control over his environment, and mastery of a subject gives him some feeling of control over a part of his environment. Interest in a subject is both a cause of mastery of the subject as well as a result of mastery. Motivation for further learning is one of the more important consequences of mastery.

At a deeper level is the student's self-concept. Each person searches for positive recognition of his worth and he comes to view himself as adequate in those areas where he receives assurance of his competence or success. For a student to view himself in a positive way, he must be given many opportunities to be rewarded. Mastery and its public recognition provide the necessary reassurance and reinforcement to help the student view himself as adequate. It is the opinion of this writer that one of the more positive aids to mental health is frequent and objective indications of self-development. Mastery learning can be one of the more powerful sources of mental health. We are convinced that many of the neurotic symptoms displayed by high school and college students are exacerbated by painful and frustrating experiences in school learning. If 90 percent of the students are given positive indications of adequacy in learning, one might expect such students to need less and less in the way of emotional therapy and psychological help. Contrariwise, frequent indications of failure and learning inadequacy must be accompanied by increased self-doubt on the part of the student and the search for reassurance and adequacy outside the school.

Finally, modern society requires continual learning throughout life. If the schools do not promote adequate learning and reassurance of progress, the student must come to reject learning—both in the school and later life. Mastery learning can give zest to school learning and can develop a lifelong interest in learning. It is this continual learning which should be the major goal of the educational system.

Reprinted from *Evaluation Comment*, May, 1968, Vol. 1, No. 2. Copyright 1968 by The Center for the Study of Evaluation of Instructional Programs. Dr. Bloom is the Charles H. Swift Distinguished Professor of Education at the University of Chicago.

References

Atkinson, R. C., "Computerized Instruction and the Learning Process." Technical Report No. 122, Stanford, California. Institute for Mathematical Studies in the Social Sciences, 1967.

Bloom, B.S., *Stability and Change in Human Characteristics*. New York: John Wiley & Sons, 1964.

Bloom, B. S. (Ed.), *Taxonomy of Educational Objectives: Handbook I, Cognitive Domain*. New York: David McKay Company, 1956.

Bowman, M. J., "The New Economics of Education." *International Journal of Educational Sciences*, 1966, 1:29–46.

Bruner, Jerome, *Toward a Theory of Instruction.* Cambridge, Massachusetts: Harvard University Press, 1966.

Carroll, John, "A Model of School Learning," *Teachers College Record,* 1963, 64:723–733.

Congreve, W. J., "Independent Learning." *North Central Association Quarterly,* 1965, 40:222–228.

Dave, R. H., "The Identification and Measurement of Environmental Process Variables that are Related to Educational Achievement." Unpublished doctoral dissertation, University of Chicago, 1963.

Gagné, Robert M., *The Conditions of Learning.* New York: Holt, Rinehart, & Winston, 1965.

Glaser, R., "Adapting the Elementary School Curriculum to Individual Performance." Proceedings of the 1967 Invitational Conference on Testing Problems. Princeton, New Jersey: Educational Testing Service, 1968.

Goodlad, J. I. and Anderson, R. H., *The Nongraded Elementary School.* New York: Harcourt, Brace & World, 1959.

Hunt, J. McV., *Intelligence and Experience.* New York: Ronald Press Co., 1961.

Husen, T. (Ed.), *International Study of Educational Achievement in Mathematics: A Comparison of Twelve Countries.* Volumes I and II. New York: John Wiley & Sons, 1967.

Morrison, H. C., *The Practice of Teaching in the Secondary School.* Chicago: University of Chicago Press, 1926.

Schultz, T. W., *The Economic Value of Education.* New York: Columbia University Press, 1963.

Scriven, Michael, "The Methodology of Evaluation." In Stake, R. (Ed.), Perspectives of Curriculum Evaluation. Chicago: Rand McNally & Co., 1967.

Skinner, B. F., "The Science of Learning and the Art of Teaching." *Harvard Educational Review,* 1954, 24:86–97.

Suppes, P., "The Uses of Computers in Education." *Scientific American,* 1966, 215:206–221.

2

A Model of School Learning

John B. Carroll

The primary job of the educational psychologist is to develop and apply knowledge concerning why pupils succeed or fail in their learning at school, and to assist in the prevention and remediation of learning difficulties.

This job is inherently difficult because behavior is complex and has a multiplicity of causes. To deal with it, educational psychologists have evolved a number of concepts which they find useful in classifying the phenomena of behavior. Textbooks in the field are commonly organized around such concepts as maturation, individual differences, learning, thinking, motivation, and social development. These are useful categories, but because they overlap or refer to different levels of organization in the subject matter, it is difficult to build them into an integrated account of the process of school learning. What is needed is a schematic design or conceptual model of factors affecting success in school learning and of the way they interact. Such a model should use a very small number of simplifying concepts, conceptually independent of one another and referring to phenomena at the same level of discourse. It should suggest new and interesting research questions and aid in the solution of practical educational problems.

With the aid of such a framework, the often conflicting results of different research studies might be seen to fall into a unified pattern.

Many such formulations, perhaps, are possible. A conceptual model will be presented here that seems to have the advantage of comprehensiveness combined with relative simplicity. The model is amenable to elaboration, but for our immediate purposes, we will leave aside any such elaborations.

Scope of the Model

We need first to define learning task. The learner's task of going from ignorance of some specified fact or concept to knowledge or understanding of it, or of proceeding from incapability of performing some specified act to capability of performing it, is a learning task. To call it a task does not necessarily imply that the learner must be aware that he is supposed to learn or be aware of what he is supposed to learn, although in most cases it happens that such awarenesses on the part of the learner are desirable.

Most, but not all, goals of the school can be expressed in the form of learning tasks or a series of such tasks. Teaching the child to read, for example, means to teach him to perform certain acts in response to written or printed language. Examples of other learning tasks taught in the schools can be multiplied at will: learning to spell all the words in common use, learning to perform certain operations with numbers, learning to explain or otherwise demonstrate an understanding of the subject matter of biology, learning to speak a foreign language, learning to perform in competitive sports, and learning to carry out certain responsibilities of a citizen. Some of these tasks are very broadly defined, such as learning to read printed English, but we can also consider narrowly defined tasks like mastering the content of Lesson 20 in a certain textbook of French, or even mastering a certain grammatical construction covered in that lesson. The model presented here is intended to apply equally well to all such tasks, no matter how broad or narrow. It is required, however, that the task can be unequivocally described and that means can be found for making a valid judgment as to when the learner has accomplished the learning task—that is, has achieved the learning goal which has been set for him.

It will be seen that as many as possible of the basic concepts in the model are defined so that they can be measured in terms of time in order to capitalize on the advantages of a scale with a meaningful zero point and equal units of measurement. An effort is made to provide for a mathematical description of the degree to which a learning task is achieved. Although the model applies only to one learning task at a time, it should be possible in principle to describe the pupil's success in learning a series of tasks (e.g., all the work of the fifth grade) by summating the results of applying the model successively to each component task.

The model is admittedly oversimplified. The assumption that the work of the school can be broken down into a series of learning tasks can be called into question. In actual school practice, the various tasks to be learned are not necessarily treated as separate and distinct, and the process of teaching is often organized (whether rightly so or not) so that learnings will take place "incidentally" and in the course of other activities. Nevertheless, a conceptual model requires certain simplifying assumptions, and the assumption of discrete learning tasks is a useful one to make.

The model can be regarded as applying even to those educational goals ordinarily formulated in terms of "transfer"—that is, the ability to apply in a "new" situation something learned previously. The concept of the learning task is defined to include the attainment of that degree of competence which will make "transfer" essentially as automatic as demonstration of performance in the original setting. "Transfer," correctly viewed, is a term in a metalanguage which states the conditions under which particular learnings occur or manifest themselves. Thus, when we say that "learning which occurred in situation A transfers to situation B," we are really saying that "something learned in situation A also manifested itself in situation B, there being sufficient commonality between the two situations to elicit the learned performance in both."

The model is not intended to apply however, to those

goals of the school which do not lend themselves to being considered as learning tasks. Such, for example, are those goals having to do with attitudes and dispositions. Educating a child so that he has tolerance for persons of other races or creeds, respect for parental or legal authority, or attitudes of fair play, is thought to be largely a matter of emotional conditioning or of the acquisition of values and drives. Learning tasks may indeed be involved in the cognitive support of such attitudes (as where the child learns facts about different races or creeds), but the acquisition of attitudes is postulated to follow a different paradigm from that involved in learning tasks. Perhaps the distinctions made by Skinner (6) are of use in this connection: We could say that whereas learning tasks typically involve "operants," the attitudinal goals of education typically involve "respondents."

Overview of the Model

Briefly, our model says that the learner will succeed in learning a given task to the extent that he spends the amount of time that he needs to learn the task. The terms of this statement, however, require special definition, explication, and interpretation if the statement is to be properly understood.

First, it should be understood that "spending time" means actually spending time on the act of learning. "Time" is therefore not "elapsed time" but the time during which the person is oriented to the learning task and actively engaged in learning. In common parlance, it is the time during which he is "paying attention" and "trying to learn."

Second, there are certain factors which determine how much time the learner spends actively engaged in learning.

Third, there are certain factors which determine how much time a person needs to spend in order to learn the task. These factors may or may not be the same as, or associated with, those which influence how much time he spends in learning.

The major part of this article is devoted to a presentation of the factors conceived as determining the times needed or actually spent in the course of a learning task and the way in which these factors interact to result in various degrees of success in learning. Four of these factors are convenient intervening variables or constructs which may, in turn, be regarded as functions of still other factors or variables; one, however, is in principle a directly manipulable and measurable factor ("opportunity").

This model of school learning should not be confused with what is ordinarily called "learning theory," that is, with the exact scientific analysis of the essential conditions of learning and the development of systematic theory about this process. Rather, the model may be thought of as a description of the "economics" of the school learning process; it takes the fact of learning for granted.

The five factors or variables in the model will be presented under two headings: (1) determinants of time needed for learning, and (2) determinants of time spent in learning.

Time Needed in Learning

■ *Aptitude*—Suppose that a randomly selected group of children is taught a certain learning task by a teacher (or teaching device) with the best possible teaching techniques. Suppose further that each child is willing to stick attentively with the learning task for the number of minutes, hours, or days required for him to learn it to the specified criterion of success, and that each child is in fact given the opportunity to do this. Common experience, as well as abundant research evidence, suggests that the amounts of time needed by the children even under these ideal conditions will differ widely. Let us think, then, of the amount of time the pupil will need to learn the task under these conditions as the primary measure of a variable which we shall call his aptitude for learning this task. In ordinary parlance, learners who need only a small amount of time are said to have high aptitude; learners who need a large amount of time are said to have low aptitude. Some learners, it may be, will never learn even under these optimal conditions; we may say that these learners would need an indefinitely large (or an infinite) amount of time to learn the task.

It will be noted that this variable is measured in the

opposite direction from the usual way of measuring aptitude—the shorter the time needed for learning, the higher the aptitude.

Furthermore, it will be noted that the measure of aptitude is specific to the task under consideration. Aptitude may be regarded as a function of numerous other variables. For one thing, it may depend upon the amount of prior learning which may be relevant to the task under consideration. A learner who has already progressed far towards the mastery of a task may not need much time to complete his learning. On the other hand, aptitude may also depend upon a series of traits or characteristics of the learner which enter into a wide variety of tasks; whether these traits can be accounted for solely on the basis of generalized prior learnings, or whether they reflect genetically determined individual characteristics, is of no immediate concern here. It may be useful, however, to conceive that a learner's estimated needed time, α_t, for learning a given task, t, may be written as a mathematical function of a series of basic aptitudes, symbolized with Greek letters and subscripts, minus the amount of time, s_t, saved by virtue of prior learnings relevant to the task. Thus:

$$\alpha_t = f(\alpha_1, \alpha_2, \ldots, \alpha_n) - s_t$$

The exact form of this formula would vary for different tasks. Presumably, the basic aptitudes $\alpha_1, \alpha_2, \ldots, \alpha_n$ could be measured with considerable exactitude by appropriate tests.

■ *Ability to understand instruction*—We find it useful to postulate as a variable separate from those we consider under "aptitude" the ability to understand instruction, since this variable (in contrast to pure aptitude variables) is thought of as interacting with the method of instruction in a special and interesting way. The ability to understand instruction could be measured, one would suppose, as some combination of "general intelligence" and "verbal ability"; the former of these two would come into play in instructional situations where the learner is left to infer for himself the concepts and relationships inherent in the material to be learned, rather than having them carefully spelled out for him, while the latter would come into play whenever the instruction utilized language beyond the grasp of the learner. The way in which ability to understand instruction is postulated to interact with the type of instruction will be explained after we introduce a third variable affecting time needed for learning, the quality of instruction.

■ *Quality of Instruction*—One job of the teacher (or any person who prepares the materials of instruction) is to organize and present the task to be learned in such a way that the learner can learn it as rapidly and as efficiently as he is able. This means, first, that the learner must be told, in words that he can understand, what he is to learn and how he is to learn it. It means that the learner must be put into adequate sensory contact with the material to be learned (for example, one must insure that the learner will adequately see or hear the materials of instruction). It also means that the various aspects of the learning task must be presented in such an order and with such detail that, as far as possible, every step of the learning is adequately prepared for by a previous step. It may also mean that the instruction must be adapted for the special needs and characteristics of the learner, including his stage of learning. All these things may be summarized in what we call *quality of instruction*. This variable applies not only to the performance of a teacher but also to the characteristics of textbooks, workbooks, films, teaching-machine programs, etc.

Now, if the quality of instruction is anything less than optimal, it is possible that the learner will need more time to learn the task than he would otherwise need. Some learners will be more handicapped by poor instruction than others. The extent of this handicap is conceived to be a function of the learner's ability to understand instruction. Learners with high ability in this respect will be able to figure out for themselves what the learning task is and how they can go about learning it; they will be able to overcome the difficulties presented by poor quality of instruction by perceiving concepts and relationships in the teaching materials which will not be grasped by those with lesser ability.

For the purposes of this conceptual model, we shall say that the amount of time actually needed by a person to learn a given task satisfactorily is a function not only of aptitude (as defined previously), but also of the quality of instruction insofar as it is less than optimal. And the amount of additional time he will need is an inverse function of his ability to understand instruction.

We could, of course, apply Occam's razor and get rid of both of the two preceding variables by conceiving that a change in the quality of instruction causes an essential change in the learning task itself. In this case, we would deal only with a learner's aptitude for learning a given task, subscripted with the quality of instruction attached to it. Such a modification of our model seems undesirable, however, for one would tend to lose sight of instructional quality as one of the important manipulable variables in educational psychology.

Time Spent in Learning

■ *Time allowed for learning ("opportunity")*—It may come as a surprise to some to be told that the schools may allow less than adequate time for learning any task, but second thought will make one realize that this is very often the case. It is partly a consequence of the very large amount of material that the schools are expected to teach; the available time must somehow be distributed among many things. And it is partly a consequence of the very great variation that exists in the amounts of time that children need for learning, even under a good quality of instruction, and particularly when the instructional quality is such that many children of lower ability to understand instruction require much more time than they might otherwise need.

The school responds to differences in learning rates (for that is what differences in aptitude are) in many ways. Sometimes the policy of the school is, in effect, to ignore these differences; a certain amount of time is provided for everybody to learn, and no more. (For example, at some military academies, study time is prescribed and scheduled uniformly for all cadets.) At the opposite extreme is the case where each student is allowed to proceed exactly at his own rate; private instruction in music or foreign languages and self-instruction by teaching machine or other means are approximations to this case. The middle position is occupied by learning situations in which there is some kind of "ability grouping": Pupils are assigned to different groups, classes, or curricula on the basis of estimated learning rates.

Even when there is some constraint upon the amount of time "officially" provided for learning, teachers and instructional programs vary in the amount of time they allow for learning. Some programs present material at such a rapid pace that most students are kept under continual pressure; only the apter students can keep up with this instruction, while the others fall back or out, sometimes never to get caught up. In other programs, the instruction is paced for the benefit of the slower student. The faster student is fortunate if the teacher takes appropriate steps to "enrich" his instructional content; but this will not always happen, and it is undoubtedly the case that many fast learners lose some of their motivation for learning when they feel that their time is being wasted or when they are not kept at the edge of challenge.

Perseverance

Obviously, failure to allow enough time for learning produces incomplete learning. If a person needs two hours to learn something and is allowed only one hour, and if we assume that learning proceeds linearly with time, the degree of learning is only 50 per cent. Probably one of the most aversive things which a school can do is not to allow sufficient time for a well-motivated child to master a given learning task before the next is taken up. Children meet such frustrations by indifference or the more extreme avoidance reactions and are, in any case, handicapped in undertaking the next task.

■ *The time the learner is willing to spend in learning ("perseverance")*—The term perseverance is used here, rather than persistence, because of the somewhat pejorative connotations of the latter. Nevertheless, the concept is similar to what Paul Brandwein describes in the following passage:

> The characteristics grouped under the Predisposing Factor . . . include a spectrum of traits which the writer places under the head of Persistence. This is defined

as consisting of three attitudes: (1) A marked willingness to spend time, beyond the ordinary schedule, in a given task (this includes the willingness to set one's own time schedules, to labor beyond a prescribed time, such as nine to five). (2) A willingness to withstand discomfort. This includes adjusting to shortened lunch hours, or no lunch hours, working without holidays, etc. It includes withstanding fatigue and strain and working even through minor illness, such as a cold or a headache. (3) A willingness to face failure. With this comes a realization that patient work may lead to successful termination of the task at hand (1, pp. 9-10).

But the variable of perseverance applies not only in the case of the "gifted student" and not only in the case of long durations of effort, but also to all other learners and also to learning tasks which require only short times for mastery. That is, in the general case, a learner who (in view of his aptitude, the quality of the instruction, and his ability to understand the instruction) needs a certain amount of time to learn a task may or may not be willing to persevere for that amount of time in trying to learn. It is not a matter of his predicting how long he will be willing to learn: we simply postulate that there is a certain time over and above which he will not continue active learning of a task, and this time may lie anywhere on the scale from zero to infinity. The learner may not be motivated to learn at all, or he may regard the task as something too difficult for him to learn; in either case, he may spend no time at all in trying to learn. He may start to learn and later become distracted or bored, or he may lose confidence in his ability. He may go far toward mastery and then overestimate his achievement, thus prematurely terminating his efforts to learn. He may, of course, be so highly motivated that he would be willing to spend more time than he needs in order to reach a specified criterion of mastery. Nevertheless, for the purposes of our conceptual model, it will be assumed that the learner will never actually spend more time than he needs to master the task as defined, that is, that he will stop learning as soon as he has mastered the learning task. (In this way we avoid, for the present, the necessity of incorporating a concept of "overlearning" in the model.)

This variable, which may be called *perseverance-in-learning-to-criterion,* is thus measured in terms of time, and if it is not sufficiently great to allow the learner to attain mastery, it operates in our conceptual model to reduce the degree of learning. Assume, as before, that learning proceeds as a linear function of time. Then if a child needs two hours to learn something, is allowed one hour, but will persevere only thirty minutes, the degree of learning is only 25 per cent. Perseverance-in-learning is measured only in terms of the amount of time the child is actively engaged in learning; a child who is actively engaged in learning for various periods totaling only thirty minutes during an hour is presumably not paying attention to learning for the other thirty minutes, and this time is not counted.

Perseverance-in-learning is itself a function of many other variables which will not be separately treated in this conceptual model. It is a function partly of what is ordinarily called "motivation" or desire to learn. But there are many reasons for desiring to learn a given thing. To please the teacher, to please one's parents or friends, to get good grades or other external rewards, to achieve self-confidence in one's learning ability, to feed one's self-esteem, to avoid disapproval—all these can operate in place of or in addition to any incentives for learning which may derive from the intrinsic interest or perceived utility of the thing being learned. And there are probably just as many reasons which one may adopt (consciously or unconsciously) for not learning: to avoid the exertion of learning, to behave consistently with one's image of oneself as a non-learner, or to avoid wasting time on learning tasks of no perceived importance.

Perseverance-in-learning may also be a function of what are ordinarily called emotional variables. One may desire to learn but be unable to endure frustrations caused by difficulties in the learning task or distractions from external circumstances. It may also interact with the quality of instruction; poor quality of instruction may reduce perseverance-in-learning even beyond the toll it takes in wasted minutes or even weeks.

The Complete Model

It will be noticed that the model involves five elements —three residing in the individual and two stemming from external conditions. Factors in the individual are (1) aptitude—the amount of time needed to learn the task under optimal instructional conditions, (2) ability to understand instruction, and (3) perseverance—the amount of time the learner is willing to engage actively in learning. Factors in external conditions are (4) opportunity—time allowed for learning, and (5) the quality of instruction—a measure of the degree to which instruction is presented so that it will not require additional time for mastery beyond that required in view of aptitude.

Three of the factors are expressed purely in terms of time. If ability to understand instruction corresponds to a combination of general and verbal intelligence, it can be assessed in relative terms by currently available measuring devices. The most elusive quantity in this model is that called quality of instruction, but both it and the ability to understand instruction are interconnected with temporally measurable variables in such a way that by appropriate experimental manipulations, they could eventually be indexed in terms of time. Temporarily, let us put quality of instruction on a scale from 0 (poor) to I (optimal), and ability to understand instruction on a standard score scale with mean $= 0$ and $\sigma = $ I.

The five factors can be worked into a tentative formula which expresses the degree of learning, for the ith individual and the tth task, as a function of the ratio of the amount of time the learner actually spends on the learning task to the total amount he needs. Thus:

$$\text{Degree of learning} = f\left(\frac{\text{time actually spent}}{\text{time needed}}\right)$$

The numerator of this fraction will be equal to the smallest of the following three quantities: (1) opportunity—the time allowed for learning, (2) perseverance—the amount of time the learner is willing to engage actively in learning, and (3) aptitude—the amount of time needed to learn, increased by whatever amount necessary in view of poor quality of instruction and lack of ability to understand less than optimal instruction. This last quantity (time needed to learn after adjustment for quality of instruction and ability to understand instruction) is also the denominator of the fraction. It is not necessary or worthwhile here, however, to pursue the detailed mathematical formulation, which has been given elsewhere (3).

As an illustration of the usefulness of this model in clarifying other educational concepts, let us see how it provides a framework for interpreting the notion of "under-achievement" as criticized by Henry Dyer (4). While we are at it, let us also look at the notion of "overachievement." It is our contention that these terms are useful and salvage-able if properly defined.

Underachievement and overachievement, like under-weight and overweight, are ordinarily taken with reference to some norm or baseline of expectation. The under-achiever does poorer than we expect him to, and the overachiever does better than we expect him to. The issue is this: Upon what do we base our expectation? The approved manner of doing this is to make predictions from those tests or other measurements which in fact yield the best predictions of success, and statistical theory tells us how to make best use of these predictors (i.e., by making our predictions along a regression line). There is, however, a paradox here. Suppose our predictions were perfect: Then there would be no "underachievers" and no "over-achievers." An unlikely eventuality to be sure! Neverthe-less, our intuitive rejection of the case of perfect prediction lends credence to the following analysis of what we mean by "underachievement": Underachievement is a situation in which there is a discrepancy between actual achieve-ment and that expected on the basis of a certain kind of evidence—evidence concerning the "capacity" or "apti-tude" of the individual to achieve in a particular context. Such evidence is recognized as being quite distinct from evidence concerning other factors in achievement, e.g., "motivation," "opportunity for learning," etc., and these latter factors would not figure in forming our expectations. Instead, we would hope to gather as much evidence as possible concerning the "capacity" or "aptitude" of the individual, defined as his learning rate when all other factors are optimal.

Achievement and Expectancy

With reference to the conceptual model presented earlier, our expectation of an individual's achievement in a given learning task would in the strictest sense be that which he would attain when he spends all the time he needs—that is, when the ratio of the time spent to the time needed is unity. Anything less than this is, to some degree, underachievement. From this point of view, all learners are underachievers unless they are superhuman beings in an ideal world. Perseverance sometimes flags; the quality of instruction is seldom optimal, and time allowed for learning is not always sufficient.

Let us, therefore, strike some sort of average for perseverance, instructional quality, and opportunity for learning. Our expectation of the degree of learning will be somewhat less than unity because, on the average, individuals will spend less time in learning than they need. And we may gauge underachievement and overachievement with reference to this expectation. In effect, this is what we do by the customary regression techniques based on aptitude measures, although in a less precise way than might be done if we were able to measure each of the components of achievement as stated by the model. In the framework of the model, however, underachievement is now seen to be a state of affairs which results whenever perseverance is less than some "reasonable value," whenever the quality of instruction is poor, whenever time allowed for learning has not been sufficient, or whenever some combination of these conditions has occurred. "Overachievement," contrariwise, may occur when there is an especially favorable combination of attendant events: high perseverance, instruction of high quality, or ample opportunity for learning.

We have a feeling about the relative amenability of different factors in achievement to manipulation or treatment: "Aptitude" is regarded as relatively resistant to change, whereas it is the hope of the psychologist that he can readily intervene to modify "perseverance," "quality of instruction," or "opportunity for learning." To some extent, this feeling is justified not only by logic but also by research findings—by the research on the apparent constancy of the IQ, on the effect of various instructional variables, etc. On the other hand, if aptitude is largely a matter of prior learnings, it may be more modifiable than we think, whereas, conversely, some kinds of clinical findings suggest that motivational characteristics of the individual may be much harder to change than one might think. These considerations, however, need not detract from the basic utility of the concepts of underachievement and overachievement. The concept of "underachievement" does not automatically imply the possibility of remediation any more than the concept of illness does. Some patients never get well, and some underachievers remain underachievers.

Babies and Bathwater

Henry Dyer (4) has drawn attention to possible dangers in the concept of underachievement—for example, the dangers of making predictions from unreliable or invalid predictors, of assuming that ability is innate or fixed, of making unwarranted inferences from school marks, and of overlooking determinants of school performance which are external to the pupil. Nevertheless, in suggesting that we kill the notion of underachievement, it would seem that he wants to throw out the proverbial baby with the bathwater. The concepts of underachievement and of overachievement are meaningful from both a statistical and a clinical point of view, as shown by the many fruitful studies of "underachieving" groups of students (e.g., 5). Careful attention to the elements of the conceptual model presented here will afford a safeguard against misuse of the concepts: Aptitude must be estimated by relevant and reliable measures (in actuality, all of them measures of past performance); the degree of learning must be accurately appraised, and the possible role of instructional variables must be considered. Above all, the variable which we have called perseverance must be validly assessed; the most direct evidence concerning it, our model would suggest, would come from observations of the amount of time the pupil actively engages in learning.

Before leaving this topic, let us consider another way in which the term "overachievement" is sometimes used. When a person is designated as an overachiever, it is often implied that his achievements derive more from his perseverance than from his aptitude or his intelligence. In terms of our model, this can occur when the learning task can be broken down into a series of subtasks of varying difficulty with difficulty roughly gauged in terms of average learning time. Because of his great perseverance, the overachiever masters to a criterion more of the easy tasks—tasks which are within the compass of his aptitude—than the student of average perseverance. While he may fail to learn some of the more difficult tasks, the net result may be a high score on an achievement test—a score considerably higher than predicted from aptitude measures. This concept of over-achievement is distinctly different from the concept of overachievement suggested previously; responsible users of the term must clearly state which of these meanings they intend.

Future Research

Our conceptual model could lead, it would seem, to almost endless possibilities for research. It should provoke renewed effort to develop measures of each of the basic variables included in the model. The measurement of aptitudes is a fairly well advanced art, although the exact ways in which these aptitudes are relevant to school learning tasks remain to be worked out. The same remark may be made about the measurement of ability to understand instruction. But measurements of perseverance and of instructional quality are practically nonexistent. It should be intriguing to attempt to provide a general way of measuring opportunity to learn, that is, the actual time available to individual students to learn in view of the pacing of instruction; for it is our hypothesis that variations in the pacing of instruction have remained largely unrecognized in pedagogical discussions.

Research is also needed on the interactions of the several variables in the model. Is the model correctly put together? To what extent are the variables interdependent? For example, how does instructional quality affect perseverance? In what way is the degree of learning a function of the ratio of the amount of time spent in learning to the amount of time needed? Are we correct in postulating an interaction between instructional quality and ability to understand instruction such that pupils low in the latter ability suffer most from poor instructional quality?

One of the most exciting possibilities suggested by the model is that of being able to state parameters for different types of learning by learners of varying characteristics under stated instructional conditions. Perhaps ultimately such parameters could be tied back to the data of pure learning theory. One of the bolder hypotheses implicit in the model is that the degree of learning, other things being equal, is a simple function of the amount of time during which the pupil engages actively in learning. Psychologists have paid little attention to this variable of pure time in human learning. A recent experiment by Bugelski (2) is one of the few to consider time factors in the field of paired-associate learning; and interestingly enough, it supports the hypothesis that more parsimonious descriptions of learning may be obtained by the use of time as a variable rather than, say, number of trials.

What is important to emphasize is that this conceptual model probably contains, at least at a superordinate level, every element required to account for an individual's success or failure in school learning (at least in the learning tasks to which the model applies). The explication and refinement of these factors and the exploration of their interactions constitute a major task of educational psychology. Its other major task is to account for those types of school learning (e.g., attitudinal and emotional conditioning) to which the present model is not intended to apply and for which a separate model might well be constructed.

Reprinted from *Teachers College Record*, 1963, 64: 723–733. Reprinted by permission of the author and the publisher. Dr. Carroll is senior research psychologist, Educational Testing Service, Princeton, N.J.

References

[1]Brandwein, P. F. *The Gifted Student as Future Scientist.* New York: Harcourt Brace, 1955.

[2]Bugelski, B. R. "Presentation Time, Total Time, and Mediation in Paired-Associate Learning." *Journal of Experimental Psychology.*, 1962, 63, 409–412.

[3]Carroll, J. B. "The Prediction of Success in Intensive Language Training." In Glaser, R. (Ed.) *Training Research and Education.* Pittsburgh: University of Pittsburgh Press, 1962, 87–136.

[4]Dyer, H. S. "A Psychometrician Views Human Ability." *Teachers College Record.*, 1960, 61, 394–403.

[5]Goldberg, Miriam, et al. *A Three-Year Experimental Program at DeWitt Clinton High School to Help Bright Underachievers.* High Points, 1959, 41, 5–35.

[6]Skinner, B. F. *Science and Human Behavior.* New York: Macmillan, 1953.

3

The Science of Learning and the Art of Teaching

B. F. Skinner

Some promising advances have recently been made in the field of learning. Special techniques have been designed to arrange what are called "contingencies of reinforcement"—the relations which prevail between behavior on the one hand and the consequences of that behavior on the other—with the result that a much more effective control of behavior has been achieved. It has long been argued that an organism learns mainly by producing changes in its environment, but it is only recently that these changes have been carefully manipulated. In traditional devices for the study of learning—in the serial maze, for example, or in the T-maze, the problem box, or the familiar discrimination apparatus—the effects produced by the organism's behavior are left to many fluctuating circumstances. There is many a slip between the turn-to-the-right and the food-cup at the end of the alley. It is not surprising that techniques of this sort have yielded only very rough data from which the uniformities demanded by an experimental science can be extracted only by averaging many cases. In none of this work has the behavior of the individual organism been predicted in more than a statistical sense. The learning processes which are the presumed object of such research are reached only through a series of inferences. Current preoccupation with deductive systems reflects this state of the science.

Recent improvements in the conditions which control behavior in the field of learning are of two principal sorts. The Law of Effect has been taken seriously; we have made sure that effects do occur and that they occur under conditions which are optimal for producing the changes called learning. Once we have arranged the particular type of consequence called a reinforcement, our techniques permit us to shape up the behavior of an organism almost at will. It has become a routine exercise to demonstrate this in classes in elementary psychology by conditioning such an organism as a pigeon. Simply by presenting food to a hungry pigeon at the right time, it is possible to shape up three or four well-defined responses in a single demonstration period—such responses as turning around, pacing the floor in the pattern of a figure-8, standing still in a corner of the demonstration apparatus, stretching the neck, or stamping the foot. Extremely complex performances may be reached through successive stages in the shaping process, the contingencies of reinforcement being changed progressively in the direction of the required behavior. The results are often quite dramatic. In such a demonstration one can see learning take place. A significant change in behavior is often obvious as the result of a single reinforcement.

A second important advance in technique permits us to maintain behavior in given states of strength for long periods of time. Reinforcements continue to be important, of course, long after an organism has learned how to do something, long after it has acquired behavior. They are necessary to maintain the behavior in strength. Of special interest is the effect of various schedules of intermittent reinforcement. Charles B. Ferster and the author are currently preparing an extensive report of a five-year research program, sponsored by the Office of Naval Research, in which most of the important types of schedules have been investigated and in which the effects of schedules in general have been reduced to a few principles. On the theoretical side we now have a fairly good idea of why a given schedule produces its appropriate performance. On

the practical side we have learned how to maintain any
given level of activity for daily periods limited only by the
physical exhaustion of the organism and from day to day
without substantial change throughout its life. Many of
these effects would be traditionally assigned to the field of
motivation, although the principal operation is simply the
arrangement of contingencies of reinforcement.[2]

These new methods of shaping behavior and of maintaining it in strength are a great improvement over the
traditional practices of professional animal trainers, and it is
not surprising that our laboratory results are already being
applied to the production of performing animals for commercial purposes. In a more academic environment they
have been used for demonstration purposes which extend
far beyond an interest in learning as such. For example, it is
not too difficult to arrange the complex contingencies
which produce many types of social behavior. Competition
is exemplified by two pigeons playing a modified game of
ping-pong. The pigeons drive the ball back and forth across
a small table by pecking at it. When the ball gets by one
pigeon, the other is reinforced. The task of constructing
such a "social relation" is probably completely out of reach
of the traditional animal trainer. It requires a carefully
designed program of gradually changing contingencies and
the skillful use of schedules to maintain the behavior in
strength. Each pigeon is separately prepared for its part in
the total performance, and the "social relation" is then
arbitrarily constructed. The sequence of events leading up
to this stable state are excellent material for the study of the
factors important in nonsynthetic social behavior. It is
instructive to consider how a similar series of contingencies
could arise in the case of the human organism through the
evolution of cultural patterns.

Cooperation can also be set up, perhaps more easily
than competition. We have trained two pigeons to coordinate their behavior in a cooperative endeavor with a precision which equals that of the most skillful human dancers.
In a more serious vein these techniques have permitted us
to explore the complexities of the individual organism and
to analyze some of the serial or coordinate behaviors
involved in attention, problem solving, various types of

self-control, and the subsidiary systems of responses within a single organism called "personalities." Some of these are exemplified in what we call multiple schedules of reinforcement. In general a given schedule has an effect upon the rate at which a response is emitted. Changes in the rate from moment to moment show a pattern typical of the schedule. The pattern may be as simple as a constant rate of responding at a given value, it may be a gradually accelerating rate between certain extremes, it may be an abrupt change from not responding at all to a given stable high rate, and so on. It has been shown that the performance characteristic of a given schedule can be brought under the control of a particular stimulus and that different performances can be brought under the control of different stimuli in the same organism. At a recent meeting of the American Psychological Association, Dr. Ferster and the author demonstrated a pigeon whose behavior showed the pattern typical of "fixed-interval" reinforcement in the presence of one stimulus and, alternately, the pattern typical of the very different schedule called "fixed ratio" in the presence of a second stimulus. In the laboratory we have been able to obtain performances appropriate to nine different schedules in the presence of appropriate stimuli in random alternation. When Stimulus 1 is present, the pigeon executes the performance appropriate to Schedule 1. When Stimulus 2 is present, the pigeon executes the performance appropriate to Schedule 2. And so on. This result is important because it makes the extrapolation of our laboratory results to daily life much more plausible. We are all constantly shifting from schedule to schedule as our immediate environment changes, but the dynamics of the control exercised by reinforcement remain essentially unchanged.

It is also possible to construct very complex sequences of schedules. It is not easy to describe these in a few words, but two or three examples may be mentioned. In one experiment the pigeon generates a performance appropriate to Schedule A where the reinforcement is simply the production of the stimulus characteristic of Schedule B, to which the pigeon then responds appropriately. Under a third stimulus, the bird yields a performance appropriate to

Schedule C where the reinforcement in this case is simply the production of the stimulus characteristic of Schedule D, to which the bird then responds appropriately. In a special case, first investigated by L. B. Wyckoff, Jr., the organism responds to one stimulus where the reinforcement consists of the clarification of the stimulus controlling another response. The first response becomes, so to speak, an objective form of "paying attention" to the second stimulus. In one important version of this experiment, as yet unpublished, we could say that the pigeon is telling us whether it is "paying attention" to the shape of a spot of light or to its color.

One of the most dramatic applications of these techniques has recently been made in the Harvard Psychological Laboratories by Floyd Ratliff and Donald S. Blough, who have skillfully used multiple and serial schedules of reinforcement to study complex perceptual processes in the infrahuman organism. They have achieved a sort of psychophysics without verbal instruction. In a recent experiment by Blough, for example, a pigeon draws a detailed dark-adaptation curve showing the characteristic breaks of rod and cone vision. The curve is recorded continuously in a single experimental period and is quite comparable with the curves of human subjects. The pigeon behaves in a way which, in the human case, we would not hesitate to describe by saying that it adjusts a very faint patch of light until it can just be seen.

In all this work, the species of the organism has made surprisingly little difference. It is true that the organisms studied have all been vertebrates, but they still cover a wide range. Comparable results have been obtained with pigeons, rats, dogs, monkeys, human children, and most recently, by the author in collaboration with Ogden R. Lindsley, human psychotic subjects. In spite of great phylogenetic differences, all these organisms show amazingly similar properties of the learning process. It should be emphasized that this has been achieved by analyzing the effects of reinforcement and by designing techniques which manipulate reinforcement with considerable precision. Only in this way can the behavior of the individual organism be brought under such precise control. It is also important to note that through a gradual advance to complex interrelations among responses, the same degree of rigor is being extended to behavior which would usually be assigned to such fields as perception, thinking, and personality dynamics.

From this exciting prospect of an advancing science of learning, it is a great shock to turn to that branch of technology which is most directly concerned with the learning process—education. Let us consider, for example, the teaching of arithmetic in the lower grades. The school is concerned with imparting to the child a large number of responses of a special sort. The responses are all verbal. They consist of speaking and writing certain words, figures, and signs which, to put it roughly, refer to numbers and to arithmetic operations. The first task is to shape up these responses—to get the child to pronounce and to write responses correctly, but the principal task is to bring this behavior under many sorts of stimulus control. This is what happens when the child learns to count, to recite tables, to count while ticking off the items in an assemblage of objects, to respond to spoken or written numbers by saying "odd," "even," "prime," and so on. Over and above this elaborate repertoire of numerical behavior, most of which is often dismissed as the product of rote learning, the teaching of arithmetic looks forward to those complex serial arrangements of responses involved in original mathematical thinking. The child must acquire responses of transposing, clearing fractions, and so on, which modify the order or pattern of the original material so that the response called a solution is eventually made possible.

Now, how is this extremely complicated verbal repertoire set up? In the first place, what reinforcements are used? Fifty years ago the answer would have been clear. At that time educational control was still frankly aversive. The child read numbers, copied numbers, memorized tables, and performed operations upon numbers to escape the threat of the birch rod or cane. Some positive reinforcements were perhaps eventually derived from the increased efficiency of the child in the field of arithmetic and in rare cases some automatic reinforcement may have resulted from the sheer manipulation of the medium—from the solution of problems or the discovery of the intricacies of the number system. But for the immediate purposes of education the child acted to avoid or escape punishment. It was part of the reform movement known as progressive education to make the positive consequences more immediately effective, but any one who visits the lower grades of the average school today will observe that a change has been made, not from aversive to positive control, but from one form of aversive stimulation to another. The child at his desk, filling in his workbook, is behaving primarily to escape from the threat of a series of minor aversive events—the teacher's displeasure, the criticism or ridicule of his classmates, an ignominious showing in a competition, low marks, a trip to the office "to be talked to" by the principal, or a word to the parent who may still resort to the birch rod. In this welter of aversive consequences, getting the right answer is in itself an insignificant event, any effect of which is lost amid the anxieties, the boredom, and the aggressions which are the inevitable by-products of aversive control.[3]

Secondly, we have to ask how the contingencies of reinforcement are arranged. When is a numerical operation reinforced as "right"? Eventually, of course, the pupil may be able to check his own answers and achieve some sort of automatic reinforcement, but in the early stages the reinforcement of being right is usually accorded by the teacher. The contingencies she provides are far from optimal. It can easily be demonstrated that, unless explicit mediating behavior has been set up, the lapse of only a few seconds between response and reinforcement destroys most of the effect. In a typical classroom, nevertheless, long periods of time customarily elapse. The teacher may walk up and down the aisle, for example, while the class is working on a sheet of problems, pausing here and there to say right or wrong. Many seconds or minutes intervene between the child's response and the teacher's reinforcement. In many cases—for example, when papers are taken home to be corrected—as much as 24 hours may intervene. It is surprising that this system has any effect whatsoever.

A third notable shortcoming is the lack of a skillful program which moves forward through a series of progressive approximations to the final complex behavior desired.

A long series of contingencies is necessary to bring the organism into the possession of mathematical behavior most efficiently. But the teacher is seldom able to reinforce at each step in such a series because she cannot deal with the pupil's responses one at a time. It is usually necessary to reinforce the behavior in blocks of responses—as in correcting a work sheet or page from a workbook. The responses within such a block must not be interrelated. The answer to one problem must not depend upon the answer to another. The number of stages through which one may progressively approach a complex pattern of behavior is therefore small, and the task so much the more difficult. Even the most modern workbook in beginning arithmetic is far from exemplifying an efficient program for shaping up mathematical behavior.

Perhaps the most serious criticism of the current classroom is the relative infrequency of reinforcement. Since the pupil is usually dependent upon the teacher for being right, and since many pupils are usually dependent upon the same teacher, the total number of contingencies which may be arranged during, say, the first four years, is of the order of only a few thousand. But a very rough estimate suggests that efficient mathematical behavior at this level requires something of the order of 25,000 contingencies. We may suppose that even in the brighter student a given contingency must be arranged several times to place the behavior well in hand. The responses to be set up are not simply the various items in tables of addition, subtraction, multiplication, and division; we have also to consider the alternative forms in which each item may be stated. To the learning of such material we should add hundreds of responses concerned with factoring, identifying primes, memorizing series, using shortcut techniques of calculation, constructing and using geometric representations or number forms, and so on. Over and above all this, the whole mathematical repertoire must be brought under the control of concrete problems of considerable variety. Perhaps 50,000 contingencies is a more conservative estimate. In this frame of reference the daily assignment in arithmetic seems pitifully meager.

The result of all this is, of course, well known. Even

our best schools are under criticism for their inefficiency in the teaching of drill subjects such as arithmetic. The condition in the average school is a matter of wide-spread national concern. Modern children simply do not learn arithmetic quickly or well. Nor is the result simply incompetence. The very subjects in which modern techniques are weakest are those in which failure is most conspicuous, and in the wake of an ever-growing incompetence come the anxieties, uncertainties, and aggressions which in their turn present other problems to the school. Most pupils soon claim the asylum of not being "ready" for arithmetic at a given level or, eventually, of not having a mathematical mind. Such explanations are readily seized upon by defensive teachers and parents. Few pupils ever reach the stage at which automatic reinforcements follow as the natural consequences of mathematical behavior. On the contrary, the figures and symbols of mathematics have become standard emotional stimuli. The glimpse of a column of figures, not to say an algebraic symbol or an integral sign, is likely to set off—not mathematical behavior—but a reaction of anxiety, guilt, or fear.

The teacher is usually no happier about this than the pupil. Denied the opportunity to control via the birch rod, quite at sea as to the mode of operation of the few techniques at her disposal, she spends as little time as possible on drill subjects and eagerly subscribes to philosophies of education which emphasize material of greater inherent interest. A confession of weakness is her extraordinary concern lest the child be taught something unnecessary. The repertoire to be imparted is carefully reduced to an essential minimum. In the field of spelling, for example, a great deal of time and energy has gone into discovering just those words which the young child is going to use, as if it were a crime to waste one's educational power in teaching an unnecessary word. Eventually, weakness of technique emerges in the disguise of a reformulation of the aims of education. Skills are minimized in favor of vague achievements—educating for democracy, educating the whole child, educating for life, and so on. And there the matter ends; for, unfortunately, these philosophies do not in turn suggest improvements in techniques. They offer little or no help in the design of better classroom practices.

There would be no point in urging these objections if improvement were impossible. But the advances which have recently been made in our control of the learning process suggest a thorough revision of classroom practices and, fortunately, they tell us how the revision can be brought about. This is not, of course, the first time that the results of an experimental science have been brought to bear upon the practical problems of education. The modern classroom does not, however, offer much evidence that research in the field of learning has been respected or used. This condition is no doubt partly due to the limitations of earlier research. But it has been encouraged by a too hasty conclusion that the laboratory study of learning is inherently limited because it cannot take into account the realities of the classroom. In the light of our increasing knowledge of the learning process we should, instead, insist upon dealing with those realities and forcing a substantial change in them. Education is perhaps the most important branch of scientific technology. It deeply affects the lives of all of us. We can no longer allow the exigencies of a practical situation to suppress the tremendous improvements which are within reach. The practical situation must be changed.

There are certain questions which have to be answered in turning to the study of any new organism. What behavior is to be set up? What reinforcers are at hand? What responses are available in embarking upon a program of progressive approximation which will lead to the final form of the behavior? How can reinforcements be most efficiently scheduled to maintain the behavior in strength? These questions are all relevant in considering the problem of the child in the lower grades.

In the first place, what reinforcements are available? What does the school have in its possession which will reinforce a child? We may look first to the material to be learned, for it is possible that this will provide considerable automatic reinforcement. Children play for hours with mechanical toys, paints, scissors and paper, noise-makers, puzzles—in short, with almost anything which feeds back significant changes in the environment and is reasonably free of aversive properties. The sheer control of nature is itself reinforcing. This effect is not evident in the modern school because it is masked by the emotional responses generated by aversive control. It is true that automatic reinforcement from the manipulation of the environment is probably only a mild reinforcer and may need to be carefully husbanded, but one of the most striking principles to emerge from recent research is that the net amount of reinforcement is of little significance. A very slight reinforcement may be tremendously effective in controlling behavior if it is wisely used.

If the natural reinforcement inherent in the subject matter is not enough, other reinforcers must be employed. Even in school the child is occasionally permitted to do "what he wants to do," and access to reinforcements of many sorts may be made contingent upon the more immediate consequences of the behavior to be established. Those who advocate competition as a useful social motive may wish to use the reinforcements which follow from excelling others, although there is the difficulty that in this case the reinforcement of one child is necessarily aversive to another. Next in order we might place the good will and affection of the teacher, and only when that has failed need we turn to the use of aversive stimulation.

In the second place, how are these reinforcements to be made contingent upon the desired behavior? There are two considerations here—the gradual elaboration of extremely complex patterns of behavior and the maintenance of the behavior in strength at each stage. The whole process of becoming competent in any field must be divided into a very large number of very small steps, and reinforcement must be contingent upon the accomplishment of each step. This solution to the problem of creating a complex repertoire of behavior also solves the problem of maintaining the behavior in strength. We could, of course, resort to the techniques of scheduling already developed in the study of other organisms but in the present state of our knowledge of educational practices, scheduling appears to be most effectively arranged through the design of the material to be learned. By making each successive step as small as possible, the frequency of reinforcement can be raised to a maximum, while the possibly aversive consequences of being wrong are reduced to a minimum. Other ways of designing material would yield other programs of reinforcement. Any supplementary reinforcement would probably have to be scheduled in the more traditional way.

These requirements are not excessive, but they are probably incompatible with the current realities of the classroom. In the experimental study of learning it has been found that the contingencies of reinforcement which are most efficient in controlling the organism cannot be arranged through the personal mediation of the experimenter. An organism is affected by subtle details of contingencies which are beyond the capacity of the human organism to arrange. Mechanical and electrical devices must be used. Mechanical help is also demanded by the sheer number of contingencies which may be used efficiently in a single experimental session. We have recorded many millions of responses from a single organism during thousands of experimental hours. Personal arrangement of the contingencies and personal observation of the results are quite unthinkable. Now, the human organism is, if anything, more sensitive to precise contingencies than the other organisms we have studied. We have every reason to expect, therefore, that the most effective control of human learning will require instrumental aid. The simple fact is that, as a mere reinforcing mechanism, the teacher is out of date. This would be true if a single teacher devoted all her time to a single child, but her inadequacy is multiplied many-fold when she must serve as a reinforcing device to many children at once. If the teacher is to take advantage of recent advances in the study of learning, she must have the help of mechanical devices.

The technical problem of providing the necessary instrumental aid is not particularly difficult. There are many ways in which the necessary contingencies may be arranged, either mechanically or electrically. An inexpensive device which solves most of the principal problems has already been constructed. It is still in the experimental stage, but a description will suggest the kind of instrument which seems to be required. The device consists of a small box about the size of a small record player. On the top surface is a window through which a question or problem printed on a paper tape may be seen. The child answers the question by moving one or more sliders upon which the digits 0 through 9 are printed. The answer appears in square holes punched in the paper upon which the question is printed. When the answer has been set, the child turns a knob. The operation is as simple as adjusting a television set. If the answer is right, the knob turns freely and can be made to ring a bell or provide some other conditioned reinforcement. If the answer is wrong, the knob will not turn. A counter may be added to tally wrong answers. The knob must then be reversed slightly and a second attempt at a right answer made. (Unlike the flash-card, the device reports a wrong answer without giving the right answer.) When the answer is right, a further turn of the knob engages a clutch which moves the next problem into place in the window. This movement cannot be completed, however, until the sliders have been returned to zero.

The important features of the device are these: Reinforcement for the right answer is immediate. The mere manipulation of the device will probably be reinforcing enough to keep the average pupil at work for a suitable period each day, provided traces of earlier aversive control can be wiped out. A teacher may supervise an entire class at work on such devices at the same time, yet each child may progress at his own rate, completing as many problems as possible within the class period. If forced to be away from school, he may return to pick up where he left off. The gifted child will advance rapidly, but can be kept from getting too far ahead either by being excused from arithmetic for a time or by being given special sets of problems which take him into some of the interesting bypaths of mathematics.

The device makes it possible to present carefully designed material in which one problem can depend upon the answer to the preceding and where, therefore, the most efficient progress to an eventually complex repertoire can be made. Provision has been made for recording the commonest mistakes so that the tapes can be modified as experience dictates. Additional steps can be inserted where pupils tend to have trouble, and ultimately the material will reach a point at which the answers of the average child will almost always be right.

If the material itself proves not to be sufficiently reinforcing, other reinforcers in the possession of the teacher or school may be made contingent upon the operation of the device or upon progress through a series of problems. Supplemental reinforcement would not sacrifice the advantages gained from immediate reinforcement and from the possibility of constructing an optimal series of steps which approach the complex repertoire of mathematical behavior most efficiently.

A similar device in which the sliders carry the letters of the alphabet has been designed to teach spelling. In addition to the advantages which can be gained from precise reinforcement and careful programming, the device will teach reading at the same time. It can also be used to establish the large and important repertoire of verbal relationships encountered in logic and science. In short, it can teach verbal thinking. As to content instruction, the device can be operated as a multiple-choice self-rater.

Some objections to the use of such devices in the classroom can easily be foreseen. The cry will be raised that the child is being treated as a mere animal and that an essentially human intellectual achievement is being analyzed in unduly mechanistic terms. Mathematical behavior is usually regarded, not as a repertoire of responses involving numbers and numerical operations, but as evidences of mathematical ability or the exercise of the power of reason. It is true that the techniques which are emerging from the experimental study of learning are not designed to "develop the mind" or to further some vague "understanding" of mathematical relationships. They are designed, on the contrary, to establish the very behaviors which are taken to be the evidences of such mental states or processes. This is only a special case of the general change which is under way in the interpretation of human affairs. An advancing science continues to offer more and more convincing alternatives to traditional formulations. The behavior in terms of which human thinking must eventually be defined is worth treating in its own right as the substantial goal of education.

Of course the teacher has a more important function than to say right or wrong. The changes proposed would free her for the effective exercise of that function. Marking a set of papers in arithmetic—"Yes, nine and six are fifteen; no, nine and seven are not eighteen"—is beneath the dignity of any intelligent individual. There is more important work to be done—in which the teacher's relations to the pupil cannot be duplicated by a mechanical device. Instrumental help would merely improve these relations. One might say that the main trouble with education in the lower grades today is that the child is obviously not competent and knows it and that the teacher is unable to do anything about it and knows that too. If the advances which have recently been made in our control of behavior can give the child a genuine competence in reading, writing, spelling, and arithmetic, then the teacher may begin to function, not in lieu of a cheap machine, but through intellectual, cultural, and emotional contacts of that distinctive sort which testify to her status as a human being.

Another possible objection is that mechanized instruction will mean technological unemployment. We need not worry about this until there are enough teachers to go around and until the hours and energy demanded of the teacher are comparable to those in other fields of employment. Mechanical devices will eliminate the more tiresome labors of the teacher but they will not necessarily shorten the time during which she remains in contact with the pupil.

A more practical objection: Can we afford to mechanize our schools? The answer is clearly yes. The device I have just described could be produced as cheaply as a small radio or phonograph. There would need to be far fewer devices than pupils, for they could be used in rotation. But even if we suppose that the instrument eventually found to be most effective would cost several hundred dollars and that large numbers of them would be required, our economy should be able to stand the strain. Once we have accepted the possibility and the necessity of mechanical help in the classroom, the economic problem can easily be surmounted. There is no reason why the school room should be any less mechanized than, for example, the kitchen. A country which annually produces millions of refrigerators, dish-washers, automatic washing-machines, automatic clothes-driers, and automatic garbage disposers can certainly afford the equipment necessary to educate its citizens to high standards of competence in the most effective way.

There is a simple job to be done. The task can be stated in concrete terms. The necessary techniques are known. The equipment needed can easily be provided. Nothing stands in the way but cultural inertia. But what is more characteristic of America than an unwillingness to accept the traditional as inevitable? We are on the threshold of an exciting and revolutionary period, in which the scientific study of man will be put to work in man's best interests. Education must play its part. It must accept the fact that a sweeping revision of educational practices is possible and inevitable. When it has done this, we may look forward with confidence to a school system which is aware of the nature of its tasks, secure in its methods, and generously supported by the informed and effective citizens whom education itself will create.

Reprinted from *Harvard Educational Review*, Vol. XXIV, No. 2, Spring, 1954. Reprinted by permission of the author and the publisher. Dr. Skinner is a Professor of Psychology at Harvard University.

References

[1]Paper presented at a conference on Current Trends·in Psychology and the Behavioral Sciences at the University of Pittsburgh, March 12, 1954.

[2]The reader may wish to review Dr. Skinner's article, "Some Contributions of an Experimental Analysis of Behavior to Psychology as a Whole," *The American Psychologist*, 1953, 8, 69-78.

[3]Skinner, B. F. *Science and Human Behavior*. New York: Macmillan, 1953.

4

The Impending Instruction
Revolution

Harold E. Mitzel

First, let me explain my choice of the above title. It is
fashionable in these days of rhetorical excess to describe
change as revolutionary in scope. The mass media remind
us daily that revolutions are occurring right under our
noses. We hear of (and see) the Social Revolution, the
Sexual Revolution, the Technology Revolution, the Student
Revolt, the Faculty Revolt, and so on. Apparently any
complete or sudden change in the conduct of human affairs,
with or without violent confrontation or an exchange of
power, may properly be called a revolution.

It is my thesis that the last three decades of the
twentieth century will witness a drastic change in the
business of providing instruction in schools and colleges.
Change by the year 2000 will be so thoroughgoing that
historians will have no difficulty in agreeing that it was a
revolution. You will note the omission of words like "teaching" and "learning" in describing the coming revolution.
Teaching connotes for most of us an inherently person-
mediated activity and the vision of the "stand-up" lecturer
comes most immediately to mind. One of the concomitants
of the impending change is a major modification of the role
of teacher. It is likely that future terms for teacher may be

"instructional agent" or "lesson designer" or "instructional programmer." As for learning, we take the position that the word is not a way of describing an activity of the student, but rather a way of characterizing change in the student's behavior in some desired direction between two definite time markers. Pask[1] has pointed out that teaching is "exercising control of the instructional environment by arranging scope, sequence, materials, evaluation, and content for students." In other words, instruction is the general term for the process and learning is the product.

My objective is to challenge you with the shape of the instruction revolution, to point out how you as a teacher or administrator can cooperate and cope with it, and to suggest some of the social changes which are currently fueling this revolution.

Individualized Instruction

At the secondary school level, American educators, beginning with Preston W. Search[2] in the late nineteenth century, have been interested in the goal of individualization. Between 1900 and 1930, disciples of Frederick Burk (see Brubacher[3] and Parkhurst[4]) devised and implemented several laboratory-type plans for self-instruction in the lower schools. These were self-pacing plans for the learner and demanded a great deal of versatility on the part of the teacher. Additional impetus for the theoretical interest of educators in individualization stemmed from the mental testing movement, beginning with the seminal work of Binet[5] about 60 years ago. Early intelligence tests clearly showed differences in speed of task completion among pupils, and these differences were easily confirmed by a teacher's own observations of mental agility. At the practical level, a great deal of individualization took place in rural America's one-room schools. Fifteen to 25 children spread unevenly through ages 6 to 14 necessarily committed the teacher to large doses of individual pupil direction, recitation, and evaluation. With population increases and school consolidations, most village and rural schools began to look like rigidly graded city schools. Teachers found themselves responsible for larger and larger groups of children of approximately the same age and about the same physical size. It is little wonder that some of the zest, enthusiasm, and obviousness of need for individualized teaching was lost. When teachers complained about too-large classes, the lack of time to spend with individual pupils, the wide diversity of pupil ability levels, many not-so-smart administrators introduced "tracking" or "streaming" strategies. Separating children into homogeneous classes according to measured mental ability within age groups has been shown conclusively to fail to increase the achievement level of groups as a whole.[6] Homogeneous ability grouping has, on the other hand, seriously exacerbated social problems connected with race and economic levels by "ghettoizing" classrooms within the schools, even though the schools served racially and economically mixed neighborhoods.

Whereas the common schools have some history of experimentation with individualized instruction methods, higher education, led by the large state universities, has pushed the development of mass communication methods in instruction. The large-group lecture and the adaptation of closed-circuit television are examples of higher education's trend away from individualized instruction. Of course, the outstanding accomplishments of American university graduate schools could never have been achieved without the cost-savings introduced by mass communications techniques in their undergraduate colleges.

Interest in individualized instruction had a surge about 15 years ago when Harvard's B. F. Skinner[7][8] advocated an education technology built around the use of rather crude teaching machines. It soon became apparent that there was no particular magic in the machines themselves, since they contained only short linear series of questions and answers to word problems called "frames." These programs were quickly put into book form and the programmed text was born. Although it enjoyed initial success with some highly motivated learners, the programmed text has not caught on in either the lower schools or in higher education as a major instructional device. Industry and the military forces seem to have made the best use of programmed texts, perhaps because of a high degree of motivation on the part of many learners in those situations.

Most recently, an educational technique for the lower schools has been developed out of the work of the Learning Research and Development Center at the University of Pittsburgh. The method, called "individually prescribed instruction" or IPI, is described by Lindvall and Bolvin,[9] by Glaser,[10] and by Cooley and Glaser.[11] Behind the method lies the careful development of a technology based on precise specification and delineation of educational objectives in behavioral terms. Pupils work individually on a precisely scaled set of materials with frequent interspersed diagnostic quizzes.

It must be clear, even after this sketchy review of the history of individualized instruction, that the concept has been pursued in a desultory fashion. I have heard hour-long conversations on individualization by educators who have only the vaguest notion of what is encompassed by the concept. Let me review five different concepts of individualization and acknowledge that I am indebted to Tyler[12] for some of these distinctions.

First, most educators agree that instruction is "individual" when the learner is allowed to proceed through content materials at a self-determined pace that is comfortable for him. This concept of self-paced instruction is incorporated into all programmed texts and is perhaps easiest to achieve with reading material and hardest to achieve in a setting that presents content by means of lectures, films, and television. Oettinger,[13] in his witty but infuriating little book, *Run, Computer, Run,* refers to this self-pacing concept of individualization as "rate tailoring."

A second concept of individualized instruction is that the learner should be able to work at times convenient to him. The hard realities of academic bookkeeping with the associated paraphernalia of credits, marks, and time-serving schedules make this concept difficult to implement in colleges or in the common schools.

That a learner should begin instruction in a given subject at a point appropriate to his past achievement is a third way of looking at individualization. This concept makes the assumption that progress in learning is linear and that the main task is to locate the learner's present position on a universal continuum. Once properly located, he can then continue to the goal. These notions seem to have their optimum validity for well-ordered content like mathematics or foreign languages. In fact, the advanced placement program, which provides college credit for tested subject matter achievement during secondary school, is a gross attempt to get at this kind of individualization.

A fourth concept of individualization is the idea that learners are inhibited by a small number of easily identifiable skills or knowledges. The assumption is that the absence of these skills is diagnosable and that remedial efforts through special instructional units can eliminate the difficulty. Colleges and universities seeking to enroll a higher proportion of their students from among the culturally disadvantaged and the economically deprived will be forced to bring this concept to bear if they wish to maintain current academic standards.

A fifth concept is that individualization can be achieved by furnishing the learner with a wealth of instructional media from which to choose. Lectures, audio tapes, films, books, etc., all with the same intellectual content, could theoretically be made available to the learner. The underlying notion is that the learner will instinctively choose the communication medium or combination of media that enable him to do his best work. The research evidence to support this viewpoint and practice is not at all strong.[14] Perhaps even more persuasive than the lack of evidence is the vanity of instructors who cannot understand why a student would choose a film or an audio tape in preference to the instructor's own lively, stimulating, and informative lectures.[15]

I have reviewed five concepts of individualization which have some credence in education, but by far the most prevalent interpretation is the one of self-pacing, or rate tailoring. These notions lead us directly to the idea of adaptive education in responsive environments, which I want to discuss shortly. But first, one more distinction. "Individual instruction," where one studies in isolation from other learners, should probably be distinguished from "individualized instruction," where the scope, sequence, and time of instruction are tailored in one or more of the five ways I have just described. "Individualized instruction" can still be in a group setting and, in fact, was commonly practiced in rural one-room schools, as mentioned earlier. On the other hand, "individual instruction" can be singularly rigid, monotonous, and unresponsive to the needs of the learner. You could, for instance, take programmed text material which is designed for individualized instruction and put it into an educational television format. Each frame could be shown to a large group of students for a short time, allowing the students to pick a correct option and then going on to another frame. This procedure would be individual instruction with a vengeance. But it forces a kind of lock-step on students of varying abilities and interests that is the antithesis of "individualized instruction."

Adaptive Education

I predict that the impending instruction revolution will shortly bypass the simple idea of individualizing instruction and move ahead to the more sophisticated notion of providing adaptive education for school and college learners. By adaptive education we mean the tailoring of subject matter presentations to fit the special requirements and capabilities of each learner. The ideal is that no learner should stop short of his ultimate achievement in an area of content because of idiosyncratic hang-ups in his particular study strategies.

We have seen how the concept of individualized instruction has been pretty well arrested at the level of encouraging the learner to vary and control his task completion time. Many additional, more psychologically oriented variables will have to be brought into play to achieve the goals of adaptive education, as well as the adoption of individualizing techniques. We know a great deal about individual differences among people in regard to their sensory inputs, their reaction times, their interests, their values and preferences, and their organizational strategies in "mapping" the cognitive world. What we do not know very much about is the extent to which, or how, these easily tested, individual difference variables affect the acquisition and retention of new knowledge. Psychological learning theory has been preoccupied with the study of variables in extremely simple stimulus-response situations, and investigations of meaningful learning phenomena have clearly dealt with human subjects as if they were all cut from the same bolt. The exception to this observation is, of course, the variable of measured mental ability, which has been shown to be related to achievement in conventionally presented instruction and has been carefully controlled in many learning experiments involving human subjects.

Essential to the idea of adaptive education is the means of utilizing new knowledge about individual differences among learners to bring a highly tailored instructional product to the student. As long as we are dealing with static or canned linear presentations such as those contained in books, films, video tapes, and some lectures, there seems to be little incentive to try to discover what modifications in instructional materials would optimize learning for each student. To plug this important gap in the drive toward vastly improved learning, the modern digital computer seems to have great promise. About a decade ago, Rath, Anderson, and Brainerd[16] suggested the application of the computer to teaching tasks and actually programmed some associative learning material. In the intervening decade, a number of major universities, medical schools, industries, and military establishments have been exploring the use of the computer in instruction. Five years ago we instituted a computer-assisted instruction laboratory at Penn State and have been trying to perfect new instructional techniques within the constraints of available hardware and computer operating systems.[17,18,19,20] There are, according to my estimate, some 35 to 40 active computer-assisted instruction (CAI) installations operating in the world today, and fewer than 100 completed, semester-length courses or their equivalent. Almost none of these courses have been constructed according to the ideals I mentioned for adaptive education. Indeed, many of them look like crude, made-over versions of programmed textbooks, but this does not disturb me when I recall that the earliest automobiles were designed to look like carriages without the horses. The fact is that the modern computer's information storage capacity and decision logic have given us a glimpse of what a dynamic, individualized instruction procedure could be, and some insight into how this tool might be brought to bear to achieve an adaptive quality education for every student. We do not claim that the achievement of this goal is just around the corner or that every school and college can implement it by the turn of the century. We do believe that progress toward a program of adaptive education will be the big difference between our best schools and our mediocre ones at the end of the next three decades.

What individual difference variables look most promising for adapting instruction to the individual student via CAI? At Penn State we are testing the idea that a person learns best if he is rewarded for correctness with his most preferred type of reinforcement.[21] Thus some students will, we believe, learn more rapidly if they receive encouragement in the form of adult approval. Others will perform better if they receive actual tokens for excellence at significant places in the program, the tokens being exchangeable for candy, cokes, or other wanted objects. Still others respond to competitive situations in which they are given evidence of the superiority or inferiority of their performance compared to that of their peers. It is a fairly simple matter to determine a learner's reward preference in advance of instruction and to provide him with a computer-based program in which the information feedback is tailored to his psychological preference.

Perhaps the most dynamic and relevant variable on which to base an adaptive program of instruction is the learner's immediate past history of responses. By programming the computer to count and evaluate the correctness of the 10 most recent responses, it is possible to determine what comes next for each learner according to a prearranged schedule. For example, four or fewer correct out of the most recent 10 might dictate branching into shorter teaching steps with heavy prompting and large amounts of practice material. A score of five to seven might indicate the need for just a little more practice material, and eight or more correct out of the 10 most recent problems would suggest movement into a fast "track" with long strides through the computer-presented content. The dynamic part of this adaptive mechanism is that the computer constantly updates its performance information about each learner by dropping off the learner's response to the tenth problem back as it adds on new performance information from a just-completed problem.

There are two rather distinct strategies for presenting subject matter to learners. One is deductive, in which a rule, principle, or generalization is presented, followed by examples. The other strategy is inductive and seeks, by means of careful choice of illustrative examples, to lead the learner into formulating principles and generalizations on his own initiative. In the lower schools, inductive method is called "guided discovery" and has been found useful by many teachers. Our belief at the Penn State CAI Laboratory is that these two presentation strategies have their corollaries in an individual differences variable and that, for some students, learning will be facilitated by the deductive approach; others will learn more rapidly and with better retention if an inductive mode is adopted. A strong program of adaptive education would take these and other identifiable learner variables into account in the instructional process.

Evaluation and Student Appraisal

One of the important concomitants of the instruction revolution will be a drastic revision in the approach to learner evaluation and grading practices by faculty. Even the moderate students on campus are saying that letter grades are anachronistic. On many campuses, including our own, students have petitioned for, and won, the right to receive "satisfactory" and "unsatisfactory" evaluations of their work in certain non-major courses. Other students have attacked all grades as a manifestation of a coercive, competitive, materialistic society. Without admitting to being a tool of a sick society, we should change this part of the business of higher education as rapidly as possible.

It seems to me that most formal instruction has been

predicated on the notion that a course is offered between two relatively fixed points in time. In addition, the tools of instruction, such as lectures, textbooks, references, and computer services, are all relatively fixed and are the same for all learners. To be sure, the students do vary the amount of time they spend with these tools. Even there, the college catalogue tells the students that they should all study three hours outside of class for every hour in class. At the close of the period of instruction or end of the course, usually the end of the term, we give the students an achievement test that is constructed in a way that will maximize the differences among their scores. To get this seemingly important differentiation between our students in achievement, we have to ask extremely difficult questions. Sometimes we even go so far as to ask questions about footnotes in the text. In fact, we often have to ask questions on topics or objectives that we have made no attempt to teach. Our rationalization for this tactic is that we want the students to be able to transfer their knowledge. After obtaining the achievement examination results, we consult the trusty "normal curve" and assign A's, B's, C's, D's, and F's according to our interpretation of the grading mores of the institution. With time and materials fixed, we are essentially capitalizing upon the same human abilities that are measured by intelligence tests. Thus it is not surprising that intelligence and teacher-assigned grades tend to be highly correlated.

We could, as collegiate educators, do society and ourselves a big favor by making a fundamental shift in our approach to teaching and examining. (Incidentally, we might generate some relevance "points" with our students.) First, we should say (and mean) that our job is helping each of our students to achieve mastery over some operationally defined portion of subject matter.[22] Furthermore, failure by any student putting forth an effort is a failure on our part as teachers, or a breakdown of the selection system. Now, to do this job we will have to get rid of a lot of the present practices and irrelevancies of higher education. There is no point in maintaining an adversary system in the classroom, with the students against the instructor and each of the students against each other. Society may think that it wants us to mark our students on a competitive scale, but how much more sensible it would be if we could say, on the basis of accumulated examination evidence, that John Jones has achieved 85 percent of the objectives in Engineering 101, rather than say that he got a "B." If our job is to help the student master the subject matter or come close— say, achieve 90 percent or greater of the objectives—then we are going to have to adapt our instruction to him. As a starter, we could individualize by letting the student pace his own instruction. We know, for example, from preliminary work with class-sized groups in computer-assisted instruction, that the slowest student will take from three to five times as long as the fastest student in a rich environment of individualized teaching material. During a recent computer-mediated in-service teacher education course presented by Penn State in Dryden, Virginia, to 129 elementary school teachers, the average completion time was 21 clock hours. The fastest student finished in 12 hours and the slowest took 58 hours.[23]

Student evaluations should also be based on the concept that an achievable mastery criterion exists for each course. We should no longer engage in the sophistry of classical psychometrics, in which we prepare a test or examination deliberately designed to make half the students get half the items wrong. It is true that such a test optimally discriminates among the learners, which we justify by claiming need for competitive marking information. If, however, 50 percent of the students get 50 percent of the items wrong, then either we are asking the wrong questions or there is something seriously wrong with our non-adaptive instructional program.

Under optimum circumstances, we might get an enlightened view of the faculty's need to adopt mastery-type student evaluation procedures and we might get professors to talk less, but we would still be faced with the psychological problem of instructor dominance or instructor power. The power over students which the "giving" of grades confers on professors would not be yielded easily by many in college teaching today. As Pogo says, "We have met the enemy and he is us."

If we, as faculty and administrators in higher education, embraced the notion of teaching for student mastery

by means of individually adaptive programs, then these are
some of the concomitants:

1. Instructors would have to state their course objectives in behavioral terms.

2. Achievement tests keyed to course objectives would
have to be constructed and used as both diagnostic placement and end-of-course determiners.

3. The bachelor's degree might take from two to eight
years instead of the traditional four, because of the wide
variability in mastery achievement.

4. Instead of telling three times a week, instructors
might have to spend their time listening to students individually and in small groups where progress toward subject
mastery required careful monitoring.

5. Instead of being primarily concerned with a discipline or with a specialization, those who profess for undergraduates would have to make the student and his knowledge their first concern.

6. Evaluation for promotion and salary increments for
college teachers would be based on measured amounts of
growth exhibited by their students and on numbers of
students who achieved a specific mastery criterion.

If professors and deans ignore the reasoned demands
for reform of undergraduate instruction which come from
the students, the government, and a concerned citizenry,
then the revolution will be ugly and wrenching. The so-
called "free universities," with their obvious shortcomings,
are already harbingers of the chaos into which traditional
higher education could slip if there is not responsiveness
on the part of a majority of academicians to the need for
change.

In the current wave of student unrest, many of the best
articulated issues are local in nature, like the quality of food
in the cafeteria or the relaxation of dormitory visiting rules
for members of the opposite sex. Underneath these surface
issues, however, lies the one big issue, which the students
themselves haven't spelled out clearly. This is the issue of
the relevance of contemporary collegiate instruction for
students' lives. It seems to me students are saying, albeit
not very clearly, that they want some wise adult to care

about them, to pay attention to them, to listen and to guide them. We sit on our status quo's and ignore their cry for help at our peril.

Increasing Heterogeneity

Part of the fuel breeding the revolution in instruction is the increasing heterogeneity in mental ability and scholastic preparation among college students. The combined power of the teaching faculty, regional accrediting agencies, and shortage of spaces for students has, until recently, enabled many public universities to become increasingly selective. In fact, prestige among higher education institutions has been closely correlated with the height of the norms for entrance test scores. Even the great state universities, which began under the land-grant aegis as people's colleges, have a kind of "elitest" aura about them. Rising aspirations of minority groups, particularly blacks, have pointed up the fact that the poor, the disadvantaged, and the dark-skinned of our society do not share equally in whatever benefits a post-secondary college experience confers. A recent study and report by John Egerton for the National Association of State Universities and Land-Grant Colleges[24] was based on 80 public universities which enroll almost one-third of the nation's college students. He found that less than two percent of the graduate and undergraduate students were Negro in these institutions and that less than one percent of the faculty were black. Yet approximately 11 percent of the total U.S. population is black. It seems irrefutable that, with society's new awareness of the inequality in higher education, university entrance standards will have to be lowered for sizeable groups of blacks who have been poorly educated in the nation's secondary schools. Accounts of City University of New York's open admissions plan for fall, 1970, provide ample proof of the beginning of this trend, and Healy's[25] recent article firms up the humanitarian and social theory for the change in this great university. The lowering of entrance requirements will inevitably increase the heterogeneity of scholastic skills which makes the conventional teaching job so difficult.

Another source for increasing individual differences among college undergraduates is their stiffening resistance to required courses. Students clearly want more freedom of choice in devising their education programs. They want to determine what subjects are relevant to their lives and are increasingly impatient with elaborate prerequisites and multi-course sequences. Although the activists are not likely to win a complete victory on this score, the pressure which they generate will serve to breach the walls and gates around courses that have carefully been built by faculty over the years in order to make the conventional job of teaching somewhat more manageable. In addition to the student rejection of required courses, there is a corresponding need for the teaching of interdisciplinary subjects. Students see, perhaps more clearly than the faculty, that solution of the nation's problems such as urban decay, congestion, air and water pollution, and war and peace are not going to be solved by the unitary application of knowledge from traditional disciplines. For purposes of this discussion, the drive toward more interdisciplinary courses of study can only increase the heterogeneity among students which the faculty has labored to minimize.

Conclusion

I have argued that we are now living with the early stages of a revolution in instruction which will be more or less complete by the turn of the century. The major changes will be primary characterized by individualization of instruction leading to sophisticated systems of adaptive education. Two concomitants of the revolution which seriously concern college faculty and administrators are the need for new fundamental concepts of student appraisal and adaptation to increasing heterogeneity among the students in our charge.

Reprinted from *Phi Delta Kappan,* 1970. Copyright, 1963, by Phi Delta Kappan, Bloomington, Indiana. Reprinted by permission of the author and the publisher. Dr. Mitzel is a Professor of Educational Psychology at Pennsylvania State University.

References

[1]G. Pask, "Computer-Assisted Learning and Teaching," paper presented at Seminar on Computer-Based Learning, Leeds University, September 9–12, 1969.

[2]P. W. Search, "Individual Teaching: The Pueblo Plan," *Education Review*, February, 1894, pp. 154–70.

[3]J. S. Brubacher, *A History of the Problems of Education*, 2nd ed. New York: McGraw-Hill, 1966.

[4]H. H. Parkhurst, *Education on the Dalton Plan*. New York: E. P. Dutton & Co., 1922.

[5]A. Binet and T. Simon, *The Development of Intelligence in Children*, trans. Elizabeth S. Kite. Vineland, N.J.: The Training School, 1916.

[6]J. I. Goodlad in Encyclopedia of Educational Research, 3rd ed., ed. C. Harris, New York: Macmillan, 1960.

[7]B. F. Skinner, "The Science of Learning and the Art of Teaching," *Harvard Educational Review*, Spring, 1954, pp. 86–97.

[8]B. F. Skinner, "Teaching Machines," *Science*, 128, 1958, pp. 969–77.

[9]C. M. Lindvall and J. O. Bolvin, "Programed Instruction in the Schools: An Application of Programing Principles in Individually Prescribed Instruction," in *Programed Instruction*, ed. P. C. Lange. The Sixty-Sixth Yearbook of the National Society for the Study of Education, Part II. Chicago: The University of Chicago Press, 1967, pp. 217–54.

[10]R. Glaser, *The Education of Individuals*. Pittsburgh, Pa.: Learning Research and Development Center, University of Pittsburgh, 1966.

[11]W. W. Cooley and R. Glaser, "An Information Management System for Individually Prescribed Instruction," working paper No. 44, Learning Research and Development Center, University of Pittsburgh, mimeographed, 1968.

[12]R. W. Tyler, "New Directions in Individualizing Instruction," in *The Abington Conference '67 on New Directions in Individualizing Instruction*. Abington, Pa.: The Conference, 1967.

[13]A. G. Oettinger and S. Marks, *Run, Computer, Run.* Cambridge, Mass.: Harvard University Press, 1969.

[14]S. N. Postlethwait, "Planning for Better Learning," in *In Search of Leaders,* ed. G. K. Smith, Washington, D.C.: American Association for Higher Education, NEA, 1967, pp. 110–13.

[15]D. T. Tosti and J. T. Ball, "A Behavioral Approach to Instructional Design and Media Selection," BSD Paper Number 1, Observations in Behavioral Technology, Albuquerque, N.M.: The Behavior Systems Division, Westinghouse Learning Corporation, 1969.

[16]G. J. Rath, N. S. Anderson, and R. C. Brainerd, "The IBM Research Center Teaching Machine Project," in *Automatic Teaching: The State of the Art,* ed. E. H. Galanter. New York: Wiley, 1959, pp. 117–30.

[17]H. E. Mitzel, "The Development and Presentation of Four College Courses by Computer Teleprocessing." Final Report, Computer-Assisted Instruction Laboratory, The Pennsylvania State University, June 30, 1967. Contract No. OE-4-16-010, New Project No. 5–1194, U.S. Office of Education.

[18]H. E. Mitzel, B. R. Brown, and R. Igo, "The Development and Evaluation of a Teleprocessed Computer-Assisted Instruction Course in the Recognition of Malarial Parasites." Final Report No. R-17, Computer-Assisted Instruction Laboratory, The Pennsylvania State University, June 30, 1968. Contract No. N00014-67-A-0385-0003, Office of Naval Research.

[19]H. E. Mitzel, "Experimentation with Computer-Assisted Instruction in Technical Education." Semi-annual progress report, R-18, Computer-Assisted Instruction Laboratory, The Pennsylvania State University, December 31, 1968.

[20]"Inquiry," Research Report published by Office of the Vice President for Research, Penn State.

[21]C. A. Cartwright and G. P. Cartwright, "Reward Preference Profiles of Elementary School Children," mimeographed, Computer-Assisted Instruction Laboratory, The Pennsylvania State University, 1969. Paper presented at the meeting of the American Educational Research Association, Los Angeles, February, 1969.

[22]B. Bloom, "Learning for Mastery," UCLA Evaluation Comment, 1968.

[23]K. H. Hall, et al., "Inservice Mathematics Education for Elementary School Teachers via Computer-Assisted Instruction." Interim Report, No. R-19, Computer-Assisted Instruction Laboratory, The Pennsylvania State University, June 1, 1969.

[24]B. Nelson, "State Universities: Report Terms Desegregation 'Largely Token,'" *Science*, June 6, 1969, pp. 1155–56.

[25]T. S. Healy, "Will Everyman Destroy the University?" *Saturday Review*, December 20, 1969, pp. 54–56+.

5

Individuals and Learning: The New Aptitudes

Robert Glaser

In this paper, I propose to show how certain developments in psychology have influenced present educational methods, and to show further how recent work in learning theory, developmental psychology, and psychometrics strongly suggests new directions for educational research and practice. I shall discuss this theme in the context of a central problem in education—the individualization of instruction or, in other terms, adapting educational environments to individual differences. I shall focus on the education of the young child in the pre-school and elementary school years, although what I have to say seems applicable to all levels of our educational system.

The problem obviously has been a persistent one; it has been recognized and proclaimed at least since the beginning of this century, three generations ago. Very early in the century, Edward L. Thorndike (1911) published a monograph entitled "Individuality." His editor's introduction summarizes the then current situation by noting that the teaching profession and education in general were showing signs of a violent reaction against the uniformity of method that for so long clutched and mechanized the schools. The deadening effects of uniformity needed to be recognized. Parents and students had been the first to notice this; now the professional consciousness was deeply penetrated because the teachers themselves realized that they were caught in the iron machinery of their own making. These turns of phrase were written in 1911, and throughout the twentieth century, the problem has been raised again and again. In 1925, a major effort appeared in the twenty-fourth yearbook of the National Society for the Study of Education entitled, "Adapting the Schools to Individual Differences." Carleton Washburne's introduction states in forceful terms that the widespread use of intelligence and achievement tests has made every educator realize that children vary greatly as individuals, and "throughout the educational world, there has therefore awakened the desire to find some way of adapting schools to the differing individuals who attend them (Washburne, 1925)."

Shouts of alarm have been ubiquitous; many suggestions have been made, a few sustained experiments have been launched. Nevertheless, it is now 1972, and time goes by with still only a recognition of the problem, and as yet, no directions towards solution realized. This is the situation that I would like to examine. I am encouraged to do so by the fact that work in the study of human behavior over the past 10 to 20 years now points to possible solutions. Unfortunately, I cannot point to new directions in a simple way by listing a few principles that ring with self-evident truth, although this is the fashionable road to current educational reform. The story is complicated, its roots are deep, and its complexities need to be examined.

An analysis of the problem involves the idiosyncracies of two major fields of psychology. As is known, the English and German traditions of the nineteenth century gave rise to two separate disciplines of scientific psychology: psychometrics and experimental psychology. It was the psychometricians with their emphasis on technology who had significant impact upon educational methods. Indeed, the major activity in educational psychology revolved around measurement and psychometric practice. Psychometrics emphasized the nature of individual differences and the utility of measuring these differences for education. Learning variables and modification of the educational environment, however, were not part of this field. Meanwhile, the experimental psychologists went into the laboratory to work on the basic foundations of their science, and concentrated on discovering and formulating general laws of behavior unencumbered by the additional complication of individual differences. For the most part, individual differences became the error variance in experimental design.

The separation of these two fields, both of which are necessary for a complete conception of instructional theory, led to assumptions about individual differences uninfluenced by knowledge of learning and cognitive processes, and led to theories of learning uninfluenced by the effect of individual difference parameters. In this climate, characterized by the parallel, but not combined, labors of two major disciplines relevant to education, the search for an educational system that responds to individuality has been going on. To be as clear as I can, I will overstate the case by contrasting two kinds of educational environments. One I shall call a selective educational mode, and the other, an adaptive educational mode. It appears that we have produced a selective educational mode while aspiring toward an adaptive one.

A *selective* mode of education is characterized by minimal variation in the conditions under which individuals are expected to learn. A narrow range of instructional options is provided, and a limited number of ways to succeed are available. Consequently, the adaptability of the system to the student is limited, and alternative paths that can be selected for students with different backgrounds and talents are restricted. In such an environment, the fixed or limited paths available require particular student abilities, and these *particular* abilities are emphasized and fostered to the exclusion of other abilities. In this sense, the system becomes selective with respect to individuals who have particular abilities for success—as success is defined and as it can be attained by the means of instruction that are available. The effectiveness of the system, for the designers of the system and for the students themselves, is enhanced by admitting only those students who score very highly on measures of the abilities required to succeed. Furthermore,

since only those students who have a reasonable probability of success are admitted, little change in the educational environment is necessary, and the differences among
individuals that become important to measure are those
that predict success in this special setting.

In contrast to a selective mode, and *adaptive* mode of
education assumes that the educational environment can
provide for a wide range and variety of instructional
methods and opportunities for success. Alternate means of
learning are adaptive to and are in some way matched to
knowledge about each individual—his background, talents,
interests, and the nature of his past performance. An individual's styles and abilities are assessed either upon entrance or during the course of learning, and certain educational paths are elected or assigned. Further information is
obtained about the learner as learning proceeds, and this, in
turn, is related to subsequent alternate learning opportunities. The interaction between performance and the subsequent nature of the educational setting is the defining
characteristic of an adaptive mode. The success of this
adaptive interaction is determined by the extent to which
the student experiences a match between his specific
abilities and interests, and the activities in which he engages. The effect of any election of or assignment to an
instructional path is evaluated by the changes it brings
about in the student's potential for future learning and goal
attainment. Measures of individual differences in an adaptive educational mode are valid to the extent that they help
to define alternate paths that result in optimizing immediate learning, as well as long-term success.

A selective educational mode operates in a Darwinian
framework, requiring that organisms adapt to, and survive
in, the world as it is; an alternative is that the environment
can be changed. If we design only a relatively fixed
environment, then a wide range of background capabilities
and talented accomplishments might be lost from view
because of the exclusive reliance upon selection for sur-
vival in a particular setting. What is learned and the way in
which one learns, and learns to learn, may take on less
importance or receive less emphasis in a setting that offers
more options for learning.

When one compares a selective educational mode with adaptive educational possibilities, one asks whether the particular selective tests and sorting out devices that are part of present schooling fail to consider abilities and talents that might emerge as important in a more interactive setting where there is room for adjustment between abilities and modes of learning. In principle, and in contrast to traditional practice, there seems to be no reason why educational environments cannot be designed to accommodate more readily to variations in the backgrounds, cognitive processes, interests, styles, and other requirements of learners.

In any educational mode, then, the individual differences that take on outstanding importance are those that have ecological validity within a particular system. In our traditional selective educational mode, the individual differences that are measured in order to make educational assignments center around the concepts of intelligence and aptitude. This bears looking into.

Of the various attempts to measure intellectual ability that began at the turn of the century, Binet's work emerged strongly. It was a practical endeavor to predict school success. The Minister of Public Education in France supported Binet's attempts to determine what might be done to ensure the benefits of instruction to retarded children. It was decided that children suspected of retardation be given an examination to certify that, because of the state of their intelligence, they were unable to profit from instruction as given in ordinary schooling. Scholastic success in an essentially fixed educational mode was the predictive aim toward which this test was directed, for which its items were selected, and in terms of which its overall effectiveness was validated; although to be fair to Binet, his writings do indicate a great deal of sensitivity to the possibilities for individual differential diagnosis. Nevertheless, the validation of a test is a very specific procedure in which individuals are exposed to particular kinds of test items that are constructed to predict a particular criterion measure. No test is simply valid in general, but for a specific purpose and a particular situation. The concept of Binet's work has persisted, and as Cronbach points out in the 1970 edition of his well-known book on the essentials of psychological testing: "Current tests differ from those of the earlier generation just as 1970 automobiles differ from those of about 1920; more efficient, more elegant, but operating on the same principles as before (Cronbach, 1970)."

At the present time, our most respected textbooks on the subject (Cronbach, 1970; Tyler, 1965) carefully point out that if we base our conclusions about what intelligence tests measure on their most effective use—that is, their predictive validity—then the verdict is that they are tests of scholastic aptitude or scholastic ability; these tests measure certain abilities that are helpful in most school work, as it is conducted in present-day school situations. This same ideology has penetrated the entrance requirements of almost all institutions of higher education (*vide* Wing & Wallach, 1971), and strongly determines the character of primary and secondary school education. It is further to be observed that these tests of scholastic aptitude, when considered over all school levels, account for only 35 to 45 percent of the variation in school performance.

Being aware of this, we have not been remiss in attempting to probe deeper into the different facets of human behavior that might allow us to be more sensitive to individual differences. Some years ago, as a result of some dissatisfaction with the research on the IQ and together with the results of work on multiple factor analysis, there was a de-emphasis of the concept of general intelligence that led to the popularity of tests of differential aptitudes. At that time, in addition to an overall measure of "intelligence" or "general aptitude," schools began to employ tests that provided measures on a variety of factors such as spatial, mechanical, and abstract reasoning aptitudes. More than predicting overall scholastic success, these test batteries attempted to predict differential success in school programs leading to different vocations which appeared to require different aptitude patterns.

In 1964, a careful analysis was done by McNemar of the validity coefficients of certain widely used, multi-test differential aptitude batteries. He argued from his analysis that "aside from tests of numerical ability having differential value for predicting school grades in math, it seems safe to conclude that the worth of the multi-test batteries as differential predictors of achievement in school has not been demonstrated (McNemar, 1964)." McNemar further concluded that "it is far from clear that tests of general intelligence have been outmoded by the multi-test batteries as the more useful predictors of school achievement." In general, a simple, unweighted combination of tests of verbal reasoning and numerical ability predicted grades as well as, or better than, any other test or combination of more specific ability tests; and these tests of verbal and numerical ability were similar to what was measured in group tests of intelligence. More recent evidence reaffirms McNemar's conclusion. For example, a 1971 technical report of the College Entrance Examination Board points out that there is certainly no reason why the Scholastic Aptitude Test (SAT) could not include measures from other domains in addition to the verbal and mathematical skills tested, and that research to identify these other domains has been an enduring concern. Yet, over the 40 years of the SAT's existence, no other measures have demonstrated such a broadly useful relationship to the criterion of college achievement (Angoff, 1971).

All this suggests the following observation: Given the characteristics of our present educational system, certain general measures of the ability to manipulate numbers and words predict, to a limited extent, the ability to emerge victorious from the educational environment provided. However, any attempt to further differentiate specific ability patterns that relate to specific educational programs is, at best, no more successful than the usual general ability measures or intelligence measures. Why is this so, and what does it mean?

One clue to answering this question is to note that tests of general ability, intelligence, and aptitude follow the accepted practice of attempting to predict the *outcomes* of learning in our rather uniform educational programs. These tests make little attempt to measure those abilities that are related to different *ways* of learning. The generally used scholastic aptitude tests are designed for and validated in terms of predictions of the products of learning in a particular setting. They are not designed to determine the different ways in which different students learn best, to measure the basic processes that underlie various kinds of learning, nor to assess prerequisite performance capabilities required for learning a new task.

Psychologists and educational researchers, again, have not been insensitive to this state of affairs, and there has been a recent emergence of concern about the relationships between measures of individual differences and learning variables. To a large extent, this work was heralded by the 1957 book by Cronbach and Gleser entitled *Psychological Tests and Personnel Decisions* and its second edition in 1965. This book was concerned with the development of a decision-theory model for the selection and placement of individuals into various "treatments." The word treatment was given a broad meaning, referring to what is done with an individual in an institutional setting; e.g., for what job an applicant should be trained in industry, what therapeutic method a patient should be assigned, and in education, to which particular educational program or instructional method a student should be assigned or given the opportunity to select. This theoretical analysis attempted to show that neither the traditional predictive model of psychometric work nor the traditional experimental comparison of mean differences was an adequate formulation for these practical decisions, including the kinds of decisions required for the individualization of instruction.

Cronbach and Gleser pointed out that aptitude information is useful in adapting to treatments only when aptitude and treatment can be shown to interact. In a nontechnical way, this can be explained as follows: Given a measure of aptitude, and two different instructional methods, if the aptitude measure correlates positively with the success in both treatments, then it is of no value in deciding which method to suggest to the student. What is required is a measure of aptitude that predicts who will learn better from one curriculum or method of learning than from another. If such measures can be developed, then methods of instruction can be designed, not to fit the average person, but to fit an individual or group of students with particular patterns. Unless one treatment is clearly best for everyone, treatments should be differentiated in such a way as to maximize their interaction with aptitude variables.

Following up on this logic, educational psychologists have been active in experimentation and have searched deeply into the literature of their field. The line of investigation has been called the ATI problem (ATI standing for aptitude-treatment interaction). The intent of the work is different from that of the previously mentioned work on differential aptitude testing. In the differential aptitude testing research, emphasis was placed on determining the relationship between measured aptitudes and learning outcomes under relatively fixed educational programs. In the ATI work, the emphasis is on determining whether aptitudes can predict which one of several learning methods might help different individuals attain similar educational outcomes. To be clearer, the earlier differential aptitude work assumed several different educational programs, each one leading to different careers, and attempted to select potential success in each program. The ATI work essentially assumes that if within each of these several programs there were different instructional options, then aptitude patterns might predict the option in which a student would be most successful.

Several recent comprehensive reviews report detailed analyses of ATI studies (Bracht, 1969; Bracht & Glass, 1968; Cronbach & Snow, 1969). In a review by Bracht, 90 studies were each carefully assessed for the significance of appropriate aptitude-treatment interactions. The results of his survey are quite striking. In the 90 studies, 108 individual difference-treatment interactions were examined; of these, only five were identified as being significant with respect to the kind of interaction required for the purposes I have outlined. An extensive and thoughtful analysis of many of the ramifications of the ATI problem also has appeared in an informal report by Cronbach and Snow (1969). The report is far ranging, discussing the relationships between individual differences and learning from many points of view. Their conclusion, with respect to ATI research, is similar to Bracht's: few or no ATI effects have been solidly demonstrated; the frequency of studies in which appropriate interactions have been found is low; and the empirical evidence found in favor of such interactions is often not very convincing.

This is an astounding conclusion; it implies that our generally used aptitude constructs are not productive dimensions for measuring those individual differences that interact with different ways of learning. These measures derived from a psychometric, selection-oriented tradition do not appear to relate to the processes of learning and performance that have been under investigation in experimental and developmental psychology. The treatments investigated in the ATI studies were not generated by any systematic analysis of the kinds of psychological processes called upon in particular instructional methods, and individual differences were not assessed in terms of these processes.

Perhaps we should have known all this, and not have had to learn it the hard way because I am reminded of Lee Cronbach's APA presidential address in 1957. In discussing these general concerns, he said: "I believe that we will find these aptitudes to be quite unlike our present aptitude measures." He went on to say, "Constructs originating in differential psychology are now being tied to experimental variables. As a result, the whole theoretical picture in such an area as human abilities is changing (Cronbach, 1957)." I believe that Cronbach was a moment or two ahead of his time in his address 15 years ago. But, I also believe that education and psychology have since moved in directions which make adaptation to individuals in educational settings more likely; research on cognitive processes, psychometric methodologies, deeper attempts at individualization, and the cultural Zeitgeist seem to offer enabling potentials. I shall go on to describe some of this, but first let me recapitulate the question that I am attempting to answer.

The general question takes the form of the following set of questions: (1) How can knowledge of an individual's patterns of abilities and interests be matched to the method, content, and timing of his instruction? (2) How can the educational environment be adjusted to an individual's particular talents, and to his particular strengths and weaknesses as defined in terms of social and personal objectives for education? and (3) The other way around—how can an individual's abilities be modified and strengthened to meet the prerequisite demands of available means of instruction and available educational opportunities?

The implications of my discussion so far appear to support the hypothesis that the human performances that we identify with the words "general ability," "scholastic intelligence," and "aptitudes" have emerged on the basis of measurement and validation procedures in an educational system of a particular kind. These intelligence and aptitude factors have taken on significance because of their correlation with instructional outcomes, and not because of their relationship to learning processes or different educational techniques. Furthermore, since our educational system provides a limited range of educational options for adapting to different individuals, these general abilities override the influence of any more specific abilities that might be additionally useful if alternate ways of learning were available.

The question now is: What *are* these "new aptitudes"? Current lines of research indicate that a fruitful approach is the conceptualization of individual difference variables in terms of the process constructs of contemporary theories of learning, development, and human performance. There is ample evidence to show that we can experimentally identify and influence a variety of cognitive processes that are involved in new learning, and it appears that the analysis of individual differences in performance can be carried out in terms of such processes (Melton, 1967). Some exemplary studies along these lines can be referred to as illustration. For example, it is known that learning to remember a list of words takes place more effectively when the learner is provided with, or provides for himself, some visual or verbal relationship between pairs of words. Presented with the words "boy" and "horse," one pictures a boy riding a horse, or makes up a sentence containing these words. This process has been called "mental elaboration," referring to the fact that individuals recode or transform materials presented to them by elaborating the content. William Rohwer has been particularly concerned with studying the developmental and individual difference aspects of this process. As children grow older, they begin to generate their own forms of mental elaboration; young children, however, profit from being prompted or encouraged in some way to engage in elaborative activity. Rohwer's work suggests that individual differences related to children's backgrounds, influence the way in which they carry out cognitive processes of this kind. He further implies that since this kind of elaborative activity facilitates learning in general, it would be fruitful to train particular children in such elaborative techniques of learning; and there is evidence that this indeed can be done to extend the capabilities of young learners (Rohwer, 1970a, 1970b, 1971).

In another series of studies related to our work on individualized instruction at Pittsburgh, my colleague Jerome Rosner has studied perceptual processes that appear to be related to basic academic tasks in elementary school. He has studied individual differences in visual and auditory perceptual processes concerned with competence in organizing and extracting patterns of information presented in geometric patterns and in sound combinations. Rosner's work indicates that competence in these processes is differentially related to academic achievement in arithmetic and reading; visual perceptual processes are more related to arithmetic than reading, and auditory processes more related to beginning reading than arithmetic. He has also shown that these processes themselves can be effectively taught to children, and the indication is that the effects of this instruction transfer to specific accomplishment in the beginnings of verbal and quantitative literacy (Rosner, 1972, in press).

Studies such as these support the promise of a line of research on individual differences in terms of cognitive processes. I would urge that studies attempt to identify the kinds of processes required by various tasks, and to characterize how individuals perform these processes. The conditions required to learn the task could then be adapted to these individual characteristics, or the individual might be taught how to engage more effectively in these processes.

Another sign of support for the theme of process concepts as individual difference variables comes from the work on cognitive styles or personality characteristics that influence learning and performance (Kagan & Kagan, 1970). Here, the influence of individual differences in non-cognitive domains on the cognitive processes involved in problem solving is being systematically studied. This includes research on the effects of cultural background on the dominance of visual, auditory, or tactile sense modalities; the relationship between anxiety and the quality of immediate memory; the ability to hold changing images in memory, what personality theorists have called "leveling and sharpening"; and the degree to which an individual pauses to evaluate the quality of cognitive products in the course of problem solving, generally referred to as differences in reflection and impulsivity.

There have been some interesting attempts to modify cognitive style. For example, it has been shown that when first-grade children are placed with experienced teachers who have a reflective style, the children become more reflective during the school year than children who are placed with impulsive teachers (Yando & Kagan, 1968). The practical implication of this for school instruction is tailoring the tempo of the teacher to the tempo of the child so that, for example, the behavior of the impulsive child is influenced by the presence of a reflective teacher model. Another set of studies has investigated the controlling function of covert speech as a self-guidance procedure whereby impulsive children are taught to talk to themselves in order to modify their problem-solving styles (Meichenbaum, 1971; Meichenbaum & Goodman, 1969).

The processes that make up cognitive style are important to consider in the education of culturally disadvantaged children. As we know, early experience in a particular cultural environment provides the child with a set of values and a set of techniques and skills for learning to learn and for processing incoming information. It has been pointed out that the middle-class child acquires these things so that they are continuous with what will be required of him in school. Whereas, what a lower socio-economic-class child acquires may be discontinuous with what school demands. In a non-adaptive environment for learning, "cultural deprivation" is defined in terms of a set of experiences that establishes a discontinuity between pre-school experiences and school requirements. An obvious example in the conventional school is that, explicitly or implicitly, the school requires the immediate acceptance of an achievement ethic with deferred future rewards, a characteristic most consonant with middle-class values. This discontinuity has a profound effect on the child's behavior towards school and on the school's behavior toward the child. In the adaptive educational environment that I envision, it would be assumed as a matter of course that the values, styles, and learning processes that the child brings to school are of intrinsic worth. These modes of behavior have, in fact, been extremely functional in the child's environment, and an adaptive setting would work with these assets of the child's functioning as a basis for a program of education (Getzels, 1966).

The work and theories of Piaget quite directly support and influence my theme of the importance of modifiable behavioral processes in adaptive education as opposed to notions of relatively fixed intelligence and aptitude. The stages of cognitive development described in the Piagetian theory of intelligence are thought to mark major qualitative changes in the modes of thinking available to the child, and consequently, changes in the kinds of specific learning of which he or she is capable. Adaptive education, as I have indicated, looks at this in two ways: the educational environment accommodates to the existing modes and processes of a learner, and it also can influence these processes through instruction. The stages described by Piaget thus provide individual modes of performance available to different children which would have to be considered in educational design.

Recently, Lauren Resnick and I (1972) carried out a detailed survey on the possible teachability of basic aptitudes and Piagetian processes. In our examination of operational thinking, particularly the acquisition of concrete operations, with which most studies have been concerned, we noted a significant shift, as compared with a few years ago, in the balance of evidence concerning the trainability of these processes. A number of studies have appeared which offer grounds for suggesting the possibility of developing operational thinking through instruction. As we completed this survey, we were struck with the fact that our search for work on the instructability of basic abilities uncovered far fewer studies on the training of psychometrically defined aptitudes and abilities than on the training of Piagetian and related concepts. This raises the question of why the Piagetian definition of intelligence has stimulated so much more instructional research than has the psychometric one.

One answer seems to be that Piagetian theory is not concerned with differential prediction, but with explication of developmental changes in thought structures and the influence of these structures on performance. This emphasis suggests a variety of specific performances on which to focus instructional attention, and also suggests hypotheses concerning the optimal character and sequence of instructional attempts. In contrast, most psychometric tests of intelligence and aptitude consist of items chosen because of their predictive power rather than their relationship of observed or hypothesized intellectual processes. Thus, they offer few concrete suggestions as to what or how to teach. It appears, then, that successful attempts to adapt instruction to individual differences will depend upon a line of research emphasizing process variables in human performance.

There are other forms of evidence which contribute to our definition of the "new aptitudes" or processes for adaptive education. The fact that our concept of intelligence is undergoing significant change is obvious in the work of Piaget and in related work, but different areas of endeavor also show this clearly. There has been intensive activity in the field of comparative psychology on the intelligence of different animal species (Lockard, 1971). What used to be called general animal intelligence, and tested in the old experiments as general problem-solving ability, now appears to be an aggregate of special specific abilities, each ability evolving in response to environmental demands. Animals are "intelligent" in quite different ways that can be better understood in relation to the ecological demands of their particular environments than in terms of the older notion of a phyletic ordering of animals according to their intelligence. For example, because of their environmental demands, wasps are superior in delayed-response problems to Norway rats, and gophers are better at maze problems than horses and other open-range animals. Animals show a great many different talents evolved as adaptations to their different worlds. The older work in animal behavior appears to have over emphasized abstractions like general maze brightness as a criterion behavior for study. More recent work suggests that natural selection affects smaller mechanisms of behavior which permit the individual organism to perfect a behavior pattern adaptive to the detailed circumstances of the situation.

This fact of ecological validity, that is, that the demands of the environment influence behavior quite particularly, is apparent in another interpretation of intelligence. In a recent book on cognitive development by Olson (1970), intelligence is defined as the elaboration of the perceptual world that occurs in the context of acquiring skills with cultural media. Intelligence is developed through mastering and obtaining skill in the specifics of the prevalent media in society. Such an interpretation has been popularized by McLuhan (1964), who points out that we tend to confuse skill in the medium that happens to be ascendent in our own culture with a presumed universal structure of intelligence. In this sense, intelligence is specific to the particular ways in which school subjects can be learned.

The rise of the "new aptitudes" is also forecast by the notion of interactionism whereby accommodative changes in an individual's performance occur in the course of encounters with environmental circumstances. This has been emphasized by such diverse points of view as Piaget's and Skinner's, and currently is well expressed by Bandura in his writings on social learning theory (Bandura, 1969, 1971). We know now that psychological functioning is a continuing reciprocal interaction between the behavior of an organism and the controlling conditions in the environment. Behavior partly creates the environment, and the resultant environment influences the behavior. This is clearly seen in social interaction, for example, where a person plays an active role in bringing out a positive or negative response in others, and in this way, creates, to some degree, environmental contingencies for himself through his own behavior. This is a two-way causal process in which the environment might be just as influencable as the behavior it regulates. The actual environment an individual experiences can be a function of his behavior if the environment is an adaptive one.

Our penchant for a fixed educational mode arises in part from an old-fashioned psychology, from the scientific and social tendency to think in terms of fixed categories of human beings with consistent drives and dispositions (Mischel, 1969). We think this way, rather than in terms of human beings who are highly responsive to the conditions around them so that as conditions change or conditions are maintained, individuals act accordingly. Adaptive educational environments can take advantage of the fact that individuals show great subtlety in adapting their competencies to different situations, if the situation permits such adaptability. Although individuals show generalized consistent behavior on the basis of which we frequently characterize them, this does not preclude their also being very good at discriminating and reacting to a variety of experiences in different ways. The traditional measures of general ability and aptitudes err on the side of assuming too much consistency, and de-emphasize the capability of individuals to devise plans and actions depending upon the rules, needs, and demands of alternative situations. If, in our thinking about individual differences, we make as much room for the capability of individuals to adapt and change, as well as to be stable, and as much room for the capacity for self-regulation and self-development, as well as for victimization by enduring traits, then an adaptive notion of education must follow. An educational system should present alternative environments that enhance the ability of the individual for self-regulation in different possible situations for learning.

So far, I have tried to show that the state of our understanding of human behavior has in some sense precluded a fruitful approach to individualization and adaptive education. For the reasons I have outlined, we have been fixed on an essentially selective mode of education and on the concepts that underlie it. I have also attempted to indicate some directions that have been taken and some milestones that we seem to have passed that appear to make change toward our ideals for adaptive education more feasible than heretofore.

While I have so far stressed fundamental research understandings, progress will not occur by research alone. The design and development of operating educational institutions is also required. Throughout history, science and technology, research and application have forced each other's hands, and mutually beneficial relationships between the two are absolutely necessary for the development of new forms of education. The development effort with which I am most familiar is the work that my colleagues and I at the University of Pittsburgh have been carrying out for some years in the design of elementary school environments that are adaptive to individual differences. This work has been described and disseminated in a variety of ways (Bolvin & Glaser, 1971; Cooley, 1971; Glaser, 1968; Lindvall & Cox, 1969; Resnick, 1967). Now is not the time to go into it further, although I should say that we have had the privilege and opportunity not only to work with schools, but also to study and evaluate our efforts so that we might move in successive approximations toward understanding what an adaptive educational environment is, how it can be designed and built, and what is the nature of the cognitive and noncognitive processes of young children that must be considered. At the present time, certain requirements are emerging that contrast the design of an adaptive educational environment with more traditional forms of education in the elementary school. Briefly stated, some of these appear to be the following:

■ *The teaching of self-management skills and the design of educational settings in which learning-to-learn skills are fostered*—The premise here is that children can modify an environment for their own learning requirements if they command the skills to do so. For this purpose, children can be taught how to search for useful information and how to order and organize it for learning and retention. In the selection of content for the elementary school, preference can be given to information and skills that maximize the possibilities for learning new things. The orientation and attending skills of children can be encouraged so that they learn to identify the relevant aspects of tasks and can attend to them with little distraction. With such information and skills, children can help guide the process of adaptive education.

■ *The teaching of basic psychological processes*—I have indicated this throughout my discussion. We have assumed for too long the stability of "basic aptitudes"; now we need to determine how these talents can be encouraged and taught. At the Olympic Games, young men and women joyfully exceed existing limits of human capability; in the intellectual sphere, this is also possible. The talents of individuals can be extended so that they can be provided with increased possibilities for education.

■ *The design of flexible curricula with many points of entry, different methods of instruction, and options among instructional objectives*—Extensive sequential curricula that must be used as complete systems and into which entry at different points is difficult will give way to more "modular" organizations of instructional units. This does not imply the abandonment of sequence requirements inherent in the structure of the material to be learned, but does imply that prerequisites, where essential, are to be specified in terms of capabilities of the learner rather than in terms of previous instructional experiences. A flexible curriculum avoids the necessity for all individuals to proceed through all steps in a curriculum sequence, and adapts to the fact that some individuals acquire prerequisites on their own, while others need more formal support to establish the prerequisites for more advanced learning. In such a system, it should be easy to incorporate new and varied instructional materials and objectives as they are developed in response to the changing educational interests and requirements of both teachers and students (Resnick, 1972).

■ *Increased emphasis on open testing and behaviorally indexed assessment*—In an adaptive environment, tests designed primarily to compare and select students can be expected to play a decreasing role, since access to particular educational activities will be based on a student's background together with his command of prerequisite competencies. Tests will be designed to provide information directly to the learner and the teacher to guide further learning. These tests will have an intrinsic character of openness in that they will serve as a display of the competencies to be acquired, and the results will be open to the student who can use this knowledge of his performance as a yardstick of his developing ability. These tests also will assess more than the narrow band of traditional academic outcomes. Measures of process and style, of cognitive and non-cognitive development, and of performance in more natural settings than exist in the traditional school will be required. Fortunately, this trend in process-oriented, broad-band assessment is now discernible in many new efforts.

In conclusion, it should be said that the nature of a society determines the nature of the educational system that it fosters, and educational systems tend to feed into the existing social practices. If this is so, then an adaptive educational system carried to its ultimate conclusion may be out of joint with the present social structure. An adaptive environment assumes many ways of succeeding and many goals available from which to choose. It assumes further that no particular way of succeeding is greatly valued over the other. In our current selective environment, it is quite clear that the way of succeeding that is most valued is within the relatively fixed system provided. Success in society is defined primarily in terms of the attainment of occupations directly related to the products of this system. School-related occupations are the most valued, the most rewarding, and seen as the most desirable. However, if an adaptive mode becomes prevalent and wider constellations of human abilities are emphasized, then success will have to be differently defined; and many more alternative ways of succeeding will have to be appropriately rewarded than is presently the case.

Finally, basic analysis of what I have called the "new aptitudes" and the design of adaptive environments for learning is the work that is before us. The kinds of educational systems that we can consider most desirable will be drawn only from the fullest possible understanding of human behavior and from sustained, carefully studied educational innovations with the flexibility for successive incremental improvement. The traditional formulations of the nature of individual differences in learning and the traditional modes of education fail to provide enough freedom for the exercise of individual freedom for the exercise of individual talents. We admire individual performance, but we must do more than merely stand in admiration; we must design the effective conditions under which individuals are provided with the opportunities and rewards to perform at their best and in their way.

Presidential Address, American Educational Research Association, Chicago, April 1972. The preparation of this paper was carried out under the auspices of the Learning Research and Development Center at the University of Pittsburgh, supported in part by funds from the United States Office of Education, Department of Health, Education, and Welfare.

Glaser, Robert, "Individuals and Learning: The New Aptitudes," *Educational Researcher,* June, 1972, pp. 5–13. Copyright American Educational Research Association, Washington, D.C. Dr. Glaser is Director of the Learning Research and Development Center at the University of Pittsburgh.

References

Angoff, W. H. (Ed.) *The College Board Admissions Testing Program: A Technical Report on Research and Development Activities Relating to the Scholastic Aptitude Test and Achievement Tests.* New York: College Entrance Examination Board, 1971.

Bandura, A. *Principles of Behavior Modification.* New York: Holt, Rinehart & Winston, 1969.

Bandura, A. *Social Learning Theory.* New York: McCaleb-Seiler, 1971.

Bolvin, J. O., & D. W. Allen & E. Seifman (Eds.). *The Teacher's Handbook.* Glenview, Illinois: Scott, Foresman, 1971. Pp. 270–279.

Bracht, G. H. *The relationship of treatment tasks, personological variables and dependent variables to aptitude-treatment interaction.* Boulder: University of Colorado, Laboratory of Educational Research, 1969.

Bracht, G. H., & Glass, G. V. "The External Validity of Experiments." *American Educational Research Journal,* 1968, 5, 437–474.

Cooley, W. W. "Methods of Evaluating School Innovations." Invited address presented at the meeting of the American Psychological Association, Washington, D.C., September 1971.

Cronbach, L. J. "The Two Disciplines of Scientific Psychology." Address of the president at the meeting of the American Psychological Association, New York, September 1957.

Cronbach, L. J. *Essentials of Psychological Testing.* (3rd ed.) New York: Harper & Row, 1970.

Cronbach, L. J. & Gleser, G. C. *Psychological Tests and Personnel Decisions.* (2nd ed.) Urbana: University of Illinois Press, 1965.

Cronbach, L. J., & Snow, R. E. *Individual Differences in Learning Ability as a Function of Instruction Variables.* Stanford: Stanford University, School of Education, 1969.

Getzels, J W "Pre-school Education."*Teachers College Record.* 1966, 68, 219–228.

Glaser, R. "Adapting the Elementary School Curriculum to Individual Performance." In *Proceedings of the 1967 Invitational Conference on Testing Problems.* Princeton: Educational Testing Service, 1968. Pp. 3–36.

Glaser, R., & Resnick, L. B. "Instructional Psychology." In P. H. Mussen & M. R. Rosenweig (Eds.), *Annual Review of Psychology.* Palo Alto: Annual Reviews, 1972. Pp. 207–276.

Kagan, J., & Kogan, N. "Individual Variation in Cognitive Processes." In P. H. Mussen (Ed.), *Carmichael's Manual of Child Psychology,* Volume I. (3rd ed.) New York: Wiley, 1970. Pp. 1273–1365.

Lindvall, C. M., & Cox, R. C. The Role of Evaluation in programs for Individualized Instruction. In *Sixty-Eighth Yearbook of the National Society for the Study of Education, Part II.* Chicago: NSSE, 1969. Pp. 156–188.

Lockard, R. B. "Reflections on The Fall of Comparative Psychology: Is There a Message for Us All?" *American Psychologist,* 1971, 26, 168–179.

McLuhan, M. *Understanding Media: The Extensions of Man.* Toronto: McGraw-Hill, 1964.

McNemar, Q. "Lost: Our intelligence? Why?" *American Psychologist.* 1964, 19, 871–882.

Meichenbaum, D. H. *The Nature and Modification of Impulsive Children: Training Impulsive Children to Talk to Themselves.* Ontario: University of Waterloo, Department of Psychology, 1971.

Meichenbaum, D. H., & Goodman, J. "Reflection-Impulsivity and Verbal Control of Motor Behavior." *Child Development.* 1969, 40, 785–797.

Melton A. W. "Individual Differences and Theoretical Process Variables: General Comments on the Conference." In R. M. Gagne (Ed.), *Learning and Individual Differences.* Columbus: Charles E. Merrill, 1967. Pp. 238–252.

Mischel, W. "Continuity and Change in Personality." *American Psychologist.* 1969, 24, 1012–1018.

Olson, D. R. *Cognitive Development: The Child's Acquisition of Diagonality.* New York: Academic Press, 1970.

Resnick, L. B. *Design of an Early Learning Curriculum.* Pittsburgh; University of Pittsburgh, Learning Research and Development Center, 1967.

Resnick, L. B. "Open Education: Some Tasks for Technology." *Educational Technology,* 1972, 12(1), 70–76.

Rohwer, W. D., Jr. "Images and Pictures in Children's Learning." *Psychological Bulletin,* 1970, 73, 393–403.

Rohwer, W. D., Jr. "Mental Claboration and Proficient Learning." In J. P. Hill (Ed.), *Minnesota Symposia on Child Psychology.* Minneapolis: University of Minnesota, 1970. Pp. 220–260.(b)

Rohwer, W. D., Jr. "Learning, Race and School Success." *Review of Educational Research,* 1971, 41, 191–210.

Rosner, J. *A Formative Evaluation of the Perceptual Skills Curriculum Project.* Pittsburgh: University of Pittsburgh, Learning Research and Development Center, 1972, in press.

Thorndike, E. L. *Individuality*. Boston: Houghton Mifflin, 1911.

Tyler, L. E. *The Psychology of Human Differences*. (3rd ed.) New York: Appleton-Century-Crofts, 1965.

Washburne, C. N. "Adapting the Schools to Individual Differences." In *Twenty-Fourth Yearbook of the National Society for the Study of Education, Part II*. Chicago: NSSE, 1925.

Wing, C. W., Jr., & Wallach, M. A. *College Admissions and the Psychology of Talent*. New York: Holt, Rinehart & Winston, 1971.

Yando, R. M., & Kagan, J. "The Effect of Teacher Tempo on the Child." *Child Development*. 1968, 39, 27–34.

SECTION II

Some Approaches to Individualization

This section deals with the most prominent systems and modes of individualized instruction and individualized learning which are being planned and implemented across the nation.

Ronald E. Hull, in "An Individualized Learning Continuum," uses Edling's model as a basis for matching goals of the school with the goals and the strengths of four major approaches of individualized instruction. These four approaches—Individually Prescribed Instruction (IPI), Individually Guided Education (IGE), The Plan System for Individualizing Education (Project PLAN), and the Open Classroom—are placed on a continuum in terms of school versus pupil selection of learning objectives (what is to be learned), and school versus pupil determination of means of achieving the learning (how the objectives are to be reached).

John O. Bolvin in his article, "Individually Prescribed Instruction," provides the reader with the basic rudiments of IPI. Dr. Bolvin was one of the architects of the IPI System which was developed at the Learning Research and Development Center at the University of Pittsburgh. Basically, IPI consists of planning and conducting with each student a program of studies that is tailored to his learning needs and to his characteristics as a learner. The system takes into account such parameters of individual differences as rate of learning, amount of practice, and, to some extent, preference for mode of instruction. IPI is the most highly structured system of individualization presented in this section of the book.

Herbert J. Klausmeier, as the Director of the Research and Development Center for Cognitive Learning at the University of Wisconsin, was a major force behind the development of the Individually Guided Education model. IGE, with its Multiunit School organizational structure, is designed to bring about far reaching permanent improvements in elementary education. Major modifications of traditional educational organizations, staffing patterns, administration, and instruction can be observed in schools which are now implementing the model on a nationwide scale.

John C. Flanagan in his article, "The Plan System for

Individualizing Education," provides the reader with the basic components of the Program for Learning in Accordance with Needs (Project PLAN). The author is the father of PLAN as well as quite a few other research and development projects in education and psychology. PLAN is a cooperative demonstration program in computer-managed individualized instruction which was initiated by Westinghouse Learning Corporation, the American Institutes for Research, and a number of independent school districts across the nation. The computer is utilized as an informational system which records and monitors on a day-to-day basis the performance of youngsters as they progress through the program.

Open classroom differs markedly from the other three major approaches to individualization in that it is not truly a system of education. However, open classroom warrants consideration because of the great impact it is now making on American education.

Thomas A. Petrie's article, "Open Education: Considerations for Implementors," is unique in that he developed a theoretical construct which orders the instructional interactions in the teaching-learning process ideally taking place in the open classroom approach to individualization. Heretofore, open classroom has meant many different things to educators. This article brings order to the open classroom concept of education.

John B. Bouchard and Kenneth G. Nelson's "Pupil Oriented and Individualized Systems of Education (POISE model)" is an example of an eclectic approach to individualization which leans heavily upon the IGE model. POISE is a special adaptation of IGE which has been implemented in western New York State. It also uses various other individualization modes suggested in Hull's article, "An Individualized Learning Continuum." The POISE model is offered as an example of one way to adapt various modes of individualization into a workable system applicable to a particular locale.

6

An Individualized Learning Continuum

Robert E. Hull

Educators at all levels in cities, suburbs, and towns are embracing individualized education as a promising way to meet the needs of students (Edling, 1969). Literally thousands of elementary schools in America are now implementing some system of individualized instruction. Individually Prescribed Instruction (IPI) (Education U.S.A., 1970) is presently serving 50 thousand students in 164 schools and will expand to serve 75 thousand students in 264 schools next fall; Individually Guided Education in the Multiunit School, Elementary (IGE/MUS-E) (Wisconsin R and D Center, 1972) claims installation in over 500 schools located in over eighteen different states; Program for Learning in Accordance with Needs (Project PLAN) (Aurora Public Schools, 1971) claims implementation in thirteen school districts which serve 1 thousand students, grades 1 through 12; and concepts from open or informal education (Silberman, 1970) are having a profound effect on education.

As an educator strives to individualize his instructional program, the question which he must necessarily ask is, what will work best for us? That is a difficult question to answer without some systematic comparisons of the programs.

The paragraphs that follow use Edling's (1970) relatively uncomplicated model as a basis for matching goals of the school with the goals and strengths of various systems of individualized instruction. Edling's model compares school versus pupil selection of learning objectives (what is to be learned), and school versus pupil selection of media for achieving the learning (how the objectives are to be reached).

<table>
<tr><td></td><td colspan="2" align="center">**OBJECTIVES**</td></tr>
<tr><td>MEDIA</td><td>(School Determined)</td><td>(Learner Selected)</td></tr>
<tr><td>(System
Determined)</td><td>"Individually
Diagnosed and
Prescribed"</td><td>"Personalized"</td></tr>
<tr><td>(Learner
Selected)</td><td>"Self-Directed"</td><td>"Independent Study"</td></tr>
</table>

When the school selects both the learning objectives and the media for attainment, the category is termed *Individually Diagnosed and Prescribed Learning.* When the school determines what is to be learned but allows the learner freedom to determine how he will attain the objectives, the category is termed *Self-Directed Learning.* In situations where the learner selects the objective but the media is determined by the school, the category is termed *Personalized Learning.* If the student selects both *what* is to be learned and *how* to learn it, the category is termed *Independent Study.*

Few school situations fall neatly into these categories. However, this two-dimensional perspective provides a point of departure, or better yet, a basis for placing individualization efforts on a *continuum* in terms of a school/pupil selection of objectives and/or media.

The following discussion describes several systems or modes of individualized instruction in terms which will help educators match, at least in gross terms, their school needs with the strengths of each of four approaches to individualization.

Individually Prescribed Instruction (IPI)

The developers of IPI (Research for Better Schools, 1972) have devised a systematic approach to individualization. Both the learning objectives and the media for attaining those objectives are carefully programmed. Using the IPI system, a sequenced and detailed listing of behaviorally-stated instructional objectives is prescribed for the child. These objectives are determined as the child places himself on the learning continuum by taking tests in each subject-matter area. Learning materials are then geared exactly to the objectives and are such that pupils can proceed quite independently with a minimum of direct teacher instruction.

The unique feature of IPI is its requirement that each pupil's work be guided by written prescriptions prepared to meet his individual needs and interests. The system hinges on a wealth of materials sequentially ordered for systematic progress toward behavioral goals. Pupil progress is then evaluated daily through the use of curriculum embedded tests.

As is true of more traditional classrooms, the teacher is important, but her role has changed in that little time is spent teaching a group. Much of the IPI teacher's time is spent evaluating pupil performance, diagnosing pupil needs, and preparing learning prescriptions for each child. In other words, most of the time is spent helping individual pupils.

Frequent staff conferences help insure that each child's prescriptions are effective in moving him toward fulfillment of *his* behavioral objectives. The IPI system may be implemented in a self-contained classroom structure, or children may *move* from one learning area to another. Teachers' aides are an essential part of the IPI System inasmuch as they handle practically all test scoring, recording of scores, and management of materials.

The primary objectives are to enable each pupil to work at his own *rate* through units of study in a learning sequence, to develop in each pupil a demonstrable degree of mastery, to develop self-initiation and self-direction of learning, to foster the development of problem-solving thought processes, and to encourage self-evaluation and motivation for learning.

In terms of Edling's model, IPI falls into the Individually Diagnosed and Prescribed Learning category with some overlap into the Self-Directed Learning area. Schools which have the following commitments and resources should find the IPI system compatible with their individualization thrust: (1) a heavy investment in students' cognitive skill development, especially for special education and slow learners; (Research for Better Schools, 1969) (2) a predisposition to retain a basically age-graded organizational structure; (3) a desire for accountability; (4) resources in the neighborhood of ten dollars per pupil per year for instructional materials and resources for employing one paraprofessional per classroom; and (5) a willingness on the part of the staff (including the principal) to act in new ways.

Individually Guided Education in the Multiunit School, Elementary (IGE/MUS-E)

Individually Guided Education (IGE) (Klausmeier, 1972) features the multiunit organizational structure, a model of instructional programing for the individual pupil, a model for measurement and evaluation, a program of home-school communications, and continuing research and development. The multiunit school organization is arranged according to three decision-making levels: System-wide Policy Committee, Instructional Improvement Committee, and Instructional Teams or Units.

IGE is unique among the systems presented here because it *demands* the restructuring of the school organization. Instruction of pools of different age children becomes the responsibility of units or teams of teachers. Multiunit combines theory and practice regarding instructional programming for individual students, horizontal and vertical organization for instruction, role differentiation, shared decision-making by groups, and open communication.

The multiunit program requires distinct changes made in the roles of the principal and teacher. The principal assumes greater and more direct responsibility for developing improved educational practices, managing the preservice and inservice teacher education activities in his building, and administering research and development activities. IGE has established one new position, that of unit leader or lead teacher. This team leader is a career teacher who chairs unit meetings and performs a liaison function between the team and the principal, consultants, and parents. Other instructional unit members are professional teachers, the teacher aide, an instructional secretary, and one or more interns.

The IGE system attends to differences in a child's rate and style of learning, level of motivation, and unique educational needs. Curriculum materials are geared to the instructional objectives as they are selected by the staff, for each child, based on his characteristics as a learner. This, of course, requires that information concerning pupil characteristics be utilized in curriculum decision making.

IGE provides a design for measurement and evaluation that includes preassessment of the child's readiness, assessment of progress, and final achievement. Tests inform both the child and the teacher regarding the attainment of learning objectives. IGE also attends to home-school communications in order that the school's efforts be reinforced by the interest and encouragement of parents and other adults.

In terms of Edling's model, IGE/MUS-E seems to fit into all the categories with heavier emphasis on Diagnosed and Prescribed Learning and Self-Directed Learning than on Personalized Learning and Independent Study. A major distinction between IGE and IPI instruction is that IGE leaves most instructional decisions in the hands of the teachers; IPI materials are more prescriptive, thus, teacher decision making is minimized.

Schools which have the following commitments and resources should find IGE/MUS-E compatible with their individualization thrust: (1) a willingness to completely restructure the school organization from the age-graded structure to multiunit; (2) a commitment to a three-year staff development program to insure probable success in approximating the plan; (3) a desire for accountability; and (4) resources to hire one instructional aide per unit and approximately ten dollars per pupil during the first two years of implementation for materials and consultative help.

*Program for Learning in Accordance With Needs (Project
PLAN)*

Unlike the systems of individualization discussed previously, PLAN (Westinghouse Learning Corp., 1973) is a
computer-managed educational system. The developers of
PLAN recognized that in order to develop a suitable educational program for each student, a great deal of information
must be processed efficiently. Then each student can plan
an educational program suited to his values, interests, and
potential abilities, especially when the guidance component is included.

In Project PLAN the overall educational program is
broken down into sets of behavioral objectives which can
be assigned as learning tasks to the individual student.
Early in the year, the teacher confers with each student
about his general program for the year. The objective is not
organized into a single, rigid plan or sequence—rather it is
intended that each student select his own educational
objectives with the help of his teacher. About five objectives are grouped together in a module, and each objective
requires approximately two or three hours to achieve, thus
making the module about a two-week segment of instruction.

Based on knowledge of the main curriculum demanded
by the local district and knowledge of the student's ability,
the teacher indicates which objectives are required for him
to reach and which are recommended for him to achieve.
Based on his own knowledge of his aptitudes, skills, and
abilities and his long-range goals and interests, the student
selects optional objectives.

Appropriate Teaching Learning Units are then provided the student. The various TLU's, as they are called,
are based on currently available instructional materials.
Thus, schools can adapt the PLAN system to materials they
already have on hand. PLAN makes use of audiovisual
media and capitalizes on such differences as there are in
the instructional methods used by different authors and
publishers. One TLU may make use of tape-recorded
materials, another may require the use of printed materials,
and another a slide presentation. The student uses the TLU

best suited to his own learning style to achieve that particular objective in the module.

Monitoring and evaluating pupil progress is accomplished by using specific test questions related to the objectives in a particular module. When desired mastery has been attained, a pupil moves to the next TLU, but if test results indicate more work is needed, the student goes back and reviews or does further work before retaking the test. Other tests measure long-range objectives, such as reading comprehension, attitudes, appreciations, and originality. Quick decisions regarding the assignment of TLU's are made as a result of computer printouts which keep track of each child's performance as he progresses with his studies.

In contrast with some other computer-assisted programs, students in Project PLAN are never on-line with the computer. The computer in PLAN serves an administrative function. It scores tests, updates students' files in terms of performance, provides teachers with weekly status reports, monitors students' schedules, and recommends specific TLU assignments based on empirical data from past performances of other similar students.

In terms of Edling's model, Project PLAN, like IGE/MUS-E, stresses a programmed set of objectives. However, Project PLAN seems to allow more freedom for pupil selection of learning objectives and modes of learning than does IGE/MUS-E. In contrast with IPI, in which the learning experiences are prescribed by the system, and with IGE/MUS-E, in which teachers make most decisions, Project PLAN stresses teacher and pupil decision making. This, coupled with the computer-managed data system for each pupil, provides equal emphasis in Edling's four categories.

Schools which have the following commitments and resources should find Project PLAN compatible with their individualization thrust: (1) a staff commitment for a few weeks of inservice training in the PLAN system; (2) resources in the neighborhood of 50 dollars per pupil per year for the PLAN computer service (Education U.S.A., 1970); (3) a desire for accountability; and (4) a desire to individualize instruction in grades 1 through 12.

The Open Classroom

The Open Classroom (Martin, et al., 1971) is an example of a system of individualized instruction which is more free and unstructured than any of the systems presented above. Open classroom concepts of education have succeeded in many British primary schools, and many schools in America are experimenting with the idea. Its primary goals are to help children learn how to think, to form judgments, and to discriminate. In contrast to the three systems of individualized instruction discussed earlier, the open classroom does *not* require sets of behavioral objectives. Rather, its objectives are developmental in nature and center around the quality of human interaction which in turn leads to achievement in conventional and humanistic terms.

In the open classroom the emphasis is on each child's interests and style, lots of informal verbal interaction among the children, an abundance of fascinating concrete materials, and a teacher who stimulates and sometimes steps back. Advocates of the open classroom recognize the variety in speed and style of learning among children as well as their ability to copy one another. Moreover, in a rich environment organized so that a variety of learning experiences are inevitable, rigid expectations are unnecessary.

During the day there is no real difference between one subject in the curriculum and another, or even between work and play. A few school students may be in "family" groups of children of various ages, and in all schools they will each have a wide choice of materials and activities—some commercial, many homemade—to which they can devote their attention *where* and *for* as long as they wish, limited only by the demand for the materials among other students.

While some teachers may insist on some regular reading and writing, there are generally no required subjects or assignments that students must, at some time, concentrate upon. There are generally no examinations or report cards as such. Rather, parents receive detailed "histories" reporting what the student has accomplished. Discipline is relaxed and when a student causes a disturbance the teacher attempts to find more appropriate materials and approaches rather than deny the privilege of independence of the student who may need it most.

It is evident that open classroom concepts offer maximum freedom for students' selections of school experiences. When submitted to Edling's model, the open classroom is heavily weighted on the Personalized Learning and Independent Study categories.

Schools which have the following commitments and resources should find the open classroom approach to individualization compatible with their needs: (1) a bent in favor of humanistic education; (2) teachers, administrators, and parents who are willing to "let go" of children and allow them freedom to explore, to initiate, and occasionally to be wrong; and (3) resources for buying *more* things for classrooms (ten dollars per child for the first two years).

The dimensions of Edling's model are appropriate for viewing each individualization system in terms of a continuum. In light of the characteristics of each system discussed above, the following continuum is offered to help in the selection of the appropriate individualization system for each school situation.

School Determined Learning Objectives and Means for Attaining Objectives ———— Pupil Selected Learning Objectives and Means for Attaining Objectives

IPI   IGE/MUS-E   Project PLAN   OPEN CLASSROOM

Obviously, to insure probable success in individualization efforts, a school must first identify and make explicit its educational objectives. Once commitment to these objectives is shared by the staff and community, an appropriate system, or an eclectic approach using parts of various individualization modes, can be selected. Regardless of the approach used, it seems certain that it will take more resources (at least in the beginning) and more work on the part of all persons involved to insure realization of individualized learning objectives.

Reprinted from *Planning and Changing,* March, 1973. Reprinted by permission of the copyright holder. Ronald E. Hull is Associate Professor—Research, State University College, Fredonia, New York.

Notes

1. Jack V. Edling. *An Interpretive Study of Individualized Instruction Programs. Phase I: Analysis and Interpretation. Final Report.* Monmouth, Oregon: Oregon State System of Higher Education, May, 1969.

2. *Education U.S.A.: The Weekly Newsletter on Educational Affairs.* Washington, D.C. February 2, 1970.

3. Wisconsin Research and Development Center for Cognitive Learning. *Multiunit Schools 1971–1972 Directory.* Madison: 1972.

4. Aurora Public Schools. *PLAN.* Aurora, Illinois: 1971.

5. Charles E. Silberman. *Crisis in the Classroom.* New York: Random House, 1970, p. 120.

6. Jack V. Edling. *Individualized Instruction: A Manual for Administrators.* Corvalis, Oregon: Teaching Research Division, Oregon State System of Higher Education, 1970, p. 2.

7. *Individually Prescribed Instruction,* Research for Better Schools, Inc., 1700 Market Street, Philadelphia, Pa., 19103, 1971.

8. *A Progress Report: Individually Prescribed Instruction,* Research for Better Schools, Inc., 1700 Market Street, Philadelphia, Pa., 19103, September, 1969, p. 11.

9. Herbert J. Klausmeier, et al. *Individually Guided Education and the Multiunit School.* Madison, Wisconsin: Wisconsin Research and Development Center for Cognitive Learning, 1972.

10. Westinghouse Learning Corp. *A Look at PLAN.* New York: 1973.

11. Peter A. Martin, et al. Information and planning kit for use in developing open education programs. Albany, New York: The University of the State of New York, The State Education Department, 1971.

7

Individually Prescribed
Instruction

John O. Bolvin

Educators have long professed the need for an educational system attuned to the background and abilities of individual students. This concern has, in fact, been the basis for most of the recent changes and innovations in school organizations.

Due to the importance of this problem and the potential contribution to educational practice that could result from any significant progress in the development of procedures for providing for the many individual differences among students, the Learning Research and Development Center at the University of Pittsburgh is devoting major attention to this problem. Another reason for centering attention on this problem is that problems of this nature demand rather long-term commitments to develop and are the types of problems research and development centers, now being funded by the U.S. Office of Education, have the unique opportunity to investigate.

The Project on Individually Prescribed Instruction represents an investigation of the problems encountered in the individualization of instruction and involves the development of one type of program for achieving this goal. The essential aspects of individualization that are presently being provided for in this program as operating are: 1) individualization of rate at which students proceed through a carefully sequenced set of objectives for a given subject; 2) mastery of subject-matter content by individuals to enhance discovery or creativeness as they proceed through a set of objectives; 3) some self-direction, self-evaluation, and to a limited degree, self-initiation on the part of the learners; and 4) individualized techniques and materials of instruction. These aspects are predicated upon the definition of individualized instruction as an instructional system which provides for the planning and implementation of an individualized program of studies. This system can be tailored to each student's learning needs and his characteristics as a learner that can facilitate his acquisition of new skills.

Six Major Components

The model for individualization is conceived of as consisting of the following components: 1) sequentially established curricular objectives in each area stated in behavioral terms; 2) a procedure and process for diagnosis of student achievement in terms of objectives of the curriculum and the proficiency level desired for each student and each objective; 3) the necessary materials for individualizing learning to provide a variety of paths for attainment of mastery of any given objective; 4) a system for individually prescribing the learning tasks the student is ready to undertake; 5) the organization and management practices of the total school environment to facilitate individualization; and 6) strategies for continuous evaluation and feedback of information for teacher decision-making as well as information for continuous evaluation of the curricula for the curriculum developers.

As presently operating, the project involves students for that portion of each school day set aside for study in the three basic content areas: 1) reading, 2) mathematics, and 3) primary science. For the remainder of the day, students are engaged in study under procedures followed in most elementary schools.

Implementation

The curricula presently being implemented in the Individually Prescribed Instruction Project represents a consensus of recent thinking in each of these areas. Members of the project staff, including teachers, psychologists, and subject specialists, examined a variety of curricula currently being offered in each of the subjects to define a sequence of learning experience which could provide the necessary flexibility involved in individualizing instruction. Since it is important that students be able to work through the sequence with a minimum amount of teacher direction, it is necessary to express the curricula in carefully defined objectives with each succeeding objective built upon what preceded. These objectives tend to insure that lessons be directed toward specific student competencies so that more precise evaluative devices could be developed to determine pupil achievement. Each of the curricula is divided into levels, units and objectives, or skills. A level consists of a set of operational tasks grouped into categories and represents a level of achievement at the end of a large sequence of work. Each category within a level is called a unit. Within each unit the sub-tasks needed to master the unit are called objectives or skills.

Once the sequenced objectives in each area had been stated, diagnostic instruments were developed to measure the specific tasks to be learned. As presently operating, there are four general types of instruments being utilized: placement tests, pre-unit tests, curriculum-embedded tests, and post-unit tests.

Placement tests are administered at the beginning of each academic year to determine general placement in each of the units of each curriculum. From the results of the placement tests, the teacher assigns each child to a pre-unit test for a particular unit. These pretests measure each skill within a unit. Mastery of any of the skills within a given unit means that the child can skip these particular skills and concentrate on the skills within the unit for which there is lack of mastery. Once the child has been assigned work in a given skill and indicates from his manipulation of the tasks that he has mastered that skill, the student is given a curriculum-embedded test—a test which measures the particular skill which he has been assigned. Mastery on this instrument indicates that he is ready to move to the next skill within the unit. When a child has completed all of the work assigned within a unit and successfully indicates mastery on the curriculum-embedded tests, he is assigned a post-unit test covering all of the skills. The post-tests are, in essence, an alternate form of the pre-unit tests which the student took prior to working on a unit.

Necessary Flexibility

Materials for individually prescribed instruction have been selected and developed to teach each of the objectives. These materials, for the most part, must be developed for self-study, leading the child from what he knows to what he must know next to progress through the curriculum. Presently there is considerable reliance upon worksheets, tape and disc recordings, programmed materials, individual readers, and manipulative devices. In some instances, it is necessary and desirable for the teacher to present new ideas and processes in each of the subject areas and this is done individually, in small groups, or in large group discussions.

The basic materials for each of the subjects have been organized according to the objectives of the curriculum. For example, for each objective within the mathematics curriculum there is a master file of materials that can be utilized in teaching a single objective. A major task of the Learning Research and Development Center is to develop alternative sets of materials to provide a variety of approaches to the same objectives.

Once the placement testing has been completed, the teacher can determine where each pupil is ready to begin instruction. On the basis of the diagnosis of the student's weakness, a prescription is developed for each child. This prescription, one for each student for each subject, lists the materials for the objectives in which the child should begin studying. For this initial prescription the teacher will generally consider the following factors: 1) the ability level of the child in each subject being prescribed, 2) the general maturity of the child, 3) certain learner characteristics as they relate to the particular learning, and 4) the student's general reaction to IPI. These prescriptions are prepared prior to the scheduled time for the subject and arranged for ease of dissemination as the class begins.

The student then begins work independently on the

prescribed materials. This is done in a large room which provides space for all the students from a particular group, e.g., primary, first, second, and third graders. In this area there are, generally, three or four teachers and two or three teacher aides assigned to these students. Most of the students can proceed through the prescribed materials with a minimum of teacher direction and instruction. When assistance requiring extended explanations or instruction is required the team of teachers will decide cooperatively who should give this instruction and to how many. The team responsible for the instruction of a particular group also decides on the sharing of other responsibilities such as administration of pre- and post-tests, large group instruction, and prescription writing that may be necessary during class period.

Evaluation Program

In order to free the teacher for instructional decision-making, tutoring and evaluation of student progress, the scoring of worksheets, tests, etc., is either done by the teacher aides or by the children themselves. The teacher aides also assist the children in locating materials and performing other non-instructional tasks.

An essential aspect of individualized instruction is the provision for charting progress of each student as he moves through the curriculum and the availability of these reports for teacher use. A program for computer-assisted management for the project is presently being developed and will be in operation within the next few months. With the implementation of this management system, teachers will be able to obtain more quickly relevant information on a particular student, reports as to how many and which students are working in the same units or objectives, and daily summaries of the progress of each student. Additional functions of this system will be added as we are able to move the system into operation and train teachers to utilize the system more efficiently.

As indicated earlier, work on this type of a problem demands a rather long-term commitment for development on the part of all parties concerned. Thus far, evaluation on the program has been limited to information feedback that assists in improving the program itself. Assisting in this evaluation, Research for Better Schools, Inc., the U.S. Office of Education sponsored Regional Laboratory in Philadelphia, is field testing the project in 23 elementary schools to obtain data on the model in various settings to determine its reproducibility, cost factors involved, types of teacher training needed in the various settings, and variables related to the implementation and monitoring of an individualized program. In general, what has been accomplished to date in the development of the program has convinced the staff that some degree of individualization of instruction is possible with this type of program.

Reprinted from *Educational Screen and Audiovisual Guide,* April, 1968. Reprinted by permission of the author and the publisher. John O. Bolvin is a professor of Education, Learning Research and Development Center, at the University of Pittsburgh.

8

IGE: Multiunit Elementary School

Herbert J. Klausmeier

"Planned change, evolution in education without revolution—a careful analysis by people who understand the importance of learning and how it happens."

IGE: A Comprehensive System

The above quote is what Norman Graper, principal of Wilson Elementary School in Janesville, Wisconsin, says about individually guided education (IGE) in the multiunit elementary school (MUS-E). Wilson school is in its fifth year of operation as an IGE-multiunit school. Principal Graper and his staff participated in developing the first MUS-E in 1965-66. Today, in 1970-71, there are 170 principals, 80 superintendents, and 2700 teachers implementing IGE in 170 of the nation's schools.

Developed by the Wisconsin Research and Development Center for Cognitive Learning and cooperating educational institutions, IGE is a system for formulating and carrying out instructional programs for individual children in which planned variations are made in what each child learns, how rapidly he learns, and how he goes about learning. IGE designers believe that in order for higher achievement to be realized, each child's unique characteristics must be taken into account.

Center researchers find that elementary school practitioners want to improve educational practices. Indeed many continuously attempt to improve single components such as instructional materials, teaching methods, or inservice training. However, changing one area of the educational process does not necessarily yield educational improvement. IGE has emerged as a comprehensive system for educational improvement and includes seven components. When all components are properly integrated into a school, improvements in teacher morale, administrator-teacher communication, student achievement, and personal-social development are often dramatic. The components must function simultaneously as a system.

1. The multiunit elementary school (MUS-E) is the organization for instruction and related administrative arrangements at the building and central office levels. It provides for educational and instructional decision-making at appropriate levels, open communication, and accountability. The MUS-E has been developed, field tested, and refined in school settings since 1965. An inservice program including multimedia materials has been developed.

2. A model of instructional programming for the individual student has been designed to provide for differences in children's rates and styles of learning, level of motivation and other characteristics within the context of the school's educational objectives. This model is used by Center personnel in developing curriculum materials and by school staff in implementing IGE.

3. A design for developing measurement tools and evaluation procedures includes preassessment of children's readiness, assessment of progress and final achievement with criterion-referenced tests, feedback to the teacher and child, and evaluation of the IGE design and its components. School personnel use this model to develop their own instruments and procedures and Center staff use it to develop tests which accompany curriculum materials.

4. Curriculum materials, related statements of instructional objectives, and criterion-referenced tests which can be adopted or adapted by schools are needed. There is a

shortage of these materials. The Center is developing materials and instructional procedures in reading, prereading, mathematics, environmental education, and motivation.

5. A program of home-school communications that reinforces the school's efforts by generating community interest and support is essential.

6. Facilitative environments in school buildings, school system offices, state education agencies, and teacher education institutions must be created. Inservice and campus-based educational programs prepare personnel for the new and changing roles implied by IGE. State networks involving the state education agency, local school systems, and teacher education institutions demonstrate, install, and maintain IGE schools. Local networks of school systems and support agencies generate ideas and secure consultant help. Statewide and local networks have been established in Wisconsin and Colorado.

7. Research and development is a continuing effort to generate knowledge and produce tested materials and procedures. The Center is engaged in development and development-based research to refine all the IGE components. In addition, each school must engage in practical research in order to design, implement, and evaluate instructional programs for individual students.

The Multiunit Organization

The multiunit elementary school (MUS-E) is designed to create an environment in which IGE practices can be installed and maintained. Differentiated staffing, group planning and decision-making, open communication, and accountability characterize a multiunit school. These characteristics are made possible by three organizational/administrative groups with overlapping membership. "The multiunit school's practical management tools make it really unique," asserts Principal Norman Graper.

The I & R Unit

The nongraded instructional and research (I & R) unit replaces the age-graded, self-contained classroom. Re-

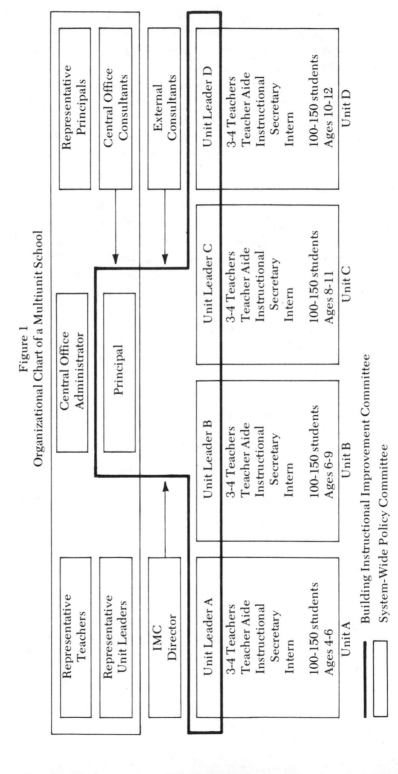

Figure 1
Organizational Chart of a Multiunit School

search is included in the title to reflect the fact that the staff must continuously do practical research in order to devise and evaluate an instructional program appropriate for each child. In the prototype of an MUS-E of 400-600 students shown in figure 1, each I & R unit has a unit leader or lead teacher, three or four staff teachers, one teacher aide, one instructional secretary, one intern, and 100-150 students. Children of a unit usually have a three- to four-year age span in contrast to traditional grades where children typically represent a two-year age span.

The main function of each unit is to plan, carry out, and evaluate each child's instructional program. Each unit engages in some inservice education. Some units plan and conduct research and development cooperatively with other agencies, and some are involved in preservice education.

The IIC

The instructional improvement committee (IIC) is at the second level of organization. It is building-wide in scope and is comprised of the principal and unit leaders.

The IIC takes primary initiative for stating the educational objectives and outlining the educational program for the entire school building. It interprets and implements system-wide and statewide policies, coordinates I & R unit activities, and arranges for the use of facilities, time, and material. The IIC deals primarily with developing and coordinating functions related to instruction.

The SPC

Substantial change is required to move from the self-contained classroom organization to the unit and the IIC. The system-wide policy committee (SPC) at the third organizational level can facilitate this transition. The SPC is chaired by the superintendent or his designee and includes consultants and other central office staff and representative principals, unit leaders, and teachers. The SPC takes initiative for identifying functions to be performed in each MUS-E of the district, recruiting personnel for each school and arranging for their inservice education, providing instructional materials, and disseminating relevant information within the district and community. A central office arrangement other than an SPC may be responsible for these functions; considerable flexibility is required since local school districts differ greatly in size.

The I & R unit, the IIC, and the SPC provide for responsible participation in decision-making by all the staff of a school system. Each element, though being responsible for certain decisions, must secure information from one or both of the other elements. Personnel who serve at each of two levels provide the communication link (see figure 1).

Differentiated Roles

Some differentiated staffing programs create a complex hierarchy and call for a proliferation of new roles and titles. The multiunit school establishes only one new position, the unit leader or lead teacher. The roles of the building principal, staff teacher, teacher intern, teacher aide, and instructional secretary are altered somewhat. Other specialized roles are not precluded. Essential roles are outlined below.

Principal

As instructional leader, the principal is primarily responsible for initiating and refining the IGE system, managing the preservice and inservice teacher education activities, and administering the research and development program. It is not assumed, however, that the principal is the expert in any subject field, in research design, or in teacher education. In many areas the unit leaders and staff teachers are expected to have more knowledge than the principal, therefore decisions are made collectively through the IIC. The principal is responsible, however, for organiizing and chairing the IIC and for assuring implementation of its decisions. In addition, he supervises and evaluates staff and makes sure the building has adequate resources.

How do principals react to sharing decision-making power with staff? One principal gave us a typical reaction. "I've been scared a few times," he admitted. "Often my teachers have better ideas than I do. But I feel security, too. I don't go out on a limb alone—maybe get it sawed off—for every decision I make. My staff and I crawl out there together."

Unit Leader

The unit leader has responsibilities as a member of the IIC, as a leader of a unit, and as a teaching member of a unit. The unit leader is not a supervisor but a career teacher who plans and coordinates unit activities. He is responsible for demonstrating new materials and for keeping abreast of research and development. As a member of the IIC, he helps plan and develop the instructional program of the building and serves as a liaison between the unit staff and the principal and central office staff.

As unit coordinator, the leader is responsible to the principal for planning and implementing the unit's educational program. However, each teacher in the unit shares fully in decision-making and takes initiative regarding the program of specific children. Unit meetings are held at least one hour a week (during school time), giving teachers an opportunity to pool their knowledge and expertise. They cooperatively plan, carry out, and evaluate an instructional program for each child. "You share ideas," says a unit leader and 26-year teaching veteran. "It's encouraging to have someone to talk to and rewarding to help newer teachers find their way."

Staff Teacher

A staff teacher plans the program for and guides many children in cooperation with other unit members. In contrast, a teacher in a self-contained classroom works independently with a small number of children. A higher level of professionalism is required by the staff teacher in implementing an IGE instructional system. Staff teachers cooperatively formulate objectives for each child, assess each child's progress, and use new materials, equipment, and instructional procedures.

For some, teaching in the unit may threaten loss of autonomy. But as one unit teacher put it, "Freedom of choice actually increases as you grow professionally through the exchange of ideas." In the environment of the MUS-E, teachers realize that joint planning and evaluating are vital to a more complete understanding of the teaching-learning process and to an effective IGE program.

Intern

The intern engages in professional activities, not in routine or clerical duties. At first he observes but moves rapidly to full responsibility at a level similar to that of a beginning certified teacher. While the unit leader and teachers retain decision-making responsibility, the intern does implement decisions and participates in unit meetings.

Instructional Secretary and Teacher Aide

Instructional secretaries and teacher aides are non-certified members of units. The wise use of their abilities is the responsibility of the unit leader in cooperation with the principal and unit staff. The instructional secretary performs clerical tasks such as keeping attendance records, duplicating materials, typing, and filing.

The precise responsibilities of teacher aides vary greatly, depending on the aide's background and training. For example, the aide with a college degree in a subject field such as science will perform functions different from the high school graduate with no work in science after ninth grade. In general with regard to IGE, teachers have found aides especially helpful with one-to-one, small group, and independent activities.

Instructional Programing

IGE's main purpose is to help teachers design instructional programs for individual children. Ideally, each child's program will be based on how and at what pace he learns best and where he stands on mastering specific skills or concepts. Trying for this ideal involves a series of steps outlined in figure 2.

The R & D Center is developing new curriculum materials with IGE principles built into them. The Wisconsin Design for Reading Skill Development (WDRSD), an individually guided reading program, is furthest along in development. For purposes of illustration, the following explanation of the instructional programing model (figure 2) discusses the six steps as they work in schools using the word attack, or word recognition, element of the WDRSD.

Figure 2
Instructional Programing Model for IGE

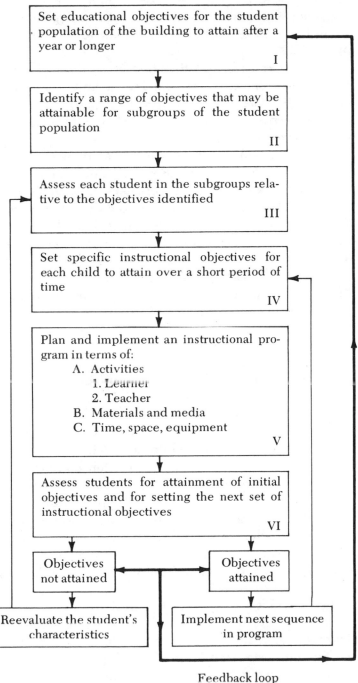

Feedback loop

Step I involves setting school-wide educational objectives in reading by the IIC. A terminal objective for reading might be: 90 percent of the children attain independence in word attack by age ten, 95 percent by age 11, and 99 percent by age 12.

Step II calls for identification of a subset of specific instructional objectives by the I & R unit staff that are appropriate for a group of children. Only part of the 45 word attack objectives, for example, are suitable for children in the early stage of reading.

Step III involves the actual assessment of each child's level of skill development. For each behaviorally stated objective of the word attack element, a short criterion-referenced test has been developed and validated for use in assessing mastery or nonmastery of the skill described. There are four levels of tests (A, B, C, and D) available. A teacher working with a unit of six- and seven-year-olds would probably start by assessing all children at level B and then test up or down a level with children for whom level B tests were too easy or too hard. This testing, supplemented with observation, indicates which of the skills each child has already mastered and which he has not.

Step IV involves setting instructional objectives for each child in the unit. Using the WDRSD, behavioral objectives related to the skills a child has not mastered become his instructional objectives.

Step V calls for the unit teachers to plan an instructional program for all unit children. Each teacher in turn assumes responsibility for the instruction of certain children, who are grouped together because they need to master one or two of the same skills. While children will be involved in several different instructional patterns in the various curriculum areas, each will have some instruction in small groups with other children working on the same skills. The word attack element of WDRSD has a Teacher's Resource File which keys published materials and suggested activities to each of the 45 skills.

Step VI of the model involves assessing students to determine their attainment of objectives. Once the student reaches the mastery level (usually an 80 percent criterion is set) on a group test, he moves on to the next sequence of the program. If he does not master the skills after additional work, the unit staff takes another look at his progress and raises questions such as—was he ready for the skills tried, were the skills appropriate to his abilities, was the instructional program appropriate for his needs?—and designs another program for the same or another objective.

Assessment & Evaluation

Assessment for pupils both prior to and following instruction is called for by the Instructional Programing Model. In both cases, pupils take criterion-referenced tests which measure their attainment of the behavioral objectives around which instruction is organized. The assessment data are used not only to plan the course of a child's instruction, but also to evaluate whether the school is meeting the objectives of its educational program. This dual use of data is at the heart of the Model for Assessment and Evaluation.

The Instructional Programing Model assumes that educational objectives have been adopted by the building staff. By summarizing individual assessment data one can determine how well groups of children of similar characteristics are performing, and thereby learn whether the staff's objectives are attained. Results of such an analysis yield information necessary to the superintendent and the public to whom the staff is accountable. Judgments about the effectiveness of a school's program can then be based directly upon performance related to specified objectives.

The Wisconsin Design for Reading Skill Development combines the wisdom of generations of teachers and reading consultants with recent research findings. It is organized into six skill areas: word attack, study skills, comprehension, self-directed reading, interpretive skills, and creative skills. The Design describes essential reading skills and related behaviors and provides machine-scorable criterion-referenced tests for assessing children's mastery of these skills from kindergarten forward. Resource materials and management procedures for teachers help them organize programs for individual children.

In 1970-71 the word attack element was tested with

primary children in schools in Alabama, Colorado, Florida, Georgia, and Wisconsin.

In 18 Wisconsin and 5 Colorado schools for which data have been analyzed, the field test group performed better on more than 90 percent of the word attack objectives after six months instruction than children of the same age in the same school had performed a year earlier without the word attack program. End-of-the-year testing showed excellent retention of skills mastered. Performance on the Cooperative Primary and Stanford Achievement tests by children who had word attack instruction was as good as or better than the performance of children who had not. Many participants made dramatic gains in phonic analysis over nonparticipants the year before.

In 1971-72 the word attack materials are under field test in more than 400 schools in 29 states. Schools interested in field testing the word attack and study skills programs during 1972-73 may apply to Quality Verification Section, Wisconsin R & D Center, 1404 Regent Street, Madison, Wisconsin 53706.

The Prereading Skills Program attempts to prevent reading failures by identifying and overcoming deficits in prereading skills at the preschool and kindergarten levels. Diagnostic tests have been developed for three visual skills (letter order, letter orientation, and word detail) and two auditory skills (sound matching and sound blending). Extensive research shows that these skills relate directly to learning to read and correlate with reading success.

Instructional packages to help children learn the skills include games, songs, and other activities. Informal assessment procedures and a handbook for teachers are also included.

In 1971 pilot tests in 3 kindergartens showed that the program is workable for teachers and successful with children. The proportion of kindergartners acquiring mastery of each skill was considerably higher in the pilot group than in the control group. In 1971-72 the program is undergoing small-scale field testing in a variety of kindergarten settings. Schools wishing to participate in field testing this program in 1973-74 may apply to Quality Verification

Section, Wisconsin R & D Center, 1404 Regent Street, Madison, Wisconsin 53706.

Curriculum Materials

Developing Mathematical Processes (DMP) integrates arithmetic, geometry, and probability and statistics as well as combining an activity approach to learning with IGE practices. Based on an empirical analysis of how children learn mathematics, DMP represents the first attempt to incorporate an activity approach in a carefully sequenced complete program of mathematics instruction for grades K-6. Early pilot studies show that children enjoy the activity approach and learn well. Teachers do not require lengthy inservice education to use the program.

The major innovation in content is investigating geometry at all levels of instruction. Integrating geometry with the study of arithmetic is done by taking a measurement approach where children themselves generate the numbers they work with. Because they are constantly generating numerical data, children also study elementary probability and statistics as they organize and analyze this data.

The complete program will include 12 curriculum packages, each containing a teacher's guide, criterion-referenced tests, and a variety of manipulative and printed materials for children. In 1970-71, the kindergarten-primary program was developed and partially pilot tested. It is projected for large-scale field testing in 1972-73, with the program for grades 4-6 to follow in 1973-74. Schools interested in testing the kindergarten-primary program in 1972 may apply to the Quality Verification Section, Wisconsin R & D Center, 1404 Regent Street, Madison, Wisconsin 53706.

Individually Guided Motivation is an inservice program to increase children's interest in learning and their self-direction. The multimedia inservice materials describe and illustrate how principles of goal-setting, modeling, feedback, reinforcement, and reasoning may be incorporated into the instructional program.

There are four motivation-instructional procedures described in sound-motion pictures: setting goals with individual children; promoting independent reading; tutoring of younger students by older students; and small group conferences to encourage self-directed behavior.

In 1970-71 the 10 teachers who conducted the small-scale field test of the goal-setting procedures found them to be effective in increasing children's rates of skill development in reading and mathematics.

The 65 adults who held conferences to promote the independent reading of 360 children reported substantial gains in the number of books the children read. Grade equivalent gains of approximately one year or more in reading speed, word recognition, and comprehension were typical for children in grades 2 and 3 during the semester the conferences were held.

Schools wanting to participate in field testing the program in 1972-73 should apply to Quality Verification Section, Wisconsin R & D Center for Cognitive Learning, 1404 Regent Street, Madison, Wisconsin 53706.

Elementary Science: Man and the Environment makes children aware of the complex relations between science and society, between man and his environment. The program is designed to teach children concepts of environmental management and related decision-making processes. Because of the urgent need for curriculum materials of this kind, readers and related materials are being developed to supplement the content of various curriculum areas.

The first two books currently under development are for children in the intermediate grade range. Each instructional package will focus on a particular problem such as air pollution and will contain an illustrated reader, an activities booklet, and audiovisual materials. Assessment exercises, a teacher's edition, and supporting inservice materials are also projected.

IGE: Cost and Requirements

It is difficult to determine the cost of becoming a multiunit school. The Center recommends that a school should have adequate funds to make necessary changes. The unit leader should be paid at least 5 and up to 20 percent above the regular schedule in compensation for increased responsibility, and to make the position of lead teacher a highly attractive career position. The school should provide one aide and one secretary per 150 children unless there are already seven or more adults to work with each unit as noted in figure 1. The school must supply additional instructional materials if it is not already equipped to provide for differences in rates and styles of learning.

The staff of the school must be able to participate, primarily at local expense, in a first-year staff development program as follows: (a) a one-day conference for the chief school officer, (b) three days of inservice training for building principals and unit leaders, (c) a one-week workshop for reading consultants, and (d) one week of inservice for the entire building staff just before the opening of school, followed by four half-days during the first year.

Recently constructed open-space buildings usually require no remodeling. Older buildings, however, often require some additions, use of portable space, or remodeling (such as eliminating walls).

Each MUS-E of 500-800 enrollment needs two well-supplied instructional resource centers: one for older children that will accommodate 90-120 children simultaneously, and one for younger children that will accommodate 60-75 children.

Principal Norman Graper reports that hiring more aides and buying additional instructional equipment and materials for IGE has added to Wilson School's operating costs. But the increase is offset by savings. The school does not, for example, use many substitute teachers since other members of the unit can fill in for an absent teacher. Also, the IGE learning environment has substantially cut both retentions and vandalism.

NEC

The National Evaluation Committee of the R & D Center which has met annually with the staff of the Center since 1965 expressed these ideas about the MUS-E in its 1970 report concerning the Center:

The Committee wishes to reiterate its strong support of the multiunit school and individually guided instruction and will here note the salient features provided by this unusual combination of educational and organizational concepts:

1. Attention is focused on the individual learner as a person with unique characteristics, concerns, and motivations.

2. Teachers and other educational personnel are helped to employ systematic problem-solving processes to the identification and satisfaction of the educational needs of individuals—both in the student body and on the staff.

3. The basic organizational units are small enough to allow every person to be known and treated as an individual and large enough to permit role differentiation and complementarity of contributions.

4. Provisions for staff training and continuing development are an essential part of the approach.

5. There is a good reconciliation of the values of autonomy and accountability, small group responsibility and intergroup coordination.

The Committee's assertions are based on facts gathered in multiunit schools over the past four years.

Evaluation of IGE/MUS-E

Impact of the Multiunit Organization

Implementing IGE in the MUS-E calls for cooperative working relationships, shared decision-making, instructional programing, and specialization of work by the instructional staff. Ronald J. Pellegrin of the Center for Advanced Study of Educational Administration at the University of Oregon conducted research in three MUS-Es and three control schools in three Wisconsin school systems. These multiunit schools were completing their initial year under the new pattern. The main conclusions of Pellegrin concerning changes that occurred during the first year of adopting the MUS-E pattern follow.

1. There was a superior recognition among MUS-E teachers of the vital role planning plays in instruction. The five most important tasks of MUS-E teachers dealt with specific types of planning and the preparation of instructional materials.

2. New specialization of labor emerged in the multiunit schools. Some teachers devoted most of their time to individual pupils, others worked mainly with small or class-sized groups, while a few worked with large groups.

3. Unit leaders were the focal points of interaction in the units and served as links between the teachers and the principal.

4. In the control schools, decision-making affecting each classroom was generally the prerogative of individual teachers, who served as primary decision-makers, and the principal, who provided advice or set limits. In the three MUS-Es decisions were typically made by the unit staff in cooperation with the principal.

5. Job satisfaction and teacher morale were much higher in the MUS-E staff.

Effectiveness of Instructional Programing

Ideally, instructional programing for the individual student should be implemented in at least one curriculum area by the end of a MUS-E's first year of operation. As of 1970-71, some children were in their fourth year in an MUS-E; however, the first supportive IGE curriculum area, reading, was not introduced until the students were in their third year.

In the 1969-70 school year the word attack element of the Wisconsin Design for Reading Skill Development (WDRSD) was used at the primary level in two smoothly functioning MUS-Es in their third year of operation. The word attack program includes 45 skills, and is designed for the first four years of schooling, including kindergarten. Group tests were administered in September of each year to identify skills the students had not mastered as well as those they had mastered; it was not anticipated that the majority of students would have mastered all the skills. Both years the tests were given to children in the second through fourth years of schooling (equivalent to grades 1-3). Therefore it is possible to compare the percentage of children at these grade levels who had mastered the various skills before the reading program was introduced with the percentages of those who had mastered the skills after experiencing the program for one year. Both schools made a special attempt to carry out excellent instruction in reading before the WDRSD was introduced. The tests showed that a higher percentage of the experienced children achieved mastery of 23 skills, fewer mastered 6 skills, and an equal percentage mastered one skill. In general, mastery by the 1970 groups was substantially higher than by the 1969 groups except in the second year of schooling, equivalent to the first grade in a traditional school. The relatively lower mastery here is attributable to the fact that the new reading program was not introduced for most children until late in the first (kindergarten) year and then only to those manifesting positive behaviors indicative of reading readiness.

The Doren Diagnostic Reading Test measures achievements similar to those implied by the objectives of the WDRSD. Two schools administered this test to third year (second grade) children who had not participated in the WDRSD in May of 1969 and to those who had participated for one year in May of 1970. The performance was higher for those children who had the program in 1969-70 than those who had not in 1968-69. The mean difference was statistically significant; higher achievements equivalent to one to four months were additionally observed on standardized reading tests at all primary school levels.

The preceding results based on criterion-referenced and standardized tests indicate the desirable combined effects of the multiunit organization and a concerted attack on curriculum improvement along the IGE model. This is not to be interpreted to mean that the organization alone will produce higher student achievement or that higher achievement will accrue in the absence of a coordinated, well-planned curriculum improvement effort. Changes in organization, instructional programing, assessment, curriculum and other elements are all necessary to produce comprehensive educational improvement.

Reprinted from booklet, *IGE Multiunit Elementary School,* Wisconsin Research and Development Center for Cognitive Learning, Center No. C-03, Contract OE 5-10-154. Herbert J. Klausmeier is V.A.C. Henmon Professor of Educational Psychology and Director of the Wisconsin Research and Developmental Center for Cognitive Learning at the University of Wisconsin, Madison.

9

The PLAN System for Individualizing Education

John C. Flanagan

Education has changed a great deal in the Twentieth Century because of changing answers to three questions— first, who should be educated; second, what should they learn; and third, how should they learn it. From a situation in the Nineteenth Century in which the prevailing view was that very few children should be educated, there has been a dramatic change to a real effort to provide both elementary and secondary education for all young people. Because of the very great individual differences among children, this change from educating a few to educating everybody has required new content and new methods.

The second question, "what should these students learn," has become a very complex one involving many factors. One of these has been termed the "knowledge explosion." The accelerating rate of our increase in knowledge has changed the scope of education from the basic skills and a classical program of history, literature, foreign languages, and mathematics to a situation in which many more choices must be made.

Education in the public schools in this country has also taken on a broader role. The responsibilities of the schools now include: preparation for effective participation in social and citizenship roles; and education for cultural, avocational, and leisure time activities.

A natural consequence of the great recent increase in the extent of available knowledge is a change in the emphasis from content to abilities. The abilities most stressed include reading comprehension, reasoning, decision-making, and similar skills. Perhaps the most important change with respect to what the student should learn is the trend towards a truly individualized educational system aimed at meeting the specific needs of each individual student.

The third question, "how should students learn," has been greatly complicated by advances in educational technology. Education is changing from a lecture, textbook, recitation program to one which involves substantially greater participation by each student through the use of audiovisual media and new forms of printed materials. The electronic computer is also becoming a resource for both learning and the management of learning.

The systems approach to education developed from experience in designing and producing various types of complex equipment. Essentially, the systems approach makes the various steps in the development of the system comprehensive, rational, and explicit rather than partial, subjective, and implicit. As applied to education, it is useful to think of the systems approach as including the following six major steps:

1. Define the objectives in specific terms.

2. Develop tests and performance standards to measure the attainment of the objectives.

3. Identify or develop the types of procedures which indicate most promise for the efficient achievement of the objectives.

4. Implement the system.

5. Evaluate the effectiveness of the system and revise the system to improve its performance.

6. Continue the implementation, evaluation, and revision cycle.

Measurement, therefore, has a central role in any application of the systems approach. It is essential that the developer have precise evaluations of the extent to which the objectives of the system are being met. These assessment procedures must be both comprehensive and valid if the system is to perform its intended function.

The trends and conditions outlined above indicate the need for a new approach to education. The more immediate cause for the development of a Program for Learning in Accordance with Needs (PLAN) was Project TALENT. The survey in 1960 of a representative sample of students in the ninth, tenth, eleventh, and twelfth grades made it quite clear that the very wide individual differences were not adequately being cared for by such make-shifts as homogeneous grouping. A large fraction of the students were being exposed to quite inappropriate educational experiences. It also appeared that the skill levels achieved in areas such as reading comprehension and arithmetic reasoning were not sufficient to prepare these students to cope with the problems of Twentieth Century living. The survey also suggested, and the one year and five year follow-ups of these students confirmed, that the guidance and planning procedures available to these students were quite ineffective in assisting them in selecting appropriate long-term goals and developing realistic plans for attaining these goals.

PLAN focuses on assisting the individual to learn about educational, occupational, avocational, and social roles and activities and to plan his own development to utilize his potentialities in ways which will be maximally satisfying to him. The functions of the PLAN system of education, with respect to individual development, are to assist each student to:

1. Acquire information about available choices regarding occupational roles, leisure time activities, and social and civic responsibilities.

2. Understand the nature of individual differences, the principles of learning and behavior modification, and the development of abilities, interests, and values.

3. Estimate, as accurately as possible, the level of development of his own abilities, the extent of his knowledge about specific fields, and his current interests, values, and related characteristics.

4. Develop skills in planning and personal decision-making.

5. Formulate immediate and long-range educational, occupational, leisure time, and social and civic goals based on the information and skills outlined in the preceding four activities.

6. Take responsibility for carrying out his individual development.

7. Develop the ability and skills required to manage his own individual development program.

The PLAN individual development system was the joint effort of the American Institutes for Research, the Westinghouse Learning Corporation, and twelve school districts* in California and the northeastern part of the country. The program included instruction in language arts, social studies, science, and mathematics as well as the student-centered aspects of the individual development program. In the first year (1966-67) the program was developed by the staff and teachers from the cooperating school districts for Grades 1, 5, and 9. In each of the next three years the program at all three levels was extended one grade so that by 1969-70 Grades 1 through 12 were covered.

The basic components of the PLAN individual development system include: (1) a set of educational objectives, (2) learning methods and materials, (3) evaluation, (4) guidance and individual planning, (5) teacher development, and (6) computer services.

A Set of Educational Objectives

In developing the educational objectives to provide the framework for the educational program, it was decided that mastering each objective should require about two or three hours of learning time. Another arbitrary decision was that about five objectives would be included in each module. Thus a module was expected to require about two weeks time for the average student.

---

*Bethel Park School District, Bethel Park, Pa.; Hicksville Public School District, Hicksville, N.Y.; Penn-Trafford School District, Harrison City, Pa.; Pittsburgh Public Schools, Pittsburgh, Pa.; Quincy Public Schools, Quincy, Mass.; Wood County Schools, Parkersburg, W. Va.; Archdiocese of San Francisco, San Francisco, Calif.; Fremont Unified School District, Fremont, Calif.; San Carlos Elementary School District, San Carlos, Calif.; San Jose Unified School District, San Jose, Calif.; Santa Clara Unified School District, Santa Clara, Calif.; Union Elementary School District, San Jose, Calif.

In addition to the module objectives from among which a student's program was selected, there were a number of intermediate objectives formulated. These required a longer period than two weeks to learn. There were also the long-range types of objectives such as the general abilities of reading comprehension, arithmetic reasoning, and similar basis skills and abilities. These were tested annually. The specific objectives written were based on a general scope and sequence developed for a particular subject matter field based on the recommendations of the national curriculum advisory panels in each of the four fields.

Learning Methods and Materials

In developing PLAN it was proposed to identify the most effective learning methods and materials available for achieving the educational objectives selected for the program. In the past 15 years the federal government has spent well over 100 million dollars on the development of new curriculum materials in various subject matter fields. Very few of these materials have been adequately evaluated. It therefore seemed more appropriate to develop a program using these materials which would make it possible to evaluate their effectiveness than to attempt to develop new instructional materials.

As indicated above, the program was built around the educational objectives. To assist the student to learn the materials necessary to indicate mastery of the objective, teaching-learning units were developed. Figure 1 gives an example of a teaching-learning unit prepared to accompany materials usually taught at the seventh grade level.

There are usually two or more teaching-learning units covering the same objectives. An effort is made to match the learning characteristics of the student with the requirements of the various teaching-learning units available. Insofar as possible, an attempt is made to provide a variety of learning experiences to assist the student to achieve each objective.

By studying the performance on the test items used to measure the achievement of a particular objective, weaknesses in the learning experiences can easily be found. Learning experiences in the teaching-learning unit used can be supplemented or replaced when the student's per-

---

Living Systems in Space

Step 1. Objective
Describe the technological advances for counteracting each of the following conditions in outer space which permit man to establish a closed ecological system in his space craft: (1) lack of gravity, (2) absence of food, (3) decreased air pressure, (4) extremes of temperature, and (5) lack of oxygen.

Use	Do
Today's Basic Science: The Molecule and the Biosphere, Teacher's Edition, John Gabriel Navarra, et al. (Harper & Row, 1965)	(a) Read pp. 428-429. For use during the next five to ten days, set up a balanced aquarium. See instruction on pp. 430–431. Set up the aquarium now, before going any further with this TLU. You may use any aquarium that may be already set up in the classroom. (b) From your readings in Activity (a), list those items that are necessary for the survival of man. (c) Your list should include all the conditions listed in the objective, except gravity, and more. Gravity is not really necessary for man to survive in space but does cause more problems when there is no gravity.
Life Science, Singer Science Series, Teacher's Edition, Helen Dolman MacCracken, et al. (The L.W. Singer Company, 1968)	(d) Read pp. 302–305, the section "What effect does weightlessness have on man." (e) Do the activity on p. 303. "Collect pictures."

Figure 1. A portion of a Teaching-Learning Unit in Science.

formance indicates the experiences were ineffective. It has been found that the comments of students and teachers provide a very valuable supplement to the item-analysis data in making such revisions.

Evaluation

The mastery of the objectives included in each module is measured when the student finishes the teaching-learning unit for that module. The answers to the module tests are recorded on IBM cards which are optically scanned at the terminal and the student's responses are scored by the central computer. The student is expected to master each of the objectives before going on to the next module. If all items on all objectives are correct, he is told to go on to the next module without further action. If he misses only one of several questions on an objective, the student is asked to review it on his own. If his performance is not quite this good, the teacher is requested to certify his mastery of the objective after he has reviewed the unit and before he goes on to the next module. If his performance on the module test indicates a failure to master some of the objectives, he is required to retake the module test after further study of the same or another teaching-learning unit.

For the most part, the items in the module test are intended to measure objectives learned in the study of this module only. Occasionally, an objective is placed in a module which represents cumulative learning over several modules. The objective is placed in the module to indicate that mastery is anticipated by the end of this particular module.

Items similar to those in the tests given at the end of the module are included in PLAN Achievement Tests given after a group of modules have been completed. This provides an opportunity to check on retention and verify the module test findings. Certain long-range goals, such as vocabulary, reading comprehension, and arithmetic reasoning, are evaluated annually in the late spring. These tests are called Developed Ability Performance Tests and are used to assist the student with his educational and vocational planning.

Pupils who are in kindergarten in the spring and anticipating entering the first grade in the fall are evaluated by the kindergarten teacher on a twenty-item Readiness Report Form. It is expected that the teacher will have much of the information and will be able to answer many of the questions without further assessment of the pupil. Ten of the items relate to the readiness of the student for reading activities, and in preliminary tests some of the items yielded biserial correlation coefficients as high as 0.40 and 0.47 with the Stanford Achievement Paragraph Meaning Test given a year later at the end of the first grade. These ten items referred to such abilities as the discrimination of "t" and "p" sounds and the naming of all of the letters of the alphabet. The results from this Readiness Report Form have been found to be very valuable in placing the beginning students in appropriate learning activities when they start school in September.

The PLAN system of education has many other important objectives which are not measurable by procedures of the types discussed above. In an effort to develop procedures for assessing some of these other objectives, the staff requested teachers to report critical incidents of effective behaviors believed to have resulted from the use of the PLAN system. The teachers were asked to "Think of a recent occasion when you observed a student exhibit an unusual amount of some quality such as resourcefulness, independence, initiative, self-confidence, responsibility, social sensitivity, etc., which appeared to result from the PLAN approach to education."

The critical incidents obtained (Jung, 1971) were grouped into six principal categories, such as, (1) did unusually thorough job on assigned task or continued beyond requirements of assigned or agreed-upon task, and (2) completed an unassigned civic, social, or playground activity without reminder or support from others. On the basis of these teacher's observations, some experimental evaluation procedures were developed. For each of the levels of students included at the intermediate and secondary levels, there were three exercises. The first two were common to all levels—they asked the student to list independent learning and community service activities which he had undertaken voluntarily during the past semester. The students were also given a 30 minute period to develop their ideas on an assigned topic such as improving the present educational system, improving the value and use of television, or getting more citizens involved in the decision-making process on the local and national levels. Although this must be regarded as only a pilot study, the comparisons of reports of activities from PLAN and Control classes all favored PLAN classes and the differences for two of the four grades studied, Grades 5 and 6, were statistically significant.

One general point which is of great importance in any evaluation program related to individual development is that the individual must be the unit. Evaluation purposes are not well served by reporting the mean and standard deviation of a group of students on a particular subject matter achievement test. It is necessary to know whether each of the items in the test is a relevant objective for the various students in the group. The point of interest is then, not the mean for the group, but how well the student performed on those items important for his educational aims and purposes.

Guidance and Individual Planning

There is a strong trend in American education at the present time to give young people an opportunity to participate in choosing their educational goals and planning their educational program. To enable the student to make responsible choices, it is essential that he be as adequately prepared as possible.

In PLAN, information about the world of work is presented as an applied economic strand in the PLAN Social Studies Program. Other relevant information is included in Language Arts, Mathematics, and Science. At the primary level, there is an introduction to the world of work which includes such topics as community and service occupations which have been observed by young children, the general nature of the work role, including making a living and achieving personal satisfactions, the social and economic functions of various occupations, and ways that people prepare for occupations.

At the intermediate level, the student is introduced to twelve occupational families which were developed on the basis of homogeneity of interests, educational requirements, and on the basis of the similarity of their ability and interest patterns as checked empirically using Project TALENT data. The twelve occupational families are shown in Table 1.

By the beginning of the secondary level, the student must have made at least tentative educational plans consistent with his occupational goals at about the level of

Table 1. Long-Range Occupational Goals

1. Engineering, Physical Science, Mathematics, and Architecture
2. Medical and Biological Sciences
3. Business Administration
4. Teaching and Social Service
5. Humanities, Law, and Social Sciences
6. Fine Arts, Performing Arts
7. Technical Jobs
8. Business, Sales
9. Mechanics, Industrial Trades
10. Construction Trades
11. Business, Secretarial-Clerical
12. General, Community Service, Public Service

specificity indicated by the twelve occupational family groups. These tentative plans need to be checked in terms of his progress in developing the required abilities, and also with a view to their relation to his developing interests and values. The student should also obtain more detailed information about the nature of the occupations in the various occupational groups.

These decisions, of course, require considerable knowledge about the student's own level of ability and his interests and values. In PLAN this information is provided in terms of the Developed Ability Performance Tests and related biographical and self-description instruments. Using the TALENT data, the student is informed of his present level of ability in relation to the requirements for typical jobs in the twelve occupational groups.

In order to interpret these data satisfactorily, the student is informed regarding the nature of learning. Thus, if the expected gain in ability level in reading comprehension is approximately six points over a three year period and the student aspires to educational and career goals which would require that he improve his performance in this period by about nine points, he needs to be informed of the extent of the effort which is likely to be required of him to achieve this amount of improvement in this particular ability.

Formulating goals and achieving them requires skill in making decisions and plans. If this were a one-time activity, it would probably be most efficient for the individual to obtain a maximum of advice and a minimum of skill. However, in present-day society, decision-making and planning are required almost continuously because of changes in the total situation. It is therefore important that the student's skills in making decisions and plans be developed as fully as possible. It is also true that decisions and plans handed to the student are not as likely to be understood, retained, and acted upon as are those which he has carefully and systematically made on his own.

To assist the student in formulating a long-range occupational goal at a particular stage in his educational development, a series of eleven modules has been developed. After completing this series, the student and his parents tentatively select the educational and general vocational aspirations and goals which seem most appropriate. The first modules in the series relate to decision-making and the consequences of decision-making. These are followed by a series of five modules describing twelve occupational families in some detail. The last module before the one in which he selects his long-range goal is related to the role of personal values in goal formulation.

The basic type of figure used in this series of modules are shown in Figure 2. For the occupational group shown in this figure, one vertical line for each of the twelve tests indicates the range from -1 standard deviation to $+1$ standard deviation. The small horizontal line indicates the

12th Grade Average

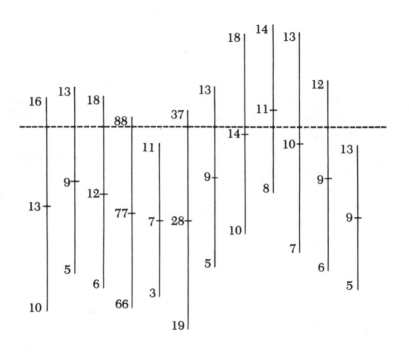

Figure 2. Means and Standard Deviations for the Scores on 12 Tests Achieved by Male Students Who Five Years Later Were Planning Careers as Carpenters.

mean for this group. Males entering careers as carpenters have a mean score above the mean for all twelfth grade males in the test for visualization in three dimensions. The mean score of those entering careers as lawyers on this test is the same as that for carpenters, but it is their lowest score on any of the twelve tests, whereas the mean score of carpenters is their highest on any of the twelve tests.

The first aim of the program is to assist the student in formulating long-range goals and developing reasonable plans for attaining them. Following this, it is essential that he accept the responsibility for his own individual development and acquire the management skills to enable him to modify his behavior to insure that he carries out this individual development program.

Teacher Development

This program consists of three segments given in the spring, late summer, and early fall. These might be described as orientation, instruction, and performance. The activities in the spring are aimed at understanding the general nature of the teacher's role in the PLAN system. Two days are devoted to structured observation by the teachers of PLAN classrooms in action. Each teacher, guided by an observation form, observes three classrooms during this period and also spends time at the end of each day discussing what has been observed. The third day of the orientation phase is spent on an individualized exercise consisting of a module on classroom organization.

In the instructional phase in August, which consists of three days of computer-supported individualized instruction, each teacher completes several modules. These are on the curriculum, the orientation of students, the computer support of the program, basic procedures for individualizing student programs, and a review of the module taken in the spring on classroom organization.

The performance phase of the teacher development activities is primarily aimed at confirmation that the instructional program has been successful in bringing the teacher to the performance standards set. The Far West Regional Educational Laboratory's mini-course on tutoring is used by the teacher. This course is self-administered and enables the teacher to verify using audio or video tape equipment that the tutoring skills have, in fact, been mastered. Each of the other instructional objectives pertaining to classroom performance is checked by the consultant with the teacher to insure that all of the necessary information and skills have been acquired.

Computer Functions

In PLAN the computer and the computer terminal located in the school building perform two main functions, (1) monitoring the student's individual progress and (2) assisting in the planning of his individual development program. The school building terminal consists of an IBM 2956 optical card reader and an IBM 2740 automatic typewriter. These are connected with the central computer by means of a telephone line. Small batches of cards are transmitted from the terminal throughout the day and checks are used to prevent incorrect data from being processed.

The computer performs its monitoring function primarily through the daily processing of module test results and status cards. The cards received by the terminal are batch-processed at the end of the day after further editing by the computer. Thus, the teacher has printout pages giving information on student test results, students ready for small group activities, changes in programs of study, etc. In addition to this daily processing, the monitoring of the student's progress is facilitated by monthly or quarterly progress reports indicating the extent to which the student is proceeding on the schedule planned at the beginning of the year.

To aid the student in planning for his individual development, the computer provides information about his present level of abilities and other learning characteristics, thus assisting him to formulate long-range goals.

The computer also assists the student in the development of a program of studies. In PLAN there are three steps in program planning. The first step is to place the student at a point on each scale where he knows the earlier modules but does not know the later ones. Placement is based on previous records and performance on PLAN Achievement

Tests which review mastery of completed modules. The second step is the assignment of a "quota" for the academic year. This is based on the number of modules completed by the student in the previous year and on his performance on the most relevant of the Developed Ability Performance Tests. The third step involves selection of the specific modules to be included in the program of studies and choice of the particular teaching-learning units to be used to master the objective. This requires extensive computer assistance and a long set of decision rules.

These rules start with state and local requirements for specific subjects. For students in the higher grades, the next important consideration is the student-parent selected long-range career goal and the data-suggested goal for this student. Using all available data supplied by the student and parent and his previous teachers, the computer recommends a specific program of studies. This program usually provides a number of opportunities for the student and teacher to make specific suggestions from among several appropriate sets of modules based on current interests or related factors. A sample Program of Studies is shown in Figure 3.

A secondary function of the computer, not directly related to the operating of the program, is the improvement of the PLAN materials. The accumulation of the data in the computer makes it possible to analyze the performance of various types of students on specific module test items. These can be related to the learning materials used and appropriate revisions made to improve the effectiveness of the learning program.

PLAN in the Dartmouth School

In the academic year 1969-70, two seventh grade classes, a total of 69 children, were enrolled in PLAN in the Dartmouth School. These students were taught by Tod Hodgdon and John Scott. Mr. Hodgdon had spent the academic year 1968-69 working with eleven other teachers from the schools participating in PLAN to develop a program for the seventh grade. John Scott received only the brief type of teacher preparation described above before undertaking this assignment. The principal, Lloyd Krelie,

0173 Landers, Paul

Program of Studies
Slippery Rock Elementary

Social Studies			Fall 1970	
Mod. No.	Module Name	Times Tested	Date Start	Date Finish
	Your test results suggest that you know some of the objectives of these modules in your program of studies. After reviewing the modules, you should consider challenging them.			
42-556-2	World Problems and Organizations The following modules are suggested for your program of studies for this year.			
44-557-2	United States Foreign Policy			
44-559-3	Races of Mankind Establishment of a Government (Complete 3 of the following 5 modules. When you are ready to begin work on this set, ask your teacher to start set number 47-329.)			
44-601-2	Government in Early Societies			
44-602-2	European Monarchism			
44-603	Development of Democracy in England			
44-604-2	Democracy in France			
44-605-2	Twentieth Century Dictatorships			

Figure 3. A portion of a Program of Studies in Social Studies.

gave these teachers a relatively free hand as was the tradition in this school and encouraged them to innovate in ways which seemed appropriate to them.

The Dartmouth School is part of the Union Elementary School District, located in San Jose, California. Some of the students entering these PLAN seventh grade classes had been in PLAN classes in the Mirassou School in this district in their fifth and sixth grades. Others were new to PLAN in the seventh grade. Mr. Hodgdon took the responsibility for instructing these students in mathematics and social studies and Mr. Scott was responsible for their work in language arts and science.

In addition to the standard PLAN program for the seventh grade, these teachers added a few modifications of their own. Thus, for part of the year, they had all 69 children together in a double classroom and allowed students a good deal of freedom in selecting the subjects they wished to study at any given time. After a few months trial, they gave this up because with this number of students together they felt they did not have time to get to students who weren't making adequate progress, but who were less aggressive about indicating their needs for help to the teachers. They reported the periodic print-outs from the computer were of considerable help to them in identifying the students who were lagging behind, but they found it difficult to ignore the bright students moving rapidly ahead who asked for assistance in favor of students who seemed to prefer just to vegetate and who didn't want to get intellectually involved in the types of materials made available to them.

John Scott reported that another innovation used was an incentive system using the yellow packing cards inserted in each package of teaching-learning units as tokens. Students were awarded one of the yellow tokens if they obtained a perfect score on the module test the first time they took it. They were also awarded a yellow token if they completed their scheduled number of modules in the month for a particular course. Each yellow token entitled the holder to a 20-minute period of recreational activity of his choosing.

In a letter written by Ted Hodgdon to Dr. William M.

Shanner last July, Mr. Hodgdon says: "Classroom involvement with Project PLAN was, without qualification, the most rewarding experience I've had in fifteen years of teaching. I cannot say that the entire year was one unbroken flow of rhythmatic bliss. It hurt a little now and then . . . Down days will undoubtedly appear next year. I look forward to them, however, because those are the days that are most instructive for me. In many ways, I was first year teacher all over again . . . The big step for me was to let go of the reins and concentrate my attention on what the students' needs were as expressed by the student. . . .

"Once the interaction started, something significant began to happen. I found that when I was talking, it was because a student had initiated the conversation. The student was displaying a need to know. . . .

"Some of the interesting outcomes for the students should be mentioned. Henry Jackson (name changed), for instance, completed the eleventh level algebra course before Easter. You may recall that he did level five math early in the fifth grade and level sixth math during the first few months of grade six at Mirassou school (in PLAN classes). The next available math at the time was level nine algebra, which he completed (skipping seventh and eighth grade mathematics). He also did a part of the eleventh level algebra before he came to Dartmouth this past year. Rather than continuing a vertical development of math after Easter, Henry devoted his math time to IBM correspondence courses in FORTRAN and the 360 computer . . . Before the year ended, I asked him to take the PLAN Achievement Test in math. His scores were higher than anyone else's in all three of the tests, even though he did not work in the level seven modules being tested. . . .

"In the area of citizenship, PLAN students were better behaved than non-PLAN students. Our vice-principal tallied the number of times each teacher in the school sent a student to the office for errant behavior in the classroom or out in the yard. The average was 65 referrals per teacher. PLAN teachers averaged seven per class. The explanation for this lies in the fact that PLAN students do not get bored in the classrooms. Classroom management is infinitely simpler because the typical stress situations do not exist. I hasten to add that we PLAN teachers are not creampuffs. Both of us are veterans of World War II and Korea."

Conclusions

The PLAN system of education represents a much more comprehensive approach to individualized education than has been previously available. The explicit statement of educational objectives and the teaching-learning units representing guides to appropriate learning materials are essential for any systematic approach to the development of an explicit and effective educational program. Objectives and guides are not enough, however, to implement an effective educational program. The module tests related to each objective, the periodic PLAN Achievement Tests to review and confirm the continued progress of the student, along with the annual PLAN Achievement Survey Tests and the Developed Ability Performance Tests provide a solid basis for assisting the student to formulate his long-range goals and develop a program of studies to achieve these goals.

The integration of the guidance and individual planning aspects of the program into the instructional phases offers real promise for the development in the student of the basic internal motivation which will enable him to take responsibility for and manage his program of studies in such a way as to prepare himself to achieve the goals he has set for himself.

In the program the computer coupled with a terminal in the school building can provide very valuable support to the teacher in the form of record-keeping, test-scoring, predicting, and utilizing extensive data inputs by both teacher and pupil to prepare a program of studies to carry out the plans and objectives of the student.

In conclusion, it should be emphasized that the availability of a comprehensive system such as PLAN does not insure that it will be automatically effective when installed in the classroom. Any such system represents only a set of instruments and procedures which make it possible for the student to plan and carry out a program of learning in accordance with his needs with extensive assistance from the teacher and the school administrator. At best, the PLAN system can only provide a framework. The responsibility for the learning must rest on the student, guided by the teacher, and supervised by the school administrator.

Reprinted from the January 1971 issue of *Measurement in Education,* Volume 2, No. 2. Published by the National Council on Measurement in Education, East Lansing, Michigan. John C. Flanagan is Chairman of the Board of American Institutes for Research, Palo Alto, Calif.

References

Dunn, James A. "The PLAN Approach to Curriculum Definition." *Education,* 1970, 90, 221-226.

Flanagan, John C. "Functional Education for the Seventies." *Phi Delta Kappan,* 1967, 49, 27-32.

Flanagan, John C. "Individualizing Education." *Education,* 1970, 90, 191-206.

Flanagan, John C. "The Implications of Project TALENT and related research for guidance." *Measurement and Evaluation in Guidance,* 1969, 2, 116-123.

Flanagan, John C. "The Role of the Computer in PLAN." *Journal of Educational Data Processing,* 1970, 1, 7-17.

Jung, Steven M. "Evaluative Uses of Unconventional Measurement Techniques in an Educational System." *California Educational Research Journal,* 1971, 22, 48-57.

Quirk, Thomas J., Steen, Margaret T., & Lipe, Dewey. "The Development of the PLAN TOS: A Teacher Observation Scale for Individualized Instruction." *Journal of Educational Psychology,* 1971, 62, 188-200.

Shanner, William M. "A System of Individualized Instruction Utilizing Currently Available Instructional Materials." Palo Alto, Calif.: American Institutes for Research, 1968. (Read at American Educational Publishers Institute meeting, Miami, May 1968.)

Wright, Calvin E. "Project PLAN Progress Report" *Education,* 1970, 90, 261-269.

10

Open Education:
Considerations for Implementors

Thomas A. Petrie

To those wishing to initiate open education programs, the problem is how to capitalize on the experiences of others. To those engaged in open education, the question is often how to improve. In any instance potential adopters, advocates, and evaluators of open education share a three-pronged challenge of: (1) defining or characterizing open education programs, (2) describing how to initiate open education, and (3) evaluating learning in open education. One aspect of the problem is concisely stated by Fetherstone, who concludes, "We could proceed more wisely if we had better notions of how to evaluate learning in informal settings" (Fetherstone, 1971, p. 23).

The purpose of this paper is to suggest some notions of how to view open education programs. Particularly germane to this task is the necessity to share a characterization of several threads pertaining to open education and the mutations of open education. This is so because helpful notions regarding the worth of open education may be intertwined with: (1) a synthesis or characterization of open education, (2) several processes through which the program is initiated and sustained, and (3) the outcomes expected of open education. In short, the means and ends of a program may be best understood in their programatic relationships.

The most common theme throughout open education is mutuality. Essentially every discussion of open education suggests creating a climate of supportive relationships. A second characteristic is participative decision making as a source for motivating and extending the child's interests. Third, open education encompasses the processes and conventions of subject matter as a primary source for task accomplishment and the development of the child's identity. The emphasis upon these three themes varies in respective programs. However, these themes of mutuality, decision making, and task accomplishment continually appear as essential features in open education programs.

The emphasis upon mutuality is derived from the communication process as a means for sharing and sustaining culturally relevant experience. Communication skills are grounded in human experience. What is it that makes child and man human? Undoubtedly, anthropologist and sociologist agree that language enables man to accumulate culture, share ideas, and view himself in a relation of time, self, and others. It is through communication that the child's sensory perceptions are organized in a particular cultural context. A child organizes, understands, and shares meaning through the communication cycle. Furthermore, within the classroom communication system the teacher and children can recapitulate and renew their human characteristics of hope, the anticipation of things to come, and respect for unique experience—a necessary condition for quality learning.

Anticipating things to come in the classroom is a complex process of building upon the developmental experiences of children. In the open classroom the teacher must sustain communication patterns which draw out of children shared verbal content. These verbalizations generally possess uniquely individual meaning to each child. Through the concern, attention, and respect characterized by mutuality while encouraging children to talk, share meaning, and clarify tasks, the child's I, self, or me comes to have significance to self and others.

Furthermore, the child's I, self, or me has an opportunity to attain a finer integration in the particular school context. This integration is particularly stimulated by sharing the child's everyday home, school, and community experiences in the language arts. These communications can be further extended through experiential activities in the humanities. The content children communicate in language arts may be further extended in their art, music, dance, and drama. The program attains quality as integrations occur through children's activities of drawing, painting, singing, dancing, and role playing. Art, music, dance, and role playing as activities enable the complementary talents of the teacher and children to be shared and extended. These media provide unlimited opportunity for articulating the second thread of open education.

The second thread of open education is the individual's need for participative decision making. The development of autonomy demands a degree of freedom to choose and create. Some freedom to examine new frontiers or to reach out for new integrations is necessary for mental health. While assuredly the need to make choices varies greatly among individuals, the continued practice of decision making in school is a necessary component of a child's development. The practice of making choices is a universal characterization of open education, open areas, and family grouping programs.

An elaboration of the relationship between shared communication, activity, and choice in open education may be in order. It often appears that open education advocates massive freedom or unlimited choice by the student. However, in open education choice is structured by the activities which extend experience. For example, a Piagetian (Piaget, 1970) view would suggest that the limits of choice complement the cognitive level of the child. From an Erikson (Evans, 1969) ego interaction perspective, the parameters of choice are established during interaction with adults. The two perspectives provide developmental ordering of activities with respect to the child's ability to select and persist in an activity.

The processes of *communicating* and *choosing* are complementary processes for schooling. The ego development of the individual while communicating tends to be closely related to developing mutuality between pupil and teacher and among pupils. On the other hand, communications benefit the child as the alternative activities from which he can choose are identified. Choice can then be exercised in the process of goal setting. Through choosing, the child actively experiences freedom and develops will power or autonomy. Furthermore, exercising will or choice is necessary for the individual to be responsible to the group (socialization). In short, as a child communicates he becomes socialized into the group while also securing an identity. Through goal setting and choosing, he becomes further socialized and integrated.

The communicative and goal setting processes provide structures for teaching children, but these two teaching processes must be sustained with respect to something. Communication and choosing pertain to activities and subject matter. Play activities in early childhood provide a mechanism for testing perceptions and securing fitness. Later questions and problems emerge which pertain to subject matter. Subject matter provides the content about which to communicate and from which to choose during the pursuit of competence. In the early grades, art, music, dance, and drama provide integrating activities. However, in the subsequent grades, questions or problem solving direct the student to subject matter that determines the conventions and processes for meaningful learning.

After goal setting, the activity selected contains operations, conventions, and prerequisite skills appropriate to the content area. For example, questions of "how much" are germane to mathematics; questions or problems about the earth, plants, and animals point to science; and concerns about ideas pertain to language as the means for sharing human experience.

In open education programs, the aforementioned communication, choice, and subject matter concerns are generally implicit. They become explicit as teachers and pupils communicate sufficiently to establish a shared frame of reference. *For the teacher,* these communications contain a *preliminary assessment* of the child's cognitive level and ego strength. Through subsequent goal setting, the child may select activities which further elaborate or extend his learning style, interest, and ego development. These selected activities serve to bring out further meanings and uniqueness of the respective subcultures which each child represents. Subsequently, with communication channels open, a refined assessment of the child's learning provides the basis for outlining the specific tasks necessary to recycle student goal setting. Then the disciplines (subject matter) provide other structures appropriate to the child's developmental level and the child's knowledge of the conventions .or processes pertaining to the subject matter scope and sequence. Assuredly, this is no small task. Yet it is a series of tasks which must be made explicit.

It is evident that the open classroom teacher must have a firm understanding of *process* and a *capacity* to sustain an exceedingly complex endeavor. Open education demands a mutuality in pupil-teacher interaction, opportunities for children to make choices, and a potential for integrating the processes and conventions of subject matter. These three themes characterize open education.

To initiate open education programs with the above three themes as guides, there are implications for communication, goal setting, and values. The communication process incorporates a sharing of meaning rather than simply telling, informing, and explaining. The skills for incorporating children's perceptions of reality are exceedingly complex and demanding. Of particular value to the teacher may be skills cited in *The Learning Encounter* by Margaret Clark and others (1971). These skills pertain to completing the communication cycle, identifying the cognitive level of the child's meanings, and bridging the generation and subcultural gaps between teachers and children. A checklist of selected communication attributes follow.

Communication Checklist
I.   Sharing a Frame of Reference
    1. denotative meaning—sharing through synonyms and literal definitions
    2. connotative meaning—sharing through feelings and interpretations
    3. characteristics or attributes of an ideal or concept
II. Developing Norms of Communication
    1. attentiveness

    2. clarification (Re: What do you mean by we?)

    3. eye contact

    4. expressiveness

III. Identifying Problems or Questions

    1. students ask own questions

    2. students share the problem or question

    3. students identify tentative answers or solutions

    4. students select ideal solution

    5. students identify requirements for the ideal solution

    6. students discuss what solution is available to the class

The implications of choice primarily pertain to goal setting. The content of shared communication is the beginning of pupil-teacher planning. Student choice is exercised with respect to activities which extend meaning or initiate investigations of questions or problems. The student and teacher may collaborate on structuring procedures through which the child can attain self-selected goals. An important resource for goal setting is the *Individually Guided Motivation* (IGM) program which was developed by the Wisconsin Research and Development Center (Klausmeier, 1972). *Organizing for Independent Learning* developed by the Far West Research and Development Laboratory (Borg, 1971) suggests organizational skills necessary for goal setting. Also, Madan Mohan's article in Section V of this volume will be helpful. In short, goal setting and instructional skills enhance student choice and their concomitant motivation in the open education classroom. The IGM program includes the following procedures.

IGM Conference Procedure

A. Opening

    1. Explain to the child that you are going to try a new way of working together and describe the goal-setting conferences. Ask questions to make sure the child understands.

    2. Tell the child that you will be meeting weekly.

    3. Give concrete examples of goals and ask the child to remember goals he has set in the past, e.g., getting to school

at a certain time, completing a school activity by a certain time, etc. Ask questions to make sure the child understands what a goal is.

B. Goal Setting

1. Look at the child when either of you speak.

2. Discuss the subject matter to be studied. Help the child recall what he already knows about the subject matter.

3. Give specific examples of the concepts and skills to be learned.

4. Explain the goal checklist.

5. Using the goal checklist, show how the subject matter has been broken down in small steps that can be learned in a short time.

6. Discuss with the student possible goals for him and help him decide which he wants to accomplish. Give as much direction as necessary.

7. Ask the child to state his goals aloud, i.e., which of the items on the goal checklist he will try to complete by the next conference.

8. Ask the child to check a copy of the goal checklist to help remember his goals. Check a second copy for your records.

C. Relating Goals to the Regular Instructional Program

1. Ask the child when he will start to work on his goals and whether he will work on them each day.

2. Suggest instructional material that might be used to help the child reach his goals.

3. Discuss with the child independent work and work with other children or his parents that might help him reach his goals.

4. Tell the child how the regular instructional program will provide an opportunity for him to reach his goals.

D. Closing

1. Encourage the child to remember his goals and to work on them during the week.

2. Have the child keep his copy of the goal checklist and show him how to use it. Suggest other ways for helping the student remember his goals if this seems necessary.

3. Tell the child when and where the next conference will be and what you will be doing at that conference.

The implications of values are with respect to the pupil-teacher reflection and teacher skill with the clarifying response. The clarifying response is generally a question intended to stimulate the learners to think about what they are really doing, saying, or being. These open-ended questions do not require the child to deliver a "right" answer, yet they enable him to reflect upon the worth and consequences of thoughts and deeds to self and others. However, in the process of reflection the child's purpose or purposes are increasingly clear. Examples of the clarifying response from *Values and Teaching* by Louis E. Raths and others (1966) are listed below.

The Clarifying Response

1. Is this something that you prize? Are you proud of that? Is that something that is important to you?
2. Are you glad about that?
3. How did you feel when that happened?
4. Did you consider any alternatives?
5. Have you felt this way for a long time? When did you first begin to believe in that idea? How have your ideas changed since you first considered the matter?
6. Was that something that you yourself chose?
7. Did you have to choose that; was it a free choice?
8. Do you do anything about the idea? How does that idea affect your daily life?
9. Can you give me some examples of that idea?
10. What do you mean by . . . ?
11. Where would that idea lead? How would that work out in practice?
12. Would you really do that or are you just talking?
13. Are you saying that . . . (repeat)?
14. Did you say that . . . (repeat in distorted way to see if child attempts to correct the distortion)?
15. Have you thought much about that idea (or behavior)?
16. What are some good things about that notion?
17. What do we have to know for things to work out that way?
18. Is that what you said earlier about . . . (note some-

thing else the child said or did that may point to an inconsistency)?

19. What other ways are there?

20. Is that a personal preference or do you think most people should believe that? Is this idea so good that everyone should go along with it?

21. What seems to be the difficulty? Where are you stuck? What is holding you up?

22. Is there a purpose back of this activity?

23. Is that very important to you?

24. Do you do this often?

25. Would you like to tell others about your idea?

26. Do you have any reasons for (saying or doing) that?

27. Would you do the same thing over again?

28. How do you know it's right?

29. Do you value that? Is that something that you value?

30. Do you think people will always believe that? Did people long ago believe that?

The initiation of an open education program is possible to the extent that teachers possess the skills of communication and goal setting. A total change to open education, however, is seldom possible because most teachers alter their instructional procedures slowly. In addition, the instructional processes of communication and goal setting also require a firm understanding of the interactive structures of children's developmental processes. Therefore, it is generally advisable that change to an open education program be initiated gradually. In this manner the skills of communication and goal setting can be initiated in one content area at a time.

The outcomes desired of open education are those characterized by a self-directed student within a culture. The developmental stage perspective holds that a self-directed student in any culture is hopeful, willful, purposeful, and competent. Hope is a function of mutuality in communications. Will is a function of participative decision making. Purpose is a function of reflection. Competence is a function of activity with the conventions and processes of the disciplines. Evaluation of an open education program must first focus upon the degree to which communication, decision making, reflection, and the conventions or processes of subject matter are evident in the teaching-learning interaction. And, second, a student assessment must be made with respect to the values of hope, will, purpose, competence, subject matter, and content. Diagramatically the evaluation would account for the process variables as tentatively outlined in the four scales below. In addition, individual and group competence should be assessed through criterion-referenced and standardized tests.

Open Education Assessment

Communication Characteristics

Teacher telling and informing	Teacher explaining	Teacher-pupil discussion or recall	Teacher seeks student comprehension	Verification of mutual communication

Goal Setting

Assignments– no alternative	Assignments to group or individuals	Teacher structured alternatives	Teacher-pupil structured alternatives	Teacher-pupil structured alternatives derived from shared comm.

Reflection

Grades paper error corrected	Explains evaluations	Teacher-pupil discussion of evaluations	Teacher-pupil or group reflection of product worth to self and others	Individual & group teacher-pupil reflection of product worth to self & others with respect to goals

Competence

Below class norm on assignment	Below norm performance on group assignments	Normative performance on individual group or class assignment	Above normative performance on individual, group, or class alternative	Task accomplishment with respect to goal setting process

The instructional steps suggested in this paper for open education will result in an instructional program which will meet the unique needs of individuals. The communication skills enable the teacher and pupil to share and build upon common meaning. Choice through goal setting insures that the child is attending to his goals and that activity and productivity are related. The clarifying response serves to further stimulate the children to define their purposes and to benefit from the unique manner by which a group of students contributes to the class.

In short, open education may be defined, initiated, and evaluated with respect to the quality of instruction pertaining to communicating, goal setting, reflection, and subject matter.

This article was specially written for this book of readings at the request of the editors. Dr. Petrie is an Associate Professor—Research at SUC, Fredonia, New York.

Notes

1. Fetherstone, Joseph. "The British and Us." *The New Republic,* September 11, 1971, p. 23.

2. Piaget, Jean. *Science of Education and the Psychology of the Child.* New York: Orion Press, 1970.

3. Evans, Richard. *Dialogue with Erik Erikson.* New York: E. P. Dutton and Co., Inc., 1969.

4. Clark, Margaret et. al. *The Learning Encounter.* Westminster, Maryland: Random House, 1971.

5. Klausmeier, Herbert J. et. al. *Individually Guided Motivation.* Wisconsin Research and Development Center, Madison, Wisconsin, 1972.

6. Borg, Walter. *Independent Learning.* Far West Laboratory for Educational Research and Development, Berkeley, California, 1971 (Draft).

7. Raths, Louis E. et. al. *Teaching for Values.* Columbus, Ohio: Charles E. Merrill Publishing Co., 1966.

11

A Pupil-Oriented and Individualized System of Education (POISE Model)

John B. Bouchard & Kenneth G. Nelson

The major purpose of the POISE Model is to propose a reorganization of the school environment which promises a better approach for meeting the interests, capabilities and needs of individual pupils than the traditional self-contained classroom organization. The installation of the Model promises to:

1. maximize opportunities for each student to be thought of and treated as an individual.

2. redirect major staff interest and effort from group-subject orientation to the capabilities, interests, and needs of individual pupils.

3. redistribute, and supplement where necessary, curriculum and instructional materials to meet the demands of an individualized rather than a group-centered educational program.

4. reallocate and modify where necessary, school facilities to permit the implementation of the proposed reorganization.

A Definition of Individualization

The concept of individualization as used in the POISE Model implies that:

1. direction of the teaching-learning process will come from the study and awareness of individual pupils.

2. pupil-selected and/or teacher-assigned learning experiences will be related to the individual child's level of mastery and interest.

3. determination of staff responsibilities for individualizing instruction will come from the study and awareness of the capabilities and interests of individual members of the staff.

4. reports of pupil progress will relate to the individual's specific performance on self-chosen and/or assigned learning tasks.

It may be prudent to indicate also that *Individualization,* as used in the POISE Model, does *not* imply an educational program in which each child's learning experiences are provided solely via a one-to-one pupil-teacher ratio. Efficient though it may prove to be, the POISE Model cannot conceivably be manipulated to produce such results. While it may well be that the most effective education for a given child, in terms of his optimum development, is achievable only through a one-to-one tutor-pupil relationship, such an arrangement appears to be beyond the resources of any school.

The hypothesis has been made that the POISE Model does appear to facilitate the use of one-to-one pupil-teacher learning experiences more so than the self-contained classroom organization. This seems to be particularly promising in such areas as the learning skills, where available individualized curriculum materials can be identified. It also appears to be possible to increase teacher efficiency, and at the same time treat individual children's needs, by grouping small numbers of pupils who are at the same level of mastery in a particular skill. Small groups with similar interests and needs should be more readily available from a pool of 150 pupils rather than from a self-contained class of 25 youngsters. The POISE Model does *not* preclude the use of small and large groups as appropriate and effective instructional procedures.

Essential Components of the Model

1. Curriculum decision making responsibilities which include:

a. at the instructional *team level*—the selection and assignment of all pupil learning experiences for which the school is accountable such as: skills, knowledge, performance, attitudes, values.

b. at the *school level*—the coordination of curriculum decisions made by the various instructional teams within the school.

c. at the *system level*—the coordination of curriculum decisions made among the various schools.

2. The development of a school information system to provide data which will distinguish:

a. *each pupil* in terms of his present levels of attainment, his potential for further learning, his special interests, his attitudes toward learning, his values, his work habits, and the effectiveness of his learning under alternative instructional procedures.

b. *each member* of the staff in terms of his special curriculum competencies, his preferences and skills in a variety of instructional procedures, and his effectiveness in working with various kinds of learners.

c. *a hierarchy of educational objectives* and means for their assessment in those areas of the cognitive and affective domains for which the school assumes responsibility so that each pupil can achieve an optimum level of growth in terms of his unique characteristics.

3. The development of an individualized reporting system which will, at established times during the school year, or upon special request, inform each student and his parents:

a. of his success in achieving the specific behavioral objectives established for him by the instructional staff.

b. about the effectiveness of his performance under alternative instructional procedures.

4. A system of instruction which seeks optimum individualization through the:

a. development and use of specific behavioral objectives for each child which are based on his present level of attainment, his rate of learning and his potential for growth.

b. identification and use of those pupil-teacher relationships which are most effective for each child (tutoring; mastery-level groups; peer teaching; independent study; pupil contracts; interest groups).

  c. identification and use of those motivational procedures which are most effective for each child (praise, knowledge of progress; cooperation; competition; ego involvement).

  d. identification and use of instructional equipment and materials which are most effective for each child (audio; visual; manipulative; multi-media).

  5. The development of differentiated staff roles which will:

  a. identify and implement the staff functions and assignments required in the individualization of instruction for all school personnel (administrative staff; supervision staff; instructional leaders; team teachers; special subject teachers; student personnel staff; internees and student teachers; teacher aides; other paraprofessionals).

  b. permit staff members to develop and use special talents for instructional skills (preparation; assessment; presentation; reporting).

  c. facilitate the induction of new staff and the retraining of present staff.

  6. Assignment of learners to an ungraded instructional pool (75–150 pupils) to provide flexibility in scheduling individualized, small group, and large group learning experiences for such pupils.

  7. Space and facilities which provide for:

  a. scheduling needs for individual, small group, and large group instruction.

  b. the development and use of a library and an instructional resources center.

  c. the use of a wide variety of instructional materials and equipment.

  8. A high degree of school-community involvement which will:

  a. identify representatives from both the community and the school for the cooperative planning of the school program.

  b. identify and use individuals and community resources for the enrichment of the curriculum and the instructional program.

  c. report progress in the development of the model program to the school board, parents, and other community agencies.

    d. establish cooperative working relationships with parent groups and other interested community organizations and agencies for the continuous development of the model program.

Staff Participation in Curriculum Decision-Making

One of the fundamental realities which must be faced by the professional staff in a POISE school is that curriculum scope and sequence is no longer neatly arranged by placing each student in a compartmentalized group and expecting him to proceed, step by step, through a chosen text. The staff's role in curriculum decision making constitutes one of the most significant elements of the proposed school reorganization—it involves a continuing planned effort to adjust curriculum and learning experiences to the needs, interests, and capabilities of students. The following are among the important guidelines which should direct the professional staff in its discharge of their important responsibility:

Limits of Decision-Making for the Staff

It is recommended that curriculum decisions be made *within* the areas of the cognitive and affective domains for which the school has assumed responsibility.

Planned Systems for Curriculum Decision-Making

It is recommended that consideration in the skill subjects be first given to highly individualized curriculum programs such as the *Wisconsin Design for Reading Skill Development* (20), or the *Pittsburgh Individually Prescribed Program in Mathematics* (12). If these or similar programs cannot be implemented, the instructional staff may approach individualization by increasing the number of skill levels from one for each of the previously established grades to as many as can be identified.

Curriculum Areas in Which Individualization Will Be Stressed

It is recommended that a school entering into the POISE Model attempt to individualize instruction in one area only during the first year. Since reading is a basic tool, it presents a good first entry into individualization efforts.

During the second year mathematics may well be added
and individualization also undertaken in one of the content
areas such as the social studies.

Adjustment of the Curriculum to the Individual

The professional staff, in the exercise of its curriculum
decision-making responsibilities, must be prepared to
make frequent and sometimes dramatic departures from
conventional curriculum practices. The following are illustrative of such departures:

1. Different children at the same "grade level" will be
provided widely differing learning experiences and substantial departures from the "pre-set" curriculum.

2. Instructional groups may, by virtue of similarity of
interest, ability, and performance level of their members,
be composed of children of different "grade levels."

3. Instructional groups studying the same curriculum
topics may use learning experiences and materials of
widely differentiated levels of difficulty.

4. It may become necessary to postpone or waive
curriculum "requirements" for some children.

5. Although such may not be appropriate for most
pupils, it may be necessary to utilize special personnel,
resources, and facilities in the provision of unique curriculum and learning experiences for some of the children
enrolled.

It is readily apparent that the professional staff, in order
to discharge its curriculum decision-making responsibilities, must have time in which to do so. The following
procedures are suggested:

1. An intensive study of the curriculum offerings of the
school, and the diagnostic data available concerning pupil
capabilities, interests, and needs must be undertaken prior
to entry in the POISE Program.

2. Plans must be established for the continued development of a comprehensive information system using college and university consultants as resources.

3. A minimum two-hour planning time, during which
all professional staff are available, must be scheduled
weekly. This may be accomplished by varying opening and
closing times, and the length of the school day.

4. Daily planning time is essential and is readily

achieved for at least part of the professional staff through the flexibility of the POISE Model itself.

Levels of Curriculum Decision Making

Curriculum decisions must be made at three levels:

1. At the *team level* the instructional staff, with the assistance of the unit leader and the principal, will select and assign all pupil learning experiences which are the responsibility of the school.

2. At the *school level* the unit leaders and the principal will coordinate the curriculum decisions made by the various units.

3. At the *system level* the principals and other selected representatives from the system-wide staff will coordinate the curriculum decisions made among the schools.

The Instructional Information System Required for the Effective Individualization of Instruction

In order to achieve the most effective interaction between learners and their instructors, it is essential that carefully planned informational systems be developed. The following guidelines are offered:

The Objectives of an Information System Designed to Promote Individualized Instruction

As a result of the information system designed to promote the effective individualization of instruction, data will be available:

1. To distinguish each learner in terms of his unique capabilities, interests and needs.

2. To help the professional staff make decisions concerning the learning experiences to be provided for each student such as:

    a. what he learns

    b. when the learning is introduced

    c. how he learns

    d. his rate of learning

    e. his optimum level of learning

3. To help the professional staff constantly reassess and report the progress of each student in terms of his unique capabilities, interests and needs.

The Nature of the Information Sought for
Individualization of Instruction

In order for the instructional staff to make sound decisions in the individualization of instruction, an information system must provide data which:

1. Distinguishes each pupil in terms of his present level of attainment, his potential for further learning, his special interests, his attitudes toward learning, his values, his work habits, and the effectiveness of his learning under alternative instructional procedures.

2. Distinguishes each member of the school staff in terms of his special curriculum competencies, his preferences and skills in a variety of instructional procedures, his effectiveness in working with various kinds of learners.

3. Distinguishes a hierarchy of educational objectives and means of their assessment in those areas of the cognitive and affective domains for which the school assumes responsibility so that each pupil can achieve an optimum level of growth in terms of his unique capabilities, interests and needs.

A Pupil Information System for Individualized
Instruction

The kind of pupil data required may be identified within such broad areas as skills, content, processes, interests, values, and attitudes.

1. *The Skills*
For the skill subjects the pupil information must provide data which:

a. distinguishes the individual learner's initial status in the skills

b. identifies particular obstacles to his learning

c. helps establish appropriate behavioral objectives

d. helps identify alternative educational experiences

e. helps in the selection of the most appropriate alternative

f. helps in the assessment of pupil progress in the attainment of the specified behavioral objective.

2. *The Content Subjects*
Despite the complexities presented by the content areas, there appears to be certain kinds of pupil information

which will greatly facilitate the individualization of instruction. Such data may include information concerning:

a. the learner's past performance in the subject

b. the learner's special interest in topics within the subject

c. the selections for study made by the learner

d. the learner's ability to cope with the instructional materials available

e. the individual's potential level of growth in the subject.

3. *The Pupil and Various Instructional Alternatives*

An information system designed to promote individualized instruction should also provide data concerning each pupil's preference for and effectiveness in using various instructional alternatives. Such data may include information about:

a. the learner's preference for such instructional modes as tutoring, membership in a small group, peer teaching, independent study.

b. the effectiveness of such various instructional modes as those above in bringing about the objectives sought for the learner.

c. the learner's preference for instructional materials and equipment (tape recorders, filmstrips, concrete materials, texts, etc.).

d. the effectiveness of various instructional materials in bringing about the desired outcomes for the learner.

e. the effectiveness of various motivational techniques on bringing about the desired outcome for the learner (praise, reproof, immediate knowledge of progress, extrinsic rewards, etc.).

A Staff Information System for Individualized Instruction

In order to effectively achieve optimum utilization of each staff member, a staff information system is required. Such a system will provide data to identify:

1. the special subject matter, interests and competencies of individual members of the team.

2. preferences for and effectiveness in using such instructional modes as tutoring, small group instruction, large

group instruction, peer instruction, individual pupil contracts.

3. preferences for and effectiveness in using such instructional skills as:

a. planning instruction for individuals, small groups,
large groups, independent study.

b. presenting instruction for individuals, small
groups, large groups, independent study.

c. development and use of observation and evaluation techniques for the diagnosis of individual pupil progress.

d. development and use of procedures for the induction of other members of the team.

e. development and use of effective procedures for
reporting the progress of individual children.

f. development and use of effective procedures for
informing and working with the community for the further
enhancement of instruction.

Some Practical Considerations in the Development of an Information System to Promote Individualization of Instruction

Several suggestions may facilitate such development:

1. Start in a skill area, such as reading or mathematics.

2. Use available individualized curriculum systems.

3. Use consultants from colleges and universities.

4. Devote a portion of staff planning time made available through large group instruction and independent pupil
study to the development of the information system.

5. Hold at least one fifteen minute conference weekly
conducted by a member of the instructional team for each
pupil in the instructional unit. Discuss and record progress,
interests, attitudes, proposed learning experiences.

6. The benefits derived from a good information system
are accumulative; once a part of the system is developed it
becomes less difficult to add other parts to the system.

Planning and Using Procedures for Individualizing Instruction

There are many possible procedures for individualizing
instruction. Some of the most promising are discussed
below.

At a practical level, teachers have long sought to cope with the problems and needs of individual pupils through tutoring, small group instruction, use of peer instructors, independent study and by differentiating assignments. Independent study is even possible in large groups through the use of highly individualized curriculums and an adequate number of monitors for checking the progress of each child. The *Individually Prescribed Instruction* (IPI) Program in Mathematics developed at the Learning Research and Development Center at the University of Pittsburgh (12) is a good example of individualization in a large group setting.

Schools which undertake the individualization of instruction as a major goal can make progress toward the realization of that goal through adjustment of:

1. A pupil's rate of progress.
2. Instructional modes.
3. Curriculum expectations.
4. Curriculum materials.

Individualization May be Achieved Through Adjusting a Pupil's Rate of Progress

Recently, John Carroll of Harvard University, in his "A Model of School Learning," (6) expressed the conviction that nearly all students enrolled in a school can achieve basic understanding of required learnings through adjustment of time. His model includes five elements—three which relate to the individual and two which come from external conditions.

Individual factors are:

1. the amount of time the learner requires to accomplish the task under desirable conditions of instruction

2. the learner's ability to understand instruction, and

3. the amount of time the learner is willing to devote to the task.

External conditions are:

4. the opportunity and time allowed for the individual's learning, and

5. the effectiveness of instruction.

Individualization Through Adjustment of Instructional Mode

These instructional modes can be identified as individualization of instruction through:

1. a teacher-pupil tutorial situation.
2. the use of small instructional groups.
3. the use of class sized or larger groups.
4. the use of other pupils as teachers—e.g., peer instruction.
5. independent pupil study, pupil contracts, or differentiated assignments.
6. the use of parents, community resource personnel.

Individualization Through Variations in Curriculum Expectation

Unfortunately, in most schools, the curriculum is typically aimed not at individual differences but at types of group differences. So-called "curriculum differentiations" usually involve the establishment of ability groups which pursue substantially the same curriculum at different rates and in different amounts according to the average, slow, or accelerated nature of the ability group.

There are exciting possibilities for the individualization of instruction through the variation of curriculum expectations for individual children. Perhaps the greatest obstacle to curriculum adaptation to individual pupil capabilities, interests, and needs is the lack of courage on the part of teachers to make such changes.

Even if the school is reluctant to permit its staff to cross content boundaries established for study from one "grade level" to another, teachers still can make decisions within the content frame which will go far more in the direction of individualization of instruction than is typical in the traditional school at the present time.

Achieving Individualized Instruction Through Variations in Instructional Materials

In recent years the schools have been virtually deluged by the appearance of innumerable new instructional materials and equipment. Recently, attention has been directed toward the use of instructional materials as a means of individualizing instruction. There is little question but that the many kinds of instructional materials now available in the schools do provide exciting new opportunities for learning for individual children. Such possibilities appear to be limited only by the imagination of the teachers and the pupils whom they instruct. No longer is there an excuse for the youngster who cannot read to sit idly at his desk while awaiting his "turn" with the teacher. Such a youngster can be guided to the school's instructional resource center and provided with single concept filmstrips which will communicate effectively to him the knowledge which is denied him via the usual route in reading. Portable tape recorders provide some excellent opportunities for peer instruction.

Differentiated Staff Roles

The specialization of staff roles in POISE follows closely the Individually Guided Education and the Multiunit School Model (14).

The Principal

The principal is an integral part of the basic unit instructional team. His most important responsibility is to provide leadership in curriculum decisions and instruction. Where a school contains both the basic POISE unit and the traditional self-contained classrooms, he will have the responsibility of coordinating the differing demands of both types of organizations on the school's facilities and resources. Where an entire school program is organized as a POISE Model, he will have the responsibility of coordinating the efforts of Unit Leaders within his school and communicating the school's efforts to appropriate system-wide authorities.

The Unit Leader

The Unit Leaders are directly responsible for the planning and implementation of the learning-experiences to be provided by the instructional team for the children enrolled in the instructional unit. This professional leader has approximately half-time teaching responsibilities and is also provided release time for planning. To avoid possible conflict with the principal's leadership status in the school, it appears to be important that no administrative authority over personnel be assigned to the Unit Leader. In recognition of the additional responsibilities such an individual assumes, however, it seems appropriate to suggest extra compensation for the Unit Leader.

Teachers

Appropriately certified teachers should be available as members of the instructional team in a ratio of approximately one teacher to every twenty-five pupils enrolled. At the elementary school level, the instructional team will be drawn from teachers normally assigned to self-contained classrooms. At the secondary level the instructional team will include those teachers normally assigned to classes serving the students now enrolled in the instructional unit.

Also included on the instructional team are the professional staff members typically described as "special" teachers in the traditional school organization (e.g., music, physical education, art, pupil personnel staff, etc.).

Each teacher member of the instructional team should assign highest priority to the responsibility for providing, in accordance with his special talents and capabilities, individualized instruction to some or all of the pupils assigned to the instructional unit. Other professional responsibilities include participation in the cooperative planning of the instructional program and discharging an appropriate share of the professional obligation identified as a result of such planning.

Special Non-Professional Aides

Two special non-professional assistants are suggested to enhance the operation of the instructional team; these are the clerical aide and the instructional aide. There appears to be little question but that the successful operation of the instructional unit will require substantial increases over the operation of a traditional school program in such services as preparation of lesson plans and daily schedules and the identification, procurement, use and return of differentiated instructional materials.

It is suggested that careful consideration be given to the appointment of both a clerical assistant and an instructional media assistant to every instructional unit on the grounds that such aides permit the teacher members of the instructional team to concentrate their time and effort on the professional tasks of planning, presentation, assessment, guidance and reporting.

Other Members of the Instructional Team

It is considered essential that arrangements be made to provide systematic and continuous college or university consultative services to members of the instructional team. Such consultants should be thoroughly familiar with the POISE program and be prepared to render such assistance as the following: continuous evaluation of the operational success of the model; in-service education programs; guidance in curriculum development; assistance in developing an information system to promote individualization; identification, procurement, and use of newly developed instructional materials for the individualization of instruction.

The Assignment of Learners to an Ungraded Instructional Pool (75-150 Pupils)

In the POISE Model the assumption is made that the capabilities, interests and needs of individual children cannot be well served if pupils are assigned, on a permanent basis, to stable learning groups. Instead, the most flexible pupil assignment procedures possible in the school must be sought to provide, on a daily basis if necessary, for the wide ranges in pupil performances as well as styles and rates of learning which exist among student populations. The basic model provides for the establishment of a pool of approximately 75-150 pupils who may be either of the same age-grade level or different age-grade levels.

Wherever possible, it is urged that the ungraded instructional pool be formed by grouping together youngsters of several age levels rather than one. This organization is much more consistent with the underlying philosophy of the POISE Model that there are wide but overlapping differences in achievement among youngsters of all grade levels. If horizontal groups are used, they may "lock in" class instruction in such subjects as the social studies and science for groups of children formed for learning the basic skills.

Depending on the size of the school, the interests of the staff and other factors, such groupings as the following may be chosen from the usual grade levels:

K-5	K-3 and 4-6
K-6	K, 1-3 and 4-6

Appropriate School Facilities

In order to implement a basic unit of the POISE Model, a school should be able to provide minimum physical facilities such as the following:

1. Space and stations for individualized instruction on a one-to-one pupil-teacher ratio, or for small groups.

2. Sufficient classroom spaces for small group instruction.

3. A classroom area or other suitable space sufficiently large to accommodate the total group of 75-150 pupils.

4. A school library sufficiently large and well-equipped to be used for small group instruction and independent study.

5. A materials resources center to provide a wide variety of audiovisual equipment and materials of instruction. This center should be sufficiently large to accommodate several instructional groups and pupils with independent studies at the same time.

Community Involvement in the POISE Model

It must be remembered that the schools belong to the people and that, before substantial departures from the existing program are undertaken, public approval is required. Once approval is secured, and the innovative program is mounted, constant feedback must be provided to the community as the program matures.

It is readily admitted that the dramatic restructuring

and redirection of the school called for in the POISE Model poses many questions for which there are only partial answers at the present time. The proposed model calls for fundamental changes in the attitudes and behaviors of teachers and other school personnel in order that each child may be treated as an important, unique human being. Such changes can take place only when there is heavy community involvement in the school. Better school-community communication is but one small part of this involvement. Parents and other community representatives must take active roles in planning the changes, in identifying the community resources which can contribute to the school curriculum, and participate in the enrichment of instruction.

There is little doubt that the proposed model will be further refined and developed as supportive research provides data for better and more complete answers to the many problems which can be raised.

This article is an abbreviated version of the POISE Model Working Paper published for discussion purposes by the Teacher Education Research Center, SUC, Fredonia, January, 1971. John B. Bouchard is Professor of Education and Kenneth G. Nelson is Director, Teacher Education Research Center, SUC, Fredonia, New York.

Selected Bibliography

1. Anderson, Robert H. *Bibliography on Organizational Trends in Schools*. Washington, D.C.: Center for the Study of Instruction, National Education Association, 1968.

2. Anderson, Robert H., and Pavan, Barbara. "Facilitating Individualized Instruction Through Flexible School Organization." Unpublished memorandum. Harvard University, Graduate School of Education, January 26, 1970.

3. Bloom, Benjamin S. (Ed.); Englehart, Max D.; Furst, Edward J.; Hill, Walker H.; and Krathwohl, David R. *A Taxonomy of Educational Objectives: Handbook I, The Cognitive Domain*. New York: Longmans, Green and Co., 1956.

4. Borg, Walter R.; Kelley, Marjorie; Langer, Philip; and Gall, Meredith. *The Minicourse–A Microteaching Approach to Teacher Education.* Beverly Hills, California: MacMillan Educational Services, 1970.

5. Bouchard, John B., "Overview and Meaning of Individualized Instruction," in *Selected Papers: Summer Workship in Individualization of Instruction,* Teacher Education Research Center, State University College at Fredonia, New York, December, 1970.

6. Carroll, John B., "A Model of School Learning," *Teachers College Record.* LXIV, 1963, 723–733.

7. "Catalog of Objective Collections." Box 24095, Los Angeles, California: The Instructional Objectives Exchange.

8. *Children and their Primary Schools: A Report of the Central Advisory Council for Education,* Vol. I, London: H.M.S.O., 1967.

9. Flanagan, John C., "Project PLAN: Basic Assumptions, Implementation and Significance." Paper presented at American Educational Research Association, Minneapolis, March 1970.

10. Gibbons, Maurice, "What is Individualized Instruction?" *Interchange—A Journal of Educational Studies,* I, No. 2, 1970, 28–32.

11. Goodlad, John I., and Anderson, Robert H. *The Non-graded Elementary School.* New York: Harcourt, Brace and World, 1959.

12. "Individually Prescribed Instruction." Learning Research and Development Center of the University of Pittsburgh, and Research for Better Schools, Inc., Philadelphia, Pennsylvania, n.d.

13. Klausmeier, Herbert J.; Schwenn, Elizabeth A.; and Lamal, Peter A.; "A System of Individually Guided Motivation." Practical Paper No. 9. Wisconsin Research and Development Center for Cognitive Learning, the University of Wisconsin, 1969.

14. Klausmeier, Herbert J.; Morrow, Richard G.; and Walter, James E.; "Individually Guided Education in the Multiunit Elementary School—Guidelines for Implementation." Bulletin 9-168. Wisconsin Research and Development Center for Cognitive Learning, the University of Wisconsin, n.d.

15. Krathwohl, David R.; Bloom, Benjamin S.; and Masia, Bertram. *A Taxonomy of Educational Objectives, Handbook II, The Affective Domain.* New York: David McKay & Co., Inc., 1964.

16. "Learning Activity Packages" (LAPS). Nova Schools, Fort Lauderdale, Florida, n.d.

17. Mitzel, Harold E., "The Impending Instruction Revolution," *Phi Delta Kappan*, LI, No. 8, April 1970, 434–439.

18. National Society for the Study of Education. Sixty-First Yearbook, Part I. *Individualizing Instruction.* Chicago: University of Chicago Press, 1962.

19. "Some Organizational Characteristics of Multiunit Schools." Address by Roland J. Pelligrin with responses by Allen T. Slagel and Lloyd N. Johansen. Working Paper No. 22, Joint Publication of the Wisconsin Research and Development Center for Cognitive Learning, the University of Wisconsin, Madison, Wisconsin, and Center for the Advanced Study of Educational Administration, the University of Oregon, Eugene, Oregon, June, 1969.

20. "Wisconsin Design for Reading Skill Development," Wisconsin Research and Development Center for Cognitive Learning, University of Wisconsin, n.d.

SECTION III

Organizing for
Individualization

Experience in working with school staffs that are studying and implementing programs of individualized instruction has taught us that organizing for individualization is a primary concern. Although teachers have been able to carry out some degree of individualization in the self-contained classroom, possibilities for facilitating individualization are enhanced when educators are able to move from traditional age-grade arrangements to a variety of other organizational procedures. Thus, the articles included in this section are directed at organizational arrangement which transcends the self-contained classroom. The articles are arranged from the general to the specific in terms of organizing variables of time, space, personnel, subject matter, and resources for attaining the goal of individualized instruction.

In his article, "Differentiated Staffing: Is It Worth the Risk?," Roy A. Edelfelt presents an objective view of the benefits and the possible pitfalls of differentiated staffing. Long-range benefits of differentiated staffing are discussed especially with regard to preparation of the instructional staff for the instruction of youngsters. Edelfelt warns that differentiated staffing, as well as other new ideas in education, requires risk taking on the part of educators. He also makes the point that some additional resources may be required to implement a program of differentiated staffing

David Pryke offers a thoughtful perspective in his article, "On Team Teaching." His basic premise is that team teaching is organization which should always be subservient to the aims of the school program. He stipulates that an important aim of education should be to facilitate cooperation rather than competition, and he offers the concept of teaming as a means to stimulate cooperation, both among staff members and among children. Pryke suggests some concrete examples of organizing the curriculum timetable for achieving the goals of developing children's basic skills, receiving facts and information, and exploring and building upon personal interests. Pryke thinks that unless a teacher has a special talent to offer, his place on a team will be of doubtful value. This has ramifications for selection of new staff and assignment of staff to various teaming situations.

Wilma H. Miller's article, "Some Less Commonly

Used Forms of Grouping," describes forms of grouping which facilitate individualization and go beyond the typical reading-ability grouping which is used most often by classroom teachers. She suggests some advantages of organizing for less commonly used forms of grouping such as needs groups, interest groups, research groups, tutorial groups, the Joplin Plan, departmentalized teaching, the ungraded primary plan, multigrade and multiage grouping, and the dual progress plan. Dr. Miller also indicates which grade levels and which situations seem most amenable for selection of a particular grouping mode.

In the article, "Teaching in Small Groups," Robert N. Bush avers that the purpose of teaching in small groups is to open wide the channels of communication amongst the members of the group. This requires a teacher who is trained to put ideas on the table and to listen to what others have to say. Dr. Bush thinks small-group leaders should take a nondirective stance once the group members begin to get involved. Continued stimulation of discussion, however, may be necessary and often the teacher must improvise as the discussion continues. Small-group discussion properly proceeds from the nature of the group and the problems and the ideas that emerge from the group.

Madan Mohan in his article, "Organizing Peer Tutoring In Our Schools," suggests that schools should make use of the older and/or brighter students to implement individualized instruction programs. Some of the steps that a teacher must be acquainted with are elaborated in the article. The author feels that effective peer tutoring can facilitate learning and motivate children.

Inasmuch as the development of self-directed learners is an ultimate goal of individualization, we have included Willard J. Congreve's article, *Independent Learning*. Dr. Congreve provides for the reader an optimistic report of a three year project in which he and his staff at the Chicago Laboratory High School have devised and field tested a systematic independent learning program. The article makes very clear that much staff interaction was required in order to mount the independent learning program. His data revealed that independence and self-direction can be taught and that students can at the same time make satisfactory achievement in subject matter. Although the study was conducted at the secondary level, the process used in developing a system of independent study seems viable for trial at other levels of education. Dr. Congreve believes that final evaluation of his project will provide a basis for his recommending that independent learning be a major curricular goal for all schools.

12

Differentiated Staffing: Is It Worth the Risk?

Roy A. Edelfelt

Since the advent of professional negotiations, there has been a perceptible shift in the balance of power in education, bringing the local association into much greater prominence. The newfound influence of the local association has been wielded largely to improve the economic welfare of teachers. However, local associations have recently begun to give attention to negotiation for non-economic matters. These are less tangible than economic welfare but perhaps more far-reaching in their impact on American education. Among the professional concerns which might be considered in this new thrust in negotiations is differentiated staffing. The concept (as defined below) has only caught the interest of educators in the last year or two, but it has achieved a distinct notoriety in that brief time. The notoriety grows from conflicting perceptions of what the concept will produce in practice: it could be used to exploit teachers but it might also make dramatic improvements in the schools. If such diverse outcomes are possible, it is crucial that teachers become well acquainted with the concept of differentiated staffing.

What Is Differentiated Staffing?

Differentiated staffing is an outgrowth and refinement of

team teaching and "the teacher and his staff" idea, both of which propose the use of auxiliary personnel in the schools to relieve teachers of their nonteaching tasks and recognize a diversity of teaching tasks. Differentiated staffing goes a step further to suggest that teaching be differentiated into various roles and responsibilities (more than a vertical heirarchy) to allow for the different interests, abilities, and ambitions of teachers. It calls for differentiating salary in terms of the responsibilities assumed and allows for both a training and a career ladder.

Why Differentiate Staffing?

Differentiated staffing could provide more manpower to diversify and individualize programs, offering alternative modes of participation in the instructional process. It could encourage varied utilization of manpower as an alternative to the uniform assignments now assumed by teachers. It could enhance teaching as a career by providing possibilities for growth in responsibility with commensurate rewards. It could provide a ladder in teacher education, eliminating the dichotomy between preservice and inservice.

Events of the last decade have demonstrated the inadequacy of schools as they are. Schools are having to reassess the needs and interests of learners in the context of an ever more unpredictable future. For the children of the 60's and beyond, learning in school is only a beginning. Today's children need preparation for a lifetime of learning and must nurture and develop the desire to learn and the skills to follow through on it. A daily fare of instruction in large groups, oriented to facts and subjects, is hardly conducive to the development of these wherewithals. Yet diversification and individualization of program clearly mean more manpower for the schools, at a time when the demand for qualified teachers already outstrips the supply. Thus education would appear to be on the classic horns of a dilemma.

On closer examination, however, the dilemma is not so distressing. The "shortage" of manpower in education may be a misnomer, the real problem may be the inefficient use of manpower. To explain, one major reason for the present manpower shortage is teacher drop-outs. Each year 30% of trained graduates fail to enter the profession and 8% of experienced professionals leave it. As a career, teaching lacks holding power. Why? As presently structured, schools offer only one basic instructional position and one basic salary schedule. Maximum responsibility for teachers is reached too soon, and the ceiling on salary is too low. Teachers who want and have the potential to assume greater responsibility must either seek promotion out of teaching or stay underemployed in teaching. Few schools are organized to use the full potential of faculty members under present staffing patterns.

Additionally, schools have no system for varied utilization of manpower. School staffing is an all-or-nothing proposition, with little range of choice. To teach, a person must have all the necessary skills and credentials and give himself full-time to the job. Education's reserves—certified personnel who could work part-time, who could re-enter with some retraining—cannot be mustered to participate in instruction because there are so few alternatives to full-time teaching.

How Would Differentiated Staffing Operate?

Differentiated staffing would provide many alternatives in teaching roles and would also give the under-employed teacher opportunities for advancement in teaching. The "omnicapable teacher"—scholar, lecturer, tutorer, curriculum planner, lesson planner, technologist, psychologist, diagnostician, and counselor—would be replaced by an omnicapable team of specialists and assistants, each performing different tasks in a close working relationship and contributing to instruction at his level of training and according to his interests.

Precise patterns of differentiated roles and responsibilities are not yet well defined. However, the following tentative definition of differentiated staffing may be helpful:

> Differentiated staffing is a plan for recruitment, preparation, induction, and continuing education of staff personnel for the schools that would bring a much

broader range of manpower to education than is now available. Such arrangements might facilitate individual professional development to prepare for increased expertise and responsibility as teachers, which would lead to increased satisfaction, status, and material reward.

This definition suggests that responsibilities could be gradated to correspond to distinct phases in the education and career aspirations of teachers and that personnel could be teamed across staffing levels. Thus, there might be a level of staffing to correspond to the recruitment phase. Persons at this level would be non-certificated and would perform as auxiliary personnel under the supervision of experienced professionals. Student teachers and interns— preprofessionals—might constitute another level of staffing, the preparation phase of teacher education. Such personnel would be considered and involved as staff members rather than as adjuncts. Teacher training would be integrated into the purposes of the school, to result in better preparation of teachers as well as improved instruction.

Beginning teachers, returning teachers, and some part-time teachers would comprise the staff in the induction phase of teacher education. Beginning teachers could be given a gradual induction into teaching instead of being thrust abruptly into full responsibility for the full range of teaching tasks. Returning teachers could work the kinks out gradually and have the assistance and counsel of experienced teachers in the retraining they need. A team arrangement would eliminate the present barrier to use of part-time teachers.

The continuing (inservice) phase of teacher education could be staffed by experienced teachers. At this level responsibilities could vary both in kind and degree, the latter allowing for advancement. For example, in addition to and related to a teacher's responsibility for specific aspects of the learning of a particular group of children, he might also be responsible for supervision of auxiliary personnel, training of preprofessionals, induction of beginning or returning professionals, or coordination of part-time professionals. He might be in charge of curriculum development or continuing education for all the members of a team. Alternatively, he might prefer to do none of these things and merely be one member of a teaching team. In this role, because of the differentiation of responsibilities, he would have more time to give individual attention to children.

Criticisms of Differentiated Staffing

Critics contend that differentiated staffing could result in the experienced and most able teacher reducing his contact hours with children and that it would therefore reduce the premium on teaching. Such a conclusion only follows if one defines teaching narrowly as time spent with children. If teaching is viewed to include such things as planning and organizing learning situations and conferring with colleagues, then reducing contact hours could ultimately enhance the quality of time spent with students. The objective, after all, is quality, not quantity.

Critics also assert that advocates of differentiated staffing will use it mainly to establish salary differentials among experienced teachers, resulting in merit pay. Merit pay means salary differentials based on the quality of performance in situations where every teacher has a similar task and the same degree of responsibility. Differentiated staffing, on the other hand, would establish salary differentials based on differences in degree of responsibility. If staffing is differentiated and there is prior agreement on various degrees of responsibilities, then a situation of merit pay will not obtain. Teacher organizations will need to be alert to ensure that new staffing patterns are fair and defensible, and teachers will need to be involved in the development of any plan for differentiated staffing, from the point of inception all the way through to evaluation and modification. Theirs are the tasks to be differentiated; hence they should participate in the judgement on how this can best be done.

What Can Teachers Do About Differentiated Staffing

Teacher involvement in the development of a plan for differentiated staffing might be initiated through the local association. A committee of local association members can collect and study information on differentiated staffing, visit school districts where experimentation is under way, assess the appropriateness of differentiated staffing to the problems confronted by local schools and teachers, and recommend what should be done about differentiated staffing in the local situation. If the prognosis is favorable, then the weight of the local association can be used to initiate the idea at the local school district level.

Differentiated staffing is not likely to result in lower operating costs for schools. It does, after all, require more, not less, personnel for instruction. In most cases, school districts will have to bear the added cost. Some funds to support experimental training for differentiated roles are available under the Education Professions Development Act. Additional financial support is available under other USOE titles and may be available from private foundations which are interested in experimentation to improve instruction.

Because the idea is still young, the bulk of material available on differentiated staffing is theoretical.[1] The best sources of empirical data are still the schools[2] which are experimenting with differentiated staffing.

Experimentation with a new idea is risky when there are no precedents on which to proceed. But risk-taking is necessary if schools are to begin to meet the great challenges of human progress.

Reprinted from *New York State Education*, March, 1970. Reprinted with permission of Roy A. Edelfelt and the New York State Teachers Association. Roy A. Edelfelt is Executive Secretary of the National Commission on Teacher Education and Professional Standards.

References

[1]McKenna, Bernard H., compiler. *A Selected Annotated Bibliography on Differentiated Staffing.* Washington, D.C.: National Commission on Teacher Education and Professional Standards, National Education Association, and ERIC Clearinghouse on Teacher Education, October 1969.

[2]National Education Association, National Commission on Teacher Education and Professional Standards. *The Teacher and His Staff: Selected Demonstration Centers.* St. Paul: 3 M Education Press, 1967. Copyright 1967 by the National Education Association.

13

On Team Teaching

David Pryke

Team teaching can mean all things to all men. Despite the fact that elements of this form of organization may have been used for some time in many of the thousands of small British rural schools, it is still considered a new phenomenon in Britain. It thus faces the risk of becoming the latest panacea for all that ails childhood education and of being adopted without much close evaluation. The freedom to determine methods and practice, jealously guarded by British schools, permits this to be so.

Over the past two years I have been working on a team-teaching venture involving fourth-year junior children—boys and girls aged ten to eleven plus, in their last years of school before transfer to some form of secondary education. The project came into being because three teachers, who happened to be in one place at one time, were interested in the possibilities of working cooperatively. We have attempted a critical examination of our process in order to improve its effectiveness. Although the situation that produced the project is a very particular one, I think certain pointers coming from it may be worthy of more general consideration.

Aims

Our basic premise has been that team teaching is organization and organization should always be subservient to aims. Our decision to try working as a team was based on the feeling that it seemed likely to help us better achieve our aims. We tried to rethink those aims in the light of demands made on children now and probable demands in the future. We wanted to bring more people and, therefore, more personalities, strengths and ideas into play.

Where did we start? About a hundred children had previously been in classes of thirty-five to forty, each with a class teacher, and grouped according to "intellectual" ability. We planned to make this group into one unit, with no rigorous divisions (we were agreed that grading by ability may well be impossible with young children). The three teachers would also work as a unit. Here then was our definition of team teaching: working with a large group of children, the teachers being equally responsible for planning, developing and evaluating the entire programme, and given scope to use specialist knowledge to the advantage of children and colleagues when help is needed.

A large group seemed to us likely to provide experiences of especial value. To look into the future may be a task of doubtful possibility, but I think it is a necessary exercise for educators. While we cannot ignore the past, we cannot go on regarding academic excellence as the only quality worth recognizing in people or keep hiving children off into small units as early as possible to find it. The class of forty with one teacher, still found in many British classrooms, may also be outmoded. Although the one-to-forty ratio may be the worst possible for adequate schooling in the 70's, I do not think that the smaller class for which we constantly cry, with a ratio of perhaps one to twenty-five, is the answer either. Perhaps the small ratio is desirable, but only along with occasional groupings of children in larger units in larger areas. At any rate, the assumption that working in large groups can be valuable was one that this project was putting to the test. The two years over which we worked were sufficient to reveal main strengths and difficulties of operating in this way.

Why the Interest in Size?

The large community seems likely to become a feature of future living and may demand a new range of social skills. Believing that an even greater demand will be put on people to cooperate in order to function optimally, our team felt that much experience of cooperative working should be given to young children. Acknowledging life as devastatingly competitive now, we shared a conviction that much more is achieved through cooperation than through competition. Because majorities may well become increasingly dominant in making decisions that will influence our lives, young children need opportunity to formulate and develop their opinions, to state their views fearlessly and to listen to those of others. Our team teachers envisaged that, with skillful handling, a large group would encourage the development of responsibility and require people to work together; these principles must be seeded into it and must grow out of it, for the group to function at all.

Teachers in Groups

Increasingly, too, teachers are finding it essential to cooperate, to consult each other, to think in terms of a whole school. They can, to be sure, do so without team teaching—as when a teacher with special skill is given the responsibility of serving as an advisor to colleagues when advice seems to be needed. Our project was conceived in such a way as to bring three teachers into constant daily and after-school contact. We knew each other well, our philosophies and temperaments were compatible, and we were dissatisfied with the relationship between our theory and practice as it stood. Without the first two conditions, teams of teachers are not viable. It also seems wise that the teaming setup be fairly durable; when a member leaves, replacing the vacancy is not easy to do at the drop of a hat.

Teachers working together should be able to give the curriculum of any group increased width and depth. Unless each teacher has a special interest he can offer, there is little point in setting up teams. On the other hand, teamwork can do away with narrow specialisation. The discussion, planning and blending of ideas that teamwork demands can vitalise the instructional programme, deepen and clarify personal philosophies, and introduce an element of retraining for the teachers concerned.

Initial Steps in Our Project

To create a large working area for our project, panels were removed from dividing walls of classrooms. This gave us three rooms in line—not an ideal shape. Every child had a "base" room and a desk in which to keep personal belongings. The teachers in turn each took a base room, in terms of special interests in math/science, language, or arts/crafts. Here each coped with registration and other chores and housed all equipment, books and hardware that had direct reference to his special interest. Here too "base grouping" began and ended (except for work in skills). Children grouped and regrouped according to need, with teachers having equal responsibility for the whole group.

Curriculum Timetable

We planned the curriculum to make possible three things: developing basic skills, receiving facts and information, and exploring and building upon personal interests in depth. To cover these we divided the day into 3 blocks of time and devoted one block to each. We found this timetable essential, because it helped give structure to the work we did. Such timetables and work schemes, and the compartmentalisation they can give, are regarded with suspicion in some informed places these days. Under the conditions that prevail in many primary schools, however, they can be useful, maybe even essential, in giving work direction.

Why did we see the above curriculum areas as important? What did we hope to do within them? In the first time-block, skills time, we were interested in the basic functions of talking, reading, mathematics and writing, skills it seems desirable for all children to have. In the second time-block we developed activities to help children learn how to learn, being concerned not with giving out masses of facts but with the ability to use facts and information when required. The third time-block gave the children a chance to explore a personal interest as far as they wanted to go, or as far as we could take them within the limits of our own specialty. We offered them an element of choice and an opportunity to do something for its own sake.

With the interconnectedness of all knowledge in mind, one central part of the work we did—occupying the second time-block—was always based on a main theme; skills from Block One and personal interests from Block Three gave it strength. Although we used the immediate environment and direct experience as useful motivation, we did not wholly subscribe to the widely held belief that the child's environment is an all-provider in the learning situation or that everything worth knowing is revealed by the child's own discovery. Teachers chose the theme to be explored over a term ("colour," for example), often planning in detail a wide range of possible development within it. The interests and wishes of individual children were always important in building activities around a theme. Teachers nevertheless controlled the topic quite tightly, stimulating thinking when ideas were lacking and broadening work that became too narrow in its development. Children were encouraged to use their own ideas about what they wanted to do and how they wanted to do it; teachers sought to help in evaluating and strengthening those ideas. Within the theme, we dealt with the traditional timetable subjects, using all the skills we had, seeking to involve everyone in the work in progress and making everyone's efforts easily available to see.

Learning how to learn brought forth such questions as these: When we need information (on a particular topic) how do we best obtain it? How do we then use it to best advantage? What is the value of this information over that? How do we formulate and test an hypothesis? How do we best communicate our knowledge? What standards do we employ? How should we involve ourselves with others in giving and sharing knowledge?

The main programme of work, then, was covered in Time-Block Two. Blocks One and Three were operated both in conjunction with, and apart from, it. In Block Three, each teacher in the team sought to guide children in extending special interests and skills. Children worked at many different levels and eventually were given some choice of activity and an extended period of time in which to explore its possibilities. Sometimes an interest in one area became linked with that in another; for example, printing in Art was used as a background for writing poetry and stories. The function of the specialist was determined by the children's demands on him, as well as by his demands on them.

Time Block One always stood somewhat apart from the other two. Children were now confined to working as a base-group in one room, whereas at all other times they moved freely and grouped and regrouped according to need. We believed that in a large primary school, skills to be taught effectively cannot depend solely on incidental learning. Work in skills-time often came from needs that appeared in the other two time-blocks but never depended on what went on in them. Since we considered talking as important as reading, we used time to develop and refine skills in both. We gave regular practice in the use of written language, considering its demands and refining basic practice in the mechanical exercise of handwriting. We related work in mathematics to everyday life and tried to give meaning to skill and process-development.

What Are the Advantages?

From our description thus far, advantages may appear to be precious few. All the things done in our three blocks of time can be accomplished without any involvement in team teaching. Teachers can organise the work of groups of any size and still function effectively as individuals with single class units. Demands on primary schools make it essential for all teachers to talk regularly, to plan collectively, to have a say in the organisation of a school as a whole unit. The complete organisational structure of primary schools, from the head teacher to the least-experienced probationary teacher, may be due for examination.

There seem to be two main advantages, however, and to explain these I return to the starting point of the project. We began by creating a large group of children because we felt that so doing would encourage the development of social relationships, removing barriers that are socially divisive. Also we believed that by doing this the teachers would find it necessary to work closely all the time, not just at the planning stage, and would thereby widen and deepen the educational process. We had a reasonable amount of success on both counts.

The close working of the team of teachers and pooling of ideas enabled us to attempt a more extensive programme than any we might have produced as individuals. We obtained a fuller knowledge of each child, because our records were compiled from three points of view, and children had one of three adults to whom they could turn initially when problems arose.

It is the potential of teamwork in fostering the development of social education which seems to be its great strength—perhaps really its only strength. The basic organisation of the group revolved around the fact that social education or the building of social relationships figured high in our list of aims. Organising a group of a hundred demands a high degree of cooperation between children and teachers for it to function at all. Children had to be involved in daily organisation, had to be prepared to cooperate and to share, had to be encouraged to communicate what they did. In short, as individuals they had some contribution to make to everything done, which had to be recognised for what it was. Produced within the group was a relaxed atmosphere, making it very satisfying to work in this way; but this is of little significance to anyone but those involved.

What Are the Limitations?

We soon became aware that team teaching obviated no special problems, that we had to deal with social, emotional, intellectual and all other problems just as we would in any other situation. In many ways it helped us to deal more purposefully with them, but we found that demands on our time beyond school hours were greatly increased. Planning, evaluating and recording—essential to the running of a project such as this—took hours. Furthermore, we probably raised as many questions as we answered because, as the work developed, team teaching was becoming more popular and greater claims were being made for it.

Despite suggestions that team teaching might be a money-saver, I would think that its demands on space and range of equipment make it entirely the opposite. There is an element of truth in the belief that it can make the strengths of teachers more available, that it can compensate for weaknesses. I think that unless a teacher has a strength or a special talent to offer, however, his place in a team will be of doubtful value. Weaknesses can be compensated for, but not in the sense that passengers can be carried. Another claim made for team teaching—that it provides a good induction for young teachers—seems to me false, because teams may give too little opportunity for young teachers to try out their own ideas, learn by their mistakes, seek advice if they want it, or be given advice in private if necessary. In teamwork, a mutually agreed plan of action has to be arrived at quickly, with straight talking and clear expression of ideas. The inexperienced teacher runs the risk of being swept along on the ideas of others. How teachers in training could be involved within teams is another matter and one crying out for exploration. But, then, the whole field of teacher preparation and retraining is screaming for attention.

Conclusion

Much more could be said about social education, about the theory behind this project, about collective planning, and about the effect of large group work on children as well as teachers. Teachers need to know more about the pressures of the school day on themselves and the children in their charge. We should never forget that education is about people. Team teaching is certainly not a method for all teachers at the moment, but the primary school concept is developing and team teaching may be able to widen this concept. The Middle School is emerging, possibly because of a realisation that children in the age range 9-13 have massive potential but have been, in some senses, deprived within our system as it has existed. Perhaps we are coming to a point where we are asking primary schools to do things within a total educational system (or lack of it) which makes the demands impossible. But that's another story.

Special thanks are due Fred Pigge, Chairman of the ACEI Research Committee, for his good services in soliciting this manuscript. We join him in welcoming response. Readers, speak out!

Reprinted from *Childhood Education*, Vol. 48, No. 2, November, 1971, pp. 85–89. Reprinted by permission of David Pryke and the Association for Childhood Education International, 3615 Wisconsin Avenue, N.W., Washington, D.C. Copyright 1971 by the Association. David Pryke is Assistant Headmaster, St. Leonard's Junior School, Bridgnorth, Shropshire, England.

Recommended Reading

Barth, Roland S. "When Children Enjoy School: Some Lessons from Britain." Childhood Education 46, 4 (Jan. 1970): 195–200.

Hapgood, Marilyn. "Letters from England." Childhood Education 47, 8 (May 1971): 412–17.

Keliher, Alice. "Effective Learning and Teacher-Pupil Ratio. ACEI Position Paper." Washington, D.C.: The Association, 1966. 4 pp., 10c; 25, $2.

14

Some Less Commonly Used Forms of Grouping

Wilma H. Miller

There are a number of different methods of grouping or class organizations that are used to expedite elementary reading instruction. Most elementary teachers use reading ability groups. However, a number of elementary teachers are not entirely cognizant of some other forms of grouping or class organization. This article describes some of the less commonly used forms of grouping; namely, needs groups, interest groups, research groups, tutorial groups, the Joplin Plan, departmentalized teaching, the ungraded primary plan, multigrade and multiage grouping, and the dual progress plan.

Needs Groups

A needs group usually is in a reading approach that does not utilize reading ability groups on a regular basis. Therefore, needs groups most often are used in the individualized reading plan and in the language-experience approach. A needs group is a short-term group that is formed when the teacher decides that a group of children in her classroom has a common word recognition or comprehension deficiency. When using individualized reading, the teacher may notice the difficulty during the individual reading conference when a child is reading a portion of his story out loud or when she is asking him comprehension questions about it. When using the language-experience approach, the teacher may notice the difficulty when she is working individually with the child in helping him to read back his experience stories.

In any case, the needs group is formed, and the specific word recognition or comprehension skills that the children needed are taught to them. A needs group may consist of able, average, and slow readers, but all of its members have certain common skill needs. The needs group is disbanded when the skills that it was formed to learn have been thoroughly mastered.

Interest Groups

An interest group also is a short-term group that may consist of fast, average, and slow readers. An interest group can be employed in any reading approach but certainly should be used in the basal reader approach to avoid the rigidity that comes from the sole use of reading ability groups.

An interest group is formed when a number of children in a classroom decide there is a certain topic that they wish to know more about. For example, a child in the class may bring in a very unusual shell that he has found on a vacation trip to Florida. A group of children then may become interested in finding out the name of the shell and its characteristics. These children then form an interest group and research information about the shell from tradebooks, science textbooks, children's magazines, and children's reference books. An interest group usually makes an oral or written report of its findings. An oral report gives the rest of the class an opportunity to share the findings of the interest group. The group is discontinued when the children in it have discovered enough about the topic to satisfy their curiosity.

Research Groups

A research group is quite similar to an interest group in some ways. The research group is a short-term group composed of children with different reading abilities. It can profitably be used in any of the reading approaches and is especially valuable in the basal reader approach. It differs from an interest group mainly in that the teacher assigns a topic to be researched to a group of children instead of allowing them to choose their own interest to study.

A research group usually is formed when the children are studying a unit in social studies or science, and the teacher wishes a portion of the unit to be studied in depth. She then assigns this portion to a research group, and they research it on their own reading levels from tradebooks, social studies or science textbooks, children's reference books, or children's newspapers or magazines. All of the research groups that are studying different aspects of a unit usually report their findings to the rest of the class orally. They also may prepare written reports. A research group is discontinued when the unit being studied is concluded.

Tutorial Groups

A tutorial group can be used in any reading method. Sometimes it is called the "buddy system" and is formed of a child-teacher and a child-pupil. Usually a good reader is the child-teacher, and a slower reader is the child-pupil. The child-teacher teaches or reviews a specific word recognition or comprehension skill that the slow reader has evidenced difficulty with in his regular reading instruction with the teacher. Usually it is more advisable for the child-teacher to review or reinforce a reading skill than it is for him to teach it. Sometimes a tutorial group consists of a good reader and a child who has been absent from school. In this case it sometimes is permissible for the child-teacher to teach some reading skills.

A tutorial group should not be formed unless both children wish to be in it. Also, a tutorial group should never continue for a long time as both children tire easily of this kind of activity. A tutorial group is discontinued when the child-pupil has mastered the reading skills that the child-teacher presented or reviewed.

The Joplin Plan (Modified Homogeneous Grouping)

One method of organizing reading instruction in the intermediate grades is called the Joplin Plan. This method of organization originated in Joplin, Missouri, and has been used since the mid-1940's. Standardized reading tests and teacher evaluation are used to place intermediate-grade pupils into various reading levels on the basis of an overall reading ability. Sometimes these reading levels are formed across fourth, fifth and sixth grade lines, while sometimes in large school buildings a reading level may only be composed of children from one grade level. The children in one reading level have approximately the same reading ability, and all children in the Joplin Plan have their instructional reading period at the same time each day. They move to the classroom in which their reading level is being taught.

There are advantages and limitations to the use of the Joplin Plan in the intermediate grades. This method of organization may reduce the wide range of reading ability that is found in a regular intermediate-grade classroom and thus make the teaching of reading easier. However, there are limitations to the use of this plan when a child is grouped with children that are younger than he. There still are differences in reading ability within each reading level that the teacher must provide for, and the teacher may not know the children as well as she would in a self-contained classroom. Reading may not be integrated with other curricular areas such as social studies and science.

Research has been inconclusive on the value of the Joplin Plan with some studies finding advantages in reading achievement by the use of this plan, and other studies finding advantages to the teaching of reading in self-contained classrooms. (1, 2, 3) Therefore, the Joplin Plan is not highly recommended for use in the intermediate grades.

Departmentalized Teaching

Departmentalized teaching sometimes is used in the intermediate grades. In this method of organization one teacher teaches reading and language arts, another teaches social studies, another teaches science and mathematics, and other teachers instruct the other curricular areas.

An apparent advantage of this method of organization is that it enables a teacher to most effectively use his subject area specialty. However, there are limitations to the use of this plan of organization, chief of which may be a teacher's lack of knowledge about the pupils he is teaching. He may be too likely to teach subject matter material instead of teaching children. Reading also may not be integrated with the remainder of the curriculum as it should be.

The Ungraded Primary Plan

Recently some elementary schools have adopted an ungraded plan or organization in the primary grades. In the ungraded primary, a number of reading and mathematics levels are established that children must master before they enter the intermediate grades. Usually children proceed through these levels at their own rate and therefore may complete the primary grades in either two, three, or four years. Children usually remain with the same teacher the entire time they are in the primary grades unless there is a teacher-pupil personality conflict.

There are several advantages to the use of this plan, foremost of which may be the individualized instruction utilized that allows pupils to proceed at their own rate. A teacher also may come to know a pupil very well if she can work with him for several years. The major limitations of this plan are the potential difficulties of organizing it and orienting primary-grade teachers and parents to it.

Multigrade and Multiage Grouping

Multigrade and multiage grouping is designed to reduce the regimentation that has characterized the graded elementary school. In philosophy it seems to be quite like the one-room country school of the past in which pupils of as many as eight grade levels were taught. This plan of organization is based on the assumption that groups should be formed using the differences rather than the similarities of children. Approximately the same number of pupils from grades one, two and three or from grades four, five and six are placed in the same classroom.

There are a few advantages to the use of this plan since children learn from those who are different as well as from those who are similar to them. Individualized instruction is used since it is not possible for a teacher of a multigrade classroom to set a common goal for every pupil. There are a number of limitations to the use of this plan, foremost among which is that the differences in the reading ability of the pupils become greater and more difficult to provide for than if they are placed in a self-contained classroom. No administrative device can assure that each pupil receives the individualized instruction that he needs as only concerned teachers can provide for this.

Dual Progress Plan

The dual progress plan is used in the intermediate grades and divides the subjects taught into two groups that are called the "cultural imperatives" and the "cultural electives". Pupils spend a half day with their homeroom teacher studying the "cultural imperatives"—reading and language arts, social studies, health, and physical education. They spend the remaining part of the day with special teachers studying the "cultural electives"—mathematics, science, art, music, and foreign language. Pupils progress through a graded sequence in the "cultural imperatives" and through an ungraded sequence in the "cultural electives."

There are several advantages to the use of the dual progress plan, perhaps the major one being that it enables pupils with special talents in an area to progress more rapidly than they could in a graded school. Teachers can use their special competencies, and this way may attract more competent teachers to elementary school teaching. The major limitation of this plan may be the criteria for designating school subjects as "cultural imperatives" and "cultural electives." It also would be difficult for the special teachers to come to know each pupil well.

Summary

This article describes a number of less commonly used methods of grouping or class organization that may be used to expedite elementary reading instruction. Needs groups are formed to teach certain word recognition and comprehension skills. Interest and research groups are short-term groups in which children research either their own interest or a topic assigned to them by the teacher. A tutorial group is composed of a child-teacher and a child-pupil who are teamed so that the child-teacher can present or review a reading skill. The Joplin Plan is an intermediate-grade plan of modified homogeneous grouping for reading instruction. Departmentalized teaching employs teacher specialists in the intermediate grades, and the ungraded primary plan is a method of organization which removes the grade lines in the primary grades. Multigrade grouping places pupils from three different grades in one classroom. The dual progress plan divides the school subjects taught into two areas to allow for more rapid progress in some areas.

Reprinted from *Elementary English*, "Some Less Commonly Used Forms of Grouping," by Wilma H. Miller. Copyright December, 1971 by the National Council of Teachers of English. Reprinted by permission of the publisher and Wilma H. Miller. Wilma H. Miller is Associate Professor of Education, Illinois State University.

References

[1]Cushenberry, Donald C. "The Joplin Plan and Cross Grade Grouping." Perspectives in Reading Number 9: Organizing for Individual Differences. Newark, Delaware: International Reading Association, 1967–68, 33–45.

[2]Kierstead, Reginald. "A Comparison and Evaluation of Two Methods of Organization for the Teaching of Reading." Journal of Education Research, LVI (February, 1963), 317–321.

[3]Moorhouse, William P. "Inter-Class Grouping for Reading Instructions." Elementary School Journal, LXIV (February, 1964) 280–286.

15

Teaching in Small Groups

Robert N. Bush

Teaching in small groups is one of the projects which has been undertaken at the Stanford Center for Research and Development in Teaching. Some speculative propositions have accrued from discussions and studies. Some troublesome questions arise concerning the ways in which teachers have been trained. Much if not most of the current training of teachers is antithetical to effective teaching in small groups. Most of what trainees are taught to do, and most of what they are learning to do, which is what they daily do in their practice is exactly what they should not be doing if they are conducting small group teaching as it should be carried out. In the first place, it has been assumed that teacher and student behavior is different from that which occurs in other contexts when the small group is genuinely operating for the purposes that it should. We have made videotape recordings in classrooms where teachers are now teaching in small groups. As anticipated, the teaching is almost identical with that which takes place in regular sized groups and in large groups. The main role is as purveyor of knowledge, lecturer. It is mostly teacher talk. What is the appropriate purpose of teaching in small groups? The assumption is accepted that it is different from that which goes on in large groups. As a beginning, two unique purposes have been identified. The first aim is to open wide the channels of communication amongst the members of the group. This means on an emotional and social as well as an intellectual level. It means between student and student as well as between teacher and student. The second aim is to provide an opportunity for individuals to apply knowledge and experience gained elsewhere to new situations, the old problem of transfer: to increase the ability to apply knowledge and experience to new problems.

With that as a beginning, we have been attempting to identify the kinds of student behavior which we want to foster in these small groups and that are uniquely appropriate for the small group. The next step is to identify the kind of teacher behavior which might reasonably be expected to produce the kind of student behavior desired. We then need to determine the kind of training programs which may be capable of producing teachers who can behave in the appropriate manner.

Here are a few illustrations of the kinds of student behavior which have been specified. We want students to become genuinely involved in the activity. We want the individual student to be willing to put his ideas on the table, to be able to listen to what others, students and teachers, have to say about his contributions, both positively and negatively, and not to react defensively when his ideas are criticized. We have not as well as in some other countries been able to separate the criticism of an individual's ideas from the criticism of him personally. We tend too much to take a criticism of whatever we say to be a personal criticism. It is important to be able and willing to put ideas on the table and to listen to what others say, and then to be able and willing to speak responsibly about another's ideas, to probe, approve, argue, and disagree. We want to have the student behave not just mainly for the teacher. According to almost all of the records we collected this seems to be most of what goes on in school. We call it "playing school." The students are trying to find out what the teacher wants and generally to give it to him or in some cases to cause him difficulty in getting it. We have lucid examples. In one recording, in attempting to model the behavior of the teacher who was trying to get students genuinely involved and reacting because of the relevancy of the situation, the situation was defined as: "We are going to select what we want to study in social studies. And after we have selected what we want to study we'll then select one of the topics and go ahead and study it." The group leader stopped after this brief definition. Quiet ruled for fifteen seconds, thirty seconds. The videotape records show the students beginning to squirm. The teacher sits quietly. After about forty-five seconds one compulsive person who can no longer keep quiet, says, "Well, uh, what about studying the origin of ancient civilizations?" The teacher replied, "Well?" And then another fifteen or twenty second period of silence and another compulsive student said: "Well, what about studying the origins of American civilization in Europe?" Is more necessary? They tried repeatedly to find out what the teacher wanted. Only very skillful teacher behavior finally brought them to the point where they were discussing hippies, drugs, and war in Vietnam, and other matters that were uppermost in their minds. Most of the behavior observed in small groups, and in all others represents students "playing school" rather than being genuinely involved, in listening thoughtfully to one another. They hide. They do not feel free to put their ideas on the table. They want to dominate or to be dominated. A further behavior we aim for is to help the student accurately to perceive himself, who he is. We aim to help him to learn to feel comfortable in the face of uncertainty, ambiguity, and change, and to act constructively in the face of such circumstances.

These are but examples of the list of behaviors to be promoted uniquely possible in small groups.

If these be the kinds of student behavior we wish to develop, then what are the teacher behaviors that are most likely to produce the desired student behaviors? It appears to be almost exactly the opposite of most of what we are trying even with our experimental programs in teacher training at Stanford, where the aim in developing the technical skills of teaching is to teach teachers to reinforce specific kinds of student behavior in the Skinnerian model.

The foregoing definitions are almost opposite to the Skinnerian model. The teacher instead of giving positive reinforcement for every "proper" behavior takes a non-evaluative stance toward pupils' comments. He also in other ways tries to bring about an open environment for the group to operate in. The teacher needs, in an appropriate small group setting, to react sensitively to the ideas, the feelings, and the actions of group members, and to convey to each member of the group and to the group itself the worthwhileness of all contributions. It is important also in small group interaction for the teacher to alter his behavior appropriately for each phase in the development of the life history of the group. In the beginning, the teacher behaves in one way; as he reaches a certain point, he behaves in another fashion, and as he comes to the end, he reacts in still another manner. This is not primarily "group dynamics" or "sensitivity training," where a small group is thrown together to work out its problems. Here the emphasis is upon responsible professional teachers teaching in small groups. The mode varies. It may at one point be necessary to get out of the way in order to get back in. Some teachers, for example, mistakenly aver that, if they talk too much they must move over to the side and let students take over. This is not the responsible role of which we speak. At this point, we are grasping for ways to train teachers to behave differently. We are groping in the dark, in new territory for the most part. To suggest in conclusion a few operational questions concerning these illustrations of experimentation, I have illustrated some of the directions. One troublesome problem is: who sets the task in the small group? How is it modified? Another is: how is work evaluated in the small group? The chief unique characteristic activity in a small group is discussion: not reading, not writing, not lecturing, not memorizing, not taking examinations, all of which now happen often in small groups.

Certain things ought not to be expected to appear in small groups. For example, it should not be assumed that what has happened in a previous large group meeting will be immediately transferred into the small group. Recall that one major purpose of the small group is to help individuals apply experience that they have gained elsewhere, maybe in the large groups, but perhaps out in the community or elsewhere. Another expectation is not to find discipline problems in small groups. When small groups are well run discipline problems simply do not appear. This alone should be enough to convince American teachers. One of the most difficult lessons to learn is that everything that happens in a small group is relevant. If the topic gets off what was considered the main track, why did it get off? Who brings it back, why, and in what form? The modus operandi of teaching in small groups is more like that of modern jazz improvization than a Mozart concerto. Unfortunately too many teachers try to conduct small groups in the style of a Mozart concerto. For large group instruction this is appropriate, but small group teaching properly proceeds from the nature of the group and the problems and the ideas that emerge from the group.

Reprinted from *New Directions for Research and Development in Teacher Education*, Research Memorandum, No. 32, May, 1968, pp. 26–28. Reprinted by permission of the publisher and Robert N. Bush. Robert N. Bush is Director of the Center for Research and Development in Teaching, Stanford University.

16

Organizing Peer Tutoring in Our Schools

Madan Mohan

Several projects (Melaragno and Newmark, 1970; Marliave and Smith, 1971) involving student tutors have been described recently in educational literature. In some of these projects older students were asked to tutor the younger (cross-grade tutoring), while in other situations bright peers tutored their low achieving classmates (peer group tutoring). Further, in some of the projects tutoring was done on a one-to-one basis, while in others it involved small groups. The outcomes of these projects have been uniformly positive: not only do the tutees benefit, but the student tutors also show gains in motivation toward learning, attitude toward school, communication skills, and school achievement. After a careful study of the procedures used in tutorial projects, two studies were undertaken at the Teacher Education Research Center, Fredonia: a pilot study (Mohan, 1971) in which testimonial evidence was gathered from students involved, the teachers, and the school principal; and a main study (Mohan, 1972) in which both testimonial and test-based evidence were gathered. The results of both these studies clearly indicated that one-to-one tutorial interaction favorably affected each participating student's knowledge, motivation, and attitude. It was further found that both consumers (students, parents) and practitioners (teachers, administrators) of education expressed their trust, understanding and full support of the program. The use of tutors is also a low-cost method for individualizing instruction. It makes use of an untapped instructional resource, namely the older and/or bright students.

The purpose of this paper is to suggest, to teachers and other personnel who professionally interact with students, some effective ways of organizing peer tutoring as a means to motivate children and to facilitate learning. The teacher must be acquainted with the following steps which have been found to encourage learners to demonstrate the desired performance. These steps are as follows:

Initiating a Program

While it is essential that all teachers in a school should be involved in the initial activities in order that there be no "surprises" at some future date, the adoption of the program should be gradual, as the adoption by all teachers and for all activities is bound to generate problems too numerous and complex to handle. It is, therefore, recommended that teachers be selected on a voluntary basis to undertake pilot projects. The volunteer group should be attentive to the following points: the critera for the selection of tutors and tutees, the subject matter in which tutoring is to be done, the objectives for the tutor, the objectives for the tutee, the development and/or compilation of instructional materials, activities and assessment exercises, the training of tutors in tutoring skills, the selection of the place, day and time for the tutoring sessions, the monitoring of tutorial sessions, and feedback to tutors and tutees.

Selection of Tutees

The selection of tutees depends upon the objectives of the program. If the objectives are to increase motivation level, self-direction in learning, and achievement in the subject matter area, then the teacher should identify unmotivated children who also lack self direction and are low in achievement in the subject matter area.

The general level of motivation of children may be assessed by using the checklist (Klausmeier, et. al., 1972) given in Appendix I. The checklist is completed by the teacher for each child in the class. An adaptation of this checklist (Appendix II) is completed by each child. Using these responses, a potential group of unmotivated children can be identified.

The achievement in the subject matter area can be determined by using criterion-referenced tests, standardized achievement tests and examination of the workbooks of the children. This data indicates which students are in need of tutoring. Generally, such information is available for each child on pupil-record cards. However, if this information is not available, assessment should be carried out to know specifically what knowledge and skills a tutee has not mastered.

In addition to the above two steps, the teacher should unobtrusively observe the classroom behavior of these children before selecting the final group of tutees for tutoring sessions.

Selection of Tutors

The selection of tutors depends upon the objectives of the program and certain characteristics of the tutors. Characteristics found to be influential are level of motivation, level of achievement in the subject matter area, self-directed social behavior, age, sex, extroversion, and willingness to tutor.

If the objective is to help the younger student only, the teacher may select a bright student from her class or from an upper grade who has a good understanding of concepts and procedures in the subject area and is good in verbalizing his thoughts and quick in doing his work. However, if the objective is to help both tutors and tutees in school achievement, motivation, attitude and self-direction, then the teacher should identify unmotivated older students using procedures suggested in the preceding section.

Tutor-Tutee Pairs

As it is very important for the tutor-tutee pair to be compatible, it is recommended that both groups of children—those who are to be taught and those who will tutor—be brought together and asked to select one student from the other grade with whom they would like to work. It is important that there should be boys and girls in both groups.

It should be emphasized to students that their participation in the program is voluntary and that they can leave the program at any time. However, the advantages of the program, to the younger child in terms of receiving individual attention and to the older child in gaining a new sense of responsibility and usefulness, should be clearly emphasized by the teacher.

Content of the Tutorial Sessions

The content of the tutorial sessions varies with objectives of the program. Usually the content selected is the one in which there are several children in need of help. Furthermore, it is recommended that the content should be a skill area, such as mathematics or reading, for which there are specific objectives, items criterion-referenced to measure objectives, multi-level instructional materials for each objective and programmed workbooks.

Besides skill subjects, the tutorial sessions may also include helping the tutee in independent work. In fact, Melaragno and Newmark (1970) find the help in independent activities a very good way to begin tutorial sessions.

Objectives of the Program

The objectives for the tutees are increase of motivational level, self-direction in learning, and achievement in the subject matter area. The objectives for the tutors are increase of motivation level, development of positive attitudes toward school, improvement in communication skills, and increase in knowledge of the subject matter area. The objectives for the school are to reach more unmotivated students through the use of tutors and to individualize instruction.

Instructional Materials

Instructional materials specifically related to the particular content and instructional objectives should be selected by the teachers of the tutees and made available to the tutors. The instructional material should be structured and should provide for student self-pacing. As different kinds of materials such as books, pamphlets, filmstrips, overlays and records are needed, it is suggested that teachers of the tutees should prepare lists of such materials.

Lists of instructional objectives and assessment exercises related to these objectives in the areas of mathematics and reading are available from the Instructional Objectives Exchange, Los Angeles, California, 90024. The Wisconsin Research and Development Center for Cognitive Learning of the University of Wisconsin at Madison also has developed objectives and assessment procedures in the areas of reading and mathematics.

Training of Tutors

It is obvious that tutors will need help from the school staff. Some areas in which a teacher should help the tutors are:

1. Content area. The teacher of the tutee should assign specific content area material to the tutor. He should make available to the tutor instructional materials on specific content and ask the tutor to review it before working with the tutee. In order to achieve mastery of the content and realize the objective, the tutor should be advised to consult books and to solicit help from the teacher and from senior students, if necessary. In short, the tutor should be fully prepared before getting into the one-to-one learning-teaching situation with the tutee.

2. Objectives and test items. The teacher of the tutee should discuss the objectives of tutoring the particular content with the tutor. A few test items criterion-referenced to measure the achievement of the objectives should also be made available to the tutor. These test items will serve two purposes. The tutor, by answering those test items, will know whether he understands the content or not, and at the same time, these items can help him in performing the tutoring sequence which consists of diagnosis, demonstration, evaluation and practice. With the help of these items, the tutor can also apprise the tutee of his progress.

3. Tutoring skills. Perhaps the most important part of

the program is the teaching of tutoring skills to the tutors. Research (Harrison, 1969) shows conclusively that trained tutors are far more successful at helping their tutees than untrained tutors. Therefore, the teacher should first explain the tutoring style and skills to the tutor, ask him to role-play and then give him feedback on his performance. It should be emphasized to the tutor that, to be an effective tutor, he must communicate his interest in the child and in the lesson. Before tutoring, the tutor should be acquainted with the following:

a. Tutoring style. The purpose of tutoring style is to create the right type of mood. Some of the tutor behaviors that have been found to be very effective in achieving this objective are (Klausmeier, et. al., 1972; Melaragno and Newmark, 1970): (1) be on time to the tutoring session; (2) be prepared with the instructional materials and activities; (3) sit next to the tutee so that both can see the material being used; (4) greet the tutee pleasantly and tell him your name and ask his name; (5) discuss the purpose of the tutorial session; (6) speak slowly and clearly so that the tutee can hear and understand; (7) relax in between the lessons and let the tutee also relax; (8) look at the tutee in order to observe many non-verbal clues about his performance; (9) be patient and wait for an answer from the tutee; and (10) allow the tutee to handle the materials. These simple behaviors of the tutor have proved successful in creating a relaxed atmosphere.

b. Beginning a tutorial interaction. Before discussing the content with the tutee, the following tutor behaviors are suggested: (11) ask the tutee about his hobbies, interests and favorite stories; (12) be a responsive audience to the things he tells; (13) gain the tutee's attention; (14) ask the tutee a question or give him the instruction; (15) request a response; (16) praise the tutee for every correct and complete answer; (17) praise the tutee for trying and making sincere efforts; (18) correct the tutee's wrong or incomplete answers before going to the next question; (19) be pleasant and try to be helpful throughout the session even though the tutee may not seem to learn or understand.

c. Ending a tutorial interaction. It is suggested that before ending the session the tutor should do the following:

(20) review with the tutee what was learned; (21) inform the tutee about the place for the next session; and (22) inform the tutee about the time for the next session.

Selection of the Place, Day, and Time

The place, day, and time for tutorial sessions should be cooperatively decided in advance by both teachers of the tutor and the tutee. It is recommended that the place for tutorial sessions should be outside the regular classroom to avoid distractions and interruptions. At the specified time of the day, the tutor should go to the tutee's classroom and take the tutee to a pre-arranged place. After the tutoring session is over, the tutor takes the tutee back to his classroom. The time and day should be so selected as to minimally affect these children's regular classwork.

Supervising Tutorial Sessions

Adult assistance and supervision should be made available. The assisting adult can be a paraprofessional who understands the program. The supervisor makes available to the tutor specific content for the next session, the objectives of the content and test items criterion-referenced to measure the objectives; provides general supervision; helps the children in recording their experiences and recommends to the tutor instructional materials specifically related to particular content and instructional objectives.

Regular monitoring of tutorial sessions should be carried out by the teacher of the tutee. Such a step provides guidance and feedback to the tutor and is an excellent means of determining the tutee's progress. In fact, it is suggested that teachers of both the tutee and the tutor should be continually involved to insure the success of the program.

Use of Work Log Book

The tutor should be asked to keep a careful record of his time, the content area and the objectives he covered, his difficulties and problems in each tutoring session, and his impressions of the interaction.

The adult supervisor may be asked to help the tutor in recording his experiences. Such a record will provide additional data on the effectiveness and efficiency of the tutorial interaction and offer specific areas where changes should be made for better results in the future.

Meeting After a Tutorial Session

The teacher of the tutee should meet the tutor after the tutorial session to share the experiences that the tutor had from this interaction. Problems encountered by the tutor should be discussed in order to improve the tutor's effectiveness. The teacher should continue to provide encouragement and guidance throughout the program.

The teacher of the tutee should discuss the experiences that the tutee had. The teacher should also review the work which the tutee did to insure that tutoring of concepts and processes is being conducted meaningfully. Such meetings with the tutee should also inform the teacher about the effectiveness of the tutor.

If, as a result of these meetings, it is found that the tutor is ineffective at his task, the tutor-tutee relationship interferes with the progress of the tutee, and/or the tutor is not keeping up with the work in his own class, he should not be allowed to work as tutor and a different tutor should be assigned to the tutee.

Assessing the Outcomes

The baseline data concerning each tutor and tutee is collected in the beginning of the program. Data is collected periodically on all these baseline variables (motivation level, self-direction in learning, achievement in the subject matter) to evaluate the effectiveness of the program. If the objective is improvement in the tutee's motivation, self-direction and achievement in the subject matter, then the tutee is the primary source of data. However, if the objectives of the program include benefits for the tutor, then both tutor and tutee are assessed to collect needed information. Although there is ample anecdotal and testimonial evidence, it is suggested that the teacher should not rely solely on this kind of data. Instead, the teacher may use checklists (Appendices I and II) for assessment of motivation level, criterion-referenced tests for subject matter achievement, work logs and unobtrusive observation for self-direction and attitude.

This paper has presented a summary of ideas related to tutoring. The present writer's interest in delineating the factors that lead to desired performance among tutees and tutors was aroused by Guilford's (1970) statement:

> Because individuals are likely to be uneven in their abilities, as well as differing from one another, much provision should be made for individual instruction and individual rate of progress. Much could be done for individuals by having older ones tutor younger ones, with benefit to both. . . .

The writer carefully studied the procedures used in tutorial projects. This paper is a result of investigation of those procedures in two studies (Mohan, 1971 and 1972).

This article was specially written for this book of readings at the request of the editors. Madan Mohan is Associate Professor—Research, State University College, Fredonia, New York.

References

Guilford, J. P. "Creativity: Retrospect and Prospect." *Journal of Creative Behavior,* Vol. 4, No. 3, 1970.

Harrison, Grant V. "The Effects of Professional and Non-professional Trainers Using Prescribed Training Procedures on the Performances of Upper-Grade Elementary Student Tutors." Dissertation, Los Angeles, California: University of California, 1969.

Klausmeier, Herbert J., et. al. "Individually Guided Motivation: Guidelines for Implementation." Madison, Wisconsin: Wisconsin Research and Development Center for Cognitive Learning, 1972.

Marliave, R. S. and Smith, K. B. "Individual Tutoring of Younger Students by Older Students (Mimeo)." Madison, Wisconsin: Wisconsin Research and Development Center for Cognitive Learning, 1971.

Melaragno, R. J. and Newmark, G. *Tutorial Community Project: Report of the Second Year, July, 1969–August, 1970.* Santa Monica, California: System Development Corporation.

Mohan, Madan. "Peer Teaching as a Technique for Teaching the Unmotivated." *Child Study Journal,* Summer, 1971.

Mohan, Madan. "Peer Tutoring as a Technique for Teaching the Unmotivated: A Research Report." Fredonia, N.Y.: Teacher Education Research Center, State University College, Fredonia, 1972.

APPENDIX I

Checklist for Assessing General Level of Motivation

Directions: Rate the child on each of the behaviors listed below.
Put a number beside the behavior to indicate how often the child
exhibits the behavior. Use this key:
1 = seldom 2 = sometimes 3 = usually

Behavior	Rating
1. Attends to the teacher, other children, or a task when attention is required.	_____
2. Begins tasks promptly.	_____
3. Seeks feedback concerning performance on tasks.	_____
4. Returns to tasks voluntarily after interruption or initial lack of progress.	_____
5. Persists at tasks until completed.	_____
6. Continues working when the teacher leaves the room.	_____
7. Does additional work during school hours.	_____
8. Works on school-related activities outside school hours.	_____
9. Identifies activities that are relevant for class projects.	_____
10. Seeks suggestions for going beyond minimum amount or quality of work.	_____
11. Works effectively as a small-group member without adult supervision.	_____
12. Works effectively for reasonable periods of time in independent study.	_____
13. Takes care of own and other people's property.	_____
14. Interacts harmoniously with other students and adults.	_____
15. States own ideas about conduct and relations with others and listens to the ideas and questions of others.	_____
16. Discusses why specific behaviors are engaged in and the effects of these behaviors on self or others.	_____
17. Discusses individual behaviors and conditions in school or at home that could be changed through personal or group actions.	_____

18. Discusses ways of changing individual behavior and school or home conditions. _____

19. Sets goals individually or as a member of a group to change behaviors or conditions. _____

20. States values related to the objectives in 1-19. _____

21. Differentiates between behaviors which are in accord with his value statements and those which are not in accord. _____

Total of Ratings _____

*Average Rating _____

*Divide total of ratings by the number of behaviors rated.

APPENDIX II

Checklist for Self-assessing General Level of Motivation

Directions: Rate yourself on each of the behaviors listed below. Put a number beside the behavior to indicate how often you exhibit the behavior. Use this key:
1=seldom 2=sometimes 3=usually

Behavior	Rating
1. I attend to the teacher, other children, or a task when attention is required.	_____
2. I begin tasks promptly.	_____
3. I seek feedback concerning performance on tasks.	_____
4. I return to tasks voluntarily after interruption or initial lack of progress.	_____
5. I persist at tasks until completed.	_____
6. I continue working when the teacher leaves the room.	_____
7. I do additional work during school hours.	_____
8. I work on school-related activities outside school hours.	_____
9. I identify activities that are relevant for class projects.	_____
10. I seek suggestions for going beyond minimum amount or quality of work.	_____

11. I work effectively as a small-group member without adult supervision.   _____

12. I work effectively for reasonable periods of time in independent study.   _____

13. I take care of my own and other people's property.   _____

14. I interact harmoniously with other students and adults.   _____

15. I state my own ideas about conduct and relations with others and listen to the ideas and questions of others.   _____

16. I discuss why specific behaviors are engaged in and the effects of these behaviors on myself or others.   _____

17. I discuss individual behaviors and conditions in school or at home that I could change through personal or group actions.   _____

18. I discuss ways of changing individual behavior and school or home conditions.   _____

19. I set goals individually or as a member of a group to change behaviors or conditions.   _____

20. I state values related to the objectives in 1-19.   _____

21. I differentiate between behaviors which are in accord with my value statements and those which are not in accord.   _____

Total of Ratings   _____

*Average Rating   _____

_____

*Divide total of ratings by the number of behaviors rated.

17

Independent Learning

Willard J. Congreve

Two years ago I reported on an experimental program at
The University of Chicago Laboratory Schools, designed to
encourage Freshman students to take responsibility for
making choices about how, where, when and to some
degree, what they would study.[1] This progress statement
will attempt to summarize the technical evolution of the
program since its inception and to demonstrate how the
project has moved from an innovative effort to a more
sophisticated inquiry.

The Freshman Project

The Freshman Project, (we never got around to meditating
on a more discriminating nomenclature) was initiated by
teachers and continues to function and improve largely as
the result of the dedication of the teachers involved to the
principle of independent learning. It is the teachers who
have worked out practically all the details, administrative
and operational. They have been both the authors and the
actors in the drama. The principal was instrumental in
getting the innovation launched and has since served as a

resource person, as a supporter, as a morale builder, and more often as a protective cushion.

The chairman and associate chairman of the Freshman Project—Ernest N. Poll (science teacher) and Edgar Bernstein (social studies teacher), respectively—have been in the program since its inception in 1961. They conceived and worked out the first pilot project and were instrumental in moving the program forward.

The staff now consists of eight teachers (two each in English, Mathematics, Science and Social Studies), a teacher-librarian (part-time), and a counselor. Twenty-two others have, over a period of three years, worked for at least one year in the program. The turnover suggests the difficult hurdles that have to be surmounted in persisting, the corollary being the intense commitment of those who have stayed with it.

Even though some of the teachers remained with the project only one or two years, it would appear that the experience was profitable. Their zest for teaching and their drive toward creative approaches to the teaching-learning process became enhanced—perhaps they had been compelled to wrestle with issues more basic than practical methodologies. One teacher moved from the freshman to the senior level and single-handedly carried on a similar program with his social studies students. Subsequently he was recruited by a large university in a neighboring state to work in its in-service teacher training program. Five others have become teachers of sophomores in our own school and have organized a staff study group to develop a program which extends and reinforces the independent-learning concepts underlying the Freshman Project. One of our teachers, who had not actually participated but was involved in the project intellectually, has moved on to an influential local college, where he is revising the freshman English program to incorporate some of the principles espoused in our Freshman Project.

The program has not been without influence at other levels at University High School. An option program has been installed which makes it possible for any teacher of juniors and seniors to release students from class on a day-to-day basis in order to form more effective teaching groups and to allow students to take class time to locate and use resource materials, on campus or off. The high school faculty as a whole has adopted an additional major goal—to develop the student who has learned how to learn and accepts responsibility for his learning. All these developments, again the result of the efforts of teachers and not of the mandates of the administration, have made University High School an exciting learning laboratory, more committed than ever before to helping each youngster realize his unique potential.

I must also give credit to the State of Illinois Plan for Program Development for Gifted Children, which supported generously the last two years of the Freshman Project, enabling us to make the endeavor a research work by providing the necessary technological assistance, materials, and clerical staff.

Inception, 1961–62

Space limitation does not permit of reviewing in detail the early evolutionary steps of the Freshman Project. These are covered in the previous report, as well as in a recent publication, *Independent Study: Bold New Venture*, edited by Beggs and Buffie.[2]

In the pilot effort of the first two years, Bernstein and Poll set out to develop a program which would explore several questions: First and foremost, could freshman high school students accept responsibility for directing a substantial portion of their learning? Then, if students assumed some direction of their class time, would they learn more or less subject matter content? Would they learn other things of value? How could audio-visual equipment and science laboratories fit into student-directed learning? Would their use of our library materials—always in heavy demand as a result of teacher-initiated assignments—increase sharply and, if so, would the library staff be able to cope with their needs? Could the students operate on schedules different from that of the rest of the school?

These questions were not so clearly stated at the time Bernstein and Poll got underway. They were implicit, however, in the teachers' desire to pursue the first and overriding question, and they were soon built into the data-gathering operations. But it is important to note that the project did not start with a precisely defined problem. More explicit definition has been in progress all along and, in fact, is still an ongoing task of the present staff.

Poll and Bernstein developed a unique plan of instruction. Every Monday the 42 youngsters assigned to the pilot program would meet for large-group instruction, at which time problems would be raised by some challenging confrontation. Each student was expected to focus on an aspect of each of the problems which was of particular interest to him. He would then devote the remainder of the week to pursuing solutions, using library and other materials, the science laboratory, fellow students and the teachers as learning resources. Near the end of the week the students would reconvene for a discussion of their findings and a summing-up.

Result? Certainly no chaos. Once the principal and faculty got accustomed to seeing students "out of their places," all was tranquil. More adjustment was required on our part than on the part of the students. At the end of the year it was found that the students had learned as much subject matter as (although not more than) they would have been expected to learn in a traditional program. They did better on the Watson-Glaser Critical Thinking Appraisal than was expected according to the norms given in the test manual. We have since come to question the usefulness of this measure, but at that time it served to bolster the idea that this program did teach students something besides subject matter knowledge.

The students made extensive use of the library. Not only did their borrowings exceed those of the other freshman students but also those of the juniors and seniors.

The two teachers found working together to be an exciting and rewarding experience. Many of the parents experienced anxiety over their children's being permitted to decide what they would do in science and social studies, but at the same time they admitted that their children were keenly interested in these subjects—often in the form of a complaint that they were spending a disproportionate amount of time on them.

Expansion, 1962–63

This first effort gave rise to a more grandiose scheme for student-direction in 1962–63, this one to involve the whole freshman class of 175, four major subjects, eight teachers, and a block of time equivalent to four periods per day. Added to the staff was a teacher-librarian, who gave part of her time to developing a liaison between the project and the library. Obviously, the carving out of the operational plan was a Herculean task. And another big question emerged: Could some better method be found to measure the additional learnings which the project sought?

It is this first full-blown project which is described in detail in my previous report.[3]

The results of the first program which involved all the freshmen were encouraging. The students had learned no less subject matter than in a regular program. Even with one-fourth of the student body on a different time schedule and with unusual opportunities to move about the building freely, the school continued to function quite normally. Using the comparative scores of a grade level before and a grade level after as controls, we found the results of the Watson-Glaser Critical Thinking Appraisal disappointing. Even though the gains were higher than could have been expected by chance, each grade level group had made equivalent gains.

When the Type I, Type II and Type III (designations of learning environments according to amount of student self-direction) students were compared in ability and achievement, it was found that they had tended to choose their mode of learning in correlation with their ability and achievement; that is, the more able the student the more self-direction he wanted or at least was willing to undertake.

A questionnaire administered to the students revealed that most of them felt that they had learned things about how to study and about their abilities to learn on their own, in addition to having increased their skill in the use of resource materials. However, the survey also revealed that many students did not like the program. Only 54% indicated that they would like to have a similar program another year.

The first year of the large project was essentially exploratory. Working out the mechanics and developing new working relationships among the teachers required considerable time and effort. The results could not be considered conclusive. There was strong feeling among us that there might have been growth in the ability to learn independently which we had not thought of a way to measure. It was decided that the 1963–64 program should be a replication.

The same staffing arrangements were maintained, except that a full-time counselor to the students was appointed. Since the mechanics of the program were "old hat," much more attention could be given to orienting the students to what was for them a drastically unfamiliar educational milieu. Again, all students were launched into some choice-making at the outset. They all attended class three days a week and exercised options as to how, when and where they would study the other two days. This arrangement obtained until after Christmas, when the Type I, II and III programs were made available. A system of recording attendance at optional activities was perfected, which committed the students to a weekly plan once made. Knowing how many would be in attendance at a particular optional activity enabled the teachers to make better preparations.

Methods of evaluation were improved, and the results provided us with greater understanding of the effects on the students. The most important findings of this second year include:

1. The fact that school-within-a-school programs can exist was reaffirmed. We are now convinced that it is not necessary to schedule a school so that all students follow the same time modules or are required at all times to be in predetermined places.

2. Again, the more able students elected more independent programs. Rather surprisingly, in comparisons of standardized tests, and also teacher-made pre- and post-tests, using multivariate analysis, we found that students in the Type I (least independent) environment made greater gains in the traditional subject matter learnings than did the Type III students. However, we have reason to believe that

the test ceilings imposed on the high-achieving Type III students caused an underrating of that group's gains. In any case, the group working most independently made the greatest gains in writing ability and in inquiry skills. These students were also more comfortable with the teacher who in the learning situation functions as a resource person rather than as a director.

3. At one time we felt that students who spent considerable time in the library were displaying independent behavior. By means of a teacher-rating of independence, a measure of the amount of time each student spent in the library, and a library skills test, we discovered that the students who do not know how to direct their own learning may well select individual study options simply because they are not aware of their educational needs or are trying to escape feelings of inadequacy and then spend their time rather aimlessly, under the accepted rubric of library study. Lest one be appalled at the thought of these students' not having the fullest possible amount of classroom instruction, a reminder is in order that many of these students also have an artful way of wasting time in class.

Can Independence Be Taught?

In the spring of 1964, we found ourselves approaching the end of the year with a well-functioning program but with the realization that we had only now succeeded in defining the basic problem: *What is the nature of student independence and how can this quality be developed in our students?*

We had not as yet found out how to measure growth in independence and therefore could not speak with assurance to a most critical question, "Is it possible to teach youngsters to be independent?" We had no proof that independence could be nurtured in a specific kind of educational program. All we could say, as a result of the high correlation between scholastic ability and selection of an independent learning milieu, was that the desire or willingness to carry on independent learning was a function of manifest ability.

The feeling persisted that the ultimate value of youngsters' learning how to learn on their own, rather than being constantly directed by an "authority," would be so great that it was worthwhile to tackle the difficult problem: What is independence; can it be taught?

Upon invitation, each Freshman Project staff member submitted a statement of his ideas to me and then we discussed them in turn. I then developed a rough statement incorporating as many of these ideas as possible. Fortunately, I was able to obtain the assistance of Richard Wolf, Research Associate and protege of Professor Benjamin S. Bloom. Wolf undertook to refine this statement into an evaluation-type design.

In final form, the design was rather simple. To get at the question "What is independence?", the two teachers in each subject would meet with Wolf and describe the attributes of a youngster whom they would consider as independent in their subject matter field. These descriptions would be translated by Wolf into behavioral terms, or measurable dimensions. The construction of a rating scale to measure the presence or absence of these dimensions in the students would then be undertaken. Using these scales, the teachers would appraise the students in their respective subjects at the beginning of the school year and again at the close. These pre- and post-ratings would provide a measurement of growth in independence as defined by the teachers, subject by subject.

Once the dimensions of independence were stated, the teachers had concrete behavior goals toward which they could direct their instruction. If the results of the pre- and post-ratings indicated that independent behaviors had indeed developed, then it would be incumbent upon the faculty to be able to report methods and techniques which would seem to have facilitated this learning. To that end, teachers had the responsibility for developing learning experiences specifically directed toward the defined behavioral dimensions and for keeping logs of these activities. They could then look back and make an appraisal as to what was conducive to student independence.

To determine the relationship between independence and manifest ability, pre- and post-testing and statistical devices would be used. Since independence would have been defined in terms of behaviors, correlations between independence and ability and achievement would be possible.

The 1964–65 Project

Once this design was established, teachers in the project and other teachers in the high school were invited to express interest in working under the rigors of the design. Appointed to the faculty of the 1964–65 Freshman Project were the two pioneers, Poll and Bernstein, three established teachers from other levels of the high school, three teachers new to the school, and two interns from the Graduate School of Education's Master of Arts in Teaching Program.

The faculty and students were divided into two subteams. Bernstein was appointed chairman of one subteam and was named associate chairman of the project. Poll was named chairman of the other subteam and overall chairman of the project, responsible for coordinating the work of the two subteams. In a sense, we had two Freshman Projects, each with a teacher for each subject and each with its own group of students.

The 1964–65 Project got underway quite smoothly. The well established organizational format enabled the teachers new to the project to take hold with little difficulty. The teachers spent two weeks early in the summer defining measurable dimensions of independence, constructing rating scales and preparing pre- and post-tests to be used in assessing gains in subject matter knowledge. They came together again during the two weeks prior to the opening of school to work out procedural details.

The project faculty devoted considerable time during the first few weeks in the fall to acquainting the youngsters with the purpose of the project and introducing them to the optional activities. Trial option periods, followed by an option day once a week and subsequently twice a week, characterized the program up to the Christmas vacation. During this period the teachers deliberated on what types of learning environments they might offer to the students at the beginning of the second quarter.

In reviewing the previous experience, involving three types, two things became apparent: 1) there was no clear-cut difference among the three types in regard to teacher behavior (didacticism was practically non-existent), and 2) the youngsters who had chosen Type III (most independent) ended up meeting the teacher as often as those who had selected Type II. Furthermore, the different types of learning environments could be viewed as lying along a continuum, with the variables being a matter of degree rather than differentiating characteristics and even the degree interchanging at times among the types. Therefore, two types of learning structure could serve as well as three.

Normally, Type II would meet three days a week and Type I would meet four days a week. This arrangement would insure that every student had some opportunity for choosing optional activities, at the same time providing greater freedom for students who felt themselves to be more independent.

At one end of the continuum, the Type I structure would be essentially teacher-directed; assignments would be specific, short-term and in sequential order; readings would be selected by the teacher; checkups of homework and review sessions would be frequent. At the other end of the continuum (representing the ideal), the Type II structure would be essentially student-directed and inquiry-oriented. Goals would be set by the students in planning sessions with the teacher. Learning could proceed in a variety of ways. A student might conduct a study of some area in depth and leapfrog other areas, filling in the gaps through reading or informal discussions with his peers. The teacher would function as a resource person and not as a purveyor of information.

All during the year the teachers would be encouraging all students to take the road of intellectual discovery or to prepare for it by defining for themselves their weaknesses in study skills or study habits and seeking help to overcome their inadequacies.

It is worthwhile to note the gradual change over the years in the orientation of the Freshman Project. As originally conceived, the project sought to give students the opportunity to be independent and to find out what would happen when they had this opportunity. The 1964–65 project sought to deliberately teach the youngsters to become independent.

Project Findings

The data on last year's project have not as yet been completely analyzed. Some of the indications, however, are interesting. When the assessment of student independence by the teachers near the beginning of the year (after they had observed their students for about four weeks) by means of the rating scales described earlier was compared with the pre-test achievement scores, a low correlation was obtained ($r = .269$). This suggests that the teachers may have found ways to describe dimensions of independence which will enable us to distinguish the attributes which must underlie student self-direction from those which are measured by achievement or ability tests. A preliminary study of the final data indicates that the distinction may have held up throughout the year.

Student and teacher adjustment to the program was better than ever before. The three major changes made in organizational format have undoubtedly contributed to this improvement. The environmental types were reduced from three to two, the project was subdivided—making possible closer relationships among faculty and student groups, and the first twelve weeks were devoted to orienting the students to the program—moving them gradually toward the degree of responsibility for their learning which they were to assume.

It appears from the data that the students again made satisfactory achievement in subject matter. There is evidence that they also made gains in their ability to learn on their own.

We expect that the substantiated findings will point to the need of more studies in this area. First, it will be advisable to refine the dimensions of independence based upon the experiences and findings of this past year and then to revise the measuring instruments. Second, some way should be found to have individual student independence rated by trained, objective observers instead of by the teachers. Third, the teacher logs need to be scrutinized meticulously to determine whether there are techniques common to all subject fields which are effective in developing independence. If such are found, they should be tested under controlled conditions. Fourth, the dimensions of independence identified by the teachers need to be validated by comparing the results of comprehensive case studies of highly independent students and highly non-independent students.

A major part of our investigation still lies before us but the direction is now set. If all goes well, we may one day be in a position to recommend that independence be included as a major curricular goal for all schools and also be able to suggest instructional methodologies for its accomplishment.

Reprinted from *North Central Association Quarterly,* Vol. 40, pp. 222–228. Reprinted by permission of the publisher and Willard J. Congreve. Dr. Congreve wrote this article while serving as Principal of the University of Chicago Laboratory High School. He now resides at 808 Saratoga Terrace, Turnersville, N.J.

References

[1]See Willard J. Congreve, "Toward Independent Learning," *North Central Association Quarterly,* Spring 1963, 298–302.

[2]See Willard J. Congreve, "The University of Chicago Project," Independent Study: Bold New Venture, edited by David W. Beggs, III and Edward G. Buffie; Chapter 3, pp. 28–50; Indiana University Press, 1965, Bloomington, Indiana.

[3]Willard J. Congreve, "Toward Independent Learning," op cit.

SECTION **IV**

Individualizing Instruction
in Various Content Areas

The collection of papers in this section focuses on individualizing instruction in various content areas. The nine articles included in the section discuss how to match and meet the needs of each child in the subject areas of reading, spelling, social studies, mathematics and science.

John B. Bouchard in his article suggests four possible approaches to the individualization of instruction. These are: the adjustment of rate of learning, instructional modes, curriculum and instructional materials. Some of the ways to adjust curriculum to meet the unique characteristics and needs of individual learners are discussed.

Lyman C. Hunt, Jr. in his article identifies six steps that have been found to lead to the installation of a highly successful individualized reading program. The reader will find in this article many helpful suggestions on how to avoid pitfalls and also on how to develop behaviors and attitudes conducive to individualization of instruction in reading.

Five strategies for an individualized spelling program are discussed by C. Glennon Rowell in "A Prototype For An Individualized Spelling Program." Many problems involved in the implementation of these strategies are identified and recommended solutions to these problems are examined.

John I. Thomas in his article, "Individualizing Learning Experiences in the Elementary School Social Studies," contends that compared to other curriculum areas, it is more appropriate to individualize instruction in Social Studies. The author takes an example of a unit on discovery of America and suggests various strategies to match and meet the needs of students. Marian Owen in her article, "Social Studies Activities," lists many helpful activities for a social studies teacher. Some of the activities are: back when; foods, where from; information swap; interviews; population density; and barter.

H. Clifford Clark in his article, "Before You Individualize Your Elementary Math. . . ," suggests five basic areas to be considered before individualizing mathematics instruction. The author contends that if the classroom techniques compare favorably with these five checkpoints, the chances for success are greatly improved.

One of the problems that teachers face in individualizing instruction is the non-availability of appropriate instructional materials. In "Developing Mathematical Processes," Thomas Romberg and Mary E. Montgomery introduce the reader to a set of instructional materials in mathematics. These materials include objectives, pre- and post-tests, enrichment activities, and manipulative materials. It is hoped that this set of materials will meet the long-felt need of teachers in elementary grades.

The last two articles in this section describe the use of the tape cartridge and tape recorder in individualizing science instruction. Joseph I. Lipson in his article, "An Individualized Science Laboratory," describes individualized science laboratory lessons and discusses the effectiveness of these lessons with elementary school children. Specific examples are given from units on magnetism and light. "An Experiment Via Tape" by George LaCava is an excellent example of the creative use of the tape recorder. The author feels that the tape recorder has unlimited possibilities as a teaching tool and can add "new dimensions to your science class."

18

Curriculum Strategies for Individualizing Instruction

John B. Bouchard

Individualized instruction may be defined as the interaction between a student and school personnel which results in the adjustment of learning experiences to the unique interests, capabilities and needs of the learner within the resources of the school.

There are at least four possible approaches to the individualization of instruction. These include:

1. The adjustment of rate of learning.
2. The adjustment of instructional modes.
3. The adjustment of curriculum.
4. The adjustment of instructional materials.

This paper will identify and discuss some of the ways in which the curriculum can be adjusted to meet the unique characteristics and needs of individual learners.

Few considerations in education are as complex as the meaning of *curriculum*. The hundred years' existence of the graded school system has witnessed many attempts to identify appropriate curriculums. Some of the major attempts to identify the learnings to be offered by the schools included:

1. *The Academic Disciplines* approach in which de-

sired learnings are organized under such courses as history, geography, biology.

2. *The Social Processes* approach in which pupils are directed to study such topics as communication, transportation and manufacturing.

3. *The Broad Fields* approach in which related subjects are grouped under such areas as the social studies, science, language arts and mathematics.

Some educators have proposed that the curriculum be focused on *Life Adjustment* with pupil studies directed toward such problems as making a living, protecting life and health, getting an education.

Other educators have proposed a problem solving focus through such approaches as the *Project Method,* or through *Inquiry* or *Discovery.*

For many years, some educators, led by John Dewey, have taken the position that it makes little difference what is learned in school—particularly at the elementary grade levels. The primary concern of the school is to create an increased desire for learning in the pupils. More recently, critics have deplored the lack of school concern for pupils as human beings and have stressed the need for developing understandings that are supportive of desired pupil attitude and value systems. Such interrelationships between cognitive and affective learnings are sought through humanized or confluent education.

Despite the many differences in opinion about what a curriculum is, each school has a curriculum, and the staff of each school, however well-directed or haphazard its efforts, seeks to use the content and learning experiences provided through its curriculum to attain the individual social goals for which the school assumes responsibility. In other words, each school has, over the period of its existence:

1. Selected and organized the learning experiences it provides for its clients.

2. Acquired instructional materials which appear likely to convey the learning sought for students.

3. Appointed staff members who have been prepared to teach the content and direct the learnings endorsed by the school.

4. Organized school facilities, staff and resources to provide the instructional program.

5. Established marking and reporting procedures to indicate pupil success in attaining learnings sought.

It is beyond the scope of this paper to discuss the considerations involved in the development of a school's curriculum or to challenge the content and learning experiences the school proposes for its clients. Unfortunately, once established, the curriculum in many schools becomes, as time goes by, much less responsive to the changing demands of its society, and the widely divergent needs of its pupils.

This is not to ignore the tremendous contributions the public schools have rendered to American society over the past hundred years. The American Public School System—with its goal of education for all, with its level of public financial support, and with its control by the people—is the world's best model of universal education. It has provided basic education for untold millions of American youth. But it can be improved.

As with any other bureaucracy, the school tends to perpetuate the established organizational structure which facilitates the achievement of its purpose. In the case of the schools, pupil learning is largely sought through group instructional procedures. The typical graded school structure has provided a highly efficient management system which makes it easy to form instructional groups, assign teachers, account for pupils, schedule classes, and purchase and distribute instructional materials.

Unfortunately, it appears to matter little in many schools that the *"efficient way"* of doing things violates not only basic principles of human learning and child development but does not even make common sense. Incredible though it may be, many schools attempt to serve pupils of widely diverging characteristics by giving them the same learning experiences, in the same sequence, with the same amount of working time. And, to cap it all, the success of pupils in the system is judged—not on what they *can do,* but on whether they are keeping up or falling behind in their groups.

This paper will identify and subsequently illustrate the implications of a system of curriculum planning for individualized instruction.

Three of the most critical considerations are:

1. The level of curriculum decision making.
2. The interaction between the teacher and each child.
3. The adjustment of educational objectives.

In order to effectively individualize instruction, curriculum decisions must be made at the teacher-pupil level. Sanction for such decision making should clearly be assigned by the school board. Any limits to the decision-making role of the teacher should be clearly defined.

Where the organizational structure of the school permits, as in the Wisconsin IGE Model, or the Fredonia POISE Model, curriculum decision making may be enhanced by placing this responsibility in the hands of an instructional team.

In any case, the professional staff, in the exercise of its curriculum decision-making responsibilities, must be prepared to make frequent and dramatic departures from conventional curriculum practice in order to determine and provide the most effective learning for each child. The following are illustrative of such departures:

1. Different children at the same "grade level" will engage in widely differing learning experiences which may depart from any "pre-set" curriculum.

2. Some instructional groups, by virtue of similarity of interest, ability, or performance level of their members, will be composed of children of different "grade levels."

3. Instructional groups studying the same curriculum will use learning experiences and materials of widely differentiated levels of ability.

4. Curriculum "requirements" will be postponed or waived for some children.

5. Special personnel, resources and facilities will be used to meet the needs of some individuals.

In order to effectively individualize instruction, the teacher must interact frequently with each child. It is readily apparent that before the teacher can make intelligent decisions about individualizing instruction, she must have data to guide her decision-making. Much of this information relates to the child's ability and his performance, in the skills and content areas.

Inasmuch as school personnel frequently exhibit more concern about *what* pupils learn than how they *feel* about their learning, successful curriculum adjustments for each child must consider the pupil's attitudes and preference for alternative learning experiences as well as his effectiveness in using them. This does not imply that the child's school day should be spent in doing "only what he likes to do." But neither should his attitudes and preferences be ignored. The teacher can, through brief weekly interviews with each child, gain much insight for participative decision-making. These interviews should be built into the weekly schedule and assigned as high a priority as any other task for which the teacher assumes responsibility. It will be useful for the teacher to think of three stages in the interview procedures:

1. Planning the Interview
2. Conducting the Interview
3. Follow-up.

In planning the interview, it will be helpful for the teacher to consider such questions as these:

1. What is unique about *this* child?
2. What progress has he made?
3. How does he feel about *his* school experience?
4. What alternatives or choices are open to *him*?

The actual interview can serve other purposes in addition to information gathering. A good interview will:

1. Provide an uninterrupted period of pupil-teacher interaction.
2. Help the child develop self-esteem.
3. Reflect the teacher's interest in the child.
4. Serve as an outlet for the child's feelings and attitudes.
5. Give the child opportunities to make choices.

The length of individual interviews will probably vary from time to time and from child to child. As a tentative guideline, until the teacher gains further experience with her own pupils, it is suggested that a ten-minute block of time be planned each week for each child.

It seems wise to inject a note of caution about the

interviews. If they are to succeed, they must not be teacher-dominated. And, at all costs, the interview must not be used as an individual scolding session in which the pupil is berated for his lack of progress.

The interviews provide a frame of reference for follow-up activities on the part of the teacher. Brief, informal checks with individual pupils will yield evidence which will support, change or reject the course of action agreed upon in the interview. Several categories of decision making are identified, including decisions related to the following:

1. The unique characteristics of the child.
2. The child's progress.
3. The child's attitudes and feelings.
4. The child's choices.

It is evident that the role of a teacher who plans, conducts and follows up individual interviews with her pupils will differ markedly from that of a teacher whose major activity is class instruction. A few of these shifts in teacher roles may be briefly illustrated.

Again, the two important strategies for adjusting the curriculum to the capabilities, interests and needs of individual children are:

1. Curriculum decisions must be made at the teacher-pupil level.
2. The teacher must interact frequently with each child.

A third critical strategy must also be discussed. *In order to effectively individualize instruction, educational objectives must be adjusted to the capabilities, interests and needs of each child.*

There is an abundance of evidence to indicate that the traditional school fails to challenge the more capable students, and, at the same time, imposes excessive demands on the slower learners. The conventional school can be indicted on yet another count—the educational outcomes by which student progress is evaluated. Even a superficial examination of a school testing program suggests that the greatest concern—perhaps because it is easier to measure— is that students can recall or reproduce information committed to memory. Such an approach is hardly consistent with a philosophy of helping each individual become all he is capable of being.

That there are ways of getting children beyond the recognition and recall stage of learning has repeatedly been demonstrated by imaginative teachers. Categories of objectives which will help to go beyond the recognition and recall stage are listed as follows:

1. Objectives relating to what the child is expected to know or understand.

2. Objectives relating to what the child is expected to do.

3. Objectives relating to exploratory learnings to be provided for the child.

4. Objectives relating to the child as human being.

At this point it seems feasible to illustrate how certain desired pupil outcomes can be sought first in terms of curriculum adjustment, and later in terms of the child as a unique human being. It must be recognized that *what* a child does and how he *feels* about it cannot be separated in the real school setting. However, it will be less confusing to discuss these one at a time.

The curriculum can be adjusted in terms of the knowledge and understandings sought for each child.

Certain basic knowledges and understandings must be achieved by each child if he is to attain higher level objectives. Knowing the number names, knowing the letters of the alphabet, knowing the number facts are all examples of such basics. There is little by way of curriculum adjustment that can be done about these basic skills and knowledges. There are, however, many possibilities for individualizing the basic knowledges and understandings through adjustment of rate, adjustment of learning mode, adjustment of instructional materials. In the school setting the basic knowledges are closely associated with performance to achieve the basic skills—rote counting, reading words in a sight vocabulary, computing the basic number facts, and the like.

While the individual classroom teacher can develop her own objectives, methods, and materials to help children

attain the basic skills, this is a questionable use of professional time. Much commercial material is available to help
the teachers in these activities. For example, an outline of
objectives is available from the Instructional Objectives
Exchange, Los Angeles, California. Carefully developed
individualized curriculum materials are also available, such
as the University of Wisconsin's Design for Reading Skill
Development, and the University of Pittsburgh's Individually Prescribed Instruction in Mathematics.

Use of such available materials can help the teacher by
providing children an individualized self-teaching mode of
instruction which can be used effectively in any kind of
teacher-pupil interaction, from the tutoring situation to the
large group.

These self-instructing materials provide pre-tests for
determining the child's entry level in the skills area,
provide a sequence of exercises designed to develop mastery, and test the child's progress through curriculum
imbedded test items.

The teacher checks the child's progress frequently and
determines whether the child will go on to the next step,
use alternative learning experiences, jump ahead, or perhaps temporarily stop work in the skill development.

Higher levels of understandings and skills

Once the child has developed certain basic skills, he can be
guided, through interaction with his teacher, to attain
higher level understandings and skills. Above the level of
the basic skills, the particular content used has less significance than the behavioral outcomes for individual children;
it will be helpful for the teacher to consider:

1. The learner's past performance in the content or
subject area.

2. The learner's special interests in topics within the
content.

3. The selections for study made by the learner.

4. The learner's ability to cope with available instructional materials.

5. The learner's potential.

Curriculum adjustments to enable individual children

to attain appropriate learning outcomes may be made either by preparing individual study units for each child, or by presenting a range of alternatives within a unit prepared for a group of children. It is suggested that the second approach be utilized until teachers become more familiar with the preparation of individual contracts.

Through such curriculum adjustments, it is now possible to help children attain educational objectives beyond the knowledge level, such as comprehension, application, analysis, synthesis, and evaluation.

It is impossible in this brief paper to give detailed illustrations concerning pupil acquisition of these objectives. However, it may be helpful to suggest some curriculum approaches which promote the development of such outcomes.

Curriculum approaches supporting individualization

In the elementary social studies, Dr. Matt Ludes at SUC, Fredonia, New York, has developed an exciting unit on Latin America. Students select a country, plan an imaginary visit, arrange transportation details, keep records of their experiences, make notes about the country and its people, and prepare a report for presentation to the class.

The elementary staff at Bemus Point Central School, Bemus Point, New York, has developed a program in which students receive at least two opportunities to explore occupational information in the field. Teachers encourage and assist continued research upon pupil return to school.

In mathematics a whole set of alternatives may be created by asking children to "spend" various amounts of money for food by making selections from newspaper prices or actually visiting a supermarket. Children would also report why they spent the money as they did and give reasons for their choices.

Again in the social studies, children might be given data about an imaginary or real land and asked to prepare reports concerning the conditions the data might reflect, whether some of the data are inconsistent, and whether they might like to live there.

Dr. Louis Raths's *Thinking Box*,[1] is an excellent collection of materials which children can use independently to promote thinking skills in science, mathematics, social studies and other school subjects. The materials can also serve as models for the teacher who wishes to develop additional learning experiences for her children.

To summarize briefly, a few illustrations have been given about curriculum adjustments which promise to individualize learning. The adjustments provide for pupil interest and choice, promote higher level skills, and offer alternative levels of these skills.

It must be recognized that worthwhile departures from a conventional curriculum not only require creative teachers but also significant investments of professional time and talent. Fortunately, locally developed curriculum materials become accumulative—good ideas can be used over again.

There are also some commercial curriculum approaches which promote the development of higher levels of learning. Programs such as: *Science–A Process Approach* (S-APA) and *Man: A Course of Study* can be extremely useful.

The curriculum can be adjusted in terms of exploratory experiences provided for each child. If the school program is to be responsive to changing interests and needs of children, their community and society as a whole, there must be some flexibility to depart from the established curriculum. It is frequently difficult to anticipate what these new learnings may be or to predict their educational outcomes. It does seem appropriate, however, to provide some opportunities within the schools to try out new ideas for their appeal and potential value for children.

A familiar exploratory experience in many schools is a music program with instruments furnished, in which children may test their interest and ability without a major investment of time, money, or effort.

Perhaps the most exciting possibility for exploratory activities lies in the identification of a special hobby, interest, or activity for each child as an important part of his school experience. A concerned teacher can, by working closely with children on these one-of-a-kind studies, truly individualize instruction, promote success feelings for her pupils, and help them achieve status in the group.

This paper has given a number of suggestions for individualizing instruction. It was pointed out that the curriculum in any school is a complex mixture of content and learning experiences directed toward the development of knowledge, understandings and skills, of each child as a student. The curriculum is also used to develop the values, appreciations and attitudes of each child as a human being. But, despite the complexity of the curriculum, educational outcomes can be adjusted to the characteristics of each learner. Three critical requirements were identified as curriculum strategies for the individualization of instruction. They are:

1. Curriculum decisions must be made at the teacher-pupil level.

2. Educational objectives must be adjusted for each child.

3. The teacher must interact frequently with each child.

Individualization efforts do not come easily—but individualization efforts can be improved in any school in the search for the best possible education for each child.

This article was written at the request of the editors for this book. Dr. John B. Bouchard is Professor of Education, SUC, Fredonia, N.Y.

References

[1]Louis Raths, et al., *The Thinking Box*. Westchester, Illinois: Benefic Press, 1971.

19

Six Steps to the Individualized Reading Program (IRP)

Lyman C. Hunt, Jr.

There are six identifiable steps to an Individualized Reading Program which, when successfully developed by the teacher, lead to four values basic to productive reading. These results are obtainable only through IRP and only when there is not too much stumbling on the steps along the way. Teachers must understand each step and its relative importance to the total program of individualized reading.

The six steps are:

1. Classroom environment
2. Silent or quiet reading time
3. Instructional guidance
4. Book talks and conferences
5. Skill development: USSR
6. Records and evaluation

The unique values resulting are:

1. Exploratory-detective type reading
2. USSR: The ultimate reading skill
3. Self-direction in the world of print
4. L.O.B.

The purpose of this paper is to prevent stumbling on

the steps, to help teachers avoid pitfalls in their efforts to build stronger classroom reading programs.

The Reading Atmosphere within the Classroom

The first step, and this is imperative to success, is to build an atmosphere for productive reading. Building this climate for reading takes careful nurturing; it also takes time. Each teacher's goal must be to develop productive reading on the part of each pupil. It is easy to make the mistake of leaving atmosphere to chance. This can be fatal to IRP. A climate for reading requires both endurance and endeavor on the part of the teacher. Two key factors for creating this climate are: (1) the concept of Quiet Reading Time and (2) skillful use of Instructional Guidance.

Quiet or Silent Reading Time

The concept underlying silent reading time is vital to developing IRP successfully. Each teacher must clearly perceive legitimate activities permissible during the Quiet Reading Period. The ideal model has each reader directing his own activities with printed material throughout the duration of the reading period. The perfect situation requires that everyone be so engaged in silent reading (or working on responses thereto) that the teacher is free to interact with pupils in a variety of ways, individually or in groups. A chart giving the framework or structure of the silent reading time helps. The chart should be very visible to each and every incipient reader. A sample chart could read:

Quiet Reading Time

1. Select a book or other printed material.
2. Read quietly (see how much you can get done).
3. Have a book talk or conference (be prepared—know what to say).
4. Record your results—write about reading—chart your progress.
5. Study vocabulary.
6. Work with a partner.

The behavior of the reader is markedly different in IRP

from that which he has used in the text program. Each must learn new ways of behaving. While natural for many, this new pattern is difficult for some. Some will need time and patient guidance to succeed. Success in IRP means:

1. Making wise and intelligent selections of reading material.

2. Spending large blocks of time in independent silent reading.

3. Preparing for and being ready to make his best contribution during the conference time.

4. Preparing reports, keeping records, and being ready to share his learning from books with others.

Teachers err in not giving sufficient time and effort to establishing the framework for the quiet reading period. Teachers frequently are too eager to move to conferences and book talks, leaving the silent reading to care for itself. Moving too quickly to conference activities doesn't work. Many young readers need constant and considered instruction in sustained silent reading prior to gaining the self-direction needed to make conference time worth-while. At first these young readers need Instructional Guidance more than they need book talks.

Instructional Guidance

Serious reading covering long stretches of print is not taken seriously by some. Many boys and some girls prefer to spend silent reading time in more noisy endeavors. The gossips, those who prefer talking to reading, are common. The wanderers, those active individuals (mostly boys) who would rather walk around than read, need considerable attention. The wanderers usually spend excessive amounts of time searching for suitable reading material. When pressed to settle down to productive reading, 101 excuses are forthcoming for not doing so. "Squirrels" collect books as their animal counterparts do nuts. "Squirrels" get a new book each day but are too busy gathering them to take time to read them. For them, the reading time is unproductive, little reading is completed.

Every teacher who tries IRP has gossips, wanderers and squirrels in varying degrees. Productive reading is most difficult for some. Typically about ¼ of the total group exhibit such evasive behaviors. IRP cannot succeed unless the teacher first works at moderating if not overcoming these disruptive behaviors. This is where instructional guidance is needed. And this is where many teachers fail.

The guiding principle, which should be held inviolate, is as follows: During the reading period no one may act so as to interfere with the productive reading of another. This means no interruption of one reader by another unless this interaction contributes in some way to the productivity of all concerned. Much legitimate interaction occurs among various readers. But this decree also means occasionally telling some to Sit Down, Keep Quiet and Start Reading.

The principle of non-interference of others and high productivity by each reader must be firmly established. IRP cannot succeed without it. Yet the teacher who finds this precept violated no more than a dozen times a day should not be discouraged. The teacher can err only by not attending to the problems which arise and by not working to ameliorate them. Little by little the wanderers, gossips and squirrels become readers. The basis for successful IRP has been established. Instructional guidance is crucial to creating the atmosphere of a successful Quiet Reading Time. The rule of non-interference must work.

Book Talks and Conferences

The Silent Reading Time, with the atmosphere of productive reading created by it, is the heart of IRP. Similarly conference time with book talks is the heart of the Silent Reading Time. Through book talks the teacher plays a key instructional role. This role must be clearly understood; otherwise efforts to build IRP will falter. In the past the role of the teacher in book talks has been poorly defined; consequently serious mistakes have been made.

First some areas of error. Teachers must not think of the first purpose of book talks as interrogating each and every reader about each and every book read. To do so is self-defeating for both teacher and reader. To the contrary, the concept that extensive reading developed within IRP is exploratory in nature (i.e. searching far and wide in print of all sorts for important ideas) must be understood by both reader and teacher. Consequently, to be successful, book talks must be based on sampling techniques. The teacher takes samples of each student's accumulated reading. Certain parts of some books are discussed; not all parts of all books. Through conversation with readers, the teacher takes samples of ideas readers have gained through a variety of situations.

To think of checking thoroughly all reading is disastrous. Thorough questioning of material read should be reserved for intensive reading which accompanies the textbook reading program; it should not be duplicated in IRP. Endeavoring to do so has been the downfall of many teachers.

Second, the conference time ought not to be used for checking oral reading errors. To think of the teacher's role as that of listening to individuals read orally is self-defeating for IRP. Again this can better be accomplished within the context of the textbook program with its oral reading groups. Teachers who try to carry the practice of oral reading checks over to the conference time of IRP find themselves overwhelmed and quickly turn back from IRP.

The essential purpose of book time is to enable each reader to reveal the significance of his reading experiences. The role of the teacher is to enable the reader to convey the true meaning of what has been read. The key to book talk time lies in the questioning used by the teacher. Perceptive, penetrating questions can give insight relatively quickly into the depth of reading. Reference is made to three articles wherein these concepts have been thoroughly developed.

1. Hunt, Lyman C. Jr. "The Key to the Conference Lies in the Questioning," Educational Comment on Individual Reading, H. Sandberg, ed., The University of Toledo, College of Education, Toledo, Ohio, 1966.

2. Hunt, Lyman C. Jr. "Evaluation Through Teacher-Pupil Conferences," The Evaluation of Children's Reading Achievement, T. Barrett, ed., Perspectives in Reading No. 8, International Reading Association, Newark, Delaware, 1967.

3. Hunt, Lyman C. Jr. "A Grouping Plan Capitalizing on the Individualized Reading Approach," Forging Ahead In Reading, J. Allen Figurel, ed., Part I, Proceedings of the Twelfth Annual Convention, International Reading Association, Newark, Delaware, 1968.

USSR: The Pinnacle of Reading Skills

Every teacher of reading should think of USSR as the pinnacle of achievement with regard to teaching skillful reading. USSR in this regard has nothing to do with our friendly Union of Soviet Socialist Republics. It is purely coincidental that the initials for this most paramount of all reading skills are identical with those of the Russian country. In this instance the initials stand for UNINTER-RUPTED SUSTAINED SILENT READING.

USSR pertains to the relativity among reading skills. Basic to the concept is the consideration that silent reading is far more significant than is oral reading. Basic to the concept is the belief that contextual reading is of greater importance than are skills of recognition at the word/letter level. Basic to the concept is that the greatest reading skill to be achieved is that of sustaining silent reading over long stretches of print without interruption and without breaks. USSR cannot be achieved unless the reader has the facility to keep his mind on and flowing with the ideas.

USSR, then, is the skill which signals that the student is able to read by himself and for himself over long spans of print. Each reader must realize that his purpose in the silent reading time is to get as many of the important and significant ideas as he can through silent reading. In USSR reading is regarded as a detective-type activity. Specifically this means that the reader is not held accountable for every single idea contained in every single sentence or parts thereof. Specifically this means that the reader is oriented to search the material for ideas which are of relatively great importance, i.e., ideas of relative importance as contrasted with details and facts of lesser importance. His task is to search out ideas that matter—ideas that make a difference.

This requires a radically different orientation to comprehension than that conveyed to the reader by the majority of current textbook programs. Both teacher and reader must understand that reading comprehension is making a series of judgments about the worthwhileness of the ideas—not remembering and repeating all that has been read.

Developing USSR in the classroom situation requires a very definite and particular set of attitudes on the parts of both the teacher and the reader. Each reader realizes that doing well means: (1) accomplishing as much silent reading as possible during the reading period; (2) keeping one's mind on the ideas; (3) responding more powerfully to high potency words and sentences; and (4) giving less attention to ideas of lesser importance.

USSR can be taught. Productive reading can be strengthened by helping each reader to realize that success means learning to sustain himself with print for longer and longer stretches of time. Any device the teacher wishes to use to help the readers attain this goal is in order. Various instructional devices help youngsters to keep track of the amount of silent reading accomplished during the reading period, i.e., through charts or through graphs or through any scheme of time-keeping which will make progress visible. Another approach is for the teacher to sit with groups in the reading circle and supervise or govern their silent reading. Here the teacher's role is simply to support and assist each youngster as he tries to get as far as he can with his printed material during his time in the reading circle. There is no oral reading around the circle; oral reading is eliminated except for having individual students verify ideas. The teacher helps with words; she assists in interpreting sentences; but more than anything else, she simply establishes the setting so that maximum amounts of silent reading can be completed by each child. The teacher helps each child to extend his own previous limits through day-to-day practice.

By using proper questions, the teacher can develop the understanding in the reader's mind that reading means getting as many big ideas out of print through sustained silent reading as he possibly can. The test for sustained silent reading consists basically of observing the youngster. Establishing situations in which sustained silent reading can be accomplished, then checking with the reader on the basic question: "Could you keep your mind on the ideas all the time you were reading?" is the essential test for USSR.

The USSR concept has significant implications for work with youngsters at the lower end of the reading scale. A gross and tragic mistake has been attempting to teach the low group readers through oral reading. The erroneous practice has been trying to get those in our low groups to sound as good while reading orally as do those in upper groups. Then, the theory goes, each will somehow become an independent reader. This approach has not worked and can not work. Just attempting to reach relatively high degrees of oral reading fluency first is going at skill tasks backwards. Helping a young reader develop power of silent reading is the first priority. Teachers should make the silent reader first, and then the oral reader, not the other way around as we currently are doing. Teachers can make silent readers first if a premium is placed on doing so; fluency in oral reading will then follow naturally. More than anything else, we must realign our priorities with regard to basic reading skill areas.

Record Keeping

Teachers who are developing the individualized approach to reading instruction have found it necessary to devise ways for keeping records of the children's development in reading. Some find that a card or notebook page for each child can be easily used to record notes during the pupil conferences. Others use a more formalized checklist on which the teacher periodically records observations concerning the children's performances and abilities. Such records serve as a guide for planning and a basis for reporting to parents on the child's progress.

Such record keeping is all to the good; however, some teachers get "hung up" on keeping track of things. Compulsive record keeping can be fatal for IRP. If keeping records, keeping track of books, answering questions or writing resumes on books read, takes more time than is spent by readers reading then the teacher has become lost—lost in non-essentials.

Realistically, teachers who are good record keepers will keep good records while teachers with messy desks and messy rooms will not. Similarly, youngsters who are high-powered readers and who are well-ordered will maintain good records. Conversely, low-powered readers and those with sloppy habits won't even be able to find the papers on which their records are kept. So be it. The object of the program is productive reading, not neat notepads filled with records.

As the saying goes:

As you ramble through life, Brother,
Whatever be your Goal,
Keep your eye upon the Doughnut
And not upon the Hole.

In this analogy, of course, the Doughnut is equated to productive reading, while record keeping can be the hole into which many well-intentioned teachers have fallen.

And Evaluation

When the goal is that of making independent, self-sufficient, and self-sustaining readers, evaluation becomes a complex matter. The evaluator must know many aspects of each child's reading. It is not enough to know whether or not each word is known. It is not enough to check on oral reading fluency. The teacher must see beyond having students answer ten questions correctly following the reading of a short passage.

The teacher must know if the young reader can perform effectively in the complex world of printed material. Does the reader find the sources important to him, and then find the truly significant ideas within them? Most important, once the proper reading material has been selected, does the reader have the staying power to follow through on long intricate passages? The ability to do this is the mark of a true reader. Any worthwhile evaluation must be predicated on this concept of reading. Fortunately each student reveals the answer to these questions through his daily performance in IRP. Evaluation becomes a self-evaluation for many. Observant teachers actually know each student's performance in reading better than in more conventional reading programs.

Four Values of IRP

The unique benefits emerging from successful development of IRP are four in number.

1. The art of extensive, exploratory reading is developed. Once the reader has learned a searching, detective approach to printed matter he has achieved a higher-level reading performance than is possible through conventional programs which concentrate on intensive types of reading.

2. USSR—the skill of sustained silent reading is acquired by some who otherwise would not have become real readers. Unless the reader can keep going with print he has not reached the highest skill level.

3. Independence and self-direction are most difficult for some to learn, so difficult for some that self-direction is never gained. Yet it is also true that as long as one must follow teacher directions, that person is not a reader. Learning to be on-your-own in the world of print is a direct benefit of IRP for some.

4. L. O. B. is the grandest result of IRP; the result teachers who have succeeded with IRP unanimously acclaim is building LOVE OF BOOKS—a passion for reading. In IRP reading becomes a personal matter. Young readers have learned to care about books and they enjoy reading them. The personal satisfaction gained from reading is genuine. This is the ultimate difference that IRP can make.

Reprinted from *Elementary English*, "Six Steps to the Individualized Reading Program," by Lyman C. Hunt, Jr. Copyright January, 1971 by the National Council of Teachers of English. Reprinted by permission of the publisher and Lyman C. Hunt, Jr. Lyman C. Hunt, Jr. is Professor of Education at the University of Vermont.

References

1. Hunt, Lyman C. Jr. "The Key to the Conference Lies in the Questioning," Educational Comment on Individual Reading, H. Sandberg, ed., The University of Toledo, College of Education, Toledo, Ohio, 1966.

2. Hunt, Lyman C. Jr. "Evaluation Through Teacher-Pupil Conferences," The Evaluation of Children's Reading Achievement, T. Barrett, ed., Perspectives in Reading No. 8, International Reading Association, Newark, Delaware, 1967.

3. Hunt, Lyman C. Jr. "A Grouping Plan Capitalizing on the Individualized Reading Approach," Forging Ahead In Reading, J. Allen Figurel, ed., Part I, Proceedings of the Twelfth Annual Convention, International Reading Association, Newark, Delaware, 1968.

20

A Prototype for an Individualized Spelling Program

C. Glennon Rowell

On Monday, every student in a classroom is introduced to the same list of spelling words. A pretest is given on Tuesday to see how many words each child already knows and on Wednesday, each child uses the weekly spelling words in sentences. Spelling activities on Thursday are designed to teach the words missed on the pretest. A final weekly spelling test is given on Friday. Every week, spelling instruction in thousands of elementary school classrooms follows this pattern or one that is strikingly similar.

Is this an effective way to teach spelling? The instruction is essentially large-group oriented. While some children do profit from such instruction, many others are undoubtedly denied the type of help that would be most useful to them. All children do not learn to spell words at the same rate of speed nor do all children have the same problems in learning to spell. While the spelling pretest is an attempt to individualize instruction, an overly rigid schedule can make it just another activity in which all children in a classroom participate.

Strategies for Individualizing Instruction

Instruction becomes individualized through the employment of the following strategies:

1. Arranging skills and concepts to be taught on a simple-to-complex continuum

2. Finding the point on the continuum at which each individual has progressed

3. Diagnosing problems that obstruct the learning of any of the skills and concepts

4. Providing activities that are appropriate for teaching the skills and concepts to one student or to a group of students

5. Streamlining procedures for keeping records of each student as he progresses through the continuum.

An individualized spelling program can be developed when these strategies are made operable. Problems involved in the implementation of these strategies and recommended solutions to these problems are discussed in the following pages.

Strategy One: Building a Spelling Continuum

In most elementary schools, children are expected to learn how to spell a large set of basic words. The identification of these words is a longstanding concern of educators but lists have been compiled from adult writings, spelling books in existence, personal and business letters, most frequently used words, and most frequently misspelled words.[2]

The extent to which the spelling needs of the individual are considered in the use of basic word lists is open to question since weekly spelling lessons usually contain words from the same spelling level and the same weekly lessons are done by everyone in a classroom. Yet children do have varying abilities to spell.[4,5,6]

Some teachers use spelling books on different grade levels in a single grade but this can be difficult to manage. It would appear that a more efficient way of providing word lists on the spelling level of each child is to duplicate a list of words that are normally taught in a two-to-six year period. When a child begins his formal spelling program at about grade two, a copy of these words would be placed in a spelling folder. The list would be used throughout the year and then along with the folder, be moved upward through the grades with the child.

The duplicated list of basic spelling words should be arranged in columns of increasing levels of difficulty, and each semester every student would be assigned words from only those columns that are on his spelling level. As an example, a fifth grade student who is at the third grade level in spelling would be assigned third grade words rather than words on a fifth grade spelling level. To make the word list even more individualized, words each child finds difficult to spell in his writing in all subjects should be added to his list.

Learning to spell a list of basic words is only one phase of a spelling program since children are expected to learn many spelling skills and generalizations that will enable them to spell words they have never studied. These skills and generalizations should be arranged on a continuum that (1) shows the order in which each major skill and generalization is introduced in the spelling curriculum and (2) reveals sub-skills that are prerequisite to learning each of the major skills and generalizations. A section of such a continuum resembles a ladder in which the skill that is directly applicable to spelling (the major skill) appears on the top rung and prerequisite skills appear on the lower rungs. Syllabication is an example of a major skill and is shown in the following diagram.

Syllabication and Prerequisite Skills
Dividing Words Into Syllables

Recognizing the Two Words in a Compound Word

Identifying the Number of Syllables a Word Has by
Counting the Vowel Sounds in the Word

Understanding the Concept of Syllable as Being a Separately Pronounced Unit of a Word

Distinguishing Between Vowel and Consonant Sounds in
Words When They are Pronounced

If all skills and generalizations taught in the elementary school spelling program are outlined on the ladder-type continuum, a series of diagrams similar to the one shown would be placed on a chart. The order in which each diagram appears on this chart would depend upon the order in which the major skill or generalization appears in the spelling curriculum.

Strategy Two: Determining Where Each Child Has Progressed in the Spelling Program

A flexible pretesting system follows the assignment of individual spelling lists. The pretests should be given to determine which words should be studied. Each child should be allowed to take pretests on clusters of words from his list whenever he has mastered the preceding group of words. The existing lock-step, weekly pretest given to all members of a class would be replaced by this flexible scheme.

How can children be given frequent and different pretests in spelling? The answer to this question is found in a practice that already exists in many classrooms—pairs of children giving out words to each other as a review for the weekly test on Friday. Through proper training children can be taught to give pretests to each other. The teacher will probably be more involved in pretesting students who have advanced to the more difficult words but student pairs can easily be formed for most of the pretesting in spelling.

What happens in an individualized spelling program after a child has been given a pretest? First, the child should mark on the basic list in his folder those words he spelled correctly. Secondly, he should become involved in activities that will enable him to learn the words he missed. When a final test indicates that the words have been learned, the child should mark these words on his basic list and refile it. The same type of flexible system that is used in spelling pretests should also operate for final tests on words studied by the individual.

It is also necessary to give pretests on skills and generalizations in the spelling program. This can be done periodically through standardized tests or informal teacher-constructed tests. These tests should be designed to survey how well a child has mastered major spelling skills and generalizations. Diagnostic tests to determine problems that might be responsible for failure to learn a particular skill will be given separately from survey tests. The diagnostic phase of the individualized spelling program is discussed in Strategy Three.

Strategy Three: Diagnosing Problems That Obstruct Spelling Achievement

Errors that students make on spelling tests and other written work provide much information that is useful in helping make the spelling program more individualized. Too often misspelled words are simply checked and the only follow-up activity is the advice given to learn the words. At the same time, the student is expected to begin studying a new lesson in spelling. While it is important for a student to learn misspelled words, it is equally necessary for spelling errors on these words to be critically examined by the teacher. The child who spells iorn for iron, gose for goes, and dsek for desk needs more help than the advice of "learn how to spell these words." If words are continuously spelled with the reversal error that is evident in the spelling of these words, this student would be better off to have activities designed to correct this particular kind of error. It is reasonable to assume that the routine activities of studying new words, writing them in sentences, and taking weekly tests on them would reenforce any type of spelling error a child has a tendency to make unless special attention is given to the error.

Several crucial problems must be dealt with in analyzing spelling errors. Identifying the types of errors made, determining the cause of each type of error, and recognizing proper corrective techniques are some of these problems but fortunately they have been explored in several sources.[1,3,7]

One of the most critical problems to be faced in the analysis of spelling errors in an individualized program is lack of time. There is a limit to how much time a teacher can devote to instruction in a particular area. This limitation, combined with the task of keeping up with the sizable number of spelling errors a group of thirty or more children will make, creates the need for a system that saves time. One time-saving procedure is to have each child write all spelling tests in a tablet that is used only for spelling. In this way a file of consecutive lessons soon develops and the teacher can easily thumb through the tablets and identify the type of error being made by each individual. One teacher, in doing this, was surprised to see how clearly errors could be classified. This teacher reported an example of one child's problem with the middle parts of words— beautiful was spelled beautful, invitation was spelled invition, and families was spelled famlies. In lesson after lesson, middle syllables of words having three or more syllables were either omitted or misspelled.*

Another procedure that aids in the analysis of spelling errors is the use of a specially prepared form to record misspelled words each child makes. This form can be as simple as a dittoed page that is divided into several squares each of which represents a week. Misspelled words on individual spelling tests as well as other written work would be recorded in the appropriate square each week. If proper instruction is given, the recording of misspelled words can be done by teacher aides or some of the students. After misspelled words have been properly recorded on a form for each student, the form should be filed in the appropriate spelling folder. It then becomes an important reference for the teacher as individualized follow-up activities are planned.

When additional information is needed concerning the type of spelling errors a child makes, standardized diagnostic spelling tests can be used. Standardized tests are available and are helpful in analyzing errors a child makes as well as methods he uses in studying words. If a spelling program is individualized, such tests are used when more informal evaluation techniques fail to supply enough information on spelling problems.

Periodic diagnosis of spelling skills and generalizations should also be made in the spelling program. If the spelling continuum of these skills and generalizations is

*This was reported by an experienced teacher who was recently enrolled in a course taught by the writer of this article.

arranged according to the model described earlier, informal diagnostic instruments can easily be constructed by the classroom teacher. Thus when a child is ready to learn a new skill, he would be given a brief inventory on the prerequisite skills. A poor performance on this inventory would indicate a need for corrective activities while an acceptable performance would indicate a readiness to learn the particular spelling skill in question. Many teachers already make these informal examinations of prerequisite skills and the development of a series of spelling continuums would merely help systematize this inventory procedure.

Strategy Four: Providing Spelling Activities to be Used With One Student or a Group of Students

In an individualized spelling program children will often need to work independently. If several activities are available on the same spelling skill, the task of individualizing instruction is made easier. A variety of materials should be provided for this purpose.

Individualization of instruction is also made easier when the teacher is well-organized and plans, from the beginning, to build a resource of activities that can be adapted to individual or group use. Some teachers file lessons on separate skills in acetate binders and when a child is ready for a particular skill, an individualized lesson is pulled from the file. Thus the child who has a reversal problem in spelling would be given a lesson on correct visual imagery at the time he needed it. When acetate binders are used, it is wise to have children write their answers on a separate sheet of paper or directly on the acetate with a special marker which permits erasure of the answers. In either instance, the skill sheet can be used at a later time with other children.

A word of caution is necessary concerning the use of individualized skill sheets. Children at different spelling levels may have the same problem in spelling but not be able to utilize the same skill sheet. The words used in the activity might be too difficult for some of these children. Consequently, it is necessary for teachers to develop a file of activities on the same skill but on different spelling levels. Caution should also be exercised in the kinds of instructional activities selected. All activities do not have to be workbook activities. The language master, tape recorder, record player, and filmstrip projector can be effectively used in an individualized spelling program.

Do children always work alone on a spelling skill in an individualized program? While it is obvious that such a program will provide more opportunities for independent work, there will be many occasions in an individualized spelling program for small clusters of children to work together. When several children have progressed to the same point on the spelling continuum at approximately the same time, instruction can be provided in a group situation. The instruction remains individualized in these situations as long as grouping patterns are highly flexible and children are constantly reshuffled.

Strategy Five: Streamlining Record-Keeping Procedures

Several references have already been made concerning the problem of keeping records of each child's progress in an individualized spelling program. The number of students in a single classroom plus the vastly different directions they will move in an individualized program demand an extremely well-organized system of record keeping.

In most individualized programs, emphasis is placed on developing outlines which show the order in which skills and concepts are introduced. These outlines are then modified and become check lists for each individual receiving instruction. As soon as a child has mastered a skill, he is given a check mark to indicate success and is then moved on to the next skill on the outline. This same approach can be followed in the spelling program with the basic word list and the continuums of spelling skills and generalizations forming the outline. Since there may be a need to recheck a child's knowledge of certain words, skills, and generalizations he has learned, vertical lines that form columns can be drawn on the outlined chart to provide appropriate check points.

The spelling folders are a vital part of an individualized spelling program since they constitute the center from which planning is done. However, these folders are important only to the extent that analyses of their content are done to guide instruction for each individual rather than for each class. The individual spelling folder should contain several different kinds of information including analyses of errors made in spelling, progress charts, and samples of spelling in written work. If the folders are well-organized, they will prove to be invaluable in planning but they become less useful as they become less organized.

Conclusion

The same spelling instruction for all individuals in a classroom fails to meet the needs of each individual child within that classroom. Since each child learns to spell at his own rate of speed and since spelling problems differ among individuals, it is time to move toward a spelling program that focuses on these differences. For this to occur, spelling continuums must be carefully outlined, each child's behavior in spelling must be better understood, a wealth of spelling materials and activities must be furnished, and record-keeping tasks must be minimized. Without proper attention to these conditions, the spelling program will continue to have a built-in neglect for the specific needs each child has in learning how to spell.

Reprinted from *Elementary English*, "A Prototype for an Individualized Spelling Program," by C. Glennon Rowell. Copyright March, 1972 by the National Council of Teachers of English. Reprinted by permission of the publisher and C. Glennon Rowell. C. Glennon Rowell is Associate Professor of Education, Florida State University.

Bibliography

[1]Anderson, Paul S. *Language Skills in Elementary Education*. New York: The MacMillan Company, 1968, pp. 160–161.

[2]Anderson, Paul S. and Patrick J. Groff. *Resource Materials for Teachers of Spelling*. Minneapolis, Minnesota: Burgess Publishing Company, 1968, pp. 9–29.

[3]Bulletin No. 54. "How to Correct Spelling Errors."

Education Today, Columbus, Ohio: Charles E. Merrill Books, Inc.

[4]Fitzgerald, James A. *The Teaching of Spelling.* Milwaukee, Wisconsin: The Bruce Publishing Company, 1951, pp. 7–8.

[5]Hildreth, Gertrude. *Teaching Spelling.* New York: Henry Holt and Company, 1955, p. 42.

[6]Horn, Thomas D. "Spelling," in Encyclopedia of Educational Research, 4th Edition. New York: The MacMillan Company, 1969, p. 1286.

[7]Otto, Wayne and Richard A. McMenemy. *Corrective and Remedial Teaching.* Boston, Massachusetts: Houghton-Mifflin Company, 1966, p. 221.

21

Individualizing Learning Experiences in the Elementary School Social Studies

John I. Thomas

Different students learn in different ways! Individualizing the learning experiences for students has different meaning for different teachers. And this is all to the good. The elementary school social studies program, a natural vehicle for personalizing the education of students, however, has too often been neglected in this respect. Indeed it is unique in that it invites unlimited opportunities for dealing effectively with the individual perceptions, needs, and interests of elementary school children.

Let's be specific. How can individualized instruction be put to work in a social studies program? We might consider, first, the school organization itself. Does the organization of the school, in fact, facilitate or inhibit the individualizing process? It would seem to me that the team-taught, non-graded school provides more optimum conditions for individualizing instruction than do the self-contained, or departmentalized organizational schemes, simply because we can more readily adjust quantity, rate, and depth emphasis to the differentiated interests, needs, and inclinations of the students. We are more apt to spread students because there are more people to whom we can distribute them. Consequently the students are not restricted to particular grades which invariably insist upon conformity rather than diversity in the all-too-typical social studies program. It is indeed unfortunate that many teachers continue to ignore the well-established theory that not all pupils master a particular skill at a particular grade.

A second way to individualize instruction in the social studies would be through the curriculum itself. The conceptual approach to social studies teaching is paramount here. Learning by the student should be viewed as a gradual process of synthesis, proceeding stepwise as more and more experiences are accumulated by the student. The conceptual approach would vary from individual to individual in the depth of the "big ideas" to which the students are exposed. Ideally students would progress from factual kinds of learning experiences to those calling for conceptual knowledge. The learning continuum would take into account students ranging from those of lesser abilities to those who are capable of dealing with refined, precise, broad social studies concepts. This is not to suggest, however, that students of lesser abilities can only handle or should be restricted to factual information. Undoubtedly these students can analyze, synthesize, apply, and evaluate data in terms of their own capacities. But it would be unrealistic to suggest that they undergo essentially the same highly complex processes of the more capable students in the derivation of concepts. Nevertheless it is important that students of lesser abilities be extended in the development of concepts so that their potential is put to the test.

Inasmuch as concepts are related to other concepts they have broad applicability. Thus the social studies program can also be individualized in terms of generalizations as hypotheses to be derived and tested by students. For some students, provisions ought to be made so that they test, for example, "Who discovered America?" Whereas other students may be called upon to discover the conditions in Europe which led to its discovery. The important consideration here is that all students be encouraged to hypothesize and generalize regardless of the degree and intensity of the differentiated tasks appropriate to the students' particular needs and interests. Some students, then, would generalize in terms of simple statements; other students in terms of more involved findings. It is essential that all generalizations, from the simple to the complex, be construed as "testable" and serve as points of departure for further processes of inquiry rather than mere summaries.

Behavioral expectations and outcomes for each student can also be differentiated in the institution of a social studies program which invites unique, appropriate learning experiences for each of the students. Skills and values to be derived as well as knowledge to be gained are to be taken into consideration. Here, for example, Bloom's taxonomy of educational objectives could be utilized with respect to individualizing instruction. Questions to be explored by students could differ in terms of experiences calling for the various levels of cognition, which include comprehension, application, analysis, synthesis, and evaluation. More than a vertical (rate) progress is involved. The horizontal (depth) progress is taken into consideration as well. Here the teacher might ask:

1. Who discovered America? (information required)

2. Was he taking a chance in doing so? (comprehension required)

3. What do you think calls for greater courage—sailing across relatively unknown waters, then, or exploring unknown space? (application required)

4. Illustrate important aspects of the discovery. (analysis required)

5. Draw some parallels between Columbus' voyage with that of John Glenn's voyage into space. (synthesis required)

6. Which of the two men do you think faced the greater obstacles? Why? (evaluation required)

As previously alluded to, it is essential that all students, regardless of achievement level, be exposed to the higher thought processes in terms of their own uniquenesses and potentials. That is, although the tasks may be differentiated for them, opportunity for each student to synthesize, and apply, and evaluate information recalled should be provided in terms of their capacities. The degree and kind of experiences called for would be based on appropriate diagnosis of the students' needs.

A third major way to individualize instruction in the social studies program is through the learning process itself. The way we view the student as a learner in process is important. Do we believe it is in the student's nature to inquire, explore, find out? Or do we believe the student to be a tabula rasa? If we believe the former, the social studies program must be individualized for us to remain consonant with our beliefs. If we accept the tabula rasa point of view, then the chances are we'll provide an environment which does not foster learning opportunities based on appropriate experiences unique to each student. Some procedures to consider in individualizing the learning process are those which utilize varied groupings, team-learning, role-playing, simulation and academic games, independent seat work, self-oriented opportunities, and problem-solving experiences.

The problem-solving approach to the individualization process is of particular pertinence. It provides the teacher with opportunities to diagnose strengths and weaknesses of the student in his development of skills. The concept of continuous progress is readily noted in that the teacher can see it in action. The manner in which a student collects, organizes, and evaluates data from a variety of sources is observable. Inasmuch as competencies in gathering, synthesizing, testing, reporting, and application of data vary from student to student, the teacher can use the problem-solving experience as an instrument for bonafide diagnosis of the student's capabilities in each of the skills called for. Consequently tasks can be differentiated in terms of motivations and purposes of the students, as well as in terms of the development of skills essential to the student's growth. Conceivably, in the problem-solving situation, one student may collect, another may diagram, one may experiment, still another may observe, and all may evaluate, thus facilitating the particular competencies and bents of each of the students. Furthermore, because predicting, inferring, and applying of tentative solutions may utilize a variety of insights and skills, the individualizing process continues to be enhanced.

A fourth major aspect to consider in the individualization of a social studies program is the utilization of source materials. To effectively meet the individual needs of the students, a wide variety is essential. These may include multi-texts, trade materials, journals and periodicals, newspapers, diaries, maps, counting rods, artifacts, case studies, simulation and academic games, and activity sheets. Full employment of such materials compels the student to compare and contrast ideas, events, cultures, and people, thus inviting the development of a variety of skills and understandings. Needless to say, the single textbook negates these possibilities because the validation of findings requires several sources for purposes of substantiation. It is essential that the student be exposed to disagreement, trial and error, experimentation, and field work conclusions of various authors. For it is through this exposure that the student's attitudes, study habits, patterns of thinking, and depths of understanding are broadened. Facts become essential, subject matter becomes means for a more creative pursuit of intellectual excellence. Instruction and learning become conceptual, problematic, integrated, and individualized as inter-relationships occur. Thus we insure—hopefully—excellent techniques and strategies for individualizing instruction through the use of source materials.

Still another way to individualize the social studies, and a way not to be discounted, is through modern technological devices. Here we'd use tapes, programmed materials, film loops and strips, open and closed-circuit television, computers, and various electronic devices now on the market. Each student would have the opportunity to use these devices as he would see fit in light of tasks to be explored and experiences necessitated.

To sum up, although individualized instruction has different connotations for different people, none deny its importance in the context of social studies instructions. The social studies deal with increasingly complex relationships of human activity. Humans are unique. The uniqueness of both student and teacher is more readily recognized when instruction and learning is differentiated for each. It goes without saying that teacher and student hear different drummers. The central task of the social studies teacher is to identify the "music" which the student hears. What the teacher brings into the classroom, what the student has going for him, the groups in which the student functions, the teaching-learning processes involved, expectations of both teacher and student, and the conditions and materials utilized all lend themselves to the individualization of instruction. Once these are taken into serious consideration, individualized instruction appropriately attuned to the uniqueness and potential of each student may well become fact in the program of the social studies.

This article was specially written for this book of readings at the request of the editors. Dr. Thomas is Assistant Professor of Education at New Mexico State University.

22

Social Studies Activities

Marian Owen

Back when—A little friendly nudging may open your local newspaper office so a group of children can inspect newspapers issued about the year they were born. Before they go, establish some differences and similarities they can hunt for. Food prices, clothing and hair styles, and cars are popular items. But newspapers should be read for deeper considerations. What were the editorials about? What was front-page news? What items told how people lived that year?

A good activity for grade 3 up. The length of time spent and the problems considered depend, of course, on the children's maturity but all need several hours to read newspapers and take notes.

Foods–where from—Divide class into seven committees— vegetables, meat, fish, dairy products, beverages, cereals, and fruits. As a "homework" assignment, students visit supermarkets to list foods in their category. Duplicate them for everyone's notebook.

If the lists were started in September, they are ready by UN Week to have the sources added. Be sure children notice how interdependent nations are for some types of food, besides the widespread growing areas in this country.

Information Swap—Think this out well and don't make any promises you won't keep, but your class can become an information swapper.

Choose between a contrasting situation or one that is similar in another part of the country. For example, a fourth grade in a town of 12,000 people in central Pennsylvania could pick out a community in Missouri or Washington. Discuss what to swap: a monthly letter in which each child writes a paragraph (be careful not to make this tiresome reading); a tape describing your community; post cards; bulletins from the Chamber of Commerce; samples of nature specimens; a movie you make or a slide series with a descriptive tape.

The teacher or principal should make the first contact with the other school. Tell them whether your class wants to swap information on a sustained basis or a one-time shot. Don't swap with more than two schools at a time. Avoid sending items of worth; don't expect anything to be returned.

Interview—Each child interviews the oldest person he knows. Advance preparation helps to obtain the desired information but don't ruin chances of success by formalizing procedures. Encourage a friendly conversational exchange rather than a question-answer dialog. If some children want to tape-record the interview—OK, but others may want to do the taping afterwards.

Population density—Make a study of the number of people living on the four sides of a block using only the sides within the dimensions. Children can either measure the block or estimate length and width. Then they knock on every door to find out how many persons live in the dwelling. From these figures, they project density. How many people would live in a square mile with a similar density? Using an encyclopedia, children can compare their estimates with figures for states and countries.

Barter—Children become barter-minded about second or third grade. Before starting, send a letter home explaining to parents what it is about and the kinds of learning involved.

To open barter, draw names of five children out of a hat. Each one brings something to school that he no longer wishes to keep. Once an item is up for barter, any child may bring something to swap. Two-way and three-way barters are likely to develop; this is good.

One teacher avoids disappointment by requiring a two-hour waiting period after each deal is made. Within that time either party can call it off; otherwise if both are satisfied, it's a deal.

23

Before You Individualize Your Elementary Math ...

H. Clifford Clark

So you're going to individualize your elementary math program! This is a popular notion being considered by many teachers today. Individualization of instruction is a rapidly growing trend in elementary school mathematics. It is viewed by some as a panacea to the problems of teaching arithmetic.

Not every program that sets out to be individualized is a success. In fact, many classroom instructors attempting to individualize mathematics are experiencing frustration and failure. Some teachers have tried to individualize mathematics by simply turning each child "loose" in his regular text to work at his own pace. With slight variations, this approach continues to be a popular practice in the name of individualization. Such shallow thinking is responsible for many of the failures teachers are experiencing today.

A few days ago I visited a classroom where such a program was in operation. The class consisted of approximately thirty sixth-grade students, each working at his own rate in a sixth-grade textbook. Answers had been duplicated and were available for periodic checking by the students. At the end of each unit in the text an individual test was administered to determine if a student were ready to proceed to the next section of the textbook. Needless to say, several problems were apparent. Neither the teacher nor the students were satisfied with this program.

The purpose of this writing is to discuss these problems and to make suggestions for individualizing instruction in elementary school mathematics. Five basic areas of consideration will be discussed with suggestions for you to consider before you individualize your elementary math program. If your plan includes techniques which compare favorably with the following five check points, your chances for success will be greatly improved.

Prepare Instructional Objectives

Preparing instructional objectives is one of the most important steps in planning to individualize instruction. It is here that a teacher must decide what a student is expected to learn. Mager stated that a teacher will function in a fog of his own making until he knows just what he wants his students to be able to do at the end of instruction.[1]

Two major functions of instructional objectives are to (1) guide the teacher in designing and planning instructional activities, and (2) facilitate evaluation procedures after instruction.

Instructional objectives for elementary school mathematics might be categorized by topic, such as addition or multiplication, and sequenced according to level of difficulty. By clearly defining the instructional goals for each mathematical topic the teacher is better able to select appropriate content, materials, and methodology. As instruction proceeds, a student's performance is evaluated according to the selected objectives. In this way a teacher will know if goals are reached.

Determine the Instructional Needs of Each Student

No program can be individualized without careful pre-assessment procedures to determine what instruction is needed. Based on the specific objectives stated for each mathematical topic, the following questions must be answered before a student begins instruction.

1. How much of what is to be learned is already known?

2. Does the student have the necessary capabilities for the instruction to follow?

3. What prerequisite skills must be mastered before beginning the instruction?

4. What skills may be omitted?

5. What specific instructional activities should be prescribed for each student?

Answers to the above questions may be obtained through the use of placement and diagnostic tests as well as informal methods. Let us consider each of the following:

Placement tests

A placement test covers an entire topic of arithmetic, e.g., addition. It enables a teacher to establish an achievement level in each topic of arithmetic for each child. (A battery of such tests were developed under the direction of Dr. Richard Cox in connection with an individualized math program undertaken at the Oakleaf School in the Baldwin-Whitehall School District near Pittsburgh.) Several other commercial achievement tests are available.

Diagnostic tests

After the level of achievement is established through placement tests as listed above, it is necessary to determine the specific operations and skills a student cannot perform. A diagnostic test identifies specific weaknesses in performance. It should be administered at the first level in which the placement test indicated lack of competence. Performance on the diagnostic test forms the basis for the instructional assignments to follow.

Informal Methods

Teacher observation of a child's daily work offers an excellent source of information about a student's performance in arithmetic. Interviews with previous teachers, anecdotal records, permanent record folders, etc., can also assist in making an assessment of the student's progress and needs. These sources are especially helpful at the beginning of the year before formal testing can be accomplished.

The sixth grade class mentioned earlier had not been carefully pretested, nor had any attempt been made to pinpoint specific weaknesses in arithmetic performance. In short, the teacher knew very little about the ability or deficiencies of these students. It was therefore impossible for her to know the instructional needs of each child.

Use Appropriate Instructional Materials

Appropriate instructional materials must be used after determining a student's needs. It is no secret that there exists a wide span of ability and achievement in a class at a given grade level. A study reported in the Sixty-first Yearbook of the NSSE indicated that students in the seventh grade varied in mental ability from grades two to eleven and in achievement from grades four to eleven.[2] An individualized program must use materials geared to meet these ranges in both ability and achievement.

In the case of our teacher discussed above, each student was studying from the same edition of a sixth-grade text. While the students were on different pages, this difference was insignificant in relation to the actual range of needs. Some students were capable of working only at a primary grade level. Meeting the individual needs of a class is not accomplished by being a few pages apart in the same text. Materials must be used which are appropriate to the instructional needs of each student. Nothing short of this will do if genuine individualization is to be achieved.

This brings up one of the biggest problems involved in individualizing instruction. The problem is finding appropriate instructional materials. Certainly basal arithmetic textbooks as published by most major companies leave much to be desired when using them as individualized texts. In the first place, these texts were not written for such a purpose. The dominating philosophy of the past decade has been "discovery" through interaction with other students and the teacher. Most basal arithmetic texts reflect this philosophy by being filled with page after page of rationale requiring teacher guidance and discussion to gain its full value. The idea that these books can be used effectively as self-directive programmed texts is questionable. Too often, the slow student becomes bogged down with difficult reading. A fast student may skip the reading pages, being accountable only for problems listed in the answer book. Thus, much of what the authors had in mind for developing mathematical ideas through discussion and discovery is omitted. Added to these problems is the fact that basal arithmetic texts are clearly identified by grade level code, a concept supposedly non-existent in a continuous progress program.

The need for specially designed individualized materials is acute if this instructional pattern is to succeed in elementary school mathematics. Several attempts are being made to modify existing materials. Some schools are cutting up the texts and placing them in folders. Others are rewriting the teacher's manual to include pre-tests, post-tests, and enrichment materials. Experimental programs are attempting to develop new individually prescribed materials. In spite of these efforts, it is a difficult task for a teacher to find a thoroughly satisfactory set of materials for this type of program. Hopefully, this will change in the near future.

Provide for Group Instruction on Major Concepts

Too often programs of individualized instruction are programs void of significant instruction. In the classroom discussed above the teacher was asked when she taught. "As they need help they come to my desk," was her reply. The idea that the typical classroom teacher can furnish every child all of his math instruction on an individual basis at the moment of need is not feasible. Most children need more than one minute of instruction per day, a possible limit in a solely one-to-one approach. In addition, much can be gained when children have an opportunity to interact with each other in discussing, explaining, and sharing mathematical ideas.

Teachers should provide small group instruction on major concepts of common need. Economy of time dictates that certain basic concepts are best taught in groups. To do otherwise would be to give instruction so diluted by pressure of time that it would be diminished in value.

The overall grouping pattern used by a school may

help reduce the range of achievement in a particular class and enhance small group instruction. A truly non-graded school seeks to identify and instruct small groups of students functioning at approximately the same level. *Individualized instruction certainly does not preclude group instruction whenever possible.*

In any event, see to it that your individualized math program has provision for adequate teacher instruction. This has been a major shortcoming of many individualized programs. After all, children deserve and need more than a correspondence course in arithmetic.

Use a Plan of Continuous Evaluation and Remediation

Learning mathematics is greatly facilitated when the learner can check the correctness of his responses immediately after they have been made. Much is lost if the reinforcement is delayed too long. A good program of individualized instruction must reflect this assumption by providing continuous evaluation and remediation.

The sixth graders previously discussed completed several pages before checking their answers. To them, checking was a tedious necessity imposed by the teacher. It was not an active part of the learning process. In one case a student completed a whole unit of multiplication using the operation of addition. The printed instruction, "Find the product," had little meaning to him. It was not until several days later that his mistake was discovered.

Specifically, here are some guidelines in evaluation for your consideration.

1. The major purpose of evaluation should be to improve the learning process.

2. The system should provide continuous feedback of errors enabling a student to immediately identify his mistakes and correct them.

3. A student must be willing to recognize when he needs help and must be able to obtain it without delay.

4. The system should have built-in check points whereby a teacher can frequently assess the progress and needs of each child. (Included is an effective record keeping system.)

5. Through effective evaluation, instruction continues to be offered at an appropriate level for each student.

6. Students, teachers, and parents must consider evaluation as an integral part of the learning process.

One cannot deny that individualizing instruction in elementary school mathematics is a significant trend with potential value. Tailoring instruction to fit the needs of a learner must as a necessity be an optimum goal in education. Let us remember, however, that this goal is not to be achieved without careful consideration of the problems discussed above. The five check points discussed in this writing should prove helpful in planning such a program.

Reprinted from *School Science and Mathematics,* Vol. LXXI, Number 8, Whole 631, November 1971, pp. 676–680. Reprinted by permission of the author and the publisher. H. Clifford Clark is Associate Professor of Education, Brigham Young University.

References

[1]Robert F. Mager, *Preparing Objectives For Programmed Instruction.* San Francisco: Fearon Publishers, 1962, p. 3.

[2]"Individualizing Instruction," *The Sixty-first Yearbook of the National Society for the Study of Education.* Chicago: University of Chicago Press, 1962, pp. 165–168.

24

Developing Mathematical Processes: A Different Kind of Individualized Program

Thomas A. Romberg & Mary E. Montgomery

During the past decade, the slogan "individualized instruction" has been used by many educational innovators as a rallying cry to bring together those opposed to the impersonal environment of contemporary classrooms. That many, if not most, schools deliberately foster a nightmarish learning environment that is joyless and repressive has been well documented. (For example, see Holt, 1964; Silberman, 1970; Sobel, 1969; and particularly on mathematics learning Berieter, 1971.) The catchword implies that schools should be for children—individual children, and somehow instructional programs should capitalize on each child's individuality.

Educators have heeded the reformer's pleas by attempting to change the technology (instructional resources and their allocation) and the organizational task structure (what teachers and students do and the associated communication and decision-making process) in their schools (Perrow, 1970). What has emerged as the stereotype of an "individualized" program is as follows. To keep track of individuals the schools instructional technology has been changed by adding a management scheme to existing resources. In mathematics, this has been accomplished by identifying a set of behavioral objectives which could be associated with the text series, writing pretests and post-tests for those objectives, and preparing a resource manual for teachers and a set of self-study booklets for children. Similarly, the organizational task structure for the school has been changed by routinizing the teacher's instructional decision making for each pupil. Student progress usually is determined by test scores used to judge mastery of objectives, and instruction is accomplished by having students work independently at different times from the same self-study booklets. Teachers during the school day are testors, record keepers, and responders to questions. Individualization is claimed because different students are learning the same things at different times. There are three implied assumptions at the roots of this type of individualization; namely, that the mathematics content, sequence and approach included in contemporary modern programs is adequate, that all children best learn in the same way only at different rates, and that the instructional process is analyzable to the extent that in most aspects it can be routinized.

■ *Developing Mathematical Processes* (DMP)—is different from the above stereotype of individualized instruction both in its technology and its task structure. It is different because the developers deny the validity of the assumptions underlying that stereotype. In developing DMP it was first assumed that the existing mathematics curricula were not adequate in content coverage, content sequence, content approach and materials for teachers and students. In spite of the nearly 20 years of curriculum reform in mathematics content, the materials and tasks for teachers and students as they appear in contemporary textbooks are inappropriate for an individualized elementary program. Simply applying a management scheme to an inadequate mathematics program would still produce an inadequate mathematics program. The content of an elementary mathematics program should contain the concepts and processes of arithmetic, geometry, and probability and statistics. The *set-theoretic* approach now in common use is psychologically inappropriate for primary children. The "self-study from printed materials" learning mode is inappropriate for elementary children.

Second, it was assumed that mathematics is best learned by children when they are actively involved in solving a mathematical problem that has caught their interest. Research from developmental psychology would indicate that children in the primary grades should participate in group activities which include physical, pictorial, and symbolic stimuli. These activities should provide students with opportunity for verbal discussion of the ideas using their natural language. From this context, rate of learning is of minor importance.

Third, the teacher in DMP is viewed as a professional. The judgment of a teacher is more important than routinized decision making. Thus, while management by objectives is helpful, behavioral objectives and associated tests should only be used as diagnostic tools in the hands of a capable professional. Since the way in which children learn is not uniform and not well understood, instruction must be flexible. This can only be accomplished by having a professional with considerable discretionary power in order to react to individual children.

Clearly, any program developed from this perspective of individualized instruction would have to be different from the stereotype presented above. DMP is different. How DMP is different can best be illustrated by examining the mathematical approach adopted, the activity approach to instruction which uses the materials that have been developed, and the professional role of the teacher advocated.

The Mathematics of DMP: Arithmetic, Geometry and Probability and Statistics from a Measurement Approach

The developers of DMP chose a measurement approach rather than a set-theoretic approach to mathematics because it is sound mathematically and because sensible activities that children can and like to do could be constructed.

From a mathematical perspective in a measurement approach to mathematics, an attribute is identified and a domain of elements established which possesses the attribute under question (Blakers, 1967). Through empirical processes a recognizable structure is imposed upon the domain. This is usually accomplished by first establishing an equivalence relation through the process of comparing the elements on that attribute. This equivalence relation partitions the domain into equivalence classes. Next, an order relation is established through the process of ordering elements from the equivalence classes. Lastly, a binary operation which is associative and commutative is defined. Through these relations and this operation, an empirical structure is imposed upon the domain. Once this has been accomplished, a set which possesses a mathematical structure must be identified and a function defined which preserves the essential characteristics of the empirical structure of the domain as it assigns to each element of the domain an element of the set with mathematical structure.

In DMP the children start by describing and classifying many objects on many attributes using their own vocabulary and concentrating on how objects are alike and different. Next children focus on the attribute of length to the exclusion of all other attributes. The child places two objects side-by-side to compare their lengths. That is, he decides whether or not two lengths are the same (or whether they belong to the same equivalence class). Next, he decides which of two lengths is longer (i.e., orders the elements). Finally, he decides how he could make the two lengths equal (the binary operation of combining lengths is invoked). Considerable time is spent with real objects just understanding the empirical structure.

Eventually DMP wants the child to associate the attribute, the relations, and the operation with a subset of the real numbers. In order to make the translation from the empirical structure to this mathematical structure, DMP takes the child through a three stage (physical, pictorial, symbolic) representation process. A problem is presented in which the child cannot compare or order two lengths directly. For example, he is asked whether the door or the window is longer. He then makes a physical representation of at least one of the lengths to see whether the door or window is longer. Later, he will pictorially and then symbolically represent the length. This last stage is analogous to assigning a measurement to the length.

Of course, in order to assign a measure to a length or to any other attribute, the child must be familiar with a set of numbers. DMP chose to begin with the whole numbers and introduced them by considering the attribute of numerousness in a way similar to the introduction of length.

Thus, in the beginning the child is constantly working with objects or sets of objects. This allows for the presentation of many problems which can be solved directly before being encumbered by symbols or by manipulating symbols. For example, long before the addition and subtraction algorithms are presented the child is given problems which require finding sums or differences. The child solves the problem physically or pictorially and later learns how to symbolically represent what he has been doing. On the other hand, he is presented symbolic problems; if he can solve symbolically, he is encouraged to validate his solution using objects, pictures, or more familiar symbolic representations and if he cannot solve symbolically, he is encouraged to model physically or pictorially to solve.

Many different attributes—weight, capacity, area, volume, time—are examined in a similar way. As a child becomes more familiar with an attribute, he becomes less satisfied with the original equivalence classes he chose. For example, all the lengths to which he assigned the measurement of 5 centimeters are not quite equal. Thus, the need for more precise measurements gives rise to the extension of the number system to include the rational numbers.

Emphasis is placed on the unit of measurement. As one changes from one unit to another, one is using the processes of grouping and partitioning. For example, if one has measured a length in inches and wants to express his answer in feet, he groups the number of inches by twelve. DMP introduces these two processes with sets of objects giving a background not only for changing units of measurements, but also for multiplication, division and place-value (grouping by tens).

It is through the attributes of movement and direction that the empirical structure is developed which is translated to the usual mathematical structure of the set of integers.

Thus, through the measurement approach the arithmetic of the rational numbers is developed. While DMP developers believe that this branch of mathematics is important, they also think that many intuitive non-metric geometry and statistical experiences are well in the reach of elementary children. In kindergarten the children describe and classify objects on geometric attributes and gradually more sophisticated relationships between geometric attributes are examined. Likewise, in kindergarten graphing is presented as a way of collecting and organizing data; the child is introduced to the beginning skills needed for statistics and probability. Thus, while most of the same concepts and skills found in contemporary programs are taught in DMP, the measurement approach utilizing attributes and processes emphasizes the relationship of mathematics to reality.

The DMP Activity Approach to Instruction

If mathematics is an abstract, but humanly created image of reality, then it can only be learned through the human activity of creating mathematics. Each child must be able to translate reality into mathematics and back, to see the intuitive bases of mathematics, to adopt the arbitrary conventions of mathematics, and to validate mathematical assertions. Thus, each child must be an active participant in the process of forming concepts and developing intellectual skills, rather than a passive recipient of information from his environment.

The main characteristics of DMP's activity approach are based on sound psychological principles. These characteristics include: having children work individually or in small groups, as well as in large groups, while the teacher acts as a resource person, not a lecturer; having children use physical materials (Unifix cubes, Lots-a-Links, games, etc.) to help make abstract mathematical ideas more concrete; having children work together, discussing the problems they are solving and justifying their answers. These characteristics of an activity approach are illustrated in the two examples that follow.

Example 1. This series of activities introduces five- and six-year-olds to graphing (DMP Level One Teacher's Guide, p. 244). The teacher begins with something close to the children—their pets. He may start by showing the class some large study prints of children in real-life situations with family pets. If he is very enterprising (and brave), he may have the children bring their pets to school, or have a collection of pets in the classroom. Once the children have had a common first-hand experience with pets to arouse their interest, they are ready to recall their own pet at home or one which they would like to have, and to make pictures of their pets on pieces of paper of uniform size.

The teacher then presents the problem: How can they make an accurate and easily read record of the number and variety of pets the children own? The children are encouraged to discover a crude type of bar graph (see Figure 1). This may be done by first having all the children with pictures of cats line up in one row, all those with dogs in another row, and so on along a given line until a human bar graph is formed. She may then ask how this can be made smaller so that everyone in the class can see it. Lining up

Figure 1

the pictures behind a baseline on the floor or on a table would establish a bar graph similar to Figure 1. To make a more permanent graph, the teacher may encourage suggestions that the pictures be arranged on the bulletin board, and that the graph be given a name. Then the group, still working as a large unit, constructs the graph and discusses what facts are apparent from looking at it. (For example, which types of pets are there more of? Fewer of? Equal numbers of? Why are there so many cats for pets? So few boa constrictors?)

Now the children have been introduced to the basic idea of graphing, and they have constructed a graph under the close supervision of the teacher. When the teacher has determined that the children have grasped the basic idea and can manage the procedure themselves, they can then extend their knowledge of bar graphs by working on similar problems, but in smaller groups, independent of the teacher. At this point, which may be some time later, each child is given a set of four picture pages. On one there are pictures of various types of food; on another, animals that children might like for pets; on a third, various ways of traveling are pictured; and on the fourth, several types of play activity are shown. The child must choose the one thing he likes best on each of the pages, color it, and cut it out. The entire group may then be divided into four committees—the food group, the pet group, the travel group, and the play group. Each committee collects all the pictures in their particular category and classifies them. The food group, for example, puts all the pictures of ice cream in one pile, the pictures of hamburgers in another, and so on. Then each group makes its own bar graph, pasting the prepared pictures in columns to show the preferences of the children, just as they did on the graph of pets made earlier. After all the graphs are completed, they can be displayed and discussed by the entire group.

This sample of an activity approach reveals some of the strengths of DMP. The children become so absorbed in a fascinating, real-to-them situation about a subject with which they are familiar (their own personal preferences) that the mathematical processes of classifying and ordering are used and practiced under conditions of maximum interest. The noise level will be reasonable, the movement well-directed to the task, the teacher free to circulate and help children individually. The final result will be used as the basis for meaningful discussion and interaction by the children. This example also shows how children are given opportunities to work in a variety of learning situations—independently, in pairs, in small groups, and in large groups—with some parts of the activity involving a great deal of teacher direction and others a minimum of teacher involvement. This is important, since variety in grouping enhances the natural social development of the child.

Example 2. One way to provide an opportunity for children to work in small groups or independently is to set up learning stations around the room. For example, after children have had experiences in graphing and in measuring distances in various standard units in the upper primary level, the following activity using learning stations provides children with opportunities to apply what they have learned in solving real-world problems. (DMP Level Four Teacher's Guide, p. 286-287).

The activity begins by having the teacher (with the help of the students) set up the different learning stations—perhaps as many as 10 to 20—according to the suggestions given in the DMP teacher's guide. (One way of arranging the stations around the room is shown in Figure 2.) Each station includes an activity card or experiment sheet and the physical materials needed to solve the problem on the card. For example, in order to generate and graph the measurements specified by the experiment sheet shown in Figure 3, the student or small group is provided with a yardstick, ruler, wooden ball, and a piece of cardboard. Other stations would have similar sheets and manipulative materials.

Once the learning stations have been set up, the teacher discusses the activity briefly with the children, perhaps relating it to earlier work on graphing or measuring distances. Since learning stations are used often in DMP, the general procedures should be familiar: Individuals or groups move from station to station, solve the problem posed at the station, and record the results on the worksheet or graph paper provided.

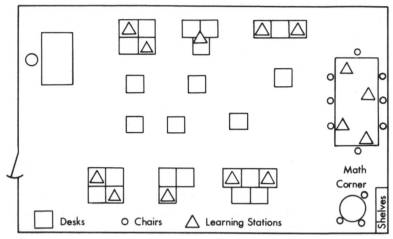

Figure 2. Possible Room Arrangement for Learning Stations

Once the teacher has finished a brief introduction to the activity, the students (individually or in small groups) can move to the different stations and begin work. The teacher also moves from station to station, helping those who are having difficulty, and asking children to tell what their graphs represent. The teacher can keep track of the progress of each child or small group by observing their graphs or worksheets.

Usually, it is not expected that every child will complete work at every station; the amount of time that a child needs to spend on the activity is determined by the teacher and student. Children who finish early may become peer tutors, or the teacher may prefer to have them move on to other activities.

When the teacher feels that the children are ready to close the activity, it is a good idea to bring the students together to summarize what has been accomplished. This is another time when the teacher can extend the activity to new ideas. For example, in Experiment 2, the teacher can ask what would happen if a longer piece of cardboard were used, if a cylinder were used instead of the ball, or would a marble roll farther than the ball. Furthermore, the teacher can relate this activity to the objectives that the children achieved earlier. For example, the children's previous experience in measuring lengths can be discussed in terms

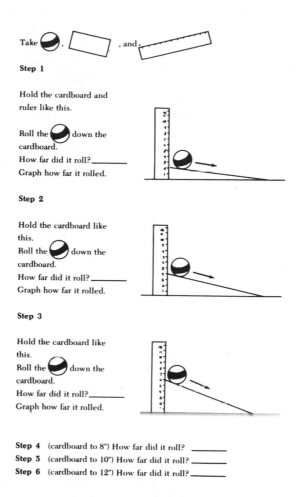

Step 1

Hold the cardboard and
ruler like this.

Roll the ball down the
cardboard.
How far did it roll?_____
Graph how far it rolled.

Step 2

Hold the cardboard like
this.
Roll the ball down the
cardboard.
How far did it roll?_____
Graph how far it rolled.

Step 3

Hold the cardboard like
this.
Roll the ball down the
cardboard.
How far did it roll?_____
Graph how far it rolled.

Step 4 (cardboard to 8") How far did it roll? _____
Step 5 (cardboard to 10") How far did it roll? _____
Step 6 (cardboard to 12") How far did it roll? _____

Figure 3. An Experiment Sheet
DMP Level Four Workbook
P. 160 Experiment 2

of the repeated measurements necessary in Experiment 2,
and previous work in addition can be utilized in finding the
total lengths.

Activities that use learning stations are found
throughout DMP. The structure of these activities is clear
and helps students understand their responsibilities in
what may be for them a new role as active learners.
Therefore, these activities are particularly useful in helping
students adjust to an activity approach, with its opportuni-

ties to move around the room, to manipulate objects, and to discuss problems with other students and the teacher. Experience has shown that both children and teachers enjoy and profit from the learning station arrangement.

From these examples, it should be clear that DMP's activity approach to math is rather different from that usually found in traditional classrooms. It should be clear, too, that activity-centered math is not turning children loose to riot; nor is it hit-or-miss random learning, with a haphazardly conducted instructional program. In fact, just the opposite is true. DMP's activities are organized and sequenced with great care, so that skills needed at a certain point have already been mastered in prior activities.

Also, from these examples it should be apparent that DMP utilizes different instructional resources allocated in different ways. The mathematics is not taught from a textbook, or from a workbook, or from self-study printed packages. When the DMP program is completely developed for K-6 there will be approximately 85 instructional packages with Teachers Guides, Pupil Texts, Pupil Workbooks, Pupil Test Booklets, and various printed and manipulative materials.

The teacher's guide is the key document in the curriculum package. It outlines the mathematical program and behavioral objectives for each topic. It provides specific suggestions for classroom organization, materials, and instruction and assessment procedures that promote an effective learning atmosphere. The guide is not prescriptive; teachers are encouraged to experiment and innovate, adapting the mathematics activities to the particular characteristics of their students.

Opportunities for practice and exploration are provided to the student through the medium of the printed page. The inclusion of a workbook in the instructional materials does not mean that the DMP program is a "page a day" mathematics program. Rather, because of its emphasis on the individual child, the intent of DMP is that the pages contained within the workbook be used with discretion. Each child does not need to work on every page. Suggestions for using the workbook pages are contained in the teacher's guide. For the intermediate grades a student text is provided because it is important for a child to learn how to read mathematics books. Non-consumable materials are also included in the text.

For several topics a materials kit containing specially manufactured items is supplied. It also contains some items that could be purchased in a grocery or hardware store by the teacher, but are used extensively and are, therefore, included as a matter of convenience. All items are an essential part of instruction. Also, included in the kit are printed, non-consumable materials for use in enriching the classroom atmosphere. Stories, pictures, sorting cards, and printed directions for experimentation at learning stations are some of the instructional materials included in this category.

Many of the objectives may be assessed by means of group-administered paper and pencil tests. The response forms for these tests are included in the test booklet.

That allocation of resources to instruction is different in DMP should also be clear from the two activities. A teacher can not simply pass out worksheets or assign problems. To assist the teacher in planning each activity described in the teacher's guide is prefaced by a description of the materials needed in the activity, new vocabulary, objectives to be observed, how the children are to be organized for each part of the activity, and specific instructions as to what preparation should be done. (See Figure 4).

Teachers who have been involved in the development and tryouts of DMP instructional materials have found that an activity approach really works. The extra bit of effort that it takes to carry out an activity approach yields a host of rewards. Students enjoy mathematics, make discoveries on their own, and become responsible and independent problem-solvers.

The Professional Role of the Teachers in IGE and DMP

DMP is the mathematics component of the Wisconsin Research and Development Center's program of Individually Guided Education (IGE) (Klausmeier, et al, 1971). The teacher in IGE is the person who guides each child through a variety of learning experiences tailored to meet his needs and learning style.

RESOURCE INFORMATION FOR ACTIVITY 1.12.2 DMP
LEVEL ONE TEACHER'S GUIDE, P. 243

MATERIALS
a piece of paper for each child (A)
crayons (A, B)
a scissors for each child (B)
paste (B)
2 or 3 large pieces of paper about 3' x 3' (B)
workbook pages 97, 99, and 101 (B)

VOCABULARY
graphing

OBJECTIVES
1   (represents set pictorially)
2△ (uses pictorial representations to compare and order sets)

ORGANIZATION
(A) individual and large group
(B) large group

PREPARATION
(B) Prepare one of the large pieces of paper for each
workbook page you will be using (see the description
for part B). Label six columns on each piece: one for
each small picture on the workbook page. This is an
example for the favorite foods on workbook page 97.

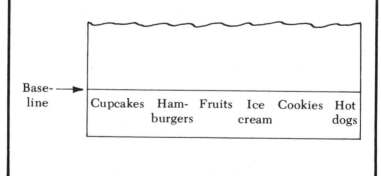

Figure 4

The multiunit elementary school (MUS-E) is the organization for instruction and related administrative arrangements at the building and central office levels for IGE. In MUS-E the nongraded instructional unit replaces the age-graded, self-contained classroom. Each unit usually has a lead teacher, three or four staff teachers, one teacher aide, one instructional secretary, one intern, and 100–150 students. Children of a unit usually have a three-to-four-year age span. The main function of each unit is to plan, carry out, and evaluate each child's instructional program.

A staff teacher in IGE plans the program for and guides many children in cooperation with other unit members. In contrast, a teacher in a self-contained classroom works independently with a small number of children. A higher level of professionalism is required by the staff teacher in implementing an IGE instructional system such as DMP. Staff teachers cooperatively formulate objectives for each child, assess each child's progress, and use new materials, equipment, and instructional procedures.

IGE's main purpose is to help teachers design instructional programs for individual children. Ideally, each child's program will be based on how and at what pace he learns best and where he stands on mastering specific skills or concepts. Trying for this ideal involves a sequence of events outlined in Figure 5.

Initially (Event I) the school staff is to state educational objectives including those dealing with mathematics. The primary objective of DMP is that children upon completion of the program will be able to translate problems from the everyday world into mathematics, solve the problems mathematically, and translate the results back into the everyday world. A second and initially less important terminal objective is that children upon completion of the program will have the conceptual background needed to examine mathematics, identify the structural properties and relationships in mathematics, and logically validate mathematical assertions in later grades. This second objective can only be reached after children have had an opportunity to develop a considerable amount of mathematics. Through task and instructional analyses a set of behavior objectives have been identified as being related to these overall objectives.

IGE: Instructional Programming Model

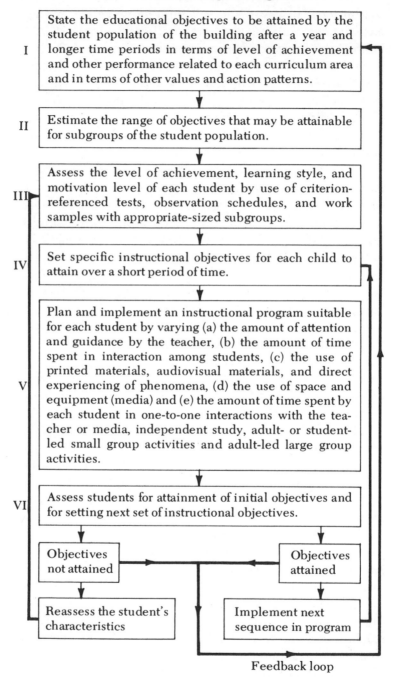

Figure 5

Guidelines are given which will assist the school staff in estimating the range and sequence of objectives that may be obtainable for subgroups of their student population. (Event II). For example, it has been found that the first 14 topics (topics are based on a subset of interrelated objectives) are suitable for kindergarteners. The next 28 topics are appropriate for grades 1 and 2.

Once an estimate has been made about which objectives may be appropriate for each student, DMP provides assessment materials that will help the teacher determine the initial level of attainment (Event III). This assessment begins with a placement inventory which may be used as a guide in identifying groups of students who need to work on the same topics.

After determining which objectives the child has attained and which he has not yet mastered, the teacher can choose objectives that are appropriate for him (Event IV). If the teacher is still uncertain about the appropriateness of the objectives, the topic inventory can be used for pre-assessment. Suggestions in the DMP assessment manual direct the teacher to the topics and activities in the teacher's guide that cover particular objectives. These suggestions will help the teacher identify children who need to work on the same objectives, and they can be placed in the same instructional group. In a Multiunit school, teachers group the children in their unit according to similar needs, and each teacher takes responsibility for one or more of the groups. DMP teachers in self-contained classrooms have followed the same procedures in choosing different activities for different groups of children.

After groups of children have been formed, the teacher plans and conducts activities that will help the children reach the objectives of a given topic (Event V). This is the heart of DMP, since the children are actively involved in learning mathematics. It is at this step also when much of the individualization is accomplished. Even within a group who are all ready for a given set of objectives there are individuals—individual in the rate they progress, in their styles of learning and in their needs.

To see how a teacher accomplishes the individualization, the following example should suffice. For each topic a sequence chart of the activities is provided (See Figure 6) like the one shown for Topic 2.9—Order Sentences. It is recommended that one begins at the bottom of the chart and goes to the top in any way suitable for the group. This means that the third and fourth activities (2.9.3 and 2.9.4) are alternate; the teacher may choose one or the other or both. In this case, the third activity focuses on the attribute of capacity while the fourth activity focuses on area. Some children may need more experience with one attribute than the other. The two activities differ also on how they are organized; the third is mainly large group and the fourth activity is individual or pair. Again, the teacher must look at the children in his group to decide which activity is appropriate.

Activity 2.9.10 is an optional activity; which provides additional practice in the objectives already presented while Activity 2.9.12, another optional activity, is an enrichment activity. Finally, the last activity provides a collection of games for additional ways to give experiences related to the objectives.

From this example it should be clear that teachers certainly have flexibility in selecting activities. There is also flexibility in carrying out activities. Table 1 presents a sequence of steps that the teacher takes in conducting most activities. The initial step, of course, is planning the activity. Will the activity be appropriate for a particular group of children or an individual child? At times, the teacher may need to revise portions of the activity to suit the needs and interest of children. The activities suggested in DMP *are* suggestions. Experienced teachers supplement DMP with appropriate activities that have worked well in the past.

After careful planning, the teacher is ready to present the activity to the children (Table 1, Step 2). This may involve specifying a problem (for example, how can the children make a record of the types of pets that they have?) that leads into a graphing activity. Or the teacher may discuss a few of the activity cards or experiment sheets that have been put at stations around the room. In other activities, stories can be read and enacted by the children to introduce a problem or a concept in an interesting way.

Topic 2.9 Sequence Chart
DMP Level Two Teacher's Guide, p. 248

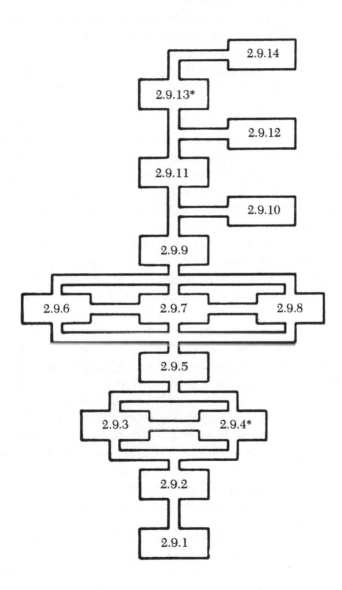

Figure 6

Teacher or student demonstrations can also actively involve students while developing the problem and a need for its solution. At this time the teacher may also want to relate the activity to earlier work.

Typically, the next step is for the teacher to organize the children into small groups to work on the problem (Table 1, Step 3). Occasionally, the entire group may work together on a project, or children may work individually or in pairs. Groups can be formed in many different ways; often teachers have used randomly chosen groups and student-formed groups early in a topic. Later, peer-teaching groups, achievement-based groups, and independent-learning or interest groups have been formed following the assessment of each individual's progress. In addition, small groups consisting of students having difficulties or special interests can work outside of the usual math period. The use of a variety of groupings serves to aid in the development of the student's social skills and verbal capacity while encouraging independent learning. A flexible approach to grouping is a definite advantage in dealing with the needs and potentialities of the individual student.

Once the problem has been presented and the children are working on the activity in small groups or individually, the teacher can move about the room (Table 1, Step 4), helping students who are having difficulty and asking students to validate their work or demonstrate what they have done. For example, DMP provides an observation schedule so that the teacher knows exactly what behavior he is to observe in each activity and to give him guidance in the questioning. Because it is often the process not the end product on a piece of a paper, the teacher must observe with the individual child as he is interacting with mathematics. Thus, the individual child, not the group, must be considered.

There are several ways provided by DMP for the teacher to assess the students on the objectives of a topic (Event VI in Figure 5). One way is to observe their work and by asking questions during the activities.

Throughout this portion of the activity, the teacher should encourage student-student interaction related to the mathematical ideas involved in the activity. Questioning

Table 1
Conducting an Activity: The Usual Steps

1. Planning the activity.	The teacher makes certain that the objectives of the activity are appropriate for the children who will be involved.
	The teacher organizes the needed materials, using children to help where possible.
2. Presenting the problem.	The teacher presents the activity to be worked on, and sometimes demonstrates the procedures to be used, usually to the entire group of children.
3. Grouping the children.	The teacher groups the children so they can work on the activity in small groups or independently.
4. Working with the children.	The teacher becomes a resource person, moving from group to group to give help, to observe for achievement of objectives, and to ask challenging questions.
5. Closing the activity.	The teacher and students summarize and extend the results by discussing the activity, and display the students' work where this is appropriate.

techniques can be used to encourage student inquiry and to assist the student in organizing his thinking. For example, the student can be asked to determine whether a given mathematical sentence is correct or incorrect, and to describe how the decision was made. Hopefully, the student's continual validation of his own work will lead not only to independent learning, but also to interaction with others concerning the validity of *their* work.

When most of the children begin to show mastery of the objectives of an activity, or when the teacher feels the children would profit more by moving on, it is time to bring the activity to a close (Table 1, Step 5). This doesn't mean just having the children put away the manipulative materials or turn in their papers. Rather, this presents an opportunity to help the children summarize what has been accomplished so far, and to relate their accomplishments to earlier work. One way to show what has been done is to have the children (individually or in groups) display their work and discuss it with the class. This is particularly appropriate for graphing activities. Another way is to have the children discuss the mathematical ideas generated during the activity and demonstrate any new skills developed. DMP teachers have used this technique to enable children to inform parents of what was learned in math. A third way of closing an activity (if time is short) is to begin the next math period with a review of previous work. This is particularly useful if the previous work leads directly into the next activity.

However, the closing of an activity should not signify its end for all time. On the contrary, putting the day's work into proper perspective can often lead to the posing of new problems for further in-depth exploration. The closing is of particular importance at the completion of an activity in which an objective is stressed for the last time in a topic. Of course, the teacher's judgment is of prime importance in determining the type and timing of an appropriate closing. Another way is through the topic inventories. These are brief criterion reference tests which cover the objectives of the topic. For the younger children these are individually administered, but for older children paper and pencil tests are available for all objectives that may be assessed in that manner.

The student's level of mastery for each objective is determined by one of these methods or by combination of the two. Each child's performance on an objective is classified as mastery (M), making progress (P) or needs considerable help (N). A rating of mastery indicates that the child has clearly demonstrated satisfactory performance, while making progress (P) is used for children who have not quite mastered the objectives, but are likely to reach mastery as they participate in a few additional experiences. Ratings of M or P on an objective indicate that a child can go on to the next topic for which the objective is prerequisite. A child who receives an N should receive special attention before he proceeds.

Once a group has completed a topic what options does a teacher have? This, of course, depends partly upon the organization of the school. He and the other teachers might wish to regroup their children according to their levels of mastery. The Topic Chart (See Figure 7) as well as suggestions in the teachers guide will help the teachers make these regroupings. For example, suppose Mr. Jones's group, Mrs. Smith's group, Miss Brown's group have completed Topics 2.7, 2.9 and 2.11 respectively. They assess their children and find these results.

	M(Mastery) No. of Students	P(Progressing) No. of Students	N(Non-mastery) No. of Students
Mr. Jones Topic 2.7	16	8	3
Mrs. Smith Topic 2.9	10	2	5
Miss Brown Topic 2.11	18	2	4

After discussing the possibilities the three teachers decide on this course of action. Miss Brown will take her entire group to Topic 2.10, a topic on movement and direction which does not depend upon Topic 2.11 the topic just completed. She notes that four children did not master all the objectives of 2.11; however, she feels that she will be able to give them additional help as they do Topic 2.10. Mr. Jones and Mrs. Smith decide to rearrange their groups. Mr. Jones will take his 24 students from Topic 2.7 who had a M or P rating on to Topic 2.9. Mrs. Smith will take her entire group and the three students from Mr. Jones who had a N rating to Topic 2.8, a topic on the attribute of capacity. However, when Mr. Jones gets to particular objectives giving Mrs. Smith's five non-masters trouble he will pick up the five for suitable activities. This would leave Mrs. Smith with a small group and she will have time to devote time to the three non-masters of 2.7, especially since 2.8 gives additional practice in writing comparison sentences, the emphasis of topic 2.7.

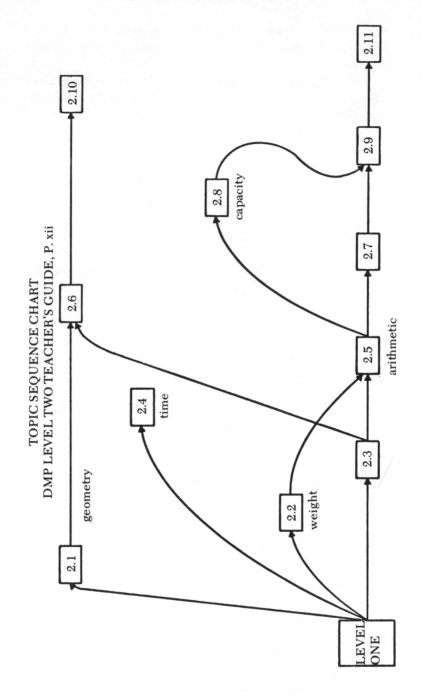

Figure 7

All of these decisions require that records must be kept. Mrs. Smith had to know that her new group did not contain children who had already mastered the objectives of 2.8 and Miss Brown had to know her group had not already done 2.10. Several different record devices are provided by DMP—those which enable the teacher to keep individual records or group records.

The components of the DMP program may be regarded as ingredients in a recipe. The professional teacher determines the success of the recipe by the procedures used in mixing and blending the various ingredients.

In summary, DMP is a different kind of individualized program. It is different in its mathematical content, sequence and emphasis. Children work first with the concrete rather than the abstract.

DMP is different in that it provides a variety of materials for teachers and students. Mathematics is no longer monotonously writing sums and equations on workbook pages, rather it becomes a natural means of expression and communication.

DMP is different in what it expects children to do. No longer is arithmetic dull drudgery. Children are expected to create their own mathematics and by so doing they think it is fun and are asking "When do we get to do math?" (Mather's, 1972).

DMP is different in what it expects teachers to do. No longer is mathematics "a page or two a day" program. Instead the typical class period may be spent with one group of children pouring liquids into containers of different sizes to discover which are equal while in a different corner of the class another group of children is using chain links to measure lengths. The teacher now is the professional guide and resource person for each child as he solves problems.

The result of these differences is a constructive, fun-learning environment where children are naturally absorbing, creating and enjoying mathematics.

Published by the Wisconsin Research and Development Center for Cognitive Learning, supported in part as a research and development center by funds from the United

States Office of Education, Department of Health, Education, and Welfare. Thomas A. Romberg is Professor of Mathematics and of Curriculum and Instruction, Wisconsin Research and Development Center for Cognitive Learning and Mary E. Montgomery is Assistant Scientist at the same center at the University of Wisconsin, Madison.

References

Berieter, C. *Does Mathematics Have to be so Awful?* LaSalle, Illinois: Open Court Publishing Company, 1971.

Blakers, A. "Mathematical Concepts of Elementary Measurement" *SMSG: Studies in Mathematics,* Volume XVII, Stanford, California, SMSG 1967.

Developing Mathematical Processes, Level One, Teacher's Guide: Developmental Edition. Chicago, Wisconsin Research and Development Center for Cognitive Learning and Rand McNally and Company, 1972.

Developing Mathematical Processes, Level Two, Teacher's Guide: Developmental Edition. Chicago, Wisconsin Research and Development Center for Cognitive Learning and Rand McNally and Company, 1972.

Developing Mathematical Processes, Level Four, Teacher's Guide: Developmental Edition. Chicago, Wisconsin Research and Development Center for Cognitive Learning and Rand McNally and Company, 1972.

*Developmental Mathematical Processes, Level Four, Pupil Workbook:*Developmental Edition. Chicago, Wisconsin Research and Development Center for Cognitive Learning and Rand McNally and Company, 1972.

Holt, J. *How Children Fail.* New York, N.Y.: Pittman, 1964.

Klausmeier, H. J., Quilling, M., Sorenson, J., Way, R., & Glasrud, C. *Individually Guided Education and the Multiunit Elementary School: Guidelines for Implementation.* Madison: Wisconsin Research and Development Center for Cognitive Learning, 1971.

Mathers, C. "This Doesn't Seem like Math—This Is Fun!" *Champaign* (Illinois) *News-Gazette,* November 12, 1972.

Perrow, C. *Organizational Analysis: A Sociological View.* Belmont, California: Wadsworth Publishing Company, Inc., 1970.

Silberman, C. E. *Crisis in the Classroom.* New York, N.Y.: Random House, 1970.

Sobel, H. W. "The Anachronistic Practices of American Education as Perpetuated by an Unenlightened Citizenry and Misguided Pedagogues Against the Inmates of the Public Schools." *Phi Delta Kappa* 51, (October 1969): 94–97.

25

An Individualized Science Laboratory

Joseph I. Lipson

The Learning Research and Development Center at the University of Pittsburgh is creating individualized science laboratory lessons. These lessons are part of an experimental project to examine innovative methods of individualized instruction in the elementary school. Reading, mathematics, and science are the subjects to which individualization procedures have been applied. The project has been underway in a Baldwin-Whitehall School (suburban area of Pittsburgh, Pennsylvania) of 220 pupils during the school years of 1964–65 and 1965–66.

Thus far in science, the project has focused upon the problems of instruction with nonreaders in grades K-3. Lessons for the K-6 grades will be instituted eventually. In the individualized system each student in a class of fifteen may be doing a different experiment. To permit each nonreading student to interact with the materials of his lesson, tape recorded voice directions, and questions are used. These tape recorded lessons are put onto an endless belt cartridge much like those being used in automobile tape systems. A sample lesson is presented on the opposite page.

A Typical Lesson

At the beginning of a class each student receives a tape cartridge and a plastic box containing the materials for his lesson. The children then take their tape and materials to a carrel. Each carrel has a tape repeater with earphones as well as a work surface. The tape repeater has easily accessible ON and OFF buttons; and once the cartridge has been plugged into the tape repeater, the child starts and stops the tape by pushing these buttons. After a direction has been given which requires a student response, a bell rings (tape recorded sound of a bell); and when the student hears the bell, he stops the tape and complies with the directions given. It is important to note that while the tape is off, the student can take as long as he likes to comply with the directions. No pressure is ever exerted to have the student turn the tape back on before he feels ready in his own mind. The child can explore the materials or convince himself of an observed effect. This freedom for the student is an important result of the philosophy of the program.

To clarify how the lessons work, let us use as an example the first lesson in magnetism. This lesson is designed (1) to show that a magnet attracts some objects and does not attract others, (2) to teach the student to be able to sort objects into two classes; those that a magnet does attract and those that a magnet does not attract. In a sense these operations define what a magnet is to the child, and in future lessons other objects will be identified as magnets if they behave similarly.

The materials for this lesson are thumb tacks, paper clips, marbles, pennies, rubber bands, stones, pieces of cardboard, nails, eight cardboard dishes, and a small red horseshoe magnet.

Using this taped demonstration as an illustration of the form and style of presenting the lessons, the following aspects of the program can now be discussed: (1) The instructional system and use of tests, (2) the instructional objectives of the program, (3) The reason for using direct experience as the basis of instruction, (4) The reason for developing individualized lessons for nonreaders, (5) Results.

Students Begin Their Lesson on Magnetism as They
Listen to the Taped Instructions Given Below.

1. Hello. I am going to tell you to do some things. The teacher will help you, too. First, we will practice. After you stop the machine, stand up, put your finger on your nose, and turn around. *Bell*

2. That was very good. Now, after you stop the machine, shake your head three times. *Bell*

3. Very good. Now you will do some things to learn something new. After you stop the machine, find the dish of thumb tacks. *Bell*

4. After you stop the machine this time, find the dish with paper clips. *Bell*

5. This time I will ask you to find two things. Find the dish with buttons and the dish with pennies. *Bell*

6. Now find the dish with rubber bands and the dish with some stones in it. *Bell*

7. We are almost finished finding things. Find the dish with the pieces of cardboard and the dish with some nails. *Bell*

8. The only thing left on the table that you have not found is called a **Magnet.** A magnet can pick up some things, but there are some things it cannot pick up. We will try to find out what things it will pick up and what things it won't pick up. The magnet is painted red to help you find it. Find the magnet. *Bell*

9. That was very good. Now take the magnet and try to pick up the thumb tacks in the dish with the magnet. Touch the thumb tacks with the magnet. *Bell*

10. If some stick to the magnet, take them off the magnet, and put them in the dish. *Bell*

11. Touch the paper clips with the magnet. If any stick to the magnet, put them back in the dish. *Bell*

12. Touch the marbles with the magnet. *Bell*

13. Touch the pennies with the magnet. *Bell*

14. Touch the rubber bands with the magnet. *Bell*

15. Touch the stones with the magnet. *Bell*

16. Touch the nails with the magnet. *Bell*

17. Now put all the dishes that have things that stuck to the magnet on one side of the table. If you are not sure, use the magnet to see if the things in the dish will stick to the magnet. Remember, put all the things that stuck to the magnet on one side of the table, away from the other dishes. *Bell*

18. Now check all the things that did not stick to the magnet to make sure that none of them do stick to the magnet. *Bell*

19. Check all the things that did stick to the magnet to make sure that they really do stick to the magnet. *Bell*

20. That was very good work. Now find the paper with the pictures. *Bell*

21. Put an X on the pictures of the things that stuck to the magnet. *Bell*

22. After you stop the machine this time, do not start it again. Goodbye. *Bell*

Instructional Systems and Use of Tests

In the individualized laboratory it is important that each child has mastered all prerequisite skills and that the students not be required to undergo formal instruction in learning areas that they have mastered already. This means that testing is very important, but it is not testing to assign a grade or to either reward or punish the student. The tests are for the purpose of diagnosis so that work can be properly assigned. In the science program the tests are now performance tests with actual materials since the objectives are phrased in terms of operations with materials.

Pre-tests have the nature of transfer lessons in which a problem is posed and no assistance is given in the solution.

Since the children have not had the lessons prior to the pre-tests, the actual lesson materials may be used. After a group of lessons has been completed, a post-test is administered with new materials. For example, if a lesson involved sorting buttons, the post-test might deal with sorting playing cards. This change of materials is designed to prevent memorization of the responses asked.

The actual tests have gone through three phases. Initially, group pencil and paper tests were used. These were not satisfactory because they did not indicate the students' ability to perform operations with real objects. The other extreme of performance tests was then tried. This called for an adult to watch a single student perform each test. The procedure had to be dropped because it involved too much time and disrupted class schedules.

A compromise testing system resulted. The tests are put on tape so that the students can perform them individually. The tests are constructed so that materials must be manipulated in order to answer the questions. After determining the answer the student must record his answer on paper. For example, in the lesson on magnetism, the test might have the materials in a box and the student would be asked to sort the objects into a group which the magnet attracts and a group of objects which the magnet does not attract. After the student has completed his task, he would be referred (by the tape voice) to a sheet of paper with pictures of the objects in the box. The student would then be asked to put an X on all the objects which the magnet attracted. The paper could then be scored later.

In order to place the student into the program, a rough-scale performance test is administered at the beginning of the school year to indicate the general level at which the student becomes unable to perform the objectives of the lesson sequence. Typically, a child stops being tested when he misses three items in succession. The student is then pre-tested in greater detail in the units for which he showed uncertain mastery. After the pre-test results are analyzed, individual laboratory lessons are assigned. After all the assigned lessons in a unit are completed, a post test is administered. If some items are still not being handled adequately by the student, the student either takes the appropriate lessons over again or he talks with the teacher in order to clear up his difficulty. As yet there is no remedial sequence of lessons to help a student who has trouble the first time around. However, the lessons are sufficiently redundant that a student who goes through all of the lessons on a concept usually encounters a theme several times in his instruction.

A typical unit consists of about fifteen lessons; in each unit there will be from one to three lessons which we call transfer lessons. These are problems which go beyond the scope of the planned curriculum, and test whether the student can apply his learning to a new, previously unseen situation. A major instructional sequence consists of about 60-75 lessons. When a sequence (e.g. Discrimination, Sorting, and Classification; Magnetism; Light; Symmetry and Measurement) is completed, a final examination is given which tests the kind of ability the student carries with him into his other activities.

Objectives of Instruction

The instructional objectives have gone through two important modifications. During the first year, 1964, the project produced approximately 45 taped lessons in magnetism and 30 taped lessons in light. These areas of science were chosen because they are topics usually included in the elementary school science curriculum and because some of the equipment problems looked more manageable in these areas. The main concern the first year of the project was to learn *how* to write lessons using the individualized tape medium so that students would understand them. It was important to discover what size step could be taken from lesson to lesson, what degree of freedom could be allowed in the lessons, and what degree of structure would be required. The lessons were really designed for the pre-reader, but during the first year the same lessons were used for all students. (grades 1-6).

The magnetism lessons begin with simple phenomena of permanent magnets and progress to include beginning electromagnetic effects. The student is shown that an electromagnet's strength increases (a) as the number of turns of wire increase (holding the core material and total wire length constant), (b) as the core material is changed from air to iron, and (c) as the number of fresh batteries supplying current increases.

The light lessons initially tackle the concept of light as an observed phenomenon by having the student identify objects which can be seen in an otherwise dark room (candle, luminous dial, flashlight bulb, etc.). The students are told that these objects emit light. Then they are asked to discriminate between things that can only be seen when light shines on them and things which can be seen because they emit light. From here the lessons explain the properties of light and eventually reflections, refraction, color properties, and image formation are observed through direct experience.

In the second year of the experiment the objectives were re-considered. In looking about the field of elementary school science, two programs seemed to have the most cohesive educational philosophy behind them. These were the AAAS program, *Science—A Process Approach* and the units of the *Science Curriculum Improvement Study* under Robert Karplus at Berkeley, California. Their lessons were adopted and modified so that they could be used with the project's equipment and procedures.

The immediate problems of the Learning Research and Development Center are to generate a set of lessons which work for the majority of students in the school and to eliminate technical, logistic, and language problems from the system. Each school year requires a minimum of 75 lessons so that the entire elementary school sequence encompasses about 1000 lessons. Not all of these lessons require tapes since we have found that a printed script is chosen by competent readers once the novelty of the tapes has worn off.

A longer term problem is to develop a comprehensive elementary school program which has a reasonable chance of adoption and execution in the public schools. This comprehensive program must, in addition to the laboratory experiences, include the following:

1. Stories which will allow the student's laboratory experiences to fit into a larger context.

2. Lessons which draw upon the experiences of all

children in order to develop a concept or reveal a pattern in the children's experiences which they might not have perceived.

3. Vocabulary development through interesting but, perhaps, scientifically irrelevant material which familiarizes the children with the sound and configuration of the words which will later be defined by experience and observation.

4. A library of science books, of audiovisual materials, and of science materials.

5. A continuing sorting and refining of the laboratory lessons in order to arrive at a sequence of lessons which will have proven value.

Verbal learning (Nos. 1 and 3 above) can be useful as long as it is not allowed to masquerade as scientific learning. The point must be stressed that verbal learning is a coding and communications device and that the scientific learning resides in the mastery of content and process in contact with the world of direct experience.

As a result of experience and analysis of the elementary school science program, the project has arrived at the conclusion that it is advantageous to use sequences of content objectives in addition to the process objectives of the AAAS and the conceptual themes of the SCIS.

Direct Experience

Confusion between the symbol and the abstraction which the symbol represents plagues many areas of learning although it is particularly inappropriate in science. In science the truth of an idea is established by observation of nature. Arguments are resolved by appeal to experiment, and ideas are abstracted from many observations. It must be obvious that this natural recourse of science to direct experiment and observation is especially important to the learning of children. It takes many encounters with dogs for young children to learn what a dog is. This classification ability comes long after the child can say the word, dog. On the other hand, the ability to answer the question, "What is a dog?" with the statement, "A dog is a carnivorous mammal," will have little to do with knowing what a dog is.

On the other side of the problem many adults think that

certain concepts are difficult for children simply because they seem esoteric to the adults. To children most things they are learning are esoteric until they become familiar with them. If adequate instances and examples are provided many concepts can be learned through direct experience which adults might think difficult (e.g. symmetry or refraction) for the children.

A favorite instance occurred when a visitor asked a class of first graders at Oakleaf, "What happens when the north pole of one magnet comes near the north pole of another magnet?" A first grader replied, "They repel each other." The visitor thought that he had trapped the youngster into giving a memorized verbal response and said, "Repel, that's a good word. What does it mean?" The boy answered, "I can't tell you, but I will demonstrate it for you." This instance illustrates the irreducible use of language as a means of coding and communication as well as the use of direct experience to enable a child to attain a concept. An elementary school science program must have a solid base in the experiences which define concepts. The number of instances and experiences which different children must have in order to form a concept which is resistant to confusion or forgetting must be determined by much observation and evaluation.

Individualized Lessons for Nonreaders

The project has generated several questions: "Why go to the trouble of making science lessons for nonreaders? Why not just wait until they are older, can read directions, and can bring more powerful intellectual tools to the problems?" "Why do you have individualized lessons when it would be so much easier to have teacher demonstrations and teacher-directed lessons?" These can be answered in the following ways.

Why lessons for nonreaders?

The reason for such lessons is that young children have the ability to learn important concepts in science which will interact with their later learning. As Karplus and others have pointed out, if children's common sense expectations are allowed to grow without guidance and structure in the early years it will be difficult to develop relationships among concepts in later learning. Experiences with college students reveal instance after instance in which the student's intuitive expectations seriously interfere with what is being taught.

Why individualize lessons for nonreaders?

The purpose in this approach lies partly in the experiment being conducted and in the dimensions of individualized instruction which are being explored. However, there are some clear reasons for attempting to individualize science lessons. The difference in scientific ability and background is often great. A few children do not know the names of the common colors. Yet, others have scientifically trained fathers and mothers who have informally enriched the education of their children with books and materials. This causes the pace of the students to vary. Any allowance in the school schedule for different completion times for an experiment must move any science program in the direction of the project. Even when a lesson is taught to a homogeneous group, some students will learn what was intended in the time allowed while others will not. Nevertheless, as soon as additional instruction is provided for those who did not master the objective, the program will once more move in the direction of the project.

While some logistic and technical problems are magnified by these procedures, the number of duplicate sets of materials the project must produce has lessened. Since the children do not all reach the same experiment at the same time as few as three sets of equipment for each experiment are needed. The use of earphones and carrels allows some interaction between children but seems to cut down distraction and allows the children to focus upon their problems.

Results

There are some conclusions which can be stated about the program and the performance of the children.

Science is by far the best-liked subject in the curriculum. The students are eager to read science books after exposure to the program. Fourth, fifth, and sixth graders had exposure to the program last year but not this year. Almost all of the fifth and sixth grade students when interviewed, said that they liked the individualized program better than the group program they are having this year.

The light lessons proved interesting and appropriate to the fourth through sixth grade children, but difficult for the younger children. An interesting comparison was made between these students and some college freshmen from the University of Pittsburgh. A comparison test was made when some physics instructors saw one of our tests and commented that they wished that entering freshmen knew the material covered in the test. Since we had been looking for a comparison group, it was decided to use a college freshman English class which included students with a wide variety of intended majors and a wide variety of high school science backgrounds. The results of the comparison need some qualification. The college students had not had their science for at least a year and only the best elementary school students got far enough in the lessons to take the test. On the other hand, none of the elementary school students had completed the lessons they were being tested on and the college students were supposedly a mature, highly selected group.

The most positive conclusion to be drawn is that the teaching of concepts by direct experience enabled the elementary school children to perform as well or better than college students who had covered much of the same material through a textbook approach in high school.

Thus, it can be seen through the testing program that there is verification students can do the things that the program expects them to do. If concepts attained through direct experience are indeed more resistant to forgetting than purely verbal learning, then there should be a high degree of retention of performance from year to year. Some indication of this was discovered when the magnetism placement tests were administered to the second- and third-grade students who had been exposed to the magnetism lessons the year before. The results indicated a high degree of retention.

All of the above does not mean that the project has initiated a significant or successful science program. The task is too great and the program is too experimental and young for any such statement. Comparison groups of children reaching for the same objectives in other ways are not yet available. The program does have the feature that the instructional procedures are so different and so controlled that they may help to define the optimal means of instruction at the same time that they provide data for the improvement of instructional materials for the future.

Reproduced with permission from *Science and Children*, December, 1966. Copyright 1966 by the National Science Teachers Association, 1201 Sixteenth Street, N. W., Washington, D. C. 20036. Joseph I. Lipson is Professor of Education, Learning Research and Development Center at the University of Pittsburgh.

26

An Experiment Via Tape

George LaCava

If you have a tape recorder collecting dust in some out-of-the way place in your school, rescue it as soon as possible. Once you have discovered the versatility of this teaching tool, you will keep it as a part of your standard room equipment.

One application which I found extremely beneficial for my class is the use of the tape recorder to facilitate group work in science. While teaching our annual unit on electricity in fourth grade, I demonstrated the construction of an electromagnet to my class. I endeavored to devise some method which would allow ample time for every student in the classroom to perform this experiment to satisfy his own curiosity, provide for him the thrill of accomplishment, and answer his own questions. I found that by using a taped lesson with my commentary, each student in the classroom could make his own electromagnet and marvel at its powers.

The setup is arranged so that each student in an average tape group of four to eight has his own headphone which is connected to a jack box. A wire with a phonograph plug attached to it leads from the jack box to the input receptacle of the tape recorder, thus carrying the electronically amplified sound of the teacher's voice to the headphones. In such a manner no one else in the room is disturbed, as only those involved in a taped lesson will hear the recording.

The most important element in the entire procedure is the lesson plan. Actually, this is a word-for-word script which must undergo careful preparation and checking before recording on magnetic tape. The wording must be clear, concise, and contain exact instructions. Keep in mind that a carefully planned script will give the listener a feeling of personal attention. This is particularly evident at the beginning of a script when you greet the student and explain the nature of the lesson.

Another important consideration in preparing the script is the time element. The number and length of pauses will depend on the material presented and personal judgment. For children in the elementary grades, the script for the tape should not exceed twelve minutes (pauses included).

Pupil participation is also important. This may be utilized at any time during a lesson in the form of a worksheet, sets of instructions, or, as in this instance, the manipulative action of utilizing the necessary materials to make the electromagnet. The worksheet included in this lesson served a dual purpose, as it helped to evaluate the effectiveness of the tape and assured me that there was understanding of the material presented.

After the tape recorder is turned off, the students proceed to complete their worksheets. The tape recorder is then ready to play over and over whenever needed. It is an invaluable asset for group work since two or three different groups may rotate to the listening station at different intervals.

Let us examine some of the advantages of this media. A student receives individual instruction since his headphone places him in isolation with only the voice of his teacher. Such exercises develop immediate concentration and accurate retention. Children become so engrossed in the "voice" on tape that their attention span is longer. The student will increase his skill in listening and evaluating what is heard.

A lesson of this nature is one excellent means of facilitating repetitive drill and enabling the teacher to be "in more than one place at one time." If so desired, he may circulate and help with individual problems while the previously made tape carries on with the details of the assignment. Such a technique enables him to become part of the listening group.

The lesson on electromagnets may be expanded by utilizing two other approaches. (1) The entire lesson can be reviewed in lecture form allowing the student to complete material on his worksheet as the lesson progresses or at the end. (2) The sequence of steps in the construction of an electromagnet may easily be produced by 2 x 2-inch colored slides accompanied by your commentary on tape. The student will focus his attention on the material presented in the slides while listening to the taped commentary.

Even though the tape recorder does not possess magical powers to accomplish any one task single-handedly, it is one of the modern teaching tools which can be personalized by the teacher. This is accomplished by introducing a lesson, creating interest in it, and using it to reach the desired objectives. The next time you are looking for a new approach to an old lesson, consider the unlimited possibilities of the tape recorder. It may add new dimensions to your science class.

"Making an Electromagnet"

Script for Tape

After a few introductory words concerning the lesson, the children are given their assignment; and one student turns on the recorder. The lesson begins:

"Good morning, boys and girls. In science yesterday, you saw how I made a magnet by using electricity. The dry cell makes electricity and the coil of wire which I used provides the path for the electricity to travel from the dry cell to the nail. The nail then becomes a magnet. Do you remember what we call this special kind of magnet? Yes, it is called an electromagnet.

"Today, we are going to make our own electromagnet. On your desk you will find the equipment which we need.

You should have a dry cell, a long wire, a long nail, some clips, thumbtacks, and pins.

"Listen carefully and follow my directions for making an electromagnet.

"First locate your nail.

Pause 5 seconds.

"Now take the long piece of insulated wire and wind the middle part of the wire around your nail.

Pause 10 seconds.

"You will notice that the covering from both ends of the wire has been scraped away and now the wire is visible at either end. Connect each end of your wire to a terminal post on your dry cell.

Pause 10 seconds.

"You have now completed the path for electricity to travel from the dry cell to your nail. Now pick up one of your paper clips and hold it near the end of your nail.

Pause 5 seconds.

"What happens? Now try a thumbtack and some pins.

Pause 10 seconds.

"What happens? You have made the nail into a magnet by using electricity.

"Suppose we were to break the path of electricity. You can easily do this—disconnect one end of your wire from the post on your dry cell.

Pause 4 seconds.

"What happens? Yes, your clips and pins fell off of the nail, because in removing the wire from the post you broke the pathway which is necessary for electricity to travel through. So you just have an ordinary nail.

"Remember, electricity helps us to make a magnet. However, the electricity must have a complete path from the dry cell to the nail before the nail can be magnetized.

"You may now disconnect the wire from the dry cell and the nail, and leave the materials on the desk.

Pause 8 seconds.

"On your desk you will find a worksheet for this lesson and a pencil. In the space provided at the top of your worksheet write your name and the date.

Pause 10 seconds.

"Listen carefully for the directions. On the first page of the worksheet there are six questions. On the lines provided write a sentence or two which will best answer each question. You will notice that the second sheet of paper is blank. On this paper I would like to have you draw a picture of your experiment, showing clearly the connections needed to generate electricity which in turn will magnetize the nail.

"I hope that you have enjoyed your experiment on tape today. The person sitting nearest the 'off' control may now turn the recorder off, after which you may start completing your worksheet.

"Thank you."

SECTION V

Evaluating Cognitive and Affective Outcomes of Individualization

The reader, by now, must have noted that an individualized instruction program should include the preparation of objectives, determination of instructional needs of each child, selection of appropriate instructional materials and activities, and evaluation of cognitive and affective outcomes. The collection in this section deals with evaluation of cognitive and affective outcomes of individualized instruction.

A potpourri of contemporary conceptions and uses of instructional objectives is considered by W. James Popham in his article, "Objectives '72." Readers will find in this article, written by a foremost objectives enthusiast, answers to many of their doubts about objectives.

John E. Bicknell in his article, "Pupil Assessment in Individualized Instruction," discusses three functions—placement, diagnosis, and prescription—of pupil assessment. This discussion is illustrated with the help of a "tree" chart and data about one particular student. Suggestions given in the paper will be of great help to teachers in individualizing instruction of their pupils.

Suggestions for implementing criterion-referenced techniques in the classroom are given by Peter W. Airasian and George F. Madaus in their article, "Criterion-Referenced Testing in the Classroom." It is pointed out that the criterion-referenced approach serves two very valuable functions: (1) it directs attention to the performances and behaviors which are the main purpose of instruction; and (2) it rewards students on the basis of their attainment relative to these criterion performances rather than relative to their peers.

In "Individual Conferences—Diagnostic Tools," Harriet Ramsey Reeves emphasizes the need for conducting individual conferences with students to acquire more specific information about them and to double check information from other sources. The author feels that by incorporating individual conferences, the teacher is in a better position to provide for individual needs.

Madan Mohan in his article, "Motivational Procedures In the Individualization of Instruction," contends that a system of individualized motivation must be built into any program of individualized instruction. The author discusses a checklist of student behaviors indicative of motivation, a procedure to identify motivated and unmotivated students, and a procedure to identify the reward preferences of students. Some of the effective and practical motivational procedures which teachers can undertake in their class-rooms are discussed. It is hoped that these procedures will help teachers become more effective in the management of the learning process.

27

Objectives '72

W. James Popham

When Sergio Mendes and his highly successful musical group Brasil '66 decided a few months ago to change their name to Brasil '77, they admitted that their prime motive was to maintain an up-to-date image. Mendes and his promoters recognized that potential record purchasers of the seventies might view recordings from a sixties group as more worthy of historical veneration than purchase.

In the field of education there is a comparable danger that when one considers the topic of instructional objectives images may arise which were more appropriate for the 1960s than for today. Instructional objectives '72 are not instructional objectives '62. And the educator who, basing his decision on an outdated notion of objectives, judges the relevance of instructional objectives to his current concerns will likely make the wrong decision. In the following paragraphs an effort will be made to inspect some of the more recent wrinkles in the rapidly changing countenance of instructional objectives. By considering a potpourri of contemporary conceptions and uses of instructional objectives, today's educator will, we hope, remain au courant.

The Furor Subsides

In the early and mid-sixties there was a goodly amount of excitement about instructional objectives, particularly behavioral objectives. America's educators had located a new tool for their instruction kit—that is, objectives stated in terms of learner post-instruction behavior—and many teachers were truly enthralled by the new toy. During that period there were enough "how-to-write-'em" workshops to stuff a horse. With a few exceptions, horse-stuffing might have been a more beneficial pursuit. This was the era of drum-pounding, and (speaking as a former drum-pounder) many zealots viewed behavioral objectives as the first step on a stairway to educational paradise.

We'll never know whether the remarkable display of interest in behavioral objectives was due to 1) the activities of programmed instructional enthusiasts (who universally employed behavioral objectives), 2) the impact of Robert Mager's little self-instruction book[1] on how to state objectives (which could be completed in 45 minutes, hence was praiseworthy on brevity grounds alone), 3) the markedly increased sales of the *Taxonomies of Educational Objectives*[2] (which may have made professors Bloom, Krathwohl, et al. regret their nonroyalty contracts with the publishers), or 4) the insistence of many U.S. Office of Education officials that instructional project proposals had to include behavioral objectives (which proposal writers often did, but project staffs often forgot).

Whatever the causes, many of our nation's educators became behavioral objectives enthusiasts. Everywhere one turned, a speaker was expounding the raptures of behavioral goals. The professional literature abounded with articles on objectives. A flood of books and filmstrips told how to state objectives behaviorally. "Behavioral" and "objectives" were, without challenge, the most persistent educational buzz words of the mid-sixties.

But much of the agitation about instructional objectives has abated. No longer behaving like newlyweds, educators and objectives are learning how to live with each other on a more permanent post-honeymoon basis. It will be interesting to see whether in this instance familiarity breeds contempt or contentment.

The Controversy Lingers

Most knowledgeable proponents of explicit instructional objectives have veered away from using the phrase behavioral objectives, for they recognize that some educators erroneously equate the adjective "behavioral" with a mechanistic, dehumanized form of behavioriam. What most objectives enthusiasts want is only clarity regarding instructional intentions, not a stipulation of the strategy (such as behaviorism) used to accomplish those intentions. Thus, because such phrases create less misdirected resistance, expressions similar to "performance objectives," "measurable objectives," or "operational objectives" are often employed these days.

Some educators use the terms objectives, goals, aims, intents, etc., interchangeably. Others use the terms differently, depending on the level of generality involved. For instance, goal is used by some to convey a broader instructional intention, while objective is reserved for more limited classroom instruction. Anyone involved in a discussion of these topics had best seek early clarification of the way the terms are being employed.

But irrespective of the particular phrase employed to depict precise instructional objectives, there are still a number of people who, individually or collectively, find fault with such goals. Some critics[3] deal with particular technical issues such as the nature of the logical connections between the goal which is sought and the pupil behaviors which are used to indicate whether the goal has been realized. In a similar vein, other writers[4] raise questions regarding the optimal level of generality at which objectives should be explicated—that is, how can objectives be both precise enough to communicate unambiguously and broad enough to avoid the thousands of objectives which would surely follow if each objective equaled a single test item. These forms of criticism are useful to those educators who would work with measurable instructional objectives, for the problems identified must be solved, at least partially, to increase the educational utility of objectives. And even in the enlightened seventies it must be noted that there are a number of technical problems regarding the uses of instructional objectives which have not yet been satisfactorily resolved, the generality-level dilemma being a good illustration.

But there are other types of critics. Anointing themselves as Defenders of the Faith, these people view proponents of performance objectives as minions of an unseen force commissioned to destroy our currently laudable educational enterprise.[5] These critics engage in all the classic forms of nonrational debate, either deliberately erecting straw men or displaying remarkable misinformation regarding current thinking on the topic of instructional objectives.

Certainly, there are abuses of instructional objectives. These are usually perpetrated by administrators who, having read Mager's little volume on objectives, feel themselves blessed with instant expertise and thus institute a free-wheeling objectives circus in their schools. Surely, there are too many examples of trivial behavioral objectives which, albeit measurable, no clear-thinking educator should ever pursue. Clearly, there are too few illustrations of really high-level cognitive goals or important affective goals. But these are rectifiable deficiencies. Those critics who wish to chuck the whole notion of measurable objectives because of such deficits would probably have rejected forever all antibiotics because some early versions of these medications were less than perfect.

One hopes that groups such as the National Council of Teachers of English, who two years ago at their national convention passed a resolution rejecting behavioral objectives almost in toto, will reappraise their stance. While teachers in fields such as English do find it difficult to frame some of their more important intentions in a form which permits subsequent assessment, they should not be excused from the task. Nor should they be applauded when they cast behavioral objectives proponents in the Arthurian role of the wicked knight. It is devilishly hard to assess many of the more profound goals of education. But if we can make some progress toward doing so, then we shall surely reap dividends for education and the learners it should serve.

Objectives Depositories

One development that seems to be catching on in educational circles is the establishment of objectives bank agencies or test item depositories.[6] These organizations collect large numbers of objectives and/or measuring instruments, thereafter making them available so that educators may select those materials of particular use in a local educational setting. The heavy demand for materials distributed by such agencies as the Instructional Objectives Exchange[7] suggests that American educators are finding these sorts of support materials useful.

There are some, critics of precise objectives, who find the provision of "ready-made" objectives particularly reprehensible. These individuals[8] contend that it is demeaning for teachers to select their objectives from an extant pool of goals. Teachers, they argue, should personally devise their own statements of objectives. This form of carping, it strikes me, is akin to asking a surgeon to manufacture his own surgical instruments. If I am about to undergo an appendectomy, I would prefer that the scalpel to be used had been professionally prepared by a surgical instrument manufacturer instead of pounded out in my doctor's toolshed. For that is precisely what objectives depositories are attempting to provide—tools for instructional designers and evaluators. The statements of objectives and pools of test items can be used, modified, or rejected by educators, depending on the suitability of the tools for a given instructional situation. To reject the provision of such tools is to yearn for the pre-hand-axe society of primitive man.

Accountability Equals Objectives

For some educators, the notion of explicit instructional objectives is inextricably tied up with the recent concern about educational accountability. They hear accountability enthusiasts attempting to devise educational monitoring systems which are anchored to behavioral objectives. They see PPBS devotees conjure up cost/effectiveness schemes in which precise objectives play a pivotal role. Thus they quite naturally assume that if you buy precise objectives you've also paid your first installment on the entire PPBS-accountability syndrome.

It is true that measurable instructional objectives can be highly useful in implementing schemes to satisfy the current quest for educational accountability; yet, to organize one's instructional thinking around precise goal statements in no way commits an instructor to the whole PPBS routine. In general, there is undoubtedly a positive correlation between educators' proclivities to employ measurable objectives and their inclinations to adopt an accountability stance. Nevertheless, a teacher who wishes to employ measurable objectives can do so while eschewing all the trappings of accountability.

Objectives and Teacher Evaluation

In part because of the general movement toward accountability, we are beginning to see measurable objectives employed in procedures designed to assess a teacher's instructional skill. In several states—for example, California, Florida, and Colorado—there is considerable activity at the state legislative level to devise schemes for evaluating the quality of the state's educational enterprise in terms of specific instructional goals.

In their recently concluded 1971 legislative session, California lawmakers enacted a statewide system of teacher evaluation in which each school district in the state must set up a systematic teacher appraisal system. Local districts have certain options regarding the final form of the evaluation scheme, but the new legislation stipulates that "standards of expected student progress in each area of study" be established by all districts. Many California educators are interpreting this to mean that local districts must adopt precise instructional goals stated in terms of learner behavior. Further, the new law requires that each teacher's competence be assessed (probationary teachers annually, nonprobationary teachers biennially) "as it relates to the established standards." Quite clearly, instructional objectives will play a central role in the attempts to implement the new California teacher evaluation law.[9]

Another teacher evaluation approach of considerable potential involves the use of short-term teaching performance tests as a vehicle for assessing one's instructional proficiency. A teaching performance test consists of determining a teacher's ability to accomplish a pre-specified instructional objective with a small group of randomly assigned learners. By controlling the ability of learners (through both randomization and statistical adjustments) and keeping constant the instructional task (that is, the objective to be achieved), it is possible to discriminate among teachers with respect to this particular instructional skill—the ability to bring about pre-specified behavior changes in learners. At least one firm[10] is now providing a limited service to evaluate teachers according to their skill with respect to teaching performance tests and, perhaps more importantly, is providing teaching improvement kits designed to enhance teachers' skills on this type of instructional task. We can readily foresee the more frequent use of such measurement strategies, whereby teachers will be judged, at least in part, by their ability to aid their pupils to achieve both cognitive and affective instructional goals.

Objectives Plus Measures

Most classroom teachers can recount stories of an earlier era when their principal asked them to write out a list of educational objectives—typically broad goals at the platitude plateau—which were dutifully prepared, then placed in the desk drawer to be trotted forth only on PTA or back-to-school nights. Such goal statements rarely, if ever, made any difference in what went on in the classroom. But these, of course, were nonbehavioral goals that were really not supposed to affect practice, only offer solace to the public. Now, however, we find educators falling into the same trap with behavioral objectives. They believe that merely by having teachers gin up a flock of performance objectives a moribund instructional operation will be magically transformed into pedagogical grandeur. It doesn't happen that way.

A well-stated instructional objective communicates an educator's aspiration for his learners. To assess the degree to which the objective has been achieved, we need measures based on the objectives. By providing the measures—and this certainly includes more than pencil-and-paper tests—we can make it easier for teachers to find out whether the objective has been attained. And we have to make it easy for teachers to live the good pedagogical life. Some religious conservatives erect hurdle after hurdle which their brethren must leap on the way to the good life. The prudent pastor makes it simple, not difficult, to live the righteous life.

Objectives with related measures can make a ton of difference in our schools. Teachers are generally well-intentioned and conscientious human beings. They want what's best for their pupils. If they discover their goals are not being achieved via current instructional strategies, they'll probably try something different. But if they only have objectives, without measures of those objectives, the odds are that they'll never find out how well their children are really doing. We desperately need more measures to match our objectives. Behavioral objectives sans measures offer only modest instructional advantages; behavioral objectives with measures can yield dramatic dividends.

Needs Assessment Enterprises

As more educators are becoming familiar with measurable instructional objectives, they are finding more uses for them, as with most new tools. One application of explicit objectives which seems particularly noteworthy involves their use in systematically deciding on the goals of an educational system, e.g., district or statewide. Stimulated largely by requirements of ESEA Title III programs which demand the conduct of an educational needs assessment in which local educational deficiencies are identified, several educators are carrying out their needs assessments by using measurable objectives. More specifically, they are either generating sets of measurable objectives or selecting them from objectives depositories, then having different clienteles, such as community representatives or students, rank the objectives in terms of their suitability for inclusion in the curriculum.

Because the use of measurable objectives reduces the ambiguity associated with statements of educational intentions, noneducators are better able to comprehend and thereby judge the importance of alternative instructional goals. By averaging the rankings of representative groups, the educational decision maker soon acquires a more enlightened estimate of the curriculum preferences of his school system's constituents.

In view of strong drives throughout the nation for legitimate community involvement in the schools, many astute school people will see the use of objectives-based needs assessments as a reasonable vehicle for allowing appropriate groups to express their educational preferences. We can anticipate increased usage of objectives in this fashion.

Objectives and Evaluation

Some educators mistakenly believe that in order to conduct a defensible evaluation of an educational enterprise one must judge the degree to which the program's instructional objectives have been achieved. Michael Scriven, perhaps America's foremost evaluation theorist, has recently argued[11] for goal-free evaluation in which one attends to the outcomes of an instructional sequence without any consideration whatsoever of what was intended by the instructional planners. After all, it is not the instructional designers' rhetoric to which we should attend, but to the results their designs produce. Scriven's suggestions pertain to the role of an independent evaluator who might be unduly constrained in his attention to consequences if he becomes too familiar with an instructional project's goals.

This does not suggest that an evaluation cannot be carried out in terms of project objectives, but if a goal-based evaluation strategy is used, then the evaluator should be certain to 1) make an assessment of the worth of the original objectives and 2) carefully search for unanticipated side effects of the instruction not encompassed by the original goal statements. As Scriven puts it, objectives may be essential for instructional planning but not necessary for certain models of educational evaluation.

All or Nothing at All?

Some classroom teachers who might otherwise organize a proportion of their instruction around measurable objectives have been so intimidated by behavioral objectives zealots demanding "measurability for each objective" that they reject the entire objectives bit. It is easy to see how those people who are enamoured of rational instructional planning can get carried away in their enthusiasm for measurability. After all, if a teacher can't tell whether a goal has been achieved, how can the teacher decide whether an instructional sequence is helping or harming the pupils' achievement of the goal? Interestingly enough, most educational goals can be operationalized so that we can tease out indicators of the degree to which they have been attained. Even for long-range goals we can usually find proximate predictors which, albeit less than perfect, can give us a rough fix on the degree to which the instruction is successful.

However, many busy classroom teachers do not possess the time, or perhaps the ingenuity, to carve out measurable indicators of some of their more elusive educational goals. These teachers, I believe, can be permitted to devote a certain portion of their instruction to the pursuit of highly important goals which, although unmeasurable by a given teacher, are so intrinsically praiseworthy that they merit the risk. The remainder of the teacher's instruction, however, should be organized around goals which are clear, hence clearly assessable.

Messing with Miscellany

In an effort to keep the reader current with respect to instructional objectives, I have attempted to skitter through a potpourri of contemporary issues regarding objectives. To me the term "potpourri" has always referred to some sort of a miscellaneous collection. I made a last-minute dictionary check as I wrote this final paragraph and discovered that Webster offers a comparable interpretation—except that the literal definition of potpourri is a "rotten pot." The reader will have to decide whether the foregoing potpourri is literal, nonliteral, or merely illiterate.

Reprinted from *Phi Delta Kappan,* copyright March, 1972. Reprinted by permission of the publisher and Dr. W. James Popham. Dr. Popham is Professor of Education at the University of California at Los Angeles.

References

[1]Robert Mager, *Preparing Instructional Objectives.* San Francisco: Fearon Publishers, 1962.

[2]B. S. Bloom et al., *Taxonomy of Educational Objectives, Handbook I: Cognitive Domain.* New York: David McKay, 1956; D. R. Krathwohl et al., *Taxonomy of Educational Objectives, Handbook II: Affective Domain.* New York: David McKay, 1964.

[3]See Philip G. Smith's essay in this issue, p. 429.

[4]For example, see E. L. Baker, "Defining Content for Objectives." Vimcet Associates, P.O. Box 24714, Los Angeles, Calif. 90024.

[5]For example, see Hans P. Guth's recent tirade in The English Journal, "The Monkey on the Bicycle: Behavioral Objectives and the Teaching of English," September, 1970, pp. 785–92. But don't pass up Peter W. Airasian's dissection of Guth's position in a later issue of that journal ("Behavioral Objectives and the Teaching of English," April, 1971, pp. 495–99).

[6]The Laboratory of Educational Research at the University of Colorado, Boulder, for example, is setting up a pool of measures in the affective domain under Gene V. Glass's leadership.

[7]Distribution statistics, Instructional Objectives Exchange, Box 24095, Los Angeles, Calif. 90024.

[8]For example, see Deborah Ruth, "Behavioral Objec-

tives: A Ratomorphic View of Man," a paper presented at the NCTE Annual Convention, Las Vegas, Nev., November, 1971.

[9]A discussion of the new California teacher evaluation law is available; see W. J. Popham, Designing Teacher Evaluation Systems. Los Angeles: Instructional Objectives Exchange, 1971 ($1.25 per copy).

[10]Instructional Appraisal Services, 105 Christopher Circle, Ithaca, N.Y., 14850; or Box 24821, Los Angeles, Calif. 90024.

[11]Michael Scriven, "Goal-Free Evaluation," an informal working paper for the Institute of Education, November, 1971.

28

Pupil Assessment in Individualized Instruction

John E. Bicknell

It is extremely difficult to discuss pupil assessment for individualized modes of education in isolation from the theory of instruction, the structure and sequencing of the subject matter, and the modes of presentation employed. All are bound inextricably together. In fact, optimal operation of an individualization model is impossible unless it incorporates a carefully designed assessment program. The purpose of individualized instruction is to adjust the learning experiences of a pupil to his unique interests, capabilities, and needs. These adjustments can only be accomplished through the use of corrective information which is obtained by a systematic program of monitoring pupil behavior during the instructional process. Pupil assessment, therefore, must be a continuous, integral part of the instruction/learning sequence.

Pupil assessment in individualized education has three major functions. The first of these, chronologically, is to identify the appropriate "entry point" in a skill development hierarchy for a particular pupil in a specific learning unit. This function is based on the assumption that pupils will vary in the number and degree of skills they already possess when they begin to work on a learning unit which is designed to achieve one or more terminal objectives through the attainment of a hierarchy of facilitating skills. The second function of assessment is to provide diagnostic data from which a teacher can infer the nature of a pupil's learning problems; his preferred learning mode; his cognitive style; and/or any of a number of his characteristics which are presumed to be related to the efficiency of his process of learning. Finally, the third function of the

Instructional Objectives hierarchy for a unit on addition operations.

1 Solves addition problems from memory for sums less than or equal to twenty.

2 Solves subtraction problems from memory for sums less than or equal to nine.

3 Solves subtraction problems from memory for two-digit sums less than or equal to twenty.

4 Solves addition problems related to single-digit combinations by multiples of ten.

5 Finds the missing addend for problems with three single-digit addends.

6 Does column addition with no carrying. Two addends with three- and four-digit combinations.

7 Does column addition with no carrying. Three- or four-digit numbers with three to five addends.

8 Adds two-digit numbers with carrying to the tens' or hundreds' place. Two addends.

9 Finds the sums for column addition using three to five single-digit addends.

10 Adds two-digit numbers with carrying to the tens' or hundreds' place. Three or four addends.

11 Adds two-digit numbers with carrying to the tens' and hundreds' place. Two to four addends.

12 Adds three-digit numbers with carrying to the tens' or hundreds' place. Two to four addends.

13 Adds three-digit numbers with carrying to the tens' and hundreds' place. Two to four addends.

14 Can generalize carrying to any number of places with any number of addends.

Figure 1.

assessment program is to determine when a pupil's skill performance reaches a prespecified criterion level.

Lest there be some misunderstanding, it should be emphasized that pupil assessment should have functions beyond the three being discussed here. There will continue to be a need for comparative and normative information which can be used to show how the pupils in a particular school perform in comparison to those in another school. These functions are largely for administrative and reporting purposes. They should be based on a schoolwide testing program with standardized tests which are used only for these functions. For our discussion of assessment in individualized modes of education, we are not concerned with these functions.

Now let's take a more detailed look at each of the three functions to determine the nature of the testing program to fulfill it. For this purpose let us assume that an instructional unit on addition operations has been planned to develop the 14 objectives shown in Figure 1. These objectives are listed in a linear sequence which is somewhat difficult to use with individual pupils. A schematic representation of these will assist discussion and may be actually used in formulating an instructional plan for each child (Figure 2). Once such a schematic hierarchy has been established for a unit of instruction, it can be duplicated so that a copy is provided for each pupil.

Having such a diagram for each pupil, the placement of each pupil in the instructional sequence can be accomplished with a pretest. The diagram can be used to ensure that the pretest is appropriate. The items on the test should be specific to the objectives and each objective should be represented by a number of items which is great enough to determine whether the pupils possess the level of skills on each objective which is prerequisite to the succeeding one in the hierarchy. However, the pretest may take one of two forms depending upon the size of the group of pupils who are taking it at a specific time.

If the number of pupils is small an individual test-interview may be used. When a pupil is ready to undertake a new learning unit it may be desirable to schedule an interview ostensibly for planning his work and acquainting

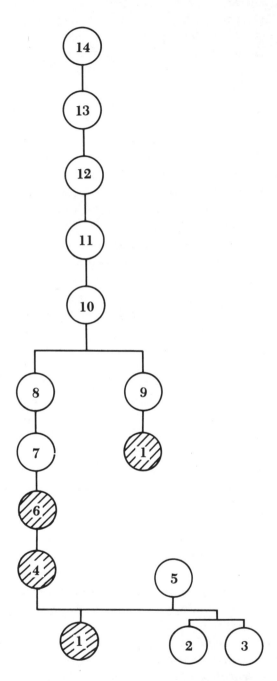

Figure 2. Diagram of Objectives for a Unit on Addition Operations

him with the objectives of the unit. During this interview, the teacher can present selected problems to the pupil. Through observing the pupils' performance the teacher can make a judgment about the appropriate "entry-point."

One advantage of the individual test-interview is that the teacher can locate quickly an approximate "entry-point" for the pupil. For example, suppose that pupil Debbie Smith is ready to begin the unit on addition operations. The teacher might logically begin her test by presenting Debbie with one or two problems from objective 8 to see if Debbie can add two-digit numbers with carrying to the "tens-place." If Debbie can do this correctly, her competence with objectives 1, 4, 6 and 7, which are basic to 8, can be inferred without actually testing them. If, on the other hand, Debbie is unable to solve the items on the 8th objective, a couple of items on the 4th objective can be presented. If she solves these satisfactorily the teacher will know that the appropriate "entry-point" for Debbie is somewhere in the span of objectives from the fifth through the seventh. Two or three more questions or problems will allow a precise identification of the objective where Debbie can be entered into the learning sequence. Thus, through the use of a testing strategy, Debbie has been properly placed in the learning sequence using only 6 or 8 test items.

A second advantage of the individual test-interview is that the teacher has great flexibility in choosing the type of problems or item formats to use in the testing.

Dr. Jerome Bruner tells us in his monograph, "Toward a Theory of Instruction,"[1] that "any domain of knowledge (or any problem within that domain of knowledge) can be represented in three ways: by a set of actions appropriate for achieving a certain result (enactive representation); by a set of summary images or graphics that stand for a concept without defining it fully (iconic representation); and by a set of symbolic or logical propositions drawn from a symbolic system that is governed by rules or laws for forming and transforming propositions (symbolic representation)." As an example of the three modes of representation, consider the concept of "carrying" to the tens place in addition. In the *enactive* mode the pupil would be engaged in manipulating cusinaire rods in boxes which would represent the units, tens and hundreds places. To "carry" from the units place he would group the units rods in bundles of 10 which would be exchanged for the tens rods, one bundle for each tens rod (regrouping). These would then be placed in the tens box. The remainder of the units rods would be left in the units box. Through these kinds of activities the pupil will build a basis in experience from which he can move to *iconic* representation. In this stage he would represent the cusinaire rods by marks of different lengths. Instead of manipulating the actual rods, he would manipulate the marks adding one of the tens length to the tens group for each group of 10 unit length marks he could cancel out of the units group. After these exercises the pupil can be introduced to the manipulation of the written numerals which are a *symbolic* representation of the number system. These forms of representation are, themselves, hierarchical. In placing the pupil in a learning unit it is important to know if he can demonstrate possession of the concept through the enactive or iconic representations if he is, for some reason, incapable of demonstrating it in symbolic representation. In an individual interview test the teacher has the flexibility of using equivalent items in two or more modes of representation.

If a larger number of pupils (ten or more) are ready to undertake a learning unit at the same time, a group test may be necessary. In this case, test items in a single mode of representation are presented to the pupils. The test usually involves symbolic representation at the oral or written levels. Thus, the test results are only indicative of the pupils' ability to demonstrate the concept at the symbolic level. A group test in symbolic representation usually is unable to determine whether a pupil who fails does so because he does not possess the concept underlying the test item or because he lacks the skill to manipulate the symbols in which it was represented. Of course, it may be argued that the objective of instruction is to enable pupils to deal with knowledge at the highest possible mode of representation (that is the symbolic mode). Therefore, he should be placed in the learning unit at the step in the objective hierarchy which immediately precedes his "failure point" on the test. However, the question of where to place the pupil in that particular step, i.e., whether to begin instruction in the enactive, iconic or symbolic mode of representation, remains unanswered. Thus, the group test is, at best, only a gross screening device. It must be followed by individual interview-tests for making the finer discriminations necessary for proper placement of individual pupils.

The group pretest, which must allow for wide variation in the skills of the pupils, should include items which test each instructional objective of the unit. The absolute minimum length of the test would be one item for each objective. However, since a pupil could select the correct response to any one item by chance, such a test would be useless to determine whether a pupil really had attained a criterion level of mastery of any of the instructional objectives. Therefore, a functional length for the pre-test must be at least three items per objective. If the test is constructed with the items arranged in the order of the instructional objectives of the unit, its scoring could be simplified. Let us suppose that a test consists of three items per objective and are arranged in the same sequence as the objectives in the unit. The proper placement in the unit for a particular pupil will be somewhere between the point in the test where he made his first incorrect response and the objective on which he failed all three items. An interview-test could then be set up to explore this range to more precisely determine the pupil's instructional entry point. Thus, the group pre-test can be used to localize the individual testing to a range of 2 to 4 of the instructional objectives.

You will note that although the test may be administered to a group of pupils at one time, each pupil's performance on the test is interpreted independently. Therefore, for purposes of pupil placement in the instructional sequence, it is unnecessary to know the pupils' total scores. It is also unnecessary to calculate means, standard deviations, norms or other group-based statistics about the test to aid in interpreting pupil performances.

On the other hand, in the interview-test used with an individual pupil, fewer items may be used, but their variety in terms of mode of representation may be greater. Direct observation of the pupil in the performance of a problem solution will allow a skillful teacher to make a better estimate of the capability of the pupil than will be possible with several multiple choice items. Furthermore, the teacher may use a strategy for quickly locating a pupil's skill level. For example, if initial testing began on the fourth objective and the pupil's response indicated a satisfactory level of skill, the teacher might next move to the eighth objective; if the responses were unsatisfactory she would then move to the sixth objective. Thus, the pupil could be placed in the learning objective hierarchy using the smallest number of test items.

The second function of pupil assessment is diagnostic. This function is best served by instructionally incorporated testing. If properly constructed, the items of the incorporated test can serve both as diagnostic and as mastery tests for the learning objective. If a pupil's error rate on these items has decreased to a previously specified level (say 2 out of 10 wrong), he may be judged to have developed the required level of skill. The items are, in this case, serving as a mastery test. However, to accomplish the diagnostic function the instructionally incorporated items must be constructed so that the nature of a pupil's learning difficulty can be inferred from his wrong responses.

The construction of diagnostic items requires that the constructor of the items and the teacher who is using them have an intimate knowledge and understanding of the possible ways in which a pupil can arrive at a wrong response to a particular item. If the item is of the multiple choice type, each distractor should appear to be a more plausible alternative than the correct one if the pupil has a particular type of difficulty, either misinformation or misconception.

Again, the first screening for diagnosis may be achieved using multiple choice items incorporated as practice exercises in the individual learning activities presented for the pupil. The teacher or aide who is supervising the pupil can observe the pupil's responses to these items and develop a tentative hypothesis concerning the pupil's difficulty. This hypothesis can then be tested and refined through an interview test using specifically chosen items.

The diagnostic procedure suggested here involves two-stage testing. Each stage utilizes items which are specifically designed to obtain a particular kind of information about the pupil.

The foregoing discussion has dealt with the identification of the type of learning difficulty that a child is encountering while working with material which may be presented in any one of the three modes of representation. Another aspect of diagnosis is the assessment of the pupil's learning-related characteristics so that instructional material in the appropriate mode of representation can be selected and the instructional strategy can be designed to fit the pupil's particular learning style. This is too large a topic to be dealt with in detail here. However, a brief discussion of some of the problems of such an assessment may be of value.

Two learning-related characteristics which warrant mention are "conceptual level" and "cognitive style." The basic work on "conceptual level" and its importance to the instructional process is being carried on by David E. Hunt at the Ontario Institute for Studies in Education.[2] The conceptual levels described by Hunt are strikingly parallel to the modes of representation suggested by Bruner.

An interesting project on the cognitive style of learners in relation to their instruction is being carried on at Oakland Community College in Michigan.[3] According to the findings of this project, the cognitive style of a student determines the kind and format of material which are meaningful for him. Through a specialized program of testing a complex cognitive style map can be developed for each pupil. With this map a teacher can determine the kind of material, the types of instructional-learning activities, and the motivational techniques which will optimize a student's development toward a particular educational objective.

Unfortunately, the tests which have been developed for Hunt's Conceptual Level Identification and Oakland's Cognitive Style mapping are suitable only for secondary and post-secondary students. Furthermore, conceptual levels and cognitive styles are defined only for the age range from 12 years to maturity. We need to build a basis in experience on which such theories can be extended into the elementary, primary, and pre-school age ranges. The best we can do at this juncture is to put our faith in the judgment of perceptive, skillful teachers aided by a system of careful observation and record keeping.

To assist in observation and record keeping we suggest that a form of anecdotal records be kept on each pupil. The purpose of these records should be to describe each child in terms of characteristics which seem to be related to the way in which he incorporates new materials and experiences into his repertoire of behavior. The teacher might start by trying to answer the following questions:

1. What kinds of things and activities seem to interest the child? Noting these for a child will suggest ways in which the child can be introduced to the study of new concepts and skills.

2. What type of play activities does the child initiate and maintain? To what extent are his play activities manipulative (moving or adjusting toys or other objects), constructive (building roads, houses, etc. with blocks or other materials), imaginative (make-believe role-playing, dramatizing stories)? These observations can give the teacher some idea of the cognitive style of the child.

3. What is the child's need for structure? Does the child seem to need a set of specific instructions for carrying out an activity; or does he prefer to work out his own procedures? These observations will allow the teacher to determine the degree to which the child can be engaged in independent, discovery type of learning.

4. To what extent does the child tolerate uncertainty and/or frustration? The answer to this question will indicate when and how frequently the teacher should intervene to resolve uncertainty and relieve frustration.

5. What are the situations in which the child displays emotion and/or behavioral changes? In these situations how quickly is the child moved to react?

6. To what extent does the child prefer group or individual activities?

7. To what extent do the other children react positively (or negatively) to the child?

These are but a few of the possible characteristics

which may be noted. However, if these and others that seem of importance are systematically noted it will be possible to relate the child's achievement of the instructional goals to them under various instructional procedures. In this sense very important exploratory research can be carried out by the instructional teams.

The third function of assessment is to determine when a pupil's performance relative to an instructional objective attains a pre-specified criterion level. The term "criterion referenced" is descriptive of this type of assessment. The major problems include the specification of an appropriate criterion level of performance for the pupil; the formulation of tasks and problems in which the pupil can demonstrate his skill (or lack of it); and fitting these into the instruction-learning sequence.

In specifying an appropriate criterion level two things must be kept in mind: the capability of the pupil and the minimum level to which a facilitating skill must be developed to allow the pupil to profitably begin work on the next step in the learning sequence. For example, if the next step in the learning sequence can be undertaken when a pupil can solve six out of ten of a certain kind of problem it would be unreasonable to require that he continue to drill upon the lower level items until he had reached a 9 out of 10 performance rate; particularly if this drill would result in boredom for the child.

Furthermore, a criterion level which is specified as 8 or 9 correct responses out of 10 items is very misleading and, to some extent, an artificial standard; particularly if the testing is instructionally incorporated. If the pupil's performance on these items is closely monitored it may be possible to evaluate his skill attainment with fewer than 10 items. For example, a pupil may fail on the first three items he attempts; the teacher or aide who is supervising his work may diagnose his difficulty from the type of errors he made and provide some tutoring; after which the pupil solves the next three items without error. This may be sufficient evidence of mastery to introduce him to the next step of the learning sequence.

From the foregoing discussion it can be inferred that the imbedded items can serve a dual purpose. They can be used for both diagnosis (if so constructed) and for mastery of the facilitating skills. Thus, the assessment program, insofar as the measurement of developed skills is concerned, should consist of a pretest at the beginning of a unit; instructionally incorporated, diagnostic-mastery items throughout the instructional sequence; and a post-test at the conclusion of the unit. This last test may profitably consist of three parts. The first of these might be made up of review items to check retention of skills from earlier units. The second, or main portion, should be made up of items to test mastery of the just completed unit. The third part might consist of the pretest for the next succeeding unit.

It should be apparent that the assessment program cannot be carried on using ad hoc items which are constructed on a spur-of-the-moment basis. As instructional objectives[4] are defined and built into sequences, evaluative items should be constructed to correspond to them. These items should be typed on 3 x 5 cards and filed according to the unit and objective to which they pertain. They should be further classified according to the particular mode of representation in which they are presented (enactive, iconic or symbolic). The resulting file will become an item bank which is readily available to the teaching team. Team members should be constantly on the lookout for items which may be added to the bank, for, like any bank account, its usefulness is expanded by regular deposits.

Since the major purpose for pupil assessment is to obtain the information necessary to make appropriate instructional decisions, the entire assessment process must be closely tied to the instructional sequence. In addition, a system of recording the information relative to the instructional decisions must be developed. To show the ways in which the assessment program is related to the instructional sequence, and to suggest a format for recording the results, let us return to the example of Debbie Smith.

Let us suppose that the pretest has shown that Debbie Smith has a sufficient level of skill on objectives 1, 4, and 6 (see figure 2) to allow her to proceed in the unit. To signify this, the circles for the objectives which she is competent can be shaded. Thus, the schematic diagram can be used as a visual record of Debbie's progress. An example is shown

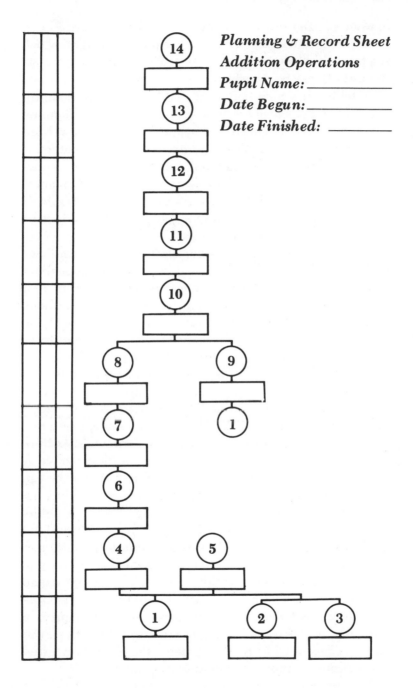

Planning & Record Sheet
Addition Operations
Pupil Name: _____
Date Begun: _____
Date Finished: _____

Figure 3. Example of Instructional Unit Planning and Record
Sheet

in Figure 3. Debbie would begin to work on objectives 2, 3, 7 and 9. Objectives 2 and 3 are prerequisite only to 5 which is a terminal objective for this unit. Therefore, her work on these skills may be done at any convenient time.

Debbie has now been "placed" in the continuum of learning objectives of the unit. The next stage of planning her program will consist of using her learning-related characteristics to select appropriate study materials, learning activities, motivational techniques for her to develop each skill. Debbie's teacher has maintained an anecdotal record in which the seven questions about Debbie's interests, preferences for structure, and working style have been tentatively answered.

From this and her previous performance record, we find that she likes to learn in a relatively independent situation; she likes to find out things for herself. In past work she has shown that she can deal easily with symbolic representations and can shift rapidly from symbols to the things they represent and back again. She also seems to be able to form concepts quickly and to express them concisely. She takes great pride in her work and is reinforced best by constructive praise. She verbalizes her thoughts and enjoys group discussions. These characteristics suggest that Debbie can achieve the objectives by being presented with a series of problems in symbolic form. With a little practice on examples of the type required by objective 7, she should be ready to work on objective 8. When she can solve objective 7 problems, the teacher can introduce an example involving carrying by saying, "Now, Debbie, we're going to try a slightly different problem. Try and tell me how it is different." When she is able to identify and describe the difference, the teacher might ask her to try to find a way of handling the difference (i.e., regrouping and carrying to the tens place). Past experience with Debbie has shown that once she recognizes and can express a principle, she is capable of generalizing it and, thus, can make a conceptual leap. At this point she should be tested to see if she can proceed immediately to objective 14.

If she can demonstrate a sufficient level of skill in addition through eighty percent or better success at objective 14, Debbie will be ready to proceed to the next unit of arithmetic. If not, she should be recycled to work on 9 and 10, then retested on 14.

A slight modification of the tree diagram can be made to show the instructional/learning sequence plans for Debbie. One modification consists of inserting rectangular boxes into the "tree" diagram immediately preceding each objective (Figure 3). These boxes represent the particular instructional strategy, materials and activities which are to be used to develop Debbie's skills. A system of abbreviations and coded identification numbers should be developed for this purpose. Library and self-instructional materials from the Instructional Resources Center can be identified by their catalogue numbers. An example of the detail which may be entered in these boxes is shown in Figure 4.

Another modification can be made by incorporating an expected time budget on the left-hand vertical margin of the plan sheet. A second vertical line on the left-hand margin of the sheet can be used in recording the actual time required. This sheet not only shows at a glance the planned activities for Debbie and her teachers during a unit of instruction, it also becomes a concise record of Debbie's performance and her experiences. These modifications are illustrated in Figure 3.

In this paper each of the three major functions of pupil assessment, placement, diagnosis and mastery determination has been discussed. A strategy for a two-stage, instructionally-incorporated testing procedure for placement and diagnosis has been suggested. An example of how the testing information can be recorded and used in the planning of a sequence of learning activities for an individual pupil in a particular unit has been presented and discussed. It is not suggested that the system described here is the ultimate answer to all of the problems of pupil assessment. However, to be successful, any effort to develop an individualized instructional system must be undergirded by an assessment program that provides a concise summarization of the information essential to individually planning the instructional sequence. It is hoped that creative teachers who are attempting to develop individualized instruction in their classes will find in this

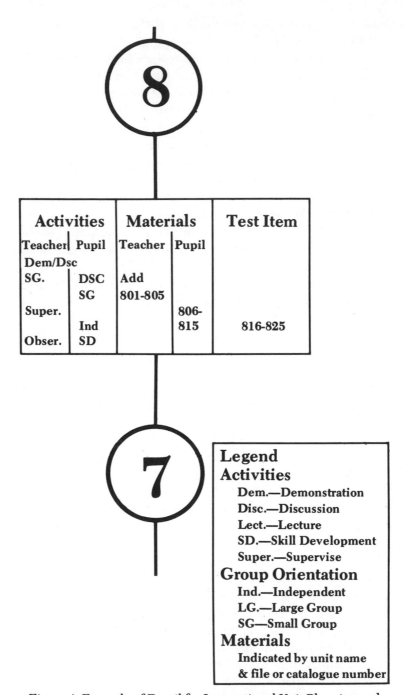

Activities		Materials		Test Item
Teacher	Pupil	Teacher	Pupil	
Dem/Dsc				
SG.	DSC	Add		
	SG	801-805		
Super.			806-	
	Ind		815	816-825
Obser.	SD			

Legend
Activities
    Dem.—Demonstration
    Disc.—Discussion
    Lect.—Lecture
    SD.—Skill Development
    Super.—Supervise
Group Orientation
    Ind.—Independent
    LG.—Large Group
    SG—Small Group
Materials
    Indicated by unit name
    & file or catalogue number

Figure 4. Example of Detail for Instructional Unit Planning and
Record Sheet

paper ideas and stimulation that will allow them to develop a system of assessment and recording to meet their individual needs.

This article was specially written for this book of readings at the request of the editors. Dr. John E. Bicknell is Research Professor, Teacher Education Research Center, SUC, Fredonia, New York.

Notes

¹Jerome Bruner. *Toward a Theory of Instruction.* New York: W. W. Norton and Company, Inc., 1966.

²David E. Hunt. "Matching Models in Education: The Coordination of Teaching Methods with Student Characteristics." Toronto: The Ontario Institute for Studies in Education, 1971.

³Laurence Wasser. *The Educational Science of Cognitive Style: An Introduction.* Oakland: Oakland Community College Press, 1971.

⁴Several objective-based instructional programs exist. These programs include instructional objectives and test items criterion-referenced to measure the objectives. For example, the Wisconsin Design for Reading Skill Development includes a system of objectives and assessment procedures for the attainment of these objectives. Lists of objectives and test items are also available from the Instructional Objectives Exchange of the Center for the Study of Evaluation, University of California, Los Angeles, California, 90024.

29

Criterion-Referenced Testing in the Classroom

Peter W. Airasian & George F. Madaus

As education has moved from a luxury to a necessity in American society and as voices for more relevant, less arbitrary stratification systems in education have increased, the problem of grading students has naturally become a focus of attention. For many years student performance has been graded on a norm-referenced, relative, basis. A student's grade is assigned on the basis of how he stands in comparison to his peers, not on the basis of any absolute criterion of what his performance is worth. Within the classroom, such grading practices have had two undesirable effects. First, they have given credence to the notion that for success or achievement to mean anything, there must be a reference group of nonattainers. The rewards system engendered by norm-referenced grading insures "winners" and "losers" in the achievement race. Second, norm-referenced practices have led to a discrepancy between the rewards system (i.e., grades) and the actual performance of students.

These effects and a series of concomitant trends to be elaborated later, have led to a renewed interest in a concept of criterion-referenced measurement. In this approach emphasis is placed upon the question "What has the student achieved?" rather than upon the question "How much has he achieved?" (Block, 1971a). The interpretation of a student's performance in a criterion-referenced situation is absolute and axiomatic, not dependent upon how other learners perform. Either a student is able to exhibit a particular skill, produce a specific product, or manifest a certain behavior, or he is not. Even in situations where some margin of error is permitted, once this margin has been specified the student's performance can be judged in terms of an "on-off" situation (Popham and Husek, 1971). Both norm- and criterion-referenced systems sort students, but there is an essential difference. In criterion-referenced measurement, interpretation of a student's performance is in no way dependent upon the performance of his classmates. In contrast, the appraisal of norm-referenced performance will differ according to the make-up of the norm group. For example, Mary's scoring higher than 90 percent of a group of academically inferior students on an algebra test will have different implications than her scoring higher than 90 percent in a group of advanced placement students (Bloom, Hastings and Madaus, 1971).

Further, and of equal importance, the criterion-referenced approach focuses attention upon a central aspect of the teaching-learning process, namely, the criterion skills. If the criterion behaviors are important, teachers should be concerned with whether the student has achieved them, not with how much he achieved relative to his peers. The teacher should design his instruction in light of the criterion behaviors and the reward system should reflect this approach.

Background

The distinction between norm and criterion-referenced tests is not a new one; few ideas in education are. In 1918, E. L. Thorndike observed that:

> There are two somewhat distinct groups of educational measurements: one . . . asks primarily how well a pupil performs a certain uniform task; the other . . . asks primarily how hard a task a pupil can perform

with substantial perfection, or with some other specified degree of success. The former are allied to the so-
called method of average error of the psychologists
[norm-referenced]; the latter, to what used to be called
the method of "right and wrong cases [criterion-refer-
enced]." Each of these groups of methods has its
advantages, and each deserves extension and refinement though the latter seems to represent the type
which will prevail if education follows the course of
development of the physical sciences (Thorndike,
1918, p. 18).

Educational measurement, however, did not develop
along the lines of the physical sciences, but adopted instead
a psychological model based on the concept of individual
differences. This psychological lineage, with its emphasis
on individual differences, normal distributions, predictions, and the like is a primary reason norm-referenced
measurement continues to dominate educational testing to
this day.

The work of the Department of Educational Investigation and Measurement of the Boston Public Schools around
1916 offers an excellent example of the course taken by
educational measurement in the face of the options Thorndike outlined. Boston teachers were required to draw up a
list of words that all students should be able to spell by
grade eight. In addition, requirements for English were
stated in very precise behavioral terms and all students had
to successfully exhibit these behaviors in order to graduate.
However, once tests in spelling and English were given to
large numbers of students the percentage passing each item
or task began to serve as a "standard by which [the teacher]
could judge whether her class [was] above or below the
general standard for the city" (Ballow, 1916, p. 62, italics
added). It was only a short step from comparing class
performance to comparing individuals' performance to such
"general city standards." Thus the emphasis shifted from
criterion to norm-referenced evaluation.

The following quote sheds light on some of the reasons
underlying such shifts:

. . . Indeed, the measurements which have been made up to this time have more than justified their costs in efforts and money, because they have dispelled forever the idea that schools should produce a uniform product or one that is perfect in its attainment . . . With the theoretical ideal of perfection overthrown, there is now an opportunity to set up rational demands. We can venture to tell parents with assurance that their children in the fifth grade are as good as the average if they misspell fifty percent of a certain list of words. We know this just as well as we know that a certain automobile engine cannot draw a ton of weight up a certain hill. No one has a right to make an unscientific demand of the automobile or of the school.

As soon as school officers recognize the fact that *measurements define for them just how much reasonably may be demanded,* they will be unafraid of measurements (Judd, 1918, pp. 153–154, italics added).

Clearly the assumption that most students could be brought to a given level of competence in skill subjects such as spelling was rejected. This rejection was due to a belief widely held at that time that native limitations in the ability of children—or poor environmental background—precluded such a goal (Judd, 1918). A corollary to this view was that reasonable demands upon student learning should be relative rather than absolute. Standardized test makers began to perfect norm-referenced tests to measure individual differences in achievement. Today, virtually all commercially available standardized tests are norm-referenced instruments.

The last three or four years have witnessed a growing interest in criterion-referenced measures, particularly in the classroom context. The interest is predicated upon a series of trends occurring both inside and outside education.

First there has been a growing criticism of testing, the focus of which has been on standardized tests of achievement and ability (e.g., Hoffman, 1962; Holt, 1968; Illich, 1971; Silberman, 1970). This criticism centers upon questions about the relevancy of tasks tested, what education is really about, and the relevancy of sorting people on any bases. However, even one of testing's most vehement critics, John Holt, admits that in at least two circumstances tests are necessary. There is a need in many occupations to demonstrate the ability to meet standards set by the occupation or profession, e.g., symphony orchestra, surgeon, translator, architect, etc. Further, there is a need for tests that allow people to check their progress toward the attainment of a certain skill or knowledge (Holt, 1968, p. 1). Both of these functions are better served by criterion-referenced than norm-referenced measures.

A second factor, closely related to the first, is the growing controversy surrounding grades. There is a growing distrust of grades per se and a reluctance to want to judge others. Critics argue that the fight for good grades engenders a competitive ethic, emphasizing "winning" the good grade race at the expense of the true purpose of education. The argument proceeds that grades become commodities to be bargained in the market place for teacher approval, college admittance, or jobs. The argument concludes, a grade of A or D tells us nothing about what a learner can do, only that he is superior or inferior to some vaguely defined reference group (Farber, 1969; New University Conference, 1972).

A third factor generating interest in criterion-referenced tests has been the growth of the instructional technology movement (Gagne, 1965; Glaser, 1971; Mechner, 1965). Instructional technologists soon realized that norm-referenced tests did not meet their needs in evaluating either individual performance or the efficacy of alternative instructional strategies. A cornerstone in instructional technology is the need for clear statements of instructional objectives. The objectives become a performance standard, for which various instructional strategies are developed. The criterion of success becomes the degree to which the student's performance corresponds to the previously set performance standard.

A fourth factor contributing to the present interest in criterion-referenced measurement is the growing belief on the part of many educators that all or at least most students can learn, benefit from, or be helped to achieve competency in most subject areas. Educators have argued that the problem of children not learning is not the result of native limitations, but instead a problem of finding better instructional strategies (see, for example, Bloom, 1968; Bruner, 1960; Carroll, 1963; Block, 1971b; Mayo, 1971). The assumption that most children can attain a given performance standard, underlies such approaches to instruction as Individually Prescribed Instruction (Lindvall and Cox, 1970), Performance Contracting (Lessinger, 1970) and Mastery Learning (Block, 1971b). A feature of all such approaches is the use of criterion-referenced measures, both in the formative, ongoing sense, and in the summative, end-of-course sense (Airasian, 1971; Bloom, Hastings and Madaus, 1971). Once one accepts the idea that most students can be helped to criterion performance, the emphasis in testing shifts from comparing individuals on a norm-referenced basis to checking and rewarding student learning in terms of that performance. If all attain the criterion, all should receive A's, passes, etc.

These four trends and their wider implications have nurtured the idea of criterion-referenced measurement. It is within the context of these trends and the value position implied by them that the classroom teacher must view criterion-referenced measurement.

Criterion-Referenced Testing and the Classroom Teacher

Is criterion-referenced testing a new concept to the teacher? It could be argued that teachers have always employed implicit, but nonetheless criterion-referenced, standards in their evaluations of pupils. For examples, there is little doubt that teachers evaluate such student characteristics as cleanliness, dress, speech patterns, conduct, and verbal fluency against an internal model they have developed as a result of their own socialization process. The model serves as a criterion, a standard, against which each individual student is judged. While the standard is internal, and highly individualistic, it nevertheless plays a powerful part in the formation of teacher expectations about a student's worth, potential, and performance

(Airasian, Kellaghan, and Madaus, 1971). This type of internal criterion is, of course, different from the common use of the term "criterion-referenced" as found in either the professional literature or in prior sections of this essay. It is not the purpose of this paper to pursue the concept of an internal criterion any further, except to point out that all classrooms are evaluative settings and while criteria may differ from teacher to teacher, and school to school, in the total evaluative context of the classroom judgments based on such internal criteria are undoubtedly pervasive and powerful in terms of their effect on teachers and pupils.

Typically, most teachers grade their classroom tests, either explicitly or implicitly, on a scale of zero to one hundred. Each test item is assigned a point value, with the total number of points generally equalling one hundred. Percentages are then translated into A's, B's, C's, D's and F's, often with gradations in between, according to widely accepted convention (90-100 = A; 89-80 = B, etc.). In this system an average grade for a marking period is easily determined.

Is the percentage grading approach an example of criterion-referenced measurement? Lynn's score of 85% was, after all, independent of her classmates' performance. She answered 17 of the 20 questions correctly. However, there are several important reasons why this widely accepted marking system does not fit the definition of criterion-referenced measurement described above.

First, the grade or percentage does not describe what Lynn can or cannot do. E. L. Thorndike recognized this problem in 1913 when he observed:

> The essential fault of the older schemes for school grades or marks was that the "86" or "B−" did not mean any objectively defined amount of knowledge of power or skill—that, for example, John's attainment of 91 in second year German did not inform him (or anyone else) about how difficult a passage he could translate; how many words he knew the English equivalents of and how accurately he could pronounce, or about any other fact save that he was supposed to be slightly more competent than someone

else marked 89 was, or than he would have been if he had been so marked (quoted in Glaser, 1971, pp. 48–49).

Second, very often teacher-made tests are built without the benefit of a prior statement of the behavioral objectives for the instructional unit. Instead, when some body of content is completed, the test items are constructed and become, after the fact, the de facto objectives of the teacher. In order to perform a criterion-referenced measurement one must possess a precise definition of objectives prior to instruction.

Third, even when objectives are clearly defined, the use of a single score to represent performance on a number of different objectives can easily mask what a student can actually do. For example, identical scores of 80% often mask the fact that Sarah did poorly on the 8 items measuring Objective A and well on the 8 items measuring Objective B, while the reverse was true for Eileen.

Fourth, the prior problem is compounded when we recognize that the meaning of identical grades on a test purporting to cover the same content can vary widely across teachers because of such factors as different objectives, item selection and scoring procedures. While it is not necessary—or likely—that every teacher will agree upon the criterion behaviors in English, or math, or reading, it is important that teachers in a department or at a grade level reach some agreement regarding at least minimum skills needed in a subject area. When this task is accomplished, record forms outlining at least the minimal essentials can be developed.

The Mathematics Goal Record Card of the Winnetka, Illinois Public Schools shown in Figure 1 is an example of one type of reporting form that is suited to criterion-referenced measurement. A check indicates that a student has mastered the particular skill. Compare the information provided in this approach to the traditional practice of using a single grade or vague verbal description such as:

distinctly superior work,

above average work,

work of average quality,

meets minimal requirements
unsatisfactory work.

While the goal card could be more specific in terms of defining behaviors (e.g. "understanding") and specifying standards for adequate performance, it does describe what the student can do rather than his rank relative to his peers. The information provided gives a better picture to teachers, students, and parents than vague letter or verbal descriptions. The goal card has a further benefit in that it is more powerful for directing teaching than are the typical norm-referenced categories. Notice also that the goal card can serve to chart student progress and identify individual needs while instruction is in progress. Most of all, however, it serves to focus attention upon the criterion behaviors.

Two additional distinctions between traditional classroom testing practices and criterion-referenced measurement are related to when tests are given and how the information derived is used. Teacher-made tests are most often summative measures, in that they are given at the conclusion of a unit of instruction for purposes of grading. Criterion-referenced measurements are amenable to use before instruction begins to properly place students; while instruction is ongoing for purposes of checking progress so that help can be given if necessary (formative testing); and at the end of the unit to see whether students have achieved the criterion (Airasian and Madaus, 1972). A portrait of group performance on a criterion-referenced test gives information about the efficacy of a particular instructional strategy.

Before describing the steps a teacher or administrator who wishes to employ criterion-based measurement might adopt, a caveat is in order. Criterion-referenced measurement is not a panacea for all the grading or sorting problems in education. The criterion-referenced approach does possess many advantages over norm-referenced approaches within the instructional context. However, criterion-referenced measurement, like all other measurement, is not value free. There is a view of what education is about, what learners are capable of, and the nature of rewards which is implicit in measurement practices based upon absolute rather than normative standards. We have tried to indicate

Recognizes number groups up to 5
Recognizes patterns of objects to 10
Can count objects to 100
Recognizes numbers to 100
Can read and write numerals to 50
Recognizes addition and subtraction symbols
Understands meaning of the equality sign
Understands meaning of the inequality signs
Can count objects:
    by 2's to 20
    by 5's to 100
    by 10's to 100
Recognizes geometric figures:
    triangle
    circle
    quadrilateral
    Recognizes coins (1c, 5c, 10c, 25c)
Knows addition combinations 10 and under using objects
Knows subtraction combinations 10 and under using
    objects
Recognizes addition and subtraction vertically and
    horizontally
Shows understanding of numbers and number
    combinations
    1. Using concrete objects
    2. Beginning to visualize and abstract
    3. Makes automatic responses without concrete
    objects
Can tell time
    1. Hour
    2. Half hour
    3. Quarter hour
Addition combinations 10 and under (automatic
    response)
Subtraction combinations 10 and under (automatic
    response)
Can count to 200
Can understand zero as a number
Can understand place value to tens
Can read and write numerals to 200
Can read and write number words to 20
Use facts in 2-digit column addition (no carrying)
Roman numerals to XII

Figure 1. Portion of the Mathematics Goal
Record Card of the Winnetka Public Schools

some of these value positions in our discussion of trends which have fostered the criterion-referenced movement. Teachers who opt for criterion-referenced techniques should be aware of the value framework implied. However, advantages of criterion-referenced information in the instructional setting do not rule out the value norm-referenced information can have to administrators, teachers, parents, and students.

Implementing Criterion-Referenced Techniques in the Classroom

It should be recognized at the outset that the steps about to be described reflect the present state of the art and that there are a number of conceptual and methodological issues concerning criterion-referenced testing which remain to be solved.

The first step in implementing criterion-referenced measurement is to develop, prior to instruction, a list of objectives which identify the performances, skills, and products which instruction is designed to help students attain. The list becomes the standard for judging learning success. It is the criterion against which each student's performance will be compared to judge learning adequacy. Implicit in the task of specifying criterion behaviors are two questions: Who should do the specifying? and What features should the criterion performances manifest?

Probably the teacher, taking into account the level and needs of the students, should have the major say in determining what the criterion behaviors will be. However, very often administrators, parents, and students can provide valuable inputs into this decision-making process. In those cases, where a particular course is a prerequisite to another course or where a number of teachers teach the same course, it is advisable that the criterion behaviors be specified by all teachers concerned. Such a recommendation is not advanced to foster total conformity across classrooms, but only to insure cohesion and direction across teachers teaching the same courses or teachers whose courses are sequential in nature.

The criterion performances, or objectives, should be

unambiguously stated. A statement of an objective should contain an operational verb, a verb that describes what the student must do to demonstrate he has learned. Often the conditions under which the behavior is expected to occur should be specified as well. For example,

> The student will demonstrate his understanding of the function of the topic sentence in a given paragraph by writing a paragraph about a given subject and under-lining the central idea. (Center for the Study of Evaluation, 1970, p. 127).
>
> When given a newspaper article, the students can distinguish between statements of fact and opinion. When given a situation he has never encountered, the student can explain what is occurring in terms of Boyle's Charles' or Bernoulli's Law.

Techniques for writing behavioral objectives are described in many books, (Gronlund, 1970; Mager, 1962; Bloom, Hastings and Madaus, 1971), and in film strips developed by Vimcet Associates and by General Program Teaching. While the reader should be aware that there are thoughtful critics of the approach to objectives described in the sources listed above, (i.e., see Eisner, 1969; Doll, 1971; Broudy, 1970), an unambiguous statement of instructional objectives is a necessary first step toward a criterion-based measurement.

The second step in implementing criterion-referenced measurement involves a decision about the standards used to judge whether a student's performance or product indicates mastery of the instructional objectives. Here we need a standard for each objective as well as a standard for the entire set of criterion behaviors. That is, if it is necessary to translate performance on a number of behaviors into pass-fail or yes-no terms, some standard for judging performance across all specific objectives is needed. It is in the area of setting standards, be they for individual objectives or sets of objectives, that criterion-referenced measurement is most in need of research. Thus far, most standards have been arrived at by arbitrary decisions on the part of teachers and researchers. Perfection, that is, perfect mastery, is simply too expensive to obtain. There is evidence (Block, 1972) that standards set in the area of 80 to 90 percent proficiency are most realistic and meaningful. However, the research is somewhat tentative and for the time being teachers will probably have to rely largely upon their own implicit standards for determining levels of adequacy for criterion behaviors.

Given an objective or set of objectives, there usually will be some standard that will define adequate performance. The standard may involve setting a permissible error rate (i.e., answers correctly 80 percent of the time). Alternatively it may consist of a list of the characteristics associated with an acceptable product or performance. For example, the standard for the previous objective concerning topic sentences and paragraph writing was as follows:

1. The paragraph must be about a single subject.

2. All other sentences in the paragraph must pertain to or support the sentence which the student has underlined.

3. The topic sentence must be underlined.

4. Capitalization and punctuation conventions must be adhered to.

The third step is to devise situations which allow the students a chance to exhibit the desired skill, behavior or product. In many cases this may mean designing paper and pencil instruments. For example, a paper and pencil test is required to assess the following objective: given a set of 10 problems calling for dividing mixed fractions, the student is able to correctly solve the problems with 90% accuracy. In form, the items look identical to items developed for a norm-referenced arithmetic test. Further, the item writing techniques do not differ for norm versus criterion-referenced tests. The reader is referred to Thorndike (1971) for a detailed description of item writing techniques. The essential difference lies in whether the items are used to determine whether a student has mastered division of mixed numbers or where he stands relative to his peers on this skill.

It should be pointed out here that the use of a criterion-referenced approach does not automatically make the testing situation diagnostic, except insofar as it identifies a particular skill a student possesses or fails to possess. In our example of dividing mixed numbers, suppose two students each answered correctly 7 of the 10 items. The conclusion is that the students have not reached the prespecified criterion and therefore have not mastered the arithmetic skill in question. By itself this piece of information is of little diagnostic value. Martha might have missed three items because she incorrectly changed the mixed numbers to fractions while Anthony missed three items because of mistakes in simple multiplication. The point is criterion-referenced information is not intrinsically diagnostic if one stops with an "on-off" statement of results. Popham and Husek (1971) describe the ideal criterion-referenced test as one in which a person's score exactly describes his whole response pattern. No such test is in sight. The point is, then, that generally the more complex the objective, the less prescriptive the test results are likely to be.

There have been efforts in the past few years to specify not only criterion behaviors in school subjects, but also ordering or sequential relationships between behaviors (Airasian, 1971; Gagne, 1965; Resnick, 1967). A body of content or a task is analyzed to determine a sequence in which performances are identified as prerequisites to or necessary products of other performances. Tests based upon such sequences are criterion-referenced, but they also possess a diagnostic value in that they are often able to shed light on the question of why a student failed to demonstrate competence on a given objective, i.e., he failed a prerequisite criterion behavior.

In building a paper and pencil criterion-referenced instrument, all of the items should represent the behavior or behaviors defined in the criterion performances so that accurate inference can be made from test results. Tyler (1967), however, points out that there is little theory "to aid in the construction of relatively homogeneous samples of exercises faithfully reflecting an educational objective" (p. 14). Until such techniques are developed, teachers will have to judge the validity of the items or exercises relative to the objective in question. The bases for this judgment can be expert opinion, experience, the face validity of the items, or group consensus. It is precisely on these bases that teachers judge item adequacy at present.

For many objectives, paper and pencil tests will be inappropriate. Actual situations in which the students' performance is observed and rated are required. For example, to determine whether a child has sufficient eye-hand coordination to handle scissors is best measured by giving the child a piece of paper and a pair of scissors. Thus, to assess this capability, Kamii (1971) describes the following measurement technique and criteria:

> Give a piece of paper and a pair of scissors to a child and ask him to cut the paper (a) in any way he likes and (b) on a line you have drawn on the paper.
>
> Criteria:
>   Cutting in any way the child likes:
>   Cuts easily without any trouble
>   Cuts with some slight difficulty
>   Cuts with considerable difficulty
>   Simply cannot cut and appears to be "all thumbs"
>   Cutting in a line: (The following criteria refer not to the child's general ability to use scissors but to his specific ability to cut along a given line.)
>   Cuts easily and accurately on the line
>   Cuts easily but with a deviation within ¼ inch from the line
>   Cuts with some difficulty with a deviation of more than ¼ inch from the line (p. 308)

A moment's reflection will reveal that it is possible to convert this measurement, either implicitly or explicitly, into a norm-referenced scale. Even though two students attain criterion performance, it is often difficult to avoid making comparisons between students on the basis of speed, fluency, smoothness, or adroitness with which they attained the criterion. Dewey (1939) points out that valuing has two aspects, one of prizing, the other appraising. The latter involves comparison and is concerned with the relational property of objects. Whether this relational aspect can be limited to the criterion in question or whether it also inadvertently spills over into comparisons between people is something one must be aware of.

In still other circumstances student products might have to be critically examined in order to infer whether or not the student has in fact attained the required skill or competency. Baldwin (1971) describes such rating scale for a woodworking project in vocational education (Figure 2). In terms of rating scales Baldwin points out that the teacher using a rating scale should also demonstrate the objectivity of the instrument for the situation for which it was designed by determining both inter and intra rater consistency in light of the criterion performance.

In summary, any classroom approach to criterion-referenced measurement should include the following steps:

1. competencies to be demonstrated by the student must be stated in explicit terms

2. criteria identifying levels or characteristics of successful accomplishment of the competencies must be made explicit

3. situations in which the student can demonstrate his competency or lack of competency must be developed

4. judgments of any student's learning success must be made in light of the predefined competencies, not in relation to other students' performance.

Conclusion

Criterion-referenced testing is not a panacea for all the grading and sorting problems which exist in education. More thoughtful reflection and research is required before all the difficulties associated with criterion-based measurement are resolved. However, the criterion-referenced approach serves two very valuable functions within the instructional context. First, it directs attention to the performances and behaviors which are the main purpose of instruction. Secondly, it rewards students on the basis of their attainment relative to these criterion performances rather than relative to their peers. Under such conditions rewards are distributed on the basis of achievement vis a vis the aims of instruction and the frequently meaningless distinctions made between students on the basis of "how

1. Evidence of excessive glue under finish/Damage from glue

1	2	3	4	5	6	7
Bubbles of glue under finish		Considerable discoloration		Slight discoloration		No evidence of glue

2. Evidence of clamp damage

1	2	3	4	5	6	7
Splitting		Deep Impressions		Marred surface		No evidence of clamps

3. Evidence of inconsistent clamping pressure in assembly (squareness)

1	2	3	4	5	6	7
Parts do not fit		Considerable warp		Some distortion		All parts square

4. Evidence of lamination problems

1	2	3	4	5	6	7
Splitting/ open joint		Buckling/ wide joint		Slight offset		Flat/tight joint

5. Evidence of the improper use of fasteners (screws)

1	2	3	4	5	6	7
Not holding/ head-stripped		Loose/head damage		Poor Seating		Secure/no head damage

6. Evidence of the improper use of fasteners (finish nails)

1	2	3	4	5	6	7
Bent nail/ surface damage		Nail showing		Under or overfilled		Fill blends with surface

Figure 2. Evaluation Form for a Woodworking Project

much" are replaced by a reward system based upon what has actually been attained.

Reprinted from NCME *Measurement in Education,* Vol. 3, No. 4, May 1972. Copyright 1972 by the National Council on Measurement in Education, East Lansing, Michigan. Dr. Airasian is Associate Professor of Education and Dr. Madaus is Professor of Education at Boston College.

References

Airasian, P. W. "A Study of the Behaviorally Dependent, Classroom Taught Task Hierachies." *Educational Technology Research Report Series,* Number 3, 1971.

Airasian, P. W. "The Role of Evaluation in Mastery Learning." In Block, J. (Ed.), *Mastery Learning: Theory and Practice.* New York: Holt, Rinehart & Winston, 1971, 81–93.

Airasian, P. W. and Madaus, G. F. "Functional Types of Student Evaluation." *Measurement and Evaluation in Guidance,* 1972, 221–233.

Airasian, P. W., Kellaghan, T., and Madaus, G. F. "Standardized Test Information, Teacher Expectancies and the Rhetoric of Evaluation." Working paper for a conference on the design of a societal experiment on the consequences of testing., Dublin, Ireland, 1971.

Baldwin, T. S. "Evaluation of Learning in Industrial Education." In Bloom, Hastings, and Madaus, *Handbook on Formative and Summative Evaluation of Student Learning.* New York: McGraw-Hill, 1971, 855–905.

Ballow, F. W., "Work of the Department of Educational Investigation and Measurement, Boston, Massachusetts." In Whipple, G. M. (Ed.), *Standards and Tests for the Measurement of the Efficiency of Schools and School Systems. Fifteenth Yearbook of the National Society for the Study of Education, Part I.* Chicago: University of Chicago Press, 1916, 61–68.

Block, J. H. *Mastery Learning: Theory and Practice.* New York: Holt, Rinehart & Winston, 1971.

Block, J. H. "Criterion-referenced Measurement: Potential." *School Review,* 1971, 79, 289–297.

Block, J. H. "Student Evaluation: Towards the Setting of Mastery Performance Standards." Paper read at the 1972 Annual Meeting of the American Educational Research Association, Chicago, Ill., 1972.

Bloom, B. S. "Learning for Mastery." *UCLA-CSEIP Evaluation Comment, 1,* 1968.

Bloom, B. S.; Hastings, J. T.; and Madaus, G. F. *Handbook on Formative and Summative Evaluation of Student Learning.* New York: McGraw-Hill, 1971.

Broudy, H. S. "Can Research Escape the Dogma of Behavioral Objectives?" *School Review,* 1970, 79, 43–56.

Bruner, J. S. *The Process of Education.* Cambridge: Harvard University Press, 1960.

Center for the Study of Evaluation. "Language Arts, 4–6. *Instructional Objectives Exchange,* 1970.

Dewey, J. *Theory of Valuation.* Chicago, Ill.: University of Chicago Press, 1939.

Doll, W. E. "A Methodology of Experience: An Alternative to Behavioral Objectives." Paper read at the 1971 American Educational Research Association Annual Meeting, New York, 1971.

Eisner, E. W. "Instructional and Expressive Objectives: Their Formation and Use in Curriculum." In *Instructional Objectives.* American Educational Research Association Monograph on Curriculum Evaluation. Chicago: Rand McNally, 1969, 1–31.

Farber, J. *The Student as Nigger.* New York: Pocket Books, 1969.

Gagne, R. M. *The Conditions of Learning.* New York: Holt, Rinehart & Winston, 1965.

Glaser, R. "A Criterion-referenced Test." In Popham, J. W. (Ed.), *Criterion-referenced Measurement.* Englewood Cliffs, N.J.: Educational Technology Publication, 1971, 41–51.

Gronlund, N. E. *Stating Behavioral Objectives for Classroom Instruction.* New York: The Macmillan Co., 1970.

Hoffman, B. *The Tyranny of Testing.* New York: Collier Books, 1962.

Holt, J. W. *On Testing.* Cambridge, Mass.: Pinck Leodas Assoc., 1968.

Illich, I. *Deschooling Society.* New York: Harper & Row, 1971.

Judd, C. H. "A Look Forward." In Whipple, G. M. (Ed.), *The Measurement of Educational Products.* Seventeenth Yearbook of the National Society for the Study of Education, Part II. Bloomington, Ill.: Public School Publishing Co., 1918, 152–160.

Kamii, C. K. "Evaluation of Learning in Preschool Education." In Bloom, Hastings & Madaus, *Handbook on Formative and Summative Evaluation of Student Learning.* New York: McGraw-Hill, 1971, 281–344.

Lessinger, L. *Every Kid a Winner.* New York: Simon and Shuster, 1970.

Lindvall, C. M. and Cox, R. *Evaluation as a Tool in Curriculum Development: The IPI Evaluation Program.* American Educational Research Association Monograph Series on Curriculum Evaluation. Chicago: Rand McNally, 1970.

Mager, R. F. *Preparing Instructional Objectives.* Palo Alto, California: Fearon Publishers, 1962.

Mayo, S. T. "Mastery Learning and Mastery Testing." *Measurement in Education.* National Council on Measurement in Education, 1070, Vol. 1, No 3

Mechner, F. "Science Education and Behavioral Technology." In Glaser, R. (Ed.), *Teaching Machines and Programmed Learning, II.* Washington, D.C.: National Education Association, 1965, 441–507.

New University Conference, "De-grading Education." Jeff Sharlett Chapter of the New University Conference, Bloomington, Ind., January 1972.

Popham, W. J. and Husek, T. R. "Implications of Criterion-referenced Measurement." In Popham, W. J. (Ed.), *Criterion-referenced Measurement.* Englewood Cliffs, N.J.: Educational Technology Publishers, 1971, 17–37.

Resnick, L. B. "Design of an Early Learning Curriculum." University of Pittsburgh Learning Research and Development Center. Working paper 16, 1967.

Silberman, C. E. *Crisis in the Classroom.* New York: Vantage Books, 1970.

Thorndike, E. L. *Educational Psychology,* 1913,

quoted in Glaser, R., "A Criterion-referenced Test." In Popham, J. W. (Ed.), *Criterion-referenced Measurement*. Englewood Cliffs, N.J.: Educational Technology Publications, 1971, pp. 48–49.

Thorndike, E. L. "The Nature, Purposes and General Methods of Measurements of Educational Products." In Whipple, G. M. (Ed.), *The Measurement of Educational Products*. Seventeenth Yearbook of the National Society for the Study of Education, Part II, Bloomington Public School Publishing Co., 1918, 16–24.

Thorndike, R. L. (Ed.) *Educational Measurement*. Washington, D.C.: American Council on Education, 1971.

Tyler, R. W. "Changing Concepts of Educational Evaluation." In Stake, R. (Ed.), *Perspectives of Curriculum Evaluation*. American Educational Research Association Monograph Series on Curriculum Evaluation, Chicago: Rand McNally, 1967, 13–18.

30

Individual Conferences—
Diagnostic Tools

Harriet Ramsey Reeves

Teaching according to each child's needs is a key phrase in education today. Seldom has so much been said on a subject—individualizing instruction—and yet so little been practiced. The key to individualized instruction in reading within a classroom is diagnosis, and the key to better diagnosis is a periodic individual conference with each child. In these conferences, teachers can determine each child's strengths and weaknesses; rapport can be established with the students; progress can be checked; students' feelings and attitudes can be ascertained.

After securing information concerning the strengths and weaknesses of students, teachers are in a position to list all students with common weaknesses and then organize instructional groups to deal with them. Individual prescriptions can be made for each student according to diagnoses made during reading conferences and from other sources of information (standardized tests, informal inventories, regular reading group activities, etc.).

Far too often teachers have been satisfied with teaching students only in groups and knowing only general information concerning a student's reading ability. Parents become concerned about a son's or daughter's reading progress and teachers are able to tell them only in vague terms about his or her reading ability. Statements commonly made by teachers are like these:

He is a poor reader.

He can't figure out new words.

He reads slowly and haltingly.

He is reading below grade level.

He doesn't understand what he reads.

He miscalls words.

While these statements may be true, they give very little information on where to start work with the student and on what types of skills to work. Few students are completely devoid of any skill in most reading areas. For instance, if a student is having problems in word recognition, he probably knows some words and perhaps has some skill in phonics. It is necessary, in order to plan the student's work, to secure information such as what level of skill in word recognition the student has attained, whether he is able to recall easily words already taught, at what level he is using phonics, why is it the student seems to be having problems in this area (illness, excessive absences, eye problems, emotional problems, etc.), and which method(s) of teaching word recognition seems to be most effective with him. While part of this information can be gathered from observing a student in reading groups, and the results of standardized tests, only individual conferences can permit more thorough diagnosis and confirmation or refutation of information gathered from the other sources.

Diagnostic Conferences

Individual reading conferences can fit in any type reading program, the traditional basal reading group system, an individualized program, a phonics program, or one based on linguistics. These conferences should be held at least once every three to six weeks, and more often if an individualized reading program is used, or if a student needs it because of problems. They should last from five to ten minutes apiece.

Many teachers, particularly those using the traditional three or more reading groups, do not feel they can find the time to conduct individual conferences and still carry on their regular programs. A slight modification in such a program will allow the time. While there is no hard and fast rule stating that every reading group must meet every day, there are many teachers who actually experience guilt feelings when they miss meeting a reading group one single day. It is not necessary to have each group meet every day as long as reading is being done. In fact, if the truth of the matter were really known, the amount of reading practice each student receives while in a group may be very little, depending on the teacher and the particular lesson being presented. It is conceivable that some students read only when called upon for direct participation (reading aloud, reading in order to answer a question) which may be anywhere up to five minutes. Such students would be receiving little, if any, practice in reading during the so-called reading group of approximately thirty minutes' duration. The point of the foregoing argument is simply to add weight to the argument that a catastrophe would not result if reading groups did not meet every day.

It is suggested that regular reading groups meet a minimum of two or three times a week, with the remainder of the time used for individual conferences, special skill groups, individual reading and reading activities, and perhaps some oral book sharing. The important thing is that reading is being done by all students every day, not that all reading groups meet every day.

Keeping Records

If individual conferences are to be a worthwhile part of reading instruction, it is important that accurate records of each student's performance be kept. At this point, many teachers might be tempted to throw up their hands in despair at the prospect of more paper work. If you are one of those, cheer up, as it is not that time consuming or onerous and the returns can be of tremendous importance. This is minimal paper work with great potential value if used properly. Several kinds of valuable information should be gathered in these conferences.

■ *Word recognition skills*—Record all mispronounced words phonetically as he said them along with the correct word. For instance, the word "worm" is pronounced "warm." Both words should be recorded with some indication of which is the correct pronunciation and which is the incorrect pronunciation. If no attempt is made to pronounce an unknown word, the word should be recorded with the indication he did not attempt it. This information will need to be written during the conference as the student misses the words since the teacher may not be able to remember such errors later. By recording this type of information, one can make some judgment on the degree of phonics the student is using; whether the student is looking at the whole word, or the first or last part; whether he is able to see syllabic divisions of words; and whether context is being used.

■ *Reading speed and fluency*—Some information on how fast the student reads is needed. Speed alone does not give a well-rounded picture of oral reading skill. For example, some students read rapidly, but in a jerky fashion. They may have occasional or frequent hesitations for one reason or another. Other students may read moderately fast with a smooth and even delivery. Fluency, the evenness of flow, needs to be recorded as this can give some indication of problems present. Unexplained pauses in relatively fast reading or slow reading can indicate a problem in keeping the place, or a problem in instant word recognition, etc. It should be determined whether the student is looking at each word as a separate entity or is able to read phrases or meaningful units. If a student is reading at about fourth grade level or above, the teacher should compare the speed of oral reading with that of silent reading, as the silent reading speed should begin to pass oral speed at about fourth grade level.

■ *Comprehension*—Contrary to the opinions of many people, there is no one single skill known as comprehension. It is, instead, a composite of many individual skills involved in understanding what is read. It is necessary for the teacher to know the kinds of comprehension in which a student may be deficient in order to make judgments concerning the kind of work to prescribe. Some of the various comprehension skills which are important for students to develop are recalling details, summarizing the main idea, making inferences, and drawing conclusions. These do not exhaust the kinds of comprehension, but they seem to be very important skills as far as elementary students are concerned. A decision needs to be made as to whether poor comprehension may be attributable to other causes such as poor word recognition. Sometimes comprehension scores are low because word identification and recognition may be faulty.

■ *Other information*—This category includes any information not listed in the above categories. Several examples follow.

a. Quality of oral reading, such as whether the student has a monotone delivery, poor phrasing, juncture, or stress.

b. Physical manifestations such as excessive nervousness, tics, twitches, many breaths in one sentence, head cocked to one side, and eyes too close to the book.

c. Attitude toward reading, amount of reading done, favorite topics.

All of the above information will probably not be collected in a single conference, but over a period of time including several conferences. Weaknesses detected in one conference should be provided for through group and individual work, and checked on in following conferences. A sample entry for a single conference might look this way:

Jack B. (fourth grade student)

3/2, 1970—Word recognition: what—that (underlined word is correct pronunciation) gasp—grasp, cotton —no attempt

Speed & fluency: Oral, medium slow rate, jerky, frequent hesitations (approx. 55 words per minute, 3rd grade material)

Comprehension: details—poor, missed 3 of 5 questions. Unable to summarize main idea satisfactorily.

Other information: Very nervous

This may be all that is recorded for that particular conference. However, one should use the information gathered in the conference to plan a course of action for the student. This course of action should be noted either on the conference record or another record as it is virtually impossible for the average teacher to recall all such information

on all students. For Jack B., the suggested course of action
might read this way:

> Suggested procedure (prescription) Further diagnosis
> necessary to determine how much phonics he knows
> and if he is able to benefit from this approach. Place in
> special skills phonics group probably (depending
> upon further diagnosis)
> Give listening test on paragraphs to check oral com-
> prehension. Place in special skills basic comprehen-
> sion group probably (depending on outcome of lis-
> tening test)
> Reading (pleasure) on or below 3' level; supply with
> easy reading on or below second grade level. Watch
> interest level of books (Butternut Bill, etc.)

Using Information from Conferences

After information is obtained on each individual, the
information should then be used to organize special skill
groups made up of people who have similar weaknesses.
For instance, all pupils who have problems with basic
phonics should be listed together; those who know most
sound-symbol relationships, but have problems pro-
nouncing multi-syllable words because of poor ability in
using syllables, accents, etc., should be placed in a group;
those who can call words satisfactorily, but cannot recall
details need to be placed together in a group. These special
skill groups should meet periodically, once or twice a week,
with follow-up assignments. Constant diagnosis is a must
when working with pupils in these groups. As a student
shows proficiency in a skill, he should be taken out of that
skill group.

These special skill groups will meet in the time re-
leased from meeting the regular reading groups. The
number of such groups will vary from class to class. There
will probably be sufficient time for approximately three
special groups at a time. In case there is a need for more,
the teacher may have to decide to emphasize certain skills
over a particular period of time and other skills at other

times. The solution to this problem lies with the individual teacher and her particular situation.

In addition to forming special skill groups, many students may need individual prescriptions for independent work. Practice work should be filed according to different skills and levels and students should be directed to the proper file and materials. Some teachers cut up workbooks and file pages according to skills. There are also commercial materials for such purposes.

Summary

Teachers need more specific information about individual pupils in order to do a better job of teaching reading. Most teachers have access to some information about each pupil's reading ability from reading group activities and standardized tests, but this is not sufficient. Individual conferences seem to provide a means to acquire more specific information about pupils and to double check information from other sources. Using information from these conferences and other sources, special skill groups should be organized and individual prescriptions, or assignments, should be made. Time for these additional reading activities can be made by reducing the number of times regular reading groups (if that happens to be the manner of organization) meet each week. Adjusting the reading program by incorporating individual conferences, special skill groups, and individual prescriptions can enable the teacher to provide for individual needs.

Reprinted from *The Reading Teacher*, February 1971, 411–415, 467. Reprinted with permission of Harriet Ramsey Reeves and the International Reading Association. Dr. Reeves is Assistant Professor of Education at University of Miami at Coral Gables, Florida.

31

Motivational Procedures in the Individualization of Instruction

Madan Mohan

Motivation is of particular significance to the classroom teacher as it helps in the selection, direction, integration, magnitude, and persistence of a child's steps in learning. The child is the principal agent in his own education and development, yet it is too often true that children apathetically go through the motions of participating in class activities without any real or lasting learning. It is at this point in the teaching-learning process that teachers badly need to know, understand, and use motivational procedures that inspire children.

As pointed out by many writers (e.g., 5, 16), a low level of motivation is the number one learning problem for children in the classes of most teachers at all levels in our schools. Yet, motivation is one area of teaching in which many teachers seem to be inadequately informed and equipped. This is due partly to the conflicting and impractical concepts and theories on motivation and partly to the fact that the teacher tries to tackle the problem on a group basis.

It is the contention of this paper that an individualized system of learning provides special opportunities to deal with motivational factors in ways that will maximize learning and, therefore, that a system of individualized motivation must be built into any program of individualized education (13). The essential characteristics of such a system as adapted from Klausmeier, et al (13) are:

1. the identification of specific behaviors that are indicative of motivation,

2. the identification of students who are motivated and who are unmotivated,

3. the identification of reward preferences of students,

4. the understanding and use of motivational procedures,

5. the carrying out of evaluation to determine the effectiveness of the above four steps in a classroom situation, and

6. the use of the results of this evaluation to improve the procedures.

These characteristics are described below. It may be pointed out that this paper does not attempt to summarize or reconcile the research or scholarly writings on motivation. Instead, it suggests some effective and practical procedures teachers can undertake regarding motivation in an individualized instructional setting within the limitations of present day knowledge, complexities of human behavior, and the realities of life in the classroom. It is hoped that these procedures will help teachers become more effective in the management of the learning process.

Specific Behaviors

As behavior is determined not only by motivation but also by the present situation and past experience, it is difficult and, at times, misleading to infer motivation from behavior. We can accurately infer motivation from behavior only if we know a person's past experience and can control the situation in which he finds himself. However, Klausmeier, et. al. (13) have suggested a tentative list of behaviors that are indicative of motivation. This list consists of four general behavioral categories, along with specific behaviors related to each category. It should be noted here that this is a tentative and beginning list and that teachers may hold certain other behaviors equally important. Klausmeier lists behaviors indicative of motivation as:

a. The student starts promptly and completes self-,

teacher-, or group-assigned tasks that together comprise the minimum requirements related to various curriculum areas.

(1) Attends to the teacher and other situational elements when attention is required.

(2) Begins tasks promptly.

(3) Seeks feedback concerning performance on tasks.

(4) Returns to tasks voluntarily after interruption or initial lack of progress.

(5) Persists at tasks until completed.

b. The student assumes responsibility for learning more than the minimum requirements without teacher guidance during school hours and outside school hours. In addition to Behaviors 1-5, the student:

(6) Continues working when the teacher leaves the room.

(7) Does additional work during school hours.

(8) Works on school-related activities outside school hours.

(9) Identifies activities that are relevant for class projects.

(10) Seeks suggestions for going beyond minimum amount or quality of work.

c. The student behaves in accordance with the school's policies and practices in connection with use of property, relations with other students, and reactions with adults.

(11) Moves quietly within and about the school building during quiet periods and activities.

(12) Interacts harmoniously with other students.

(13) Interacts harmoniously with the teacher and other adults.

(14) Conserves own and other's property.

(15) Tells other students to behave in accordance with school policies.

d. The student verbalizes a value system consistent with the preceding behaviors.

(16) When asked, gives examples of his own actions illustrative of Behaviors 1-15.

(17) When asked, gives reasons for manifesting Behaviors 1-15.

It may be pointed out here that the list above should

not be taken to mean that motivated behavior consists of listening, accepting and conformity. Instead, it is thinking, problem solving and creativity.

Identification of Students

As in many other human traits, individual differences in motivation exist. There may be many children who are highly motivated and do not require additional rewards. Indeed, there are many overly motivated youngsters who are under too much pressure to succeed. However, there are other children who do not want to learn or to behave in accordance with generally accepted rules; these children require an individualized application of reinforcers for learning and conduct. It may be profitable for members of a differentiated staff to assess each pupil on the motivational behaviors (Appendix A), then use the assessment as a basis for small group discussion or individual conferences with pupils as found necessary. Also, pupils should be asked to attempt self-assessment (see Appendix B) of their behavior. Interesting differences in teacher- and self-assessments may become apparent. Other ways of assessing motivation level, like child's written work and performance on teacher-made or published tests, should also be taken into consideration. As a result of these assessments it may be profitable to single out particular pupils for special attention and treatment. It should be kept in mind that these unmotivated students were not born this way; they have acquired their lack of motivation, initiative, responsibility, vision, interest beyond assigned tasks, and imagination in the course of their experiences at home, in school and within the community.

Identification of Reward Preferences

It quite often happens that some students do not manifest the desired behaviors even after persistent teacher effort. This may be due to the fact that these students are not being rewarded for desired behaviors with their most preferred type of reinforcements (4). Thus, it is important to determine the learner's reward preference in advance of instruction, group discussion, or individual conference. Such a step saves teachers unnecessary labor and can be expected to result in improved motivation which, in turn, should lead to an increase in learning and achievement. Perhaps one of the simplest ways of determining what an individual finds satisfying is the modified reward preference assessment procedure (MRPA) which is based on a model developed by King and Dunn-Rankin (12). Once a child's preference for rewards has been established, the next step is to reward the child in a highly consistent manner keeping the following three principles in mind: (a) liberally reward that behavior which is to be encouraged; (b) occasionally reward a stable behavior pattern in order to maintain it; and (c) avoid rewarding undesirable behaviors (4). Sometimes the length of time necessary to demonstrate marked changes may be a longer period because rewards have been found to interact not only with subject variables but also with characteristics of the task, instructions, and other situational variables to determine performance.

Motivational Practices

Some of the strategies and procedures suggested below can establish a classroom climate that should lead to an increase in learning and achievement. These practices, it is hoped, will also improve children's attitudes, motivation levels, and self-concepts.

Goal Setting

The importance of goals is very clearly brought out in the following passage in Alice in Wonderland:

> "Would you tell me, please, which way I ought to go from here?"
> "That depends a good deal on where you want to get to," said the Cat.
> "I don't much care where—" said Alice.
> "Then it doesn't matter which way you go," said the Cat.
> "—so long as I get somewhere," Alice added as an explanation.

"Oh, you're sure to do that," said the Cat, "if you only walk long enough."

In the school, instructional goals and objectives are normally specified by teachers for a group of children and the individual child is usually not given an opportunity to participate in this goal setting. It cannot be assumed, however, that the individual child has not set any goals on his own. In truth, he may have in his own mind established a goal for himself at some variance with that attempted by the teacher. To be realistic, instructional goals as well as social goals must be cooperatively established by pupils and staff and in many cases, parents. Self-involvement will result in greater effort, greater understanding, and greater enjoyment and progress toward goals. It has been pointed out that much of the problem of motivating the child will disappear if we learn to bridge the gap between those things which he should and those things he wants to learn (17). Conversely, if the student is made to do things which the teacher thinks he should learn, the teacher will have to use coercion, artificial incentives and endless repetitions, with but little success. The process of goal setting should involve the following steps (23):

(1) Encourage children to make choices freely.

(2) Help children to discover and examine available alternatives when faced with choices.

(3) Help children weigh alternatives thoughtfully, reflecting on consequences of each.

(4) Encourage children to consider what it is that they prize and cherish.

(5) Give them opportunities to make public affirmations of their choices.

(6) Encourage them to act, behave, live in accordance with their choices.

(7) Help them to examine repeated behaviors or patterns in their life.

However, children vary widely in their ability to establish realistic goals. While the more able children can be expected to set attainable goals, the disadvantaged children or the slow learning children, because of their fear of failure and their lack of practice in goal setting, normally need a lot of help in establishing realistic goals. For this group of children, goals may be set either on a small group basis or on an individual basis. Instructors in many of the Wisconsin Multiunit schools have tried to give each child the undivided attention of an educational worker for at least ten minutes per week in an individual conference. In addition to setting goals in this conference, teacher and student can carry on an assessment of progress made toward educational and social goals. Students should participate in establishing realistic, attainable, and worthy learning goals as well as determining the nature and order of this learning. Thus, outlining the task clearly and understandably would seem to be one of the most important motivational tools because the outline would guide the teacher in his teaching and the learner in his learning. This process of cooperative planning provides the bridge necessary for a healthy relationship between teacher and student. By establishing meaningful tasks the learner provides his own reinforcement and requires less time for formal instruction. However, teachers must guard against allowing this kind of participation to become "purely random activity" or a "permissive playground" for children. The skills a teacher must have for co-operative goal setting are highly developed skills which need to be discussed and developed cooperatively by members of a differentiated staff.

Incidentally, the goal setting process can also help in identifying the students who are not motivated toward the goals of the school. Such an inference is made from the goals a student selects.

Prompt Feedback

According to presently accepted learning concepts, prompt feedback is another useful motivational procedure. Instructional feedback can be defined as a process of providing a learner with information on the correctness, appropriateness or adequacy of his response to the task at hand. Too often, in our present school situation, learners do not know about the adequacy of their responses until after they have answered questions on some kind of a test and perhaps days later have found out whether their responses were correct or incorrect. In some cases, learners may not know how their responses have been evaluated and may simply be given a grade. Delayed feedback or no feedback results in slower rate of learning and interferes with effective learning (7). Feedback, therefore, is very useful in redirecting the learner's performance as it identifies areas in need of further practice and spells out how much of a correction is needed. In elementary schools, a very common way for providing this feedback is the procedure of recitation which usually includes going from child to child, getting responses, and informing the child about the correctness and incorrectness of responses. A teacher who goes about the classroom attending to the pupils and commenting on their work is more effective than the one who waits to comment at the end of the study period. Systems of individualization, which involve differentiated staff assignments, plus a variety of instructional modes, provide far better means of giving the learner prompt and effective feedback concerning the adequacy of specific responses. In individualized systems of instruction the staff typically provides feedback by working with small homogeneous groups or individuals; instructional aids or peers are often used for various kinds of practice. Auto-instructional (22) or programmed materials also provide quick feedback for individual learners; eventually computers will enable us to handle many of the subjects requiring practice and thus provide almost immediate feedback to the learner regarding his responses (18).

Peer Tutoring

This means having one student teach another student or a very small group of students. This technique is thought to have a strong motivational potential for less able and older students whose behavior and attitude toward their schooling can be favorably modified through this involvement and role reversal. Not only does it effect a favorable change in the self-image of the student, it will make a very real change in the educational climate of the school. In terms of immediate benefits to instruction, the student being helped gets help from a person who more or less talks his language and may have had the same kind of problem he is encountering. When this kind of tutoring is carried out, attention needs to be paid to the selection of compatible peers and training of peer tutors in the use of appropriate reward and reinforcement procedures, tutoring skills (diagnosis, demonstration, evaluation and practice), and content area, if necessary. Both children should be informed in advance concerning days, times, and places for the meeting. The older child should be encouraged to serve as a model for desirable behavior and to listen to the student being tutored in order to find out the student's problems. It should be emphasized to the tutor that his task, after identification of the problem, is not to give the answer or means of solution but to help the student being tutored to work through the general method needed to solve the problem. This procedure enables the student being tutored to move from his lack of understanding toward understanding and mastery of the problem using his own resources. A number of studies (13, 14) have shown that the use of less able and older students as tutors of younger children showed encouraging results for both children. Besides helping in academic subjects, peer tutors should be trained to assist their charges in improving such skills as effective study habits, taking tests, getting needed information, communicating effectively and displaying good manners and appearance.

Utilizing Rewards/Punishment

Reinforcement is one of the conditions considered essential in learning among most learning experts. Most learning research (1, 17, 21) indicates that immediate reinforcement facilitates concept attainment and that delays are detrimental to the learning process. Three principles should be kept in mind when rewarding a child in a highly consistent manner. These are: (a) liberally reward that behavior which is to be encouraged; (b) occasionally reward a stable behavior pattern in order to maintain it; and (c) avoid rewarding undesirable behaviors (4).

Writers agree that attempts to predict the effect of rewards and/or punishment must take into account a definition (age, needs, abilities and reward preference) of the kind of student or pupil involved. Thus awareness of the personal and social needs of the learner, as well as his characteristic response pattern to this kind of motivation, is necessary. Sometimes a longer period of time is needed to demonstrate marked changes because of interaction of rewards with characteristics of the task, instruction, and other situational variables besides subject variables. Rewards or positive incentives include:

■ *Adult Approval or Praise*—Research has shown praise as a motivational device to be superior to reproof which in turn, tends to be more effective than no comment (10). Adult approval may consist of teacher writing "excellent" on the paper of a child or going near the child and patting his back. However, care should be taken that such an approval or praise should not have any adverse effect on the pupil's peer status. All too often such instances have resulted in peer rejection of a so-called "teacher's pet."

■ *Consumables*—This consists of giving a child consumable things or tokens for excellence exchangeable for candy, cake, ice cream cones or other wanted objects at significant places in the program. However, such rewards are obviously limited by classroom procedures.

■ *Peer Approval*—Recently, research studies have shown the importance of the influence of peers on children, especially on issues involving attitudes toward school and learning. Peer approval through recognition, support or help is a more effective reward to some unmotivated students than adult approval or consumables.

■ *Feeling of Success*—as it leads to the development of a positive self-concept, and hence to further success and further motivation (2).

■ *Competitive Situations*—in which pupils are given evidence of the superiority or inferiority of their performance as compared to others. For example, a child is told that he was the first or the only one to answer the question correctly. This is a powerful incentive since it brings the full force of group pressure to bear upon the learner. However, individual competition tends to be more effective than group rivalry (11). Also, these extrinsic incentives should not be emphasized to the point where they supersede the real goals and provide rather convincing evidence that the activity is not worthwhile apart from the incentive. This point has been argued very convincingly by many writers (3).

■ *Freedom as an Incentive*—This means giving the child independence in selecting the activity, the place and the time. This has been found to be among the first three reward categories chosen as possessing reward value by children and adults. However, freedom to pursue favorite activities should be promised and given only after the less popular task is satisfactorily completed.

Most writers advise teachers to use positive reinformcement or the withholding of approval rather than the more punitive threat of disapproval or punishment. However, it must be remembered that each pupil is a different individual and a reinforcement technique which works well for a number of pupils may fail with others. There are times when punishment may need to be required; some maladaptive behaviors of children are much worse than the punishment it takes to eliminate them. In the study by Penny and Lupton (20), a combination of reward and punishment was found to be more effective than either reward or punishment alone.

Social Reinforcement

The classroom is a social group and social reinforcement in such a setting is the teacher's greatest ally in motivating children. It is suggested that the classroom atmosphere should be that of shared feelings of "liking," "genuine caring," or "love" and/or "mutual respect" so as to lead students to maximum growth. The teacher can easily find the students whose opinions on issues involving attitudes toward school and learning are held in the highest regard by one or more unmotivated students. The natural influence of these peers can be used to develop and reinforce desirable behavior.

Manipulating Environment

It has been found that new, unfamiliar and complex objects and events direct the attention of the individual towards them (2). Similarly, if the environment contains objects and situations which differ markedly from the individual's prior experience, the individual tries to explore the environment in order to gain knowledge about and control over it. However, there is a limit to the number and kind of stimuli that will achieve optimal results. If the amount of stimulation is below the optimal level, the individual strives to learn about the environment; if, on the other hand, the stimulation is above the optimal level, the individual strives to decrease stimulation instead of increasing knowledge about environment. Klausmeier and his associates feel that it is possible for a school staff to arrange its environment so that students become habitually curious and desire to become increasingly competent in connection with learning tasks in and out of school.

Use of Models

A number of researchers have found that children observe and imitate that behavior of models which has been rewarded. It is, therefore, suggested that the use of models can be made for the acquisition and retention of a desirable behavior. However, care should be taken in the selection of the model. The model should not only exhibit the desirable behavior but also should be influential, powerful, competent, and prestigious in the eyes of the observer. Models need not be always real-life; they can be symbolic or representational. In the school setting, peers, teachers and other members of the instructional staff are potential models. Use should be made of community resources to provide models for children to imitate.

Use of Interest-Centered Activities

The teacher, by dividing the classroom into well-planned interest centers, ensures that children encounter refreshing experiences and pursue independent work. Such activities will provide truly individualized learning developing from each child's particular interests. This approach has been reported to achieve widespread success in England and systematic efforts are being made to introduce the use of interest centers on a statewide scale in North Dakota. The "open class" is not completely free;

permission for students to pursue their favorite activities or more advanced work is given only when a less popular prior task is completed.

Use of Discussions

Discussing the objectives and performance with each student or among students is a useful motivational procedure. Discussing the "why" of the behavior by the student will give him an opportunity to verbalize and the teacher a chance to know whether the child understands and gives reasons for his behavior. Discussing such topics as the idea of success, success of a known person and the factors that lead to his success, success of a student in the class in solving problems, like grades, family relationships, social adjustment, money problems, and other school-related problems, can contribute to the motivation of the student.

Individual Conferences

Besides goal setting and diagnostic functions of such conferences, they are also major motivational sources as they preserve the student's sense of individual identity among the large groups served by educational institutions. The student will feel that he is meaningfully engaged with the teacher and the subject matter and that he is not in an impersonal educational mill.

Use of Projects

Children often follow particular individual interests with a great deal of depth. These children should be given opportunities to share their projects, which have developed from their interests, with the total class or with smaller groups of children who show interest in the project.

Participation of Parents

A number of positions, programs and surveys clearly suggest the importance of home in the development of a child's language, pattern of achievement and motives for achievement, and personality structure. Therefore, it is suggested that parents must assume the responsibility with the school in aiding the growth of the child in scholarship, health, interest, abilities and capacities as an individual and as a part of a social group. Merely informing the parents through report cards or home-school meetings is not enough. As a part of parental involvement, some parents will be given a profile of their child; others may be educated about the climate which is related to achievement motivation, language development, and general learning. Some parents may be informed about motivational practices and tutoring skills.

Behavior of Teachers

This, in the final analysis, is the key to motivation. It has been said that teachers find it easy to criticize but, when faced with the need to encourage, they are clumsy and end up doing the opposite (6). There also is the nagging teacher, who in an attempt to reward behavior by praising it, inadvertently punishes by accusing the child of not having made the correct response in the past (9). In a recent Carnegie study, Silberman (26) asserts that teachers assume that pupils cannot be trusted to act in their own best interests and suggests that there should be a much more informal atmosphere in classrooms. He argues that in such an atmosphere disciplinary and motivational problems largely disappear and that there is "great joy and spontaneity and activity" coupled with "great self-control and order." It would be useful for teachers to select and develop a variety of verbal and nonverbal response skills that can be used in appropriate situations to elicit desired pupil behavior. As the development of these skills requires practice and does not come by merely reading, talking, and thinking, it is suggested that the teacher should make use of a mirror and tape recorder in developing them. After patient practice in role playing, the teacher, it is hoped, will notice exciting new skill in the development of responses. Also, micro-teaching procedures can be helpful (e.g., The Far West Laboratory's Minicourse V, tutoring skills which provide opportunity for practice in praising skills). Sometimes a teacher may choose to practice with another person who desires to be helpful in giving the teacher appropriate feedback. Other than subject matter itself, responses available to the teacher can be classified in the following five categories (15):

(1) words (spoken-written) e.g., good, nice, bravo, well done

(2) non-verbal expressions (facial-bodily) e.g., smiling, cheering, nodding

(3) closeness (nearness-touching) e.g., patting back, leaning over, tickling

(4) activities (social-individual) e.g., displaying a student's work, decorating classroom, making a game of subject matter, and

(5) things (materials, food, playthings, awards) e.g., book covers, candy, dolls.

The examples cited in the above five categories are approval responses. A similar list of examples of disapproval responses can be given. However, it is suggested that the teacher use approval responses, as research investigating the effects of various disapproval responses and threatening words discloses that the individual exhibits greater emotional imbalance and lack of meaningful understanding in disapproval situations. Besides, by ignoring inappropriate behavior and approving all other kinds, the teacher's potential for success also improves because students then view him favorably.

This article was specially written for this book of readings at the request of the editors. Dr. Mohan is Associate Professor—Research at State University College at Fredonia, New York.

Bibliography

1. Angell, George W. "The Effect of Immediate Knowledge of Results on Final Examination Scores in Freshman Chemistry." *Journal of Educational Research*, 42, 1949, 391–394.

2. Berlyne, Daniel E. *Conflict, Arousal, and Curiosity.* McGraw-Hill, 1960.

3. Bruner, Jerome S. "The Act of Discovery." *Harvard Educational Review*, 31, 1961, 21–32.

4. Cartwright, C. A., and Cartwright, G. P. *Reward*

Preference Profiles of Elementary School Children, mimeographed. Computer-Assisted Instruction Laboratory, the Pennsylvania State University, 1969.

5. Davis, Robert A. "The Teaching Problems of 1075 Public School Teachers." *Journal of Experimental Education*, 9, 1940, 41–60.

6. Dreikurs, Rudolf. *Psychology in the Classroom*. New York: Harper and Row, Publishers, Inc., 1957.

7. Fairbanks, G., and Guttman, N. "Effects of Delayed Auditory Feedback upon Articulation." *Journal of Speech and Hearing Research* 1, 1958, 1–11.

8. Fleming, J. Carl. "Pupil Tutors and Tutees Learn Together." *Today's Education*, October, 1969.

9. Gordon, Jesse. *Personality and Behavior*. New York: Crowell-Collier and Macmillan, Inc., 1963.

10. Hurlock, Elizabeth B. "An Evaluation of Certain Incentives Used in School Work." *Journal of Educational Psychology*, 18, 1925, 149–159.

11. Jersild, Arthur T. *Child Psychology*. Englewood Cliffs, N.J.: Prentice-Hall, Inc., 1960.

12. King, F. J., and Dunn-Rankin, P. *Reward Preference Inventory*. Unpublished inventory, Florida State University, 1965.

13. Klausmeier, H. J. et. al., A System of Individually Guided Motivation. Madison: Wisconsin. February, 1969. (Not Published)

14. Lindvall, Mauritz. An Address to the Chief School Officers of Chautauqua County in Jamestown, New York, October 6, 1969. (Not Published)

15. Madsen, Charles H., Jr. and Madsen, Clifford K. *Teaching/Discipline*. Boston: Allyn and Bacon, Inc., 1970.

16. McConnell, T. R. "Learning." In A. I. Gates, et. al., *Educational Psychology*, Part III. New York: Crowell-Collier and Macmillan, Inc., 1948.

17. Meyer, Susan R. "A Test of the Principles of 'Activity', 'Immediate Reinforcement', and 'Guidance'—as Instrumented by Skinner's Teaching Machine." Doctoral dissertation. University of Buffalo, 1960.

18. Mitzel, Harold E. "The Impending Instruction Revolution." *Phi Delta Kappan*, April 1970, 434–439.

19. Neugarten, Bernice and Nelle Wright. "Encour-

aging the Child's Spontaneous Interests." In *Fostering Mental Health in Our Schools*. Washington, D.C.: Association for Supervision and Curriculum Development, 1950, pp. 134–145.

20. Penny, R. K., and A. A. Lupton. "Children's Discrimination Learning as a Function of Reward and Punishment." *Journal of Comparative and Physiological Review*, 54, 1961, 449–451.

21. Postman, Leo and Bruner, J. S. "Perception under stress." *Psychological Review*, 55, 1948, 314–323.

22. Pressey, Sidney L. "Autoinstruction: Perspectives, Problems, Potentials." In E. R. Hilgard (Ed.), *Theories of Learning and Instruction*. 63rd Yearbook, National Society for the Study of Education, Part I, pp. 354–370. Chicago: University of Chicago Press, 1964.

23. Raths, Louis E.; Harmin, Merrill; and Simon, Sidney B. *Values and Teaching*. Columbus, Ohio: Charles E. Merrill Publishing Co., 1966.

24. Sax, Gilbert. "Concept Acquisition as a Function of Differing Schedules and Delays of Reinforcement." *Journal of Educational Psychology*, 51, 1960, 32–36.

25. Sanford, Filmore H. *Psychology: A Scientific Study of Man*. Belmont, Calif.: Wadsworth Publishing Co., Inc., 1961.

26. Silberman, Charles E. *Crisis in the Classroom*. New York: Random House, 1970.

Assessment Sheet of
Positive Terminal Behavior

Name _____ Sex _____ Age _____
Date _____

	Seldom	Some-times	Most Times
1. Listens to the teacher.			
2. Begins school work promptly.			
3. Corrects mistakes.			
4. Works until the job is finished.			
5. Works when the teacher has left the room.			
6. If mistakes are made, still continues to work.			
7. Arrives at class on time.			
8. Works on learning activities in free time.			
9. Does extra school work.			
10. Participates in class projects.			
11. Reads during free time.			
12. Asks questions about school work.			
13. Has pencil and paper ready when they are needed.			
14. Moves quietly to and from classes.			
15. Listens to the ideas of others.			
16. Helps classmates with their problems.			
17. Picks up when the work is finished.			
18. Takes good care of his clothing, books, and other things.			
19. Takes good care of the school's books, desk, and other things.			
20. Does what the teacher asks.			

Self-Assessment Sheet of
Positive Terminal Behavior

Name _____ Sex _____ Age _____

Date _____

	Seldom	Some-times	Most Times
1. I listen to the teacher.			
2. I begin school work promptly.			
3. I correct mistakes.			
4. I work until the job is finished.			
5. I work when the teacher has left the room.			
6. If I make mistakes, I still continue to work.			
7. I arrive at class on time.			
8. I work on learning activities in free time.			
9. I do extra school work.			
10. I participate in class projects.			
11. I read during free time.			
12. I ask questions about school work.			
13. I have pencil and paper ready when they are needed.			
14. I move quietly to and from my classes.			
15. I listen to the ideas of others.			
16. I help my classmates with their problems.			
17. I pick up when the work is finished.			
18. I take good care of my clothing, books, and other things.			
19. I take good care of the school's books, desks, and other things.			
20. I do what the teacher asks me.			

APPENDIX A

Selected References

Instructional Objectives Exchange, A series of books on objectives and test items. Los Angeles, California: Instructional Objectives Exchange, 1971.

Klausmeier, Herbert J.; Schwenn, Elizabeth A.; and Lamal, Peter A. "A System of Individually Guided Motivation," Practical Paper No. 9. Wisconsin Research and Development Center for Cognitive Learning, the University of Wisconsin, 1969.

Lewis, James, Jr., *Administering the Individualized Instruction Program,* West Nyack, N.Y.: Parker Publishing Company, Inc., 1971.

Martin, Peter, et al., "Information and Planning Kit for Use in Developing Open Education Programs," The University of the State of New York, The State Education Department, Albany, N.Y. 12224, 1971.

National Society for the Study of Education. Sixty-first Yearbook, Part I. *Individualizing Instruction,* Chicago: University of Chicago Press, 1962.

Noar, Gertrude, *Individualized Instruction: Every Child A Winner,* New York: John Wiley and Sons, Inc., 1972.

Stahl, Dona Kofod, and Anzalone, Patricia Murphy, *Individualized Teaching in Elementary Schools,* West Nyack, N.Y.: Parker Publishing Company, Inc., 1970.

Wolfson, Bernice T., *Individualizing Instruction,* Washington, D.C.: National Education Association, December, 1966.

APPENDIX B

Materials

The following list of materials is not exhaustive. However, these materials are currently being used by schools which have individualized their instructional programs.

1. Criterion Reading, A New Assessment System in Reading, was developed by Random House School Division, 201 East 50th Street, N.Y., N.Y. 10022. Criterion Reading is a systematic individualized reading program.

2. Individually Guided Education and the Multiunit School—Elementary, University of Wisconsin Research and Development Center for Cognitive Learning, 1025 West Johnson Street, Madison, Wisconsin 53706. Curriculum materials have been developed in reading, mathematics, and motivation.

3. Individually Prescribed Instruction Materials, Learning Research and Development Center, University of Pittsburgh, Pittsburgh, Pa., and Research for Better Schools, Inc., 1700 Market Street, Philadelphia, Pa. 19103. IPI materials are currently available in elementary mathematics, reading, science, handwriting, and spelling.

4. Introduction to Individualized Instruction—Training Package. These instructional modules were developed at the Teacher Education Research Center, State University College at Fredonia, New York. This training package is designed to provide a basic understanding of individualized instruction for selected target groups (inservice school personnel, preservice personnel enrolled in teacher preparation programs, and lay personnel). The package, with its twelve module components, is designed to be self-sufficient and exportable. The package is also designed to motivate participants to the further in-depth study of individualized instruction and, at the same time, give them an understanding of the commitment such further study may require. The modules included in the training package are:

    1. Overview of Individualized Instruction
    2. Organization of Individualized Instruction
    3. Differentiated Staffing
    4. Information Systems for Individualized Instruction
    5. Curriculum Strategies for Individualization
    6. The Child in Individualized Systems of Education

5. Learning Activity Packages, NOVA-South Florida Educational Center, Fort Lauderdale, Florida. The Learning Activity Packages are basically a management system which allows the student to become involved in a diversity of individualized learning experiences.

6. Materials on "Open Classroom" and teacher preparation programs oriented to this informal approach to instruction are available at The School for Behavioral Studies in Education, The University of North Dakota, Grand Forks, N.D.

7. Mathematics Teaching Tape Program was developed by William Schall, et al. The program consists of 72 pre-recorded lessons. Thirty-two lessons comprise the Primary Level and 40 the Intermediate Level. The program is marketed by Houghton Mifflin, Pennington-Hopewell Rd., Hopewell, N.J. 08525. Each lesson is referenced to specific pages in Houghton Mifflin's *Modern School Mathematics, Structure and Use*, K-6 Series, but may be used with any other modern mathematics elementary series.

8. The Minicourses developed at the Far West Laboratory for Educational Research and Development, 1 Garden Circle, Hotel Claremont, Berkeley, California 94705, have been used effectively to develop such skills as "questioning," with both preservice and inservice educators.

9. Principles and Practices of Instructional Technology is programmed, individualized workshop produced by General Programmed Teaching, A Division of Commerce Clearing House, Inc., Palo Alto, California. This training package contains 15 audio tapes, 12 filmstrips, 10 partici-

pants' workbooks, 10 sets of unit tests and final examinations, 1 monitor's manual, and 1 script book.

10. Project PLAN Materials, Westinghouse Learning Corporation, 2680 Hanover Street, Palo Alto, Calif. 94304. The curriculum aspects of PLAN involve the writing in and coding of commercially available materials to the requirements of the computer-managed system of individualized instruction.

11. Science Research Associates, Teaching Problems Laboratory, is a set of taped teaching incidents which illustrates specific problems and provides an opportunity for small group problem solving. It is available from Science Research Associates, 259 East Erie Street, Chicago, Illinois.

12. Scott Foresman Reading Systems. Scott, Foresman and Company, Glenview, Illinois 60025. This program consists of books for elementary grades and is suitable for individualized reading programs.

13. The Story Plays, authored by Douglas and Margaret Rector, are a boxed set of self-directing materials for oral reading which contain twenty stories for boys and twenty stories for girls. In each Story Play there are four reading parts (that is, four characters), ranging from fourth grade reading level (free reading) to 2.1 or below (the least difficult). The Story Plays are marketed by Harcourt Brace Jovanovich, Inc.

14. The Thinking Box was developed by Louis E. Raths, et al., and is marketed by Benefic Press, Westchester, Illinois. The Thinking Box contains instructional materials that can help emphasize critical thinking. There are two levels of the Thinking Box available: one for primary and one for intermediate grades.

15. Utah State University Protocol Materials Project is a series of skills development lessons which can be obtained from Dr. Walter Borg, Utah State University, Logan, Utah. For example, the *Encouragement* protocol has been used successfully for developing "encouragement" skills in inservice workshops.

16. Winnetka Curriculum Materials List, Winnetka Public Schools, Winnetka, Illinois. Winnetka materials are divided into two parts, viz., common essentials and social and creative activities.

APPENDIX C

Projects on Individualizing Instruction

A persistent question for all of us is "How can I individualize instruction in mathematics?" Many are actively exploring solutions, trying various programs, and developing new approaches. Locating information on what is being tried sometimes seems to be a matter of luck, however.

In an attempt to shorten the search for information on such projects, a notice was inserted in the August 1970 issue of the NCTM "Bulletin for Leaders." We're now printing some of the replies; in every case, the person whom you can contact for additional, specific information is noted. If you are involved in a project not included here, why not send information on it today?

We hope that knowing about what is being done will help others in their search for new ways of individualizing!

Belleview Program of Individualized Instruction

The components of this program are diagnosis, prescription, commitment, implementation, and assessment. These components are implemented through the use of curriculum packages, contracts, and individual prescriptions utilizing multiple-source materials.

There are no published materials on the program itself.

Grade level: K-6.
Address for further information:

> Dr. Jack Platt, Principal
> Belleview Elementary School
> 4955 South Dayton Street
> Englewood, Colorado 80110

Current Trends and Innovations in Mathematics

This program is designed to assist in individualizing and implementing the mathematics curriculum. Three hours of graduate credit are given.

Material available: contract cards.
Grade level: K-6.
Address for further information:

Mrs. Adelyn C. Muller
Director of Mathematics
Shawnee Mission Public School, K-8
8101A West Ninety-Fifth Street
Overland Park, Kansas 66212

East High School Mathematics Laboratory

This program consists of a programmed sequence of lessons for general mathematics students. The lessons allow a student to develop his mathematics background to the extent determined by his motivation.

Materials available: Teacher-developed lesson sheets and audio tapes are utilized. Listening stations with headsets are available: there is an audio tape for each lesson. Automatic printing calculators are also available for student use.

Grade level: Grade 9 students in a four-year senior high school.
Address for further information:

Mr. Rich Meyer
East High School
515 North Forty-eighth Street
Phoenix, Arizona 85008

The Hendrix Experiment

This three-year project started in September 1969. Its major objective is the development of a program of individualized instruction for students preparing to teach mathematics in schools seeking new ways to individualize instruction. The first year of the experiment included the collection of materials, the selection of content around which behavioral objectives would be written, and the selection of educational experiences and the outlining of them in terms of a sequence of learning experiences. During stage two, the current year, behavioral objectives, learning packages, and evaluation procedures are being developed by consultants, the project director, and the students. Stage three, next year, will be the actual implementation of the program. A complete set of learning experiences will be available to each student.

Grade level: Students preparing to teach grades K-6.
Address for further information:

> Dr. Cecil W. McDermott, Project Director
> The Hendrix Experiment
> Hendrix College
> Conway, Arkansas 72032

Individualized Mathematics System (IMS)

After placement testing and pretesting in individual skills, each child is given a daily prescription according to his mathematics needs. Each child's work is corrected daily and evaluated. If mastery is achieved, this is recorded on his individual profile chart. This chart lists eleven subjects in nine different levels. The work sheets in the skill folders are laminated, thus making them usable again and again.

Material available: Brochure on the program, giving its philosophy and a sample laminated work sheet.

Grade level: 1-6; possibly 7.
Address for further information:

> Mrs. Evelyne M. Graham
> Supervisor of Mathematics
> Chesapeake Public Schools
> Post Office Box 15204
> Chesapeake, Virginia 23320

Islands of Continuous Progress (Math)

The project consists of the utilization of curriculum packages developed by Grand Forks School District staff. Open-area classrooms are served by a differentiated teaching staff; approximately 3500 students are involved. Project materials utilize behavioral objectives, performance criterion standards, pre- and post-testing, and directed learning experiences using a variety of media.

Materials available: Learning packages are available in hard copy and microfiche; also, descriptive brochures of the operational program.

Grade level: K-12.
Address for further information:

Dr. Wayne Worner
Mr. Walter Knipe
Mr. Vaughen Hesse
Post Office Box 1358
Grand Forks, North Dakota 58201

Phoenix Union High School Mathematics Laboratory

The laboratory is available for the use of all students in Phoenix Union High School. It is designed to provide self-paced instruction for students in basic mathematical skills. Twelve listening stations and three calculator stations are available. The project also emphasizes the use of games, puzzles, and other instructional aids.

Materials available: Teacher-prepared audio tapes correlated with printed materials are used in this developmental program. Other materials include forty programmed lessons on the use of the calculator. Cumulative records will be maintained for all students using the laboratory for individualized learning in basic mathematics.

Grade level: 9-12.
Address for further information:

Mrs. Charlene Hicks
Phoenix Union High School
512 East Van Buren Street
Phoenix, Arizona 85004

Saint Bernard Parish Nongraded Individualized Project

Students in grades 1-4 are grouped in one mathematics center, those in grades 5-8 in another, and those in grades 9-12 in a third. The project is individualized and nongraded.

Materials available: A course guide consisting of learning sequences for each level (1-4, 5-8, 9-12); also, individual packets.

Grade level: 1-12.
Addresses for further information:

> Mr. Buford Jones
> Associate Superintendent
> Saint Bernard Parish Schools
> Chalmette, Louisiana 70043

> Dr. Merlin M. Ohmer
> Dean, College of Sciences
> Nicholls State University
> Thibodaux, Louisiana 70301

Selma Project

A program for individualized instruction in mathematics (and in other subjects) was started in 1967 with federal funding. Teachers and aides received special training. The Cedar Park Elementary School was designed especially for this project; special features include four modules, module leaders, and a modern resource center.

Grade level: 1-6.
Address for further information:

> Miss Lorna West, Principal
> Cedar Park Elementary School
> Selma, Alabama 36701

Self-Instruction in the Arithmetic Skills

The project aims at teaching as well as reviewing the basic facts and algorithms of addition, subtraction, multiplication, and division by means of cassette tapes and student workbooks. The tapes were developed from an adequate conceptual base rooted in the theory of knowledge. The project has been successfully used at a pilot school. The tapes are designed to free the teacher of much of the drudgery of drill and review; the teacher can then devote more time to the explanation of and instruction in important underlying concepts.

Materials available: Tapes and scripts of the addition, subtraction, multiplication, and division algorithms, together with the necessary work sheets.

Grade level: 1-6, or as needed remedially.
Address for further information:

Director, Mathematics Education Research Group
University of Pennsylvania
Graduate School of Education
Philadelphia, Pennsylvania 19104

Reprinted from the *Arithmetic Teacher*, March 1971 (vol. 18, pp. 161–163), © 1971 by the National Council of Teachers of Mathematics. Used by permission.